# IN THE SHADOW
# OF THE BROCHS
## The Iron Age in Scotland

# IN THE SHADOW OF THE BROCHS
## THE IRON AGE IN SCOTLAND

*Beverley Ballin Smith and Iain Banks*
*Editors*

TEMPUS

*A celebration of the work of Dr Euan W. MacKie on the
Iron Age of Scotland*

First published 2002

PUBLISHED IN THE UNITED KINGDOM BY:
Tempus Publishing Ltd
The Mill, Brimscombe Port
Stroud, Gloucestershire GL5 2QG

PUBLISHED IN THE UNITED STATES OF AMERICA BY:
Tempus Publishing Inc.
2 Cumberland Street
Charleston, SC 29401

British Library Cataloguing in Publication Data.
A catalogue record for this book is available from the British Library.

ISBN 0 7524 2517 X

Typesetting and origination by Tempus Publishing.
PRINTED AND BOUND IN GREAT BRITAIN.

# Contents

# Acknowledgements

The idea for this volume began the afternoon Dr. Euan MacKie retired from his post at the Hunterian Museum, University of Glasgow. Several years have passed since then, but it is of great credit to each of the contributors that they have persevered through months of long silences when the pressure of their normal archaeological duties overtook the editors. Roger Miket and Graham Ritchie are to be singled out for encouraging the editors to carry on with the volume, for supplying excellent advice, help and assisting with its compilation. I would also like to thank The Carnegie Trust for the Universities of Scotland for their generosity towards the production of the colour illustrations.

Peter Kemmis Betty, the commissioning editor for Tempus Publishing Limited, is to be thanked for taking on the challenge of this volume and encouraging its completion. His positive attitude and advice have been of enormous assistance. Claire Brittain, Katherine Savage, Michelle Burns and Tim Clarke enthusiastically and inspirationally brought the words and pictures together.

Individual contributors' acknowledgements include:

**Derek Alexander:**
Mr Martin Stansfeld of Ford Esk Tower, Dr Ian Armit, Andrew Dunwell, Dr Doug Gentles, Professor Dennis Harding, Dr Euan MacKie, Callum Mitchell, George Mudie, Professor Ian Ralston, Dr David Sanderson, Professor Don Tarling and the first year archaeology undergraduates of 1999.

**Ian Armit:**
Dr Noel Fojut and Dr Richard Hingley.

**Beverley Ballin Smith:**
Torben Ballin, Stephen Driscoll, Noel Fojut, Roger Miket, Graham Ritchie, Catherine Smith and GUARD.

**Julie Bond:**
J. Ambers, Steve Dockrill, Professor John Hunter, R. Nicholson, T. O'Connor and Val Turner, BP Exploration Operating Company Ltd., EC Objective 1, Historic Scotland, Robert Kiln Trust, Scottish Hydro Electric plc, the Old Scatness/Jarlshof Environs Project, SERC, Scottish Natural Heritage, Shetland Amenity Trust, Shetland Enterprise Company, Shetland Islands Council and the University of Bradford.

**Mike Church:**
Dr Simon Gilmour, Professor Dennis Harding and Andrew Heald.

**Iain Crawford:**
Alasdair and Rebecca Crawford, Stephen Dockerill, Lesley Ferguson, Noel Fojut, Susan Hothersall Hazel Moore, Robert Tye and Marek Zvelebil.

**Stephen Dockrill:**
Dr Julie Bond, Louise Brown, Dr R.A. Nicholson, Dr Ian Simpson, BP Exploration Operating Company Ltd, EC Objective 1 Programme, Historic Scotland, Robert Kiln Trust, Scottish Hydro Electric plc, Scottish Natural Heritage, Shetland Amenity Trust, Shetland Enterprise Company, Shetland Islands Council, Shetland Islands Council (Charitable Trust), University of Bradford.

**Simon Gilmour:**
Dr Ian Armit, Dr Ewan Campbell, Catherine Flitcroft, Professor Dennis Harding, and Dr Rob Sands.

**John Hunter:**
Ian Armit, Henry Buglass, Sally Foster, Mel Johnson, Chris Lowe, Tim Neighbour the National Trust for Scotland.

**Anne MacSween:**
John Barber, Alan Braby, Noel Fojut, Andy Heald, Fraser Hunter, Ian Scott and Andrea Smith, Jim Wilson, the Archaeology Department of the Museum of Scotland and Historic Scotland.

**Roger Miket:**
Beverley Ballin Smith, Paul Booth, Caitlin Evans, Professor Lawrence Keppie, Peter McKeague, Maggie Macdonald of Armadale Castle, Murdo Nicolson, Sally Phelps, Graham Ritchie, Adam Welfare, M. Wildgoose, Peter and Janet Wilson, Clan Donald Centre, *Dualchas,* Skye & Lochalsh Museums Service, Highland Council, the Hunterian Museum, University of Glasgow and the Royal Commission for Ancient and Historical Monuments.

**Graham Ritchie**
Mrs Lesley Ferguson, Dr Iain Fraser, Dr Anna Ritchie, Miss E. Ritchie and Royal Commission on the Ancient and Historical Monuments of Scotland.

# List of illustrations and tables

**Colour plates**

**List of tables**

# Preface

*Noel Fojut*

This volume of essays has been compiled in celebration of the work of Euan MacKie who has held an honoured position in Scottish Archaeology for almost four decades, representing the tradition of independent scholarship in an era of increasing corporatism. Although employed as a curator at Glasgow University's Hunterian Museum, where his contributions to the running of the organisation and to research into its collections were distinguished, his real research work was carefully kept separate from the daily grind, and undertaken in early mornings, late evenings, weekends and holidays (**colour plate 1**). Apart from occasional modest grants from academic funding sources, Euan supported his own endeavours. He may be unique in his generation in having worked within the Scottish archaeological establishment for his entire career without ever taking funds from the state archaeology budget for projects he himself directed.

Although best known for his publications on all matters related to brochs, Euan's contributions to research and debate cover the full span of prehistory. As the papers in this volume show, his influence has extended over several generations of researchers (**colour plates 2** & **3**). The constant theme of his own work is reflected here, time and again: the relationship between explanatory theory and material evidence. It was the essence of Euan's approach to any problem that the evidence must be studied first, and that any theory must be capable of encompassing all of the material evidence. His impatience with researchers whom he regarded as putting theory before facts was legendary.

Yet Euan was simultaneously renowned for being more willing than most to advance firm and sometimes radical theories. His published arguments for the external roots of societal change, which triggered the rapid spread of the broch phenomenon, have served to stimulate several rounds of spirited debate, commencing with the 'Wessex versus Local' debate of the 1960s and today once again forming a sounding board for the post-devolution rising generation of 'made in Scotland' theorists.

His PhD research did likewise, especially the seminal extension of Angus Graham's detailed enumeration of broch origins: the 'short-fast' development school versus the 'long-slow', the 'Inner Hebrides and the West' versus the 'Orkney and the North'. It also formed a sure foundation for geographical and locational research undertaken from the late 1970s onwards, and still current today in the guise of GIS-based studies. What made Euan's analysis of over 500 sites more remarkable was that it was performed before the days of pocket computers, using optical coincidence cards: a technique which, being Euan, he meticulously described in a published paper which now stands as a source of wonder to the computer-blessed graduates of the early twenty-first century.

Those of us lucky enough to be invited to trade ideas with Euan were always sure that our own thoughts would come back to us (eventually) woven into wholly new ways of perceiving a problem, while our attempts to modify his own were met with firm but gentle scepticism. His ability to spot the one point where the grand new theory glossed over a minor factual inconsistency kept us honest, while his unflagging belief that the big questions would, eventually, be answered, kept us digging, surveying and thinking. He maintained a far view of archaeological research long into the current era of instant theoretical gratification. Perhaps this is the summary of this tribute to Euan MacKie: he has kept most of us thinking long after we were ready to turn our brains off and retire upon the laurels of our youthful publications.

Euan frequently described his more radical ideas as 'aunt sallies'. How symmetrical then, that so many of today's working population of Scottish archaeologists (unknown to him, we think) refer to 'Uncle Euan' (or Eoghan nam Bhuiribhan as he should be known, pers. comm. Iain Crawford). His genial yet slightly aloof manner, like that of all the best uncles, always promised that provided the rules are obeyed, fun is in the offing. To judge from the prospectus for his next publications, there is more fun to come.

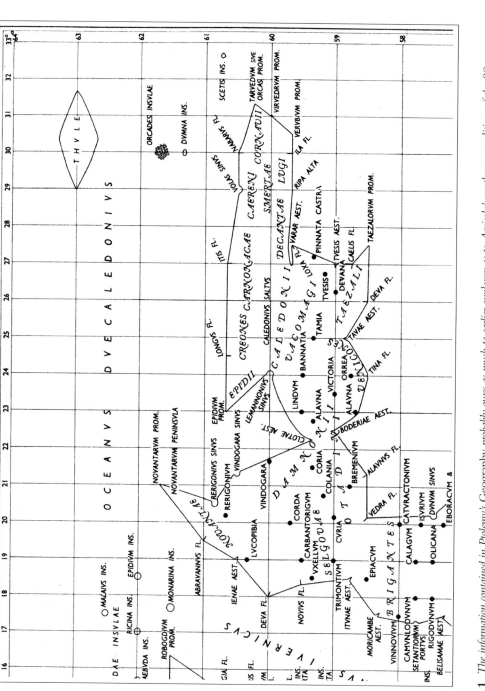

1  *The information contained in Ptolemy's Geography probably owes as much to earlier explorers as to Agricola's northern expeditions of the 80s.*
Reproduced by kind permission of the Ordnance Survey

# 1 The ancient geography of Scotland

*David J. Breeze*

## Introduction

The *Geography* of Claudius Ptolemaeus or Ptolemy of Alexandria, dating to AD 140-150, is generally assumed to have drawn heavily, albeit at second-hand, on the military and naval expeditions of Gnaeus Julius Agricola in Scotland from AD 79 to 83. In fact, the Greeks and Romans had considerable knowledge of the geography of Scotland before Agricola arrived as governor. The purpose of this paper is to explore this earlier information and consider its implications.

## Pre-Agricolan geographical information

Britain may have been known to the Greeks from at least the sixth century BC through the voyage of a captain from Massilia (Marseilles); though a reference survives in a poem of the fourth century AD it is far from clear (Rivet and Smith 1979, 114). The earliest known voyage to north Britain was by another Massaliote, Pytheas, probably sometime between 322 and 285 BC. Unfortunately, his discoveries attracted disbelief: Strabo called him a liar; rather than praising him, and accounts of his voyage only survive in brief form, heavy with sarcasm (Diodorus Siculus *History* V, 21-22 is probably drawn from Pytheas; Pomponius Mela *De Chorographia* II 6; Pliny *Natural History*; II, 186-87; IV, 102-104; Solinus *Collectanea Rerus Memorabilium* 22, 1-12; Strabo *Geography* I, 4, 2-5; II, 1, 18; 4, 1-2; 5, 7-8; IV, 2, 1; 5, 1-5; Cary and Warmington 1963, 47-56; the latest discussion of Pytheas is by Cunliffe 2001).

The purpose of the voyage was probably commercial, as indicated by Pytheas' inspection and description of the Cornish tin mines. It would appear that from Cornwall, Pytheas sailed completely round Britain, which he described as a triangle: the northernmost point he named Orcas (Cunliffe discusses Strabo's assertion that Pytheas walked around Britain, Cunliffe 2001, 98).

Pytheas, as reported by his detractors, recorded that six days' sail to the north of Britain lay the island of Thule, one day's distance from the congealed (that is, frozen) 'Cronian' sea. Around Thule, 'there is neither sea nor air, but a mixture like a sea-lung, in which the earth and sea are suspended; the sea-lung binds everything together'; Pytheas said that he saw this thing like the sea-lung himself. He also reported that there were no nights in summer and no days in winter. Finally, Pytheas noted that there was a lack of some crops and animals there, and that the people lived on millet and other vegetables and fruit and roots, and those that had grain and honey made a drink from them; the corn was pounded in large houses.

Pytheas acknowledged that he did not sail to Thule himself, but he acquired his information second-hand (Cunliffe 2001, 131 argues that Pytheas did sail to Thule). We cannot be certain where Thule lay: Cary and Warmington (1963, 52) prefer Norway while Cunliffe (2001, 116-30) supports the claims of Iceland. Thule is unlikely to have been Shetland, in spite of the statement by Tacitus that Agricola's fleet saw it (Tacitus, *Agricola*, 10). The significant point is that the existence of this land six days' sailing beyond Britain was known to the people Pytheas met and is clear evidence for travel in the north Atlantic in the fourth century BC.

Caesar knew that Britain was an island, but otherwise he offers no information on north Britain. Our next useful source dates to about the time of the invasion of Britain by Claudius in AD 43. Pomponius Mela recorded that there were 30 Orkney islands, separated from one another by narrow spaces, and seven *Haemodae*, which he stated were located towards Germany, while Thule was situated opposite the coast of the *Belgae*, who are otherwise unknown (*De Chorographia* II, 6; *Rivet* and Smith 1979, 76).

Claudius' invasion is recorded by the late fourth-century writer Eutropius, who averred that the emperor added the Orkney islands to the empire (*Breviarium ab Urbe Condita*, VII, 13, 3; Rivet and Smith 1979, 65). This passage has been discussed by Fitzpatrick in relation to the discovery of a fragment of a mid-first-century Roman amphora at Gurness broch (Fitzpatrick 1989).

Pliny the Elder died in the eruption of Vesuvius in AD 79. In his *Natural History* (IV, 103-4), published in AD 77, he mentioned not just Thule, as we have seen, but also the Orkney islands, 40 in number separated from one another by moderate distances, seven *Acmodae*, 30 *Hebudes* and *Dumna*. Pliny also mentioned the Caledonian forest (IV, 102), while the existence of the Caledonii was known to his contemporary Lucan (*Pharsalia* VI, 68),

It is also possible that other information in Ptolemy's *Geography* (**1**) was gathered before Agricola's activities. John Mann has suggested that the information in the *Geography* was acquired on at least two different occasions. He has pointed out that the Roman place-names within the tribal territories in north Britain are always placed after the Celtic names, indicating that they were added to an existing body of information (Mann and Breeze 1987, 87-8). Ptolemy's information on the land beyond the Great Glen is skeletal, with a few tribal names and geographical features (only seven river or estuary names and four promontories). The lack of place-names suggests that Agricola's army did not penetrate into these areas (Breeze 1996, 46-7). While all the known names could have been gathered by his fleet as they are coastal in nature, the possibility remains that some of Ptolemy's information relating to this part of the country came from an earlier source and was not acquired by Agricola's sailors. Watson (1926, 40) stated that the name *Dumna* (Lewis and Harris) *'first mentioned by Pliny, must have come down from Pytheas'* while Tierney (1959, 146) noted that Ptolemy's information on Scotland *'was extremely poor'* and considered it doubtful that Agricola's fleet brought back much evidence.

## The location of the islands

The pre-Agricolan writers all provide valuable information on the north and west of Scotland.

### *Orkney*

Mela records 30 and Pliny 40 islands (the number in Ptolemy is 'about 30': II, 3, 14); they agree that the islands are separated from each other by short distances. Orkney is also mentioned in relationship to the invasion of Claudius. There are, in fact, over 100 islands in Orkney, but at the beginning of this century only 29 were inhabited (*Ordnance Survey Gazetteer*: the number is now 20). Pytheas named the promontory opposite Orkney as *Orcas*, a name repeated by Ptolemy (II, 3,1). Rivet and Smith (1979, 434) suspect that the name 'probably had no real currency, being perhaps originally a deduction from the name of the Orcades because this mainland cape faced the islands'.

## Haemodae/Acmodae

Mela and Pliny both give seven for the number of islands in this group. Rivet and Smith (1979, 241) are of the view that these are the Shetland Isles not only from Mela's description of them as located 'towards Germany' (i.e. not towards Ireland: see below), but also because there is another group of islands mentioned by Pliny which are better interpreted as the Hebrides. The number of islands recorded for the group is not unreasonable: while there are over 40 Shetland isles, only seven or eight are of a significant size, while the balance of numbers with Orkney is correct.

## Hebudes

Pliny states that there were 30 islands in the archipelago and he mentions *Dumna* separately (IV, 104). A problem here is that Ptolemy states that there were only five islands in the *Ebudes* (II, 2, 10); he also (II, 3, 14) lists *Dumna* and *Scetis* (Skye). The Inner Hebrides is the location preferred by Rivet and Smith (1979, 114; 40) for the (*H*)*ebudes* because Ptolemy lists them under Ireland, to which they are correctly related, while *Dumna* is most likely to be the Outer Hebrides, or rather the Long Island of Lewis and Harris (*Domon* in Old Irish and Gaelic: Watson 1926, 40-1). There are over 40 islands in both Inner and Outer Hebrides, so Pliny's 30 is not an unreasonable figure.

## Thule

Through the activities of Pytheas, the existence of land beyond Britain is also known. Shetland was most certainly not Thule, in spite of the statement by Tacitus that Agricola's fleet sighted *Thule* from Orkney. Shetland cannot be seen from Orkney (this was checked with the captain of the inter-islands ferry in 1991), and it seems more probable that land beyond the main cluster of islands was sighted, either the northern Orkney islands or Fair Isle, and the name of *Thule* attached to it simply because this was the name given to land beyond Britain. It might be asked why this land was not called *Haemodae/Acmodae*, but, apart from the fact that the *Agricola* is not strong on geographical names, Tacitus may have been more interested in the use of a near-mythical name as a way of adding glory to the memory of his father-in-law. It also raises the question of how much geographical information was available to Agricola.

## The obtaining of information

This information was all recorded before the first known Roman incursion beyond the Tyne-Solway isthmus (though see Breeze 1996, 33-4 for the possibility of Roman movement in southern Scotland in the early 70s). Apart from the voyage of Pytheas, there is no specific evidence on how this information was obtained.

Caesar, Tacitus and Vegetius record the methods of gathering military intelligence (e.g. Caesar, *BG* V, 1; Tacitus, *Agricola* 24; Vegetius III, 6). The army obtained information from merchants, refugees and travellers (Breeze 1988, 14; Ptolemy specifically mentions obtaining information from travellers). In relation to Ireland, Tacitus stated that the Romans possessed tolerably good information on its approaches and harbours from the merchants who traded there (*Agricola 24)*. This is supported by Ptolemy's *Geography* in which the amount of information on the interior of Ireland is in sharp contrast to that available on Scotland beyond the Great Glen. It also emphasises how little explored northern Britain was and perhaps indicates a lack of mercantile expeditions.

We do, however, know of an official voyage of exploration at the time of Agricola's campaigns. Plutarch (*On the Disuse of the Oracles*, 18) recorded that in AD 83 Demetrius of Tarsus arrived in Delphi *en route* to his home from Britain. He had been commissioned by the emperor to sail to the nearest of the islands around Britain to make enquiries and observations. Demetrius said that there were many deserted islands scattered around Britain, some of which were named from spirits and heroes. The island nearest to the deserted ones did not have many inhabitants, but they were all holy men who were considered sacrosanct by the Britons. It is generally considered that the Hebrides best fit this account (Burn 1969, 3). There may have been earlier expeditions, though the coincidence of dates suggests that Demetrius' exploration was part of the Agricolan campaigns.

## The implications

It is clear that in the fourth century BC there were people able to inform Pytheas that there was land six days sail beyond Britain. Two other pre-Agricolan writers had gathered information on Orkney, Shetland, the Hebrides and established that there was a Caledonian forest. It is not known how this information was gained (assuming that it was not contained in lost accounts of the exploits of Pytheas), but merchants and travellers are the most obvious source. MacKie (e.g. 1971), following an earlier discussion by Childe (1935, 259-67), has suggested that refugees fleeing in the face of Belgic expansion and the Gallic invasion of Julius Caesar may have brought both artefacts and ideas on building techniques with them to Scotland. It has also been pointed out that the northern tribal names '*Cornavii* and *Damnonii* carry the suggestion that the peoples to which they were applied were related to the *Cornavii* and the *Dumnonii* of southern Britain' (Wainwright 1955, 50). Fitzpatrick (1989) has sought to explain the existence of the fragment of mid-first century AD Roman amphora at Gurness through the possibility of dynastic links between the southern tribes and Orkney. The above review of the early geographical evidence emphasises that we should not overlook the possibility of such links and greater communication between the north of Scotland and the rest of Britain than we normally allow. Indeed such links should not be unexpected in view of the movement of people indicated by the distribution of stone axes, for example those manufactured at Creag na Caillich in Perthshire about 3000 BC which have been found from Lewis to Buckinghamshire (Edmonds *et al.* 1992, 82; Sheridan 1992, 197).

# 2  Land and freedom

## Implications of Atlantic Scottish settlement patterns for Iron Age land-holding and social organisation

*Ian Armit*

## Introduction

Atlantic roundhouses, including the well-known broch towers, have long dominated the study of the Atlantic Scottish Iron Age. This paper examines how these monumental domestic structures may have functioned within various island landscapes of the north and west, and looks particularly at the ways in which their social and cultural significance may have varied from place to place, at both regional and local scales. The distribution of Atlantic roundhouses in certain particularly well-studied areas has important implications for the way in which we understand the potential variability of land-holding regimes in the Iron Age, even within relatively small geographical areas. It also suggests significant variation in the degree of autonomy enjoyed by individual households across Atlantic Scotland.

## Atlantic roundhouses

Atlantic roundhouses comprise a range of structures often described as brochs, galleried duns, island duns, semi-brochs, dun houses, or other variants. The term reflects the basic unity underlying the profusion of stone-built roundhouses in northern and western Scotland (cf. Armit 1992 and 1996 Chapter 7).

Atlantic roundhouses were massive-walled drystone roundhouses, forming one regional manifestation of the much wider tradition of substantial roundhouse building in Britain during the Later Bronze Age and Iron Age. The Atlantic roundhouse form is so-called because it is peculiarly characteristic of the Iron Age in the Atlantic north and west, even though sporadic examples can be found elsewhere in Scotland (cf. Macinnes 1984). Like timber roundhouses in the south, Atlantic roundhouses were primarily domestic buildings, but, in contrast to their southern equivalents, they continued to develop and become ever more elaborate until around the end of the first millennium BC.

Within the overall class of Atlantic roundhouses we can identify a sub-group of complex roundhouses which show some signs of architectural complexity, such as intra-mural galleries, cells and stairs. A still smaller sub-set of the complex roundhouse class are the broch towers, where the characteristic elements of broch architecture were combined to create a taller, more visually imposing form (**2**).

15

**2** *Dun Carloway (artist's reconstruction): Broch towers were formed of two concentric walls tied together at vertical intervals by stone slabs to form a series of superimposed galleries. The galleries were linked by stairs within the walls, while ledges, or 'scarcements', projecting from the inner wall could have supported internal timber floors and a conical thatched roof.* Copyright: Comhairle nan Eilean and Alan Braby

Crucially, however, after two millennia of stone-robbing, re-building and collapse, it is almost never possible to determine the original height of complex roundhouses, and thus we can never hope to know what proportion of complex roundhouses were originally broch towers (although occasionally we can be fairly sure that individual complex roundhouses were not broch towers, by virtue of their irregularity of construction).

# The function of Atlantic roundhouses

It has often been assumed that Atlantic roundhouses had a more or less uniform function wherever they were found. This is probably because for so long they were thought to be the product of immigrants or invaders and, as a result, there has been remarkably little study of the different contexts of their adoption and use. Brochs apparently just spread, and the long-running arguments about whether they were domestic buildings or forts, or some combination of the two, tended not to differentiate between different parts of Atlantic Scotland, far less different parts of the Hebrides.

Recent work, however, has suggested that significant differences exist between the Western Isles and Orkney and that even within relatively small geographical areas there may have been significant differences.

## Orkney and the Western Isles

Several basic differences can be identified between Atlantic roundhouses in Orkney and the Western Isles (defined as the modern local authority area of that name). The most important include:

## Simple Atlantic roundhouses

There appear, so far, to be very few, if any, simple Atlantic roundhouses in the Western Isles, i.e. those without any evidence for architectural complexity (Armit 1992 and 1996 Chapter 7). Instead, wherever Atlantic roundhouses have been excavated in the Western Isles they have shown evidence of features such as intra-mural galleries, cells and/or stairs; i.e. they were complex roundhouses.

Since, at least in Orkney, excavated simple roundhouses tend to be earlier in date than most excavated complex roundhouses, their non-appearance in the Western Isles might suggest that the period in which Atlantic roundhouses were current there began somewhat later than in the north. The scant dating evidence so far suggests a date in the middle to late centuries BC: disturbance of the vegetation in the small catchment around Loch Bharabhat in west Lewis, and the inwash of silts into the loch, may well reflect the construction of the complex roundhouse of Dun Bharabhat sometime around 450 BC (Lomax 1997, 357), since secondary occupation dates from the structure suggest construction prior to the second century BC (Harding and Armit 1990). Dun Vulan in South Uist appears to have been built by the first century BC at latest (contra Parker Pearson and Sharples 1999) since a date of 183-44 BC derives from material under a secondary revetting wall apparently indicating repair in the last centuries BC, while the surrounding midden was forming by 55 BC – AD 66 at latest (*ibid.*). Many more dates will be required, however, before the period of the Hebridean roundhouses can be established with any confidence.

## 'Broch villages'

The last centuries BC saw the emergence in Orkney and the mainland of northern Scotland of clustered and highly organised settlements focused on certain broch towers at sites like Gurness and Howe in Orkney (**3**, Hedges 1987, Ballin Smith 1994). In Orkney there seems to have been a progression over upwards of 600 years from isolated, unenclosed, simple Atlantic roundhouses, through the evolution of complex roundhouses with intra-mural cells and galleries, to the appearance of full-blown broch towers, some with attached nucleated villages (**colour plates 4** & **5**) (cf. Armit 1990). The development of broch villages has been thought to reflect the gradual centralisation of power within a relatively few hands (also cf. Foster 1989).

These 'broch villages', however, appear so far to be absent from the Western Isles. This does not mean that Atlantic roundhouses in the Western Isles did not have outbuildings and associated enclosures (Armit 1992); simply that the complexity and integration of settlement design seen in the north did not apparently develop in the west.

The layout of the Orcadian 'broch villages' would appear literally to set in stone the social relationships of dominance and subservience that presumably underpinned Orcadian society towards the end of the first millennium BC; or at least those relationships to which the emergent social leaders aspired. Architecture and settlement design were apparently manipulated to drive home the message that those who commissioned and lived in the broch tower, and their descendants, were the legitimate leaders of society.

If powerful leaders similar to those present in Orkney emerged in the Western Isles, they do not appear to have manifested their authority through the manipulation of settlement design in quite the same way.

## Decorated pottery

One clear characteristic of the Iron Age material culture of the Western Isles is the persistence and profusion of decorated ceramics over many centuries in the first millennia BC and AD, and indeed in periods before and after (Lane 1990). The relative paucity of such pottery found in association with Orcadian Atlantic roundhouses (e.g. at Howe, Ballin Smith 1994)

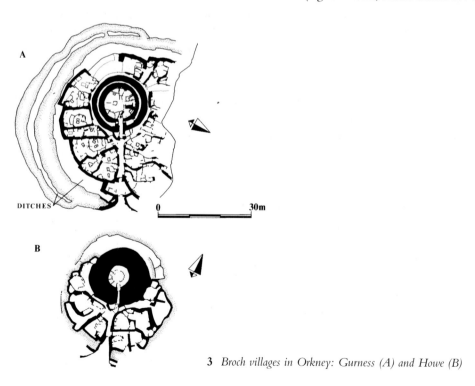

*3 Broch villages in Orkney: Gurness (A) and Howe (B)*

and those in Shetland (e.g. Hamilton 1956, 1968) shows that, although many of the ceramic forms and motifs used were far from exclusive to the Western Isles, the variety and quantity of pottery use in the Western Isles was quite regionally specific.

The persistence of such distinct regional variations in perceptions and uses of aspects of material culture suggests that much of routine domestic life within Atlantic roundhouses maintained much longer-lived local traditions, largely unaltered by the introduction of the roundhouse form of architecture. The post-broch re-emergence of settlement forms characteristic of the pre-broch period in Shetland suggests that equally distinct patterns can be demonstrated there (cf. Fojut 1985).

## Atlantic roundhouses in the Western Isles

Even within the Hebrides there is evidence that Atlantic roundhouses were adopted and inhabited by communities with quite distinct priorities and concerns. This can perhaps best be appreciated by first establishing the settlement patterns within which Atlantic roundhouses were adopted in North Uist and Barra, two of the most intensively studied islands; and contrasting the results with the patterns observed on other Hebridean islands such as South Uist.

## North Uist and Barra

North Uist is fairly typical of the physical landscapes of the Western Isles, being dominated by a sharp divide between the miles of machair sands along the north-west coast, and the bleak interior peatlands with their spine of low hills. The east coast is generally rocky and inhospitable and settlement in recent centuries has consequently been restricted to the north and west coastal areas, focusing on the machair, which has been the most productive land for agriculture.

Although considerably smaller, Barra has the same broad pattern of economically viable west coast and inhospitable east. The contrast is, however, considerably less marked than in North Uist and the landscape is fragmented into a series of well-defined catchment systems. A number of smaller islands lie to the east and south of Barra, including Vatersay, Fuday, Pabbay, Mingulay, Berneray and Sandray, and these will be included under the heading of Barra from here on. Modern and historically attested population figures show that Barra has long been more densely settled than North Uist, though with a smaller overall population.

Both areas have lengthy histories of archaeological research, and dense distributions of Atlantic roundhouses, as well as other forms of Iron Age settlement. Erskine Beveridge's exhaustive excavations in the early part of the century opened the way for later research in North Uist (Beveridge 1911, 1930, 1931), while the pioneering work of Sir Lindsay Scott on the settlement patterns of Barra (inter alia) was a landmark in the development of studies of the Atlantic Scottish Iron Age (Scott 1947).

*Atlantic roundhouses in North Uist and Barra*
North Uist has 51 Atlantic roundhouses, including probable examples, in an area of only

20 by 25km (**4**), of which a very restricted portion appears to have been inhabited (Armit 1992). The distribution of these structures is broadly similar to that of later, post-medieval settlement (i.e. they are distributed around the north and west coasts, generally in areas with access to a range of natural resources, including machair and peatland), while the interior and east of the island were apparently virtually unoccupied in this period. The east coast township of Lochmaddy had its origins as a fishing centre in the post-medieval period and represents the main area of historic settlement lacking an Iron Age pedigree. The distributions of walled and causewayed islets in North Uist, which appear to be of rather earlier date (cf. Armit 1992 Chapter Ten), show a much more even coverage, suggesting that the absence of roundhouses from certain parts of the island represents a genuine avoidance of these areas rather than being a result of fieldwork bias. In essence, then, the areas most intensively exploited by the inhabitants of the North Uist roundhouses correspond closely to those areas exploited in the post-medieval period.

There have been 18 Atlantic roundhouses identified on Barra and its associated islands (**5**). The distribution pattern in Barra itself is less obviously coastal than in North Uist, and most of the west-facing catchments were exploited. Again, later prehistoric settlement occupies essentially the same parts of the island as post-medieval settlement, with the exception of the later fishing centre of Castlebay.

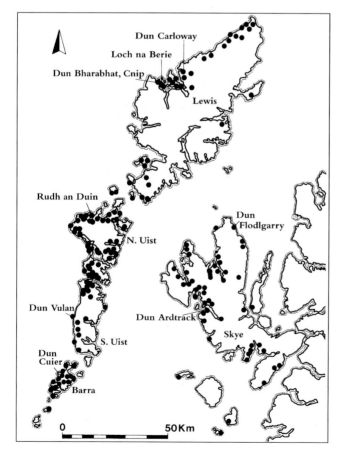

**4** *Distribution of Atlantic roundhouses in the Western Isles*

## *Survival*

There are a number of reasons to think that the presently known distributions of Atlantic roundhouses in these two islands are at least broadly representative of their original distribution. Firstly, there is the relatively high survival potential of such massively built stone structures; secondly, there is the relative lack of destructive later agricultural practices; and thirdly there is the comparatively comprehensive history of survey and research on these islands.

Nonetheless considerable problems remain: coastal erosion has made significant inroads into several sites, particularly in Barra (e.g. Dun Chlif, Armit 1992, 161), and it is quite possible that others have been entirely lost (see Ballin Smith this volume). The movement and redeposition of the machair sands may have hidden some sites, while wholesale stone-robbing could have rendered others unrecognisable. The masking of sites by subsequent settlement or other human activity may obscure still more, as is demonstrated by the relatively recent archaeological reappearance of Dun na Kille in Barra: a site suspected from place-name evidence and rediscovered built into a relatively recent cemetery wall (Armit 1992, 162).

Although the site distributions are unusually good in relation to other forms of prehistoric site, consideration of these factors suggests that they still probably under-represent the original population to some degree. Unusually for a group of prehistoric structures, however, it is at least possible to begin to approach an analysis of original site distributions.

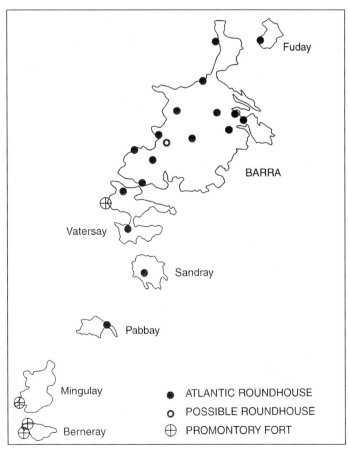

**5** *Distribution of Atlantic roundhouses and promontory forts in Barra and surrounding islands*

## Contemporaneity

Apart from how representative the surviving site distributions are, the other crucial factor in analysing the Iron Age settlement patterns is the issue of site contemporaneity. However, there is good reason to believe that the great majority, if not all, of the Atlantic roundhouses in these islands were in use at broadly the same time. Most importantly, there is the longevity of the structures themselves and the evidence from excavated sites such as Dun Cuier in Barra (Young 1955, Armit 1988), and Loch na Berie (Harding and Armit 1990) that occupation extended, perhaps continuously, from the later centuries BC to the immediately pre-Norse period. This remarkable continuity of settlement location implies a high degree of stability in land tenure and settlement foci.

The structures themselves also form a broadly homogeneous group of complex roundhouses, which seem unlikely to be far separated in their dates of construction, presumably in the second half of the first millennium BC. Additionally, the general spatial distribution of the sites, spread remarkably evenly across the most hospitable parts of the islands, suggests a more or less contemporary pattern of landscape exploitation (Armit 1988, 1992).

## Population minima and maxima

Given, then, that the site distributions represent basically coherent patterns of landscape exploitation, occupying the same land areas as were occupied in the eighteenth century, and under comparable climatic and environmental conditions, and given that the sites concerned were at least broadly contemporary, we can now look at some of their implications for social organisation. This can be approached by analogy with the post-medieval population figures which first become available for 1755 (Sinclair 1791-99).

It should be stressed at the outset that it is not being suggested that the 1755 figures are representative of likely prehistoric population levels, nor is it suggested that there is any likely correspondence in terms of social organisation or land tenure between the two periods. Comparison with the later population figures, however, is useful in assessing the implications of some alternative social interpretations of Atlantic roundhouses.

The population figures for 1755 relate to an essentially subsistence-based economy broadly analogous to that operating in earlier periods. The beginnings of the growth of the kelp industry and the commercialisation of fishing which were associated with significant growth in population a few generations later, however, have probably resulted in somewhat higher figures than would have characterised the subsistence economy of the immediately preceding medieval period.

The figures for North Uist in 1755 show a population of 1909 people. Somewhere between 1500 and 2500, therefore, might be a realistic indicative figure for the population which could have been supported under the prevailing economic regimes in these areas, with the lower figure perhaps more likely than the higher. Since 51 roundhouses occupy North Uist, a figure of 29–49 is reached on this analogy for the mean population potentially associated with any given structure. It immediately becomes apparent, therefore, that an extremely substantial population figure, enormously in excess of that for 1755, would have to be invoked to argue that these structures had anything like the status of tribal centres.

The population figure of 1150 for Barra and its southern islands in 1755, calculated on the same basis, suggests an indicative figure of around 600–1500 for the viable population supported by a subsistence economy. This area has 18 roundhouses, giving a figure of potentially 33–83 people associated with each structure.

Additional, and perhaps rather more satisfactory, data on both the likely population associated with each structure and the minimum resource base required to support such a population, comes from the smaller islands close to Barra (**5**). These islands, of assorted sizes and varying economic potential, straggle off to the south and east of Barra itself. Vatersay supported two roundhouses, while one each occupied Fuday, Sandray and Pabbay. No island under 3km² has a roundhouse.

The southernmost islands, Mingulay and Berneray, have had no definite roundhouses identified as yet, although there are possible traces of one on the east coast of Mingulay (Fojut pers. comm.); nonetheless Berneray has two promontory forts including that at Barra Head Lighthouse, a structure probably contemporary with the Atlantic roundhouses and displaying many of the same architectural traits (RCAHMS 1928, no. 450, not included in the present discussion), while Mingulay has a further example on its west coast. It is quite possible that these structures may have been occupied contemporaneously with the Atlantic roundhouses and may thus account for the absence of definite roundhouses on these islands (if so, they would increase the number of sites from 18 to 22 and alter the resulting population estimates accordingly). They have not, however, been included in this discussion.

The island of Pabbay, with Dunan Ruadh (RCAHMS 1928, no. 447) as its one roundhouse site, is more or less 3km², lacks any significant machair resource, has a rocky inhospitable coast, no land of particular agricultural value, and is not located near any other island without its own roundhouse site. Pabbay thus appears to demonstrate the minimal resource base required to support a population who were capable of constructing an Atlantic roundhouse. It is hard to imagine that such an ill-favoured location could ever have yielded sufficient resources to support even one household that could be described as part of a social elite; and the presence of similar structures on the adjacent islands suggests that the inhabitants are unlikely to have held power over any more extensive territories.

The population records for these small islands are imprecise, but they do at least give the numbers of families present, while from the overall population figures we know that the mean family size was seven individuals. The southern islands, with evidence for one roundhouse, were occupied in 1755 by three to nine families each, i.e. 21–63 individuals, and these must be regarded as high figures for extremely marginal (and now uninhabited) islands. It would be difficult to argue for substantially higher population figures in prehistory.

So what, if anything, can we make of these statistics? Essentially, the absolute number of people living on land occupied by an Atlantic roundhouse in North Uist and Barra was likely to be fairly low. Clearly not every roundhouse could have represented a centre of power over people and resources. A straightforward division of the 1755 population of the two islands by the number of known roundhouses would give 37 people per site in North Uist and 64 in Barra. Given the potential increase in population associated with the beginnings of economic growth in the eighteenth century, rather lower population estimates may be more appropriate for later prehistory, while allowance for the future discovery of further sites would lower the figures still further.

It is worth perhaps carrying this analogy just a little further. By 1755 the social elite was principally represented in the islands by 'tacksmen'. These were minor aristocracy who held land in return for administration on behalf of the landowner. Below tacksmen in the social hierarchy were the tenant farmers of joint farms, and below them a class of landless families. Crawford has calculated that the numbers of tenant and landless families in the eighteenth century were approximately equal (1965). While this social system is unlikely to have any close relationship to that pertaining in the Iron Age, it does enable comparison in terms of the likely limits of social authority and power available to communities occupying the same land in prehistory.

In 1718 there were 20 tacksmen in North Uist, and that figure had fallen to only 16 by 1764. Therefore, if broadly similar population figures were to apply to the two periods, or if Iron Age populations were lower than those of the eighteenth century, then clearly the majority of the 51 Atlantic roundhouses in North Uist were constructed and occupied by groups of relatively low social status, and certainly well below any level which could reasonably be described as elite.

It is interesting, in this context, that the number of roundhouses is similar to the number of eighteenth-century joint farms (51 compared to 54), which were the standard settlement unit of the later period. These joint farms were essentially self-sufficient economic units associated with individual areas of land. The effort put into the construction and maintenance of a permanent and monumental structure such as an Atlantic roundhouse must imply some expectation of security of land tenure: it is perhaps not unreasonable to suggest, therefore, combining these observations, that Atlantic roundhouses were built and occupied by most or all of the groups within society who held land. It is not inconceivable, although it clearly need not be the case, that the entire contemporary populations of North Uist and Barra inhabited roundhouses.

### The social role of Atlantic roundhouses

It would appear, then, that Atlantic roundhouses in North Uist and Barra were built and occupied by a variety of groups; presumably including any local elites which may have existed, but extending down to levels of society analogous to the tenant farmers of the post-medieval period (i.e. the lowest social level at which land was held on other than a casual basis). Yet, if we accept that Atlantic roundhouses in these two islands were not built solely as statements of the power and authority of local chiefs and their households, then why did island communities expend the labour and resources required to construct these monumental domestic buildings?

Part of the answer may lie in the local historical context within which Atlantic roundhouses were adopted. From the Neolithic to the post-medieval period, settlement in the Western Isles seems gradually to have retreated from the interior of the islands to the coastal belt, in the face of environmental degradation through peat growth, soil exhaustion, and deforestation (Armit 1998), factors probably exacerbated by inappropriate farming regimes. The adoption of Atlantic roundhouses in great numbers throughout the Western Isles could be interpreted in the context of increasing conflict over access to the ever-decreasing areas of usable land in the latter centuries of the first millennium BC.

Against a background of economic stress and competition for limited resources, the Atlantic roundhouse form, with its high local visibility and impression of permanence, could have come to be seen as a highly appropriate means of reinforcing claims to land. It is perhaps significant that these were the first domestic buildings in the Western Isles with walls more than a couple of metres above ground level, and their massive walls and towering conical roofs would have been an impressive sight for those used to semi-subterranean or low, cellular buildings. The massive stone roundhouses enabled individual households to make a clear imprint on the landscape. As such they may have served to reflect and legitimise the local autonomy of households occupying the small, marginal islands south of Barra, just as much as that of higher status households holding rather more productive lands in parts of Barra and North Uist.

The roundhouses inhabited by poorer communities, on islands like Fuday and Pabbay, could presumably have been constructed primarily by the households themselves; although it is quite possible that the work involved in construction, repair and maintenance, for example the quarrying and transport of stone, labouring and building, roofing and thatching, might have formed a focal point for interaction between neighbouring communities. It seems improbable, however, given the numbers of such structures relative to the likely population levels, that the inhabitants could draw upon any significant external subservient labour. This situation can presumably be contrasted with that of the Orcadian broch villages where subservience and social stratification appear to be embodied within the very design of the settlement.

## South Uist

This pattern of locally self-sufficient households, however, does not appear to hold true for all parts of the Hebrides. Some islands seem to contain far fewer roundhouses than Barra or North Uist and exhibit rather different patterns of distribution.

One such island is South Uist (**4**), where the number of roundhouses (21) is remarkably low compared to neighbouring North Uist (51), despite a comparable area of land available for settlement (although dividing the 1755 population by number of roundhouses in South Uist parish gives a figure of 64, exactly the same as in Barra, this result is distorted by the high density of roundhouses in Benbecula which nowadays forms part of South Uist parish). The dichotomy is especially intriguing as it appears to parallel directly the imbalance in the numbers of chambered tombs in the two islands, more than 2000 years earlier (Armit 1990b).

If we accept that the available distribution of sites in South Uist reflects a survey of comparable intensity to that in North Uist, we are left with a number of possible explanations for the differences in distribution: it is possible, though it seems unlikely, that South Uist had a far smaller Iron Age population than North Uist. Alternatively land-holding may have been differently organised, with lower status households having less security of tenure, and thus being less able or willing to invest in the construction of Atlantic roundhouses; or perhaps greater social stratification existed in South Uist than in North Uist and Atlantic roundhouse building in the former island was seen as inappropriate to all but a few social groups of higher social status.

Whatever the explanation it seems probable that the Atlantic roundhouses of South Uist were restricted to a smaller group within the Iron Age population than was the case in North Uist or Barra. The implication would appear to be that control over land and/or social power was concentrated in fewer hands, presumably reflecting significant local differences in social relations. There is some evidence from the study of dietary differences between Atlantic roundhouses and other sites in South Uist which might support a distinction between high status roundhouse sites and other lower status sites (Parker Pearson and Sharples 1999), although the faunal evidence is far from clear (Gilmour and Cook 1998).

The type of distribution seen in South Uist may be even more marked in Lewis where the number of Atlantic roundhouses relative to post-medieval population is very low (although the lack of intensive survey across the whole island makes statements about site distributions here less reliable). Some of the most elaborate and best-constructed of all Hebridean broch towers, such as Dun Carloway or Loch na Berie, and sites which combine high-quality construction with elaborate outworks as at Dun Loch an Duna, Bragar, are found in Lewis; these might well be examples of high status buildings, although the vagaries of preservation on potentially comparable sites elsewhere must always be borne in mind.

Nonetheless, even Dun Carloway, Loch na Berie, and Dun Loch an Duna, Bragar lack the clustered dependent villages seen in Orkney, and it is unlikely that an island such as Lewis could ever have supported 26 sites which could be described, even generously, as tribal centres. As in South Uist, it may be that the construction of Atlantic roundhouses, and perhaps by implication the secure tenure of land, was restricted to a narrower band of households towards the top of the local social scale.

## Atlantic roundhouses: context and variation

Such variations between neighbouring islands like North and South Uist may initially appear surprising, but we should bear in mind that even today there are significant differences between these very islands in terms of their social organisation and religious practices. South Uist has a strongly Catholic population in direct contrast to Free Church Presbyterian dominance in North Uist. The roadside shrines that greet the visitor arriving in South Uist from the north, and the strict observance of the Sabbath in North Uist, leave little doubt about the cultural importance of such distinctions.

The Iron Age communities across Atlantic Scotland who adopted Atlantic roundhouses were by no means a homogenous group (cf. Armit 1997). Major differences can be identified, as we have seen, between the Western Isles and Orkney, and, at a more detailed level of analysis, between on the one hand, North Uist and Barra, and on the other, South Uist and Lewis. The evidence for local autonomy at the level of the individual land-holding household in the former contrasts with the evidence for more overt social hierarchies in the latter. Such dimly perceived differences reflected in the patterns of archaeological site distribution are presumably a minimal representation of the wider differences that would have defined local groups in social and cultural terms. In each case, Atlantic roundhouse construction was seemingly adopted, as in much of the north and west, within the context of local, historically rooted, social strategies and did not, in itself, indicate a uniformity of cultural background or social structure.

# 3  Always the bridesmaid
## The Iron Age of south-west Scotland

*Iain B.J. Banks*

## Introduction

South-west Scotland essentially comprises Dumfriesshire, Galloway and southern Ayrshire. This is a beautiful part of the country, a landscape of rolling hills and valleys with dramatic coastlines, and one that receives fewer visitors than it perhaps should. The same can be said of its archaeology: it receives far less attention than it deserves. While Orkney is the best-known archaeological landscape in Scotland, the Highlands in general are fairly well studied and the archaeology has been well publicised. This is particularly true of the Iron Age. The geographical interests of the other papers in this volume demonstrate this quite clearly, as the Highlands and Islands are the main focus of study. In general, discussions of the Iron Age concentrate north of the Forth-Clyde isthmus, and when they take account of the south, limit themselves essentially to the south-east. As an example of this, a recent review of Scotland's archaeology (Edwards & Ralston 1997) covered the Iron Age in considerable detail, but virtually ignored the south-west; it was considered in less than four pages.

In a similar vein, a recent collection of hillfort excavations from southern Scotland was entitled *Hillforts of Southern Scotland* despite having no material from south of Troon in Ayrshire (Rideout *et al.* 1992). This reflects the low level of modern excavation of hillforts in south-west Scotland. Such a lack of interest is not the result of a paucity of archaeology, and certainly the Royal Commission on the Ancient and Historical Monuments of Scotland (RCAHMS) has undertaken large amounts of fieldwork for its recent *Eastern Dumfriesshire* inventory (RCAHMS 1997). However, this fieldwork has been survey in both the senses of identification of sites and of recording of the surface traces. There has been a low level of intrusive fieldwork in the area, and the situation would have been far worse had the A74 not been upgraded to motorway, thus driving a slice through the landscape.

It is the intention of this paper to direct interest toward this 'Cinderella' region of Scottish Iron Age studies, to argue for more fieldwork in the area and for the incorporation of the existing data within the accounts written of Iron Age Scotland. South-west Scotland has contributed virtually nothing to our debates on Scotland's Iron Age, a fact demonstrated quite clearly by the lack of references to sites in the south-west in the other contributions to this volume. This paper is therefore intended to provide a balance to the geographical tunnel-vision that archaeology can develop (cf. Barclay 2001).

## An Iron Age desert?

The lack of interest in the Iron Age of south-west Scotland is hard to explain. Dumfriesshire is the first part of Scotland encountered by visitors from the south travelling up the M6 onto the M74, and the motorway route runs through a rich archaeological landscape (cf. Banks forthcoming). Remoteness is frequently blamed for an area being under-researched, but this is difficult to maintain for south-west Scotland; indeed, it is far less remote than the Inner and Outer Hebrides that have received so much recent attention from English universities. The reason can hardly be the difficulty of the terrain, as the landscape is one of the more welcoming in Scotland. There are frequent towns and villages, communications are good both by road and by train and there are few of the logistical difficulties posed by working on the Islands or in remote parts of the Highlands.

There could be many reasons for the apparent lack of interest in south-west Scotland. An uncharitable suggestion might be that the very ease of working in the area makes it less attractive because it is perceived as being less of an adventure. What might be more relevant is the fact that the south-west has little in the way of brochs or duns except as outliers along the Solway Firth. The archaeology is therefore different from that of the north and west and does not form a part of the same story. It is inevitable that considerable archaeological effort in one area will detract from another area that does not deal with the same material. There are, however, impressive hillforts, such as Burnswark (**6**) that glowers over the Solway plain from the north. While this site has particular questions relating to its use during the Roman period, there are many other large forts in the area. The region is also thick with enclosures containing roundhouses of various forms, and tending to date to the Iron Age. There are many issues about society that can be addressed through study of these sites, yet the vast majority remain unexamined and are disappearing under the plough.

The history of the area is different from the Northern and Western Isles or the Highlands because of its experience of the Roman invasion. This again may direct interest away from the area. There are very different issues raised by the Roman occupation here that are of limited importance to the north and west, although there have been a few attempts to examine the impact of Rome on these distant areas (*pace* Fitzpatrick 1989). However, the impact of Rome was also felt in south-east Scotland, which has seen far greater interest in its Iron Age archaeology. Most of the literature concerning the southern Scottish Iron Age derives from excavations in south-east Scotland starting in the late 1940s with Hayhope Knowe (Piggott 1951), with a flurry of activity

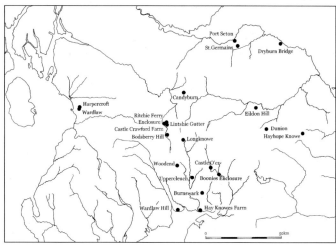

**6** *Map of sites mentioned in the text*

in the early 1980s, e.g. St Germains (Alexander & Watkins 1999) and Dryburn Bridge (Triscott 1982). This has been matched recently with the major excavations at Fishers Road in Port Seton (Haselgrove & McCullagh 2000). The south-east has not been ignored in the same way the south-west has, yet its archaeology is no better preserved, nor is there a greater quantity.

## The environment of south-west Scotland in the Iron Age

The landscape is very different from that of the Northern and Western Isles or the Highlands. Rather than the acid moorland and rocky outcrops of the north, this is a lush landscape of rolling hills and arable land. Botanical evidence suggests that the Iron Age landscape of south-west Scotland was very similar, being largely open. Clearance of the forest cover seems to have begun in the early Iron Age, with evidence from several sites indicating that this process had started by *c.*500 cal BC (Van der Veen 1992; Dumayne 1993; Ramsay, forthcoming). There was a peak in the clearance process around 150 – 50 BC, but the landscape had by then been relatively open for several centuries. This indicates that the cleared landscape was an autochthonous development and not the result of the Roman invasion. This contradicts an earlier paradigm about the southern Scottish landscape that the clearance of the forests was initiated by the Romans and was related directly to the requirements of the Roman army for grain. It is now apparent, just as on the Islands, for example, that the main episodes of forests clearance are a legacy of the Iron Age.

Again, just as in the Islands, the landscape that resulted in the south-west from the tree clearance was not necessarily an arable farming landscape. There were significant areas of marsh, particularly in the Lockerbie area, while much of the region was upland, best suited to grazing. Nonetheless, the climate was relatively temperate and much of south-west Scotland was capable of producing arable crops. An earlier idea suggested that the Iron Age was a period of cold and wet following the warm dry Bronze Age, leading to a collapse in production and societal change. It now appears that there was an increase in rainfall and certainly an increase in the levels of soil erosion (Tipping 1994), but this was not of sufficient magnitude to affect crop production. It is likely that the uplands were almost exclusively used for pastoralism in the Iron Age. Nonetheless, there were certainly Iron Age farming settlements in the uplands, such as the Bodsberry Hill platform settlement in south Lanarkshire near Beattock Summit (Terry 1994). The uplands also bear numerous hillforts and enclosures, suggesting that crop production may well have been a feature of the hills during the Iron Age. It is likely to have been located in patches, such as at Abington and Crawford, with the intervening hills being left to livestock.

Elsewhere in this volume, the environmental data from the Highlands and Islands during the Iron Age is presented (Bond). It is far more difficult to present an overview for the south-west with the relatively small amount of recent excavations in the region. There have been a number of rescue excavations, but these have produced very different results from the Highlands. As Bond's paper shows, the majority of these northern sites have produced good environmental data, with both floral and faunal evidence to work with. The situation in south-west Scotland is very different. Rather than substantial amounts of charred seeds and animal bones, the south-western sites have tended to produce large amounts of tree charcoal, very small amounts of charred seeds and infrequent animal bones. At a large enclosure at Woodend in Annandale, excavated in 1994 and 1997, small quantities of charred seeds were recovered, with no animal bone at all (Banks 2001). However, the site also produced several rotary querns, at least one of which was partially finished, suggesting that the occupants made their own querns. The enclosure quite obviously had a need for querns to process grain, and seems thus to have been an arable settlement. It appears that they did not store grain in a way that it entered the archaeological record. There was no indication of how grain would have been stored on site; there were no storage pits and no four-poster structures that might have been granaries. None of the hearths of the settlement survived, so there was no discernable difference in function between structures.

This low recovery rate for charred grain is not unusual in the region as few sites have produced much in the way of charred grain. Woodend has already been mentioned, but there are several others. Uppercleuch, also on Annandale (Terry 1993), produced a large cache of emmer grains, but this comes from an insecure context and the radiocarbon date failed in the laboratory. There is consequently no means of relating the emmer to the Iron Age use of the site. Excluding this single deposit, the rest of the site yielded very small amounts of grain. The site of Long Knowe in Eskdale produced no evidence of grain and no querns were recovered. The excavator's interpretation of this circumstance was that the site had been a seasonal livestock station (Mercer 1981); however, this site appeared very similar to Woodend, where several querns were recovered (Banks 2001). Whether the interpretation of a livestock station can be justified purely on negative evidence is open to question; the general lack of artefactual material and the very denuded nature of the archaeological remains following forestry ploughing mean that evidence has been lost. Some of the quern material from Woodend was fragmented, and such fragments might have been missed at Long Knowe. Unfortunately, the Long Knowe report has no detail about its environmental sampling strategy to indicate why there is a lack of charred grain.

The lack of animal bones is another common feature of Iron Age sites in south-west Scotland. It is likely that this is a taphonomic issue: the soils are too acid for bone to be preserved. However, there are various indications at the excavated Iron Age sites that cattle were present. Long Knowe was interpreted as a livestock station, partly because of the lack of cultivation evidence and partly because of the presence of cattle, horse and *caprine* bones (Mercer 1981). These were all poorly preserved, indicating the effect of the acid soils. This would suggest, however, that the lack of animal bone at lower altitudes does not relate to the soil conditions, as the Long Knowe soils would have been more inimical to bone survival than elsewhere. Uppercleuch was also considered by its excavator to have been heavily involved in livestock, and the cobbled area close to the excavated hut-circle was considered to have been hard-standing for cattle (Terry 1993). At Woodend, there was considerable damage to the eastern side of the enclosure that seemed to have been cattle-trample. Although this was not recent damage, it is difficult to link it directly to the period of occupation of the site. However, the micro-morphological report of the soil confirmed the presence of cattle when the settlement was in use, while the largest of the structures seems to have been a livestock pen (Banks 2001). This building would appear to represent the *lías* mentioned in early Irish texts (Lucas 1989, 25-31), an enclosure within the settlement where cattle were penned overnight.

This suggests that the economy of the Iron Age sites of south-west Scotland was based on mixed farming, with both arable and cattle playing a role. Dairying was probably involved, although without faunal remains there is no positive evidence for this. However, it is barely conceivable that it would not have been a part of the economy. There is evidence for the importance of dairying within Dark Age society in Irish literary sources (Lucas 1989), and this has been projected back for Iron Age societies. What remains unclear, due to the lack of faunal remains, is the role of the wildscape in the diet of Iron Age south-west Scotland. While red deer remains are known from Iron Age sites in the Highlands and Islands, it is unknown if the diet was supplemented by hunting in the south-west thank to the scarcity of faunal remains. Current information would suggest that hunting was not a significant element of the food resources, but this is open to discussion. South-west Scotland has considerable numbers of burnt mounds scattered across the landscape, and it is now apparent that many are found within the lower-lying arable areas. While the majority of dated examples are Bronze Age, there are outlying dates at either end of the scale. It also seems strange that such a major part of the Bronze Age landscape had absolutely no role in the Iron Age. Few examples in the low-lying areas have been excavated, and it may well be the case that the use of burnt mounds continued into the Iron Age. If so, this would suggest that hunting was part of the food strategies of communities.

## Material culture

Artefacts are relatively rare in south-west Scotland. In contrast to the south-eastern sites (**6**) that are normally considered in any discussion of the southern Scottish Iron Age, many of the excavated enclosures in south-west Scotland have produced virtually no artefacts. The Woodend enclosure, despite its excavation by hand, produced only coarse stone tools (Banks 2001). Uppercleuch produced a Roman glass bangle and a stone disc (Terry 1993), Candyburn near Biggar produced no artefacts at all (Lane 1986), while the Long Knowe site was similarly barren of finds (Mercer 1981). The Hayknowes Farm enclosure at Annan (Gregory 1996) produced two sherds of pottery tentatively identified as early Medieval, a carnelian bead and some fragments of bird bone. The only other artefact was a stone bearing incised rock art that was found in the excavated hut circle. The Boonies enclosure in Eskdale produced rather more in the way of artefacts; Jobey recovered seven sherds of local pottery and three of Roman pottery, together with a fragment of a glass bracelet, a bronze penannular brooch and a coarse stone tool assemblage (Jobey 1975). The unusual square enclosure at Rispain Camp near Whithorn (Haggarty & Haggarty 1983) produced two metal artefacts (a pair of iron tongs and a bronze object), two pieces of blue glass, and both carbonised seeds and animal bone in the small area excavated. The assemblage of animal bone was very small, but it included deer bones from the ditch in addition to domestic cattle, sheep and pigs. This may indicate some hunting in addition to the use of livestock for meat. However, the general pattern is of a lower level of recovery compared to sites in the Highlands and Islands, or in south-east Scotland.

The low recovery of finds from enclosures is not necessarily the whole story, however. The excavations at Burnswark, a large hillfort overlooking Ecclefechan in Annandale, yielded far more finds. The excavations of 1898 and 1973 produced a range of Iron Age and Romano-British artefacts (Christison *et al.* 1899; Jobey 1978), including querns, glass bracelets and locally produced pottery. However, while there was undoubtedly a larger amount of material from the site, the range of artefacts was quite small and rather unimpressive compared to some Iron Age sites in the Highlands and Islands. To some extent, this may relate to the size of the excavations. The investigations at Harpercroft and Wardlaw Hill forts, between Troon and Dundonald in Ayrshire (Halpin 1992), produced a small artefact assemblage (77 pottery sherds and five fragments of jet armlet from the Harpercroft site) compared to the large assemblages from the Dunion, between Hawick and Jedburgh in Roxburghshire (Rideout 1992a) or Eildon Hill North, also in Roxburghshire (Owen 1992). However, the excavations at the Ayrshire sites were on a smaller scale than the Roxburgh examples and this may have affected the level of recovery achieved. This is particularly the case for the Wardlaw Hill excavation, which essentially only examined the rampart on one side of the fort (Halpin 1992, 122: fig. 4.1). Certainly, the level of recovery more closely resembles that from the partial excavation at Gilles Hill, Cambusbarron, near Stirling (Rideout 1992b).

The impression that this disparity creates is that the south-west of Scotland had a poorly developed material culture in the Iron Age. This is unlikely to have been the case, as the inhabitants of this area would have had contact with artefactually-richer areas of south-east Scotland and northern England. One factor in the paucity of artefact recovery might be that much of the artefactual material was made of bone, and very little bone survives in south-west Scotland. However, this does not explain the lack of pottery and metalwork. That there is some cultural difference between the south-east and the south-west seems likely; a site such as St Germains in East Lothian produced a reasonable array of material despite being as heavily ploughed as Uppercleugh which produced virtually no artefacts (Alexander and Watkins 1999; Terry 1993). It is difficult to explain the difference in recovery rates in terms of post-depositional factors or by differences in soil chemistry; rather, cultural differences probably reduced the deposition of artefactual material. Whatever their nature, there seems to have been a genuine difference between east and west in southern Scotland, which may reveal the political entities that existed in the Iron Age.

## Social structure

There is some reason to consider a settlement hierarchy, with the enclosures acting as a middle rank between hillforts (including duns and brochs) and unenclosed hut circles. This was suggested by RCAHMS in their Eastern Dumfriesshire Inventory (RCAHMS 1997). They considered that it was possible to consider hillfort territories, where each large hillfort controlled an area with smaller hillforts and other settlement types; this was based upon the example of Castle O'er in Eskdale, Dumfriesshire (RCAHMS 1997, 82). Yet this is rather a dated approach to studying settlement patterns, and is undermined by the fact that most of the sites included in the study area are undated. It is thus impossible to know whether the range of sites are contemporary or whether they reflect changes in the structure of settlement. Nonetheless, there does appear to be some kind of hierarchy in the settlement types. There are large enclosed sites on hilltops, some with a number of houses; there are smaller enclosed sites in lower-lying areas, with one, two or several houses; and there are individual sites, frequently unenclosed. The sites that produce the most substantial artefact assemblages are the hillforts, while the other sites produce very little. However, this is based on a very small sample, and it is of course possible that more excavation will change the picture entirely.

There appears to be a case for suggesting a hierarchy, based on the range of types of settlement and their different sizes. It has been a fairly general practice to use Irish Medieval texts to provide a Jacksonian '*Window on the Iron Age*'. These texts, which preserve legal material from the first millennium AD, use the principle of social status being displayed in the architecture of settlement. One of the key elements to this is the principle of the *drécht giallnae* in the seventh-century *Críth Gablach* (Kelly 1988, 30; *Críth Gablach* 1 570). This principle of the rights of the élite to labour services could be expressed in the construction of extra banks to the rath of the lord (Graham 1950, 69; Byrne 1973, 138). This has normally been taken to mean that multivallation, particularly for enclosures, is an indication of high social status (e.g. Banks 2001). Leaving aside the difficulties of applying later material that was deliberately archaic in nature to earlier conditions, and in transporting the legal arrangements from Ireland to Scotland, there does seem some justice in suggesting that the unnecessary elaboration of banks around an enclosure reflects the social status of the inhabitants. Unfortunately, the example of Woodend could be taken to contradict this model. The banks at Woodend were quite low while the presence of stone within the trench sections suggests that they might have been partially stone-capped, indicating they were never particularly high. If this was the case, then there was no practical reason for having the extra banks. However, the excavation produced virtually no artefacts, despite the site having been in use during the Roman period and lying close to the Roman road and to the concentration of forts and marching camps in the Beattock area.

A hierarchy of settlement would contrast with the arguments advanced by Ian Armit in his paper on Atlantic roundhouses in this volume. He suggests that, in the Hebrides at least, the large stone structures do not reflect social status or a settlement hierarchy, and that some must have been the basic unit of settlement. If this were the case, then it would appear that there is a distinction between the Hebrides and south-west Scotland in terms of the organisation of society: south-west Scotland had a hierarchy of settlement and is likely to have been a ranked society, while the north had no settlement hierarchy and is likely to have been a less organised society. However, with the low level of excavation in both areas, firm conclusions cannot be drawn. It is possible to suggest that south-west Scotland has the potential to illumine issues of social status and site hierarchies with its range of Iron Age sites, as might not be possible in the north where there are fewer types.

## Case study

There is a particularly good opportunity to study this problem at Crawford in South Lanarkshire, an area rich in archaeology and excavations, particularly with the upgrade of the A74 to a motorway. There are Bronze Age unenclosed platform settlements, with Lintshie Gutter having been excavated (Terry 1995), burnt mounds in profusion (Banks 1999), Neolithic and Bronze Age burial monuments (see Banks 1995), a Roman fort and marching camps (Maxwell 1974) and a Medieval castle. There is also a number of presumed Iron Age sites, including enclosures, homesteads and a site identified as a fort (Crawford 1939). Of the latter, two groups are of particular interest: the Richie Ferry enclosure and homestead, and the Castle Crawford Farm fort and enclosure (**7**). These paired sites are very similar to one another. In both cases there is a large enclosure capable of containing a number of buildings (in the case of Richie Ferry, eight have been identified), with a smaller enclosure in near proximity that either contains a single building or has no trace of any structure. Indeed, the Richie Ferry site has three enclosures close by, only one of which seems to have a building within.

These two groups of sites are very similar in appearance. It is tempting to think of them as being of similar date. If they are of the same date, then it is possible that an element of the Iron Age settlement geography has been preserved. It is also tempting to assume that both clusters of sites had the same developmental history.

The main issue with the clusters is whether the large and small enclosures in each case were contemporary or sequential. If the large and small enclosures were sequential, then two alternative circumstances are possible. In the first the small enclosure was built as a founding settlement. As the settlement became successful then the population increased. This might have been an increase in

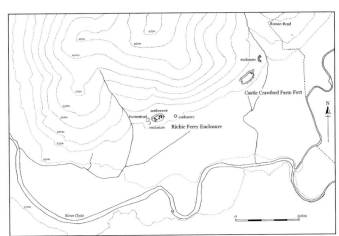

**7** *Map of Ritchie Ferry enclosure and Castle Crawford Farm fort and enclosure*

the size of the extended family, with each succeeding generation increasing the population. Alternatively, the success of the settlement might have attracted other families, so that a community of separate families emerged. In both cases, the increasing population required a larger enclosure. The smaller enclosure would then have been abandoned or used simply for stock or storage.

In the alternative situation, the larger enclosure was the founding settlement, containing an entire community. Over time, the population dwindled and the larger enclosure became redundant. Finally, what was left of the community built the small enclosure and left the larger enclosure either abandoned or used for stock or storage.

If the enclosures were contemporary, then a more interesting possibility emerges. Both were used for settlement so there may have been a difference in social status. Perhaps the leader of the community lived in the smaller enclosure, demonstrating their superiority by creating exclusive space. This may have been the impulse behind the construction of duns and brochs, the Atlantic roundhouses discussed elsewhere in this volume. It was certainly the idea behind tower houses in the medieval period, of which there are numerous examples in Dumfriesshire. Alternatively, it is possible that the smaller enclosure was a lower status settlement. It is possible that slaves were quartered in the smaller enclosure; slavery was certainly present in Dark Age Ireland, and it is possible that slavery can be pushed back into the Iron Age. Rather than living in the same enclosure as the free members of society, perhaps the *cumals* were accommodated in a separate space, again demonstrating social status through the use of space. There is a final possibility, again using space to reflect status. It is possible that the smaller enclosure was the location of something seen as dangerous or of low status. Smiths were certainly considered to have been outside normal society in the law codes of early Medieval Ireland (Banks 1996). There were dangers in the smithying process, particularly in the smelting of bronze, because of the poisonous metals used. This seems to have been quite widespread, and Classical mythology tended to show smiths as lame, possibly as the result of arsenic poisoning. It is thus possible that the smith was accommodated in a separate location to keep such perilous activities at arm's length.

The only way to investigate these possibilities would be to excavate the sites. This would have to be a long-term project, leading to the complete excavation of both clusters of sites. A note of caution should be sounded, however. Although this pair of clusters suggests the possibility of being able to investigate these issues, it must be recognised that such a cluster of enclosures is extremely unusual. Even if the results were all that could be hoped, answering every question, it would be difficult to apply them more widely because the circumstances are so unusual.

## Conclusion

The intention of this paper has been to bring south-west Scotland out of the shadows. The south-west contains a large body of material that can add substantially to our understanding of the Scottish Iron Age, yet it has been passed over in favour of the south-east and the Highlands and Islands. There has been much discussion recently about the effect of regionalism on Scottish Archaeology (cf. Barclay 2001), noting that the Neolithic of Scotland is written in terms of south-west England and Orkney. The same is true of the Scottish Iron Age, with the Highlands and Islands dominating the majority of discussions of the period, and south-east Scotland as the remainder. This is not only a problem for the Iron Age, as knowledge of other periods would be improved by breaking the grip that the traditional regions of study have always held. The intention is merely to suggest that the south-west should become a part of any study of Iron Age Scotland. Always the bridesmaid in Scottish Iron Age studies, it is time that south-west Scotland became the bride.

# 4  The Oakbank Crannog
## Building a house of plants

*Jennifer J. Miller*

## Introduction

Oakbank Crannog (NGR NN72284425) lies in shallow water at the north-east end of Loch Tay, Perthshire, Scotland (**8**). There are 18 such crannogs in the loch (Dixon 1982), and Oakbank is one of nine now permanently submerged. It exists today as a boulder capped mound of almost entirely organic material, *c.*1000 cubic metres volume (Miller, Dickson & Dixon 1998), and is the first in Scotland to have been excavated underwater to modern standards and recording techniques.

To date, financial and seasonal constraints have meant that only 25 per cent of the total area of the site has been examined, but the abundance of well-preserved organic remains recorded has served to emphasise just how much information can be retrieved from water-logged occupation sites. Radiocarbon dates from structural timbers place the occupation phases to a *c.*400-year period spanning the Late Bronze/early Iron Age transition (Dixon 1984; Barber & Crone 1993). AMS dating of two pips of cloudberry (*Rubus chamaemorus* L.) from the top of the organic mound, representing the detrital build-up of the latest *surviving* occupation, have dated this ultimate phase to the pre-Roman Iron Age (390-50 cal BC 2$\sigma$, OxA-7103) (Miller *et al.* 1998).

Numerous structural timbers have been isolated, disclosing evidence of the uprights, platform and walls of a building constructed entirely of plant materials. Identification of remains of 166 higher plant taxa from deposits within the occupation levels have indicated a peaceful, wealthy economy (Miller 1997; Miller *et al.* 1998), with arable agriculture successful enough to permit the feeding of surplus barley (*Hordeum vulgare sl* L.) to livestock as a supplement to hay fodder. The presence of emmer (*Triticum dicoccum* Schübl.) and especially spelt (*T. spelta* L.) wheat chaff, together with seeds of opium poppy (*Papaver somniferum* L.) imply high status and wealth, as well as indicating trade links with the south. Summer transhumance is suggested from the seeds of cloudberry, a montane species with low fruiting potential and an obligate requirement for blanket peat above *c.*210m altitude (Taylor 1971). The utilisation of gathered wild fruits and nuts is also evident, together with numerous miscellaneous household uses for other wild plants. Interpretation of the remains from the dwelling itself and the plant macrofossils from occupation levels have shown that the people who inhabited Oakbank Crannog in the early Iron Age had a sound understanding of how to exploit their local environment extremely successfully, and in a sustainable manner, for all aspects of living.

## The Crannog

Oakbank Crannog was a stilted timber structure with a thatched roof and hurdle walls. A reconstruction at Kenmore, on the other side of Loch Tay, is based on the evidence from Oakbank and demonstrates what the dwelling would have looked like during occupation (**colour plate 6**). Wild plants would have been gathered for specific household uses to make the dwelling warm, water-tight and comfortable. More than 2000 structural timbers encompassing at least six phases of occupation have been isolated during excavation (Dixon 1984; Sands 1994) (**colour plate 7**), as well as hundreds of wood and charcoal fragments from the organic mound. Wood was one of the most important natural resources known to prehistoric man, providing shelter, fuel, and a wide range of other daily necessities. Consequently, the identification of wood taxa found in archaeological contexts is important in explaining past woodland cover and the utilisation of forestry by ancient communities. Different trees have distinct qualities of strength, weight, flexibility and chemical constituents, and some are better than others for particular uses. At Oakbank Crannog, trees supplied timbers for housing, wood for carving into tools, utensils and other artefacts, flexible rods for wattle and basketry and fuel for domestic purposes. Selection of specific taxa for particular purposes was strongly in evidence in all areas of the site.

## Wood selection at Oakbank

Simplistically, the mean increase in girth of a tree in full crown averages 25mm per annum when taken over a prolonged period (Mitchell 1996). However, the width of the bole is dependent on the amount of space and light available, and an individual in a closed forest

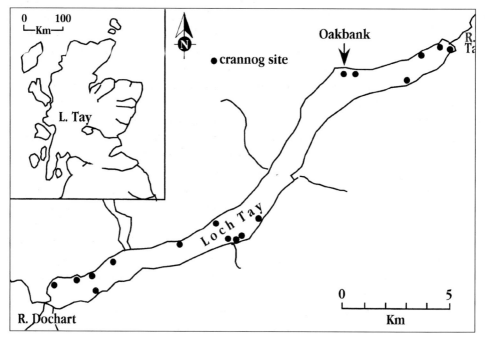

8  *Map of Loch Tay showing crannog sites*

situation may be up to 100 years older than one with a similar girth in full crown and adequate space. This has implications for Oakbank Crannog, where the piles were long, straight maiden trees, indicating they had been taken from forest situations, and thereby were likely to have been of a good age. The regeneration of this woodland could not be achieved satisfactorily with any sustained human impact, and this activity must have contributed to the forest clearance in the local area. Similar clearances are now recognised to have occurred in central Scotland during the pre-Roman Iron Age (Ramsay 1995).

At Oakbank, the choice of timbers for construction reflects both availability and selection for specific properties. Most of the uprights, platform timbers and gangway piles were alder (*Alnus*) or oak (*Quercus*), with only low numbers of other taxa, including birch (*Betula*), rowan type (Maloideae), willow (*Salix* sp L.), elm (*Ulmus* sp L.) and ash (*Fraxinus* sp L.). These few piles probably represent occasional use of resources to hand. Other wood found at Oakbank was in the form of wood-working waste chips and roundwood fragments from within organic occupation deposits. Here, species were primarily alder, oak, hazel (*Corylus*) and birch, with willow, rowan type, elm and sloe type (*Prunus spinosa* L. type) present in descending order of abundance (Miller 1997). Sands (1994) also found low quantities of charred tapers of Scots pine (*Pinus sylvestris* L.). Having a high resin content, pine is well known for torch making and fire-lighting. Very little pine was found elsewhere, suggesting purposeful selection of this wood for fire-lighting.

Alder constituted more than 50 per cent of all the structural timbers found on the site (Sands 1994), and was the most commonly identified wood and charcoal type isolated from the occupation deposits (Miller 1997), including the majority of wooden artefacts and worked chips found at Oakbank both by this author and others (Dixon 1984; Crone 1988; Sands 1994). With such an abundance of alder and oak timbers it might have been expected that it would have been possible to date the crannog using dendrochronology (i.e. dating by measuring the pattern of annual growth ring formation and comparing this to a time-line of patterns from timbers of various, known ages). In this country dendrochronology is carried out most commonly on oak. However, the oaks examined were of insufficient ages, and although the alders were older, their annual growth habits were too inconsistent to produce a satisfactory *absolute* chronology (Crone 1988). Nevertheless a *relative* chronology was calculated and Sands (1994) compared this with groups of tool signatures he had devised, tracing the signature marks found on the structural timbers to particular axes and by implication to the same phase of construction. This enabled him to calculate building phases and the approximate time scales involved. Clearly this combination of dendrochronology and signature groupings has implications for future work on other sites.

The abundance of long, straight alder timbers implies dense, unmanaged woodland with maiden (not coppiced) trees, ideal for construction. Alder grows beside water in the kind of damp woodland carr that would have been abundant around the crannog site as it is today (**colour plate 8**). This proximity to the loch means that the trees could be floated out to the construction site without too much energy expended in long distance haulage. However, the most important reason for using alder wood for construction on a wetland site is that it is extremely durable in conditions of alternate wetting and drying (Schwankl 1957; Edlin 1973; Mitchell 1996), partly due to the high tannin content of the wood. Piles of both alder and oak have been identified from other crannog sites too, including (in recent times) Buiston in South Ayrshire (Crone 2000) and Dumbuck in the Clyde Estuary (Hale 1999).

Morrison (1985) argues that any timber-built crannog would require continuous refurbishment, but this effect must have been minimised by a careful choice of construction taxa, as is suggested from Oakbank, Buiston and Dumbuck. Certainly there is only clear evidence for a few major phases of consolidation at Oakbank (Dixon 1984; Sands 1994) over an occupation estimated to span some 400 years (Dixon 1984). The durability of alder timbers in a wetland situation is demonstrated aptly by the pilings of the abandoned Loch Tay ferry pier, still upright and above water 100 years after construction.

The resistance of alder to alternate wetting and drying combined with the soft nature of the wood also enables it to be carved easily into small items which require durability when wet, such as clogs, scrubbing brushes, and bowls (Edlin 1973; Coles, Heal & Orme 1978). Intricately carved and rougher plates, a possible spoon, a canoe paddle, and a butter dish have all been found at Oakbank. One particularly fine alder plate had such ornate carving that it may have had a special purpose (Dixon 1984).

Numerous alder and oak wood chips were found in context with household detritus during the course of this study. They were of a wedged or square shape, indicative of fashioning a point or mortise joint onto a timber for a pile or stake. Such wood-working waste is characteristic of construction, consolidation, and reconstruction of an existing dwelling, although the larger construction piles are likely to have been shaped on land. Chips from wood-working would have had a multitude of uses in the dwelling, including fuel, packing and flooring. Sands (1994) took between 500 and 800 blows to reconstruct pile points with 100 facets, and clearly wood chips would have been an abundant resource. Alder wood also makes good charcoal for smelting purposes (Edlin 1973), and has been found in context with metalworking slag at Oakbank (Miller 1997), although not in significant enough quantities to imply specificity of use.

Oak wood was also utilised extensively for construction at Oakbank. Many of the dwelling piles and most of the 40 gangway timbers were oak (Dixon 1984; Sands 1994), and numerous worked chips and charcoal fragments have also been isolated from the occupation deposits (Miller 1997). Oak has been recorded frequently on crannog and lake settlement sites (e.g. Keller 1866; Munro 1882; Wood-Martin 1886; Piggott 1953; authors in Coles & Lawson 1987; Crone 2000), probably due as much to the properties of oak wood as to availability: the heartwood of oak is extremely durable because of tyloses and tannin, which block the heartwood vessels and prevent invasion by necrotising bacteria and fungi. The oak piles from Oakbank Crannog are still strong, a testament to their durability, and the leakage of tannins from the wood is partly responsible for the excellent preservation of all the organic remains on the site.

Oak is a very dense wood, making it suitable for housing, furniture, boats, bridges, and all manner of small artefacts which need to be strong, such as building dowels and wheel spokes. Three eight-year-old roundwood dowels of oak from Oakbank with cleanly cut ends are interpreted as remains of pegs to join structural timbers (Miller 1997). Oak would have been ideal for this purpose because the wood is so strong. However, oak is less easily worked than other softer woods like alder, and would not have been favoured for intricate carving at Oakbank. From signatures left by the tools, Sands (1994) has recreated the tool-kit used by the late Bronze/early Iron Age Oakbank inhabitants, and concluded that the equipment used was basic but serviceable. Consequently it is not surprising that the more easily worked alder wood was used for elaborate carving.

More than 90 per cent of all the roundwood fragments over two years old found in samples investigated by this author were hazel (Miller 1997). The incidence of Coryloid (hazel/bog myrtle) pollen in the Breadalbane area was high in the late Bronze and early Iron Age (Donner 1962), and abundant finds of hazelnut shell on the site further confirm the frequency of hazel in the vicinity. The locations of the hazel roundwood fragments were often directly attributable to wattle and hurdles from external walls or internal partitions. The abundance of them in these situations infers selective collection. Wattle waste on the site is also evident from the axe marked ends and knots found (see Miller 1997), implying ongoing house repairs.

Hurdles would have provided a lightweight, flexible material for walls and partitions, a fact especially important on a house built on stilts over water. Evidence for daub is restricted to one putative fragment near the door (Sands 1994). However, daub may not have been employed extensively anyway, due to the extra weight this would have brought. Although there is no direct evidence, the numerous discoveries of fragments of large pleurocarpous (weft-forming) mosses mixed with hazel roundwood would suggest that a system of hurdle walls packed with moss in between gaps was employed. The mosses identified for walling purposes are from large woodland species, especially *Neckera complanata* (Hedw.) Hüben, *Hylocomium splendens* (Hedw.) B., S. & G. and *Rhytidiadelphus squarrosus* (Hedw.) Warnst., all of which would have grown abundantly in suitable woodland throughout the area.

Much of the hazel roundwood found suggests coppicing (Miller 1997). This is an important discovery for a site of this age, and is very unusual for the fossil record in general. Coppicing for hurdles and basketry produces prolific shoots, which are much narrower than normal (Schwankl 1957; Edlin 1973), with a uniform diameter down the length of the stem. Coles (1987) describes these features in coppiced shoots from the Somerset Levels trackways. At Oakbank, the rods found were straight, with narrow growth rings and an average age of six to eight years. These were found in context with thicker rods approximately 12 years old, suggestive of uprights. Recent coppices involve a seven-year cycle (Edlin 1973), and this figure would fit in well with the rods discovered at Oakbank. Other possible uses for hazel rods are thatching spars (Fenton 1978) and fishing traps (Edlin 1973).

Piles and worked wood chips of birch wood were much less frequent than those of alder or oak at Oakbank, but this is to be expected as the smaller birch trees are not so suitable for large structural use. Today, birch is used more readily for small item turnery (Edlin 1973), and this is also borne out by the fossil record (e.g. Coles *et al.* 1978). Birch roundwood has been found at Oakbank with hazel roundwood in contexts indicative of use in hurdles, in this case mainly as uprights. Like hazel and willow, narrow birch rods are flexible enough to be utilised for hurdles, basketry and other woven artefacts, and birch twigs were common in some samples. Other common uses for small birch twigs in the past include bedding, roofing thatch, brooms, or rope made from the twisted fine twigs (Edlin 1973). The incidence of birch twigs at Oakbank was not sufficiently high to suggest thatch or bedding, but twisted birch wood rope is suggested from the aggregations found of small twigs (Miller 1997). However, birch charcoal was more common than worked wood chips at Oakbank, and the wood may have been gathered for firewood and kindling more frequently than for other uses. The high tar content of birch wood ensures that it burns well.

Very little can be said about the use of willow at Oakbank. Willow wood and charcoal fragments were not found abundantly, suggesting either that there was little willow in the locality, that it did not survive, or else that willow was not selected for use. Given the abundance of other well-preserved organic remains and the fact that the tall shrub willows are wetland taxa likely to have grown well around the crannog, it must be considered that willow was available but that other taxa were preferred.

## Thatching, flooring and bedding

The plants which come into this category could have been used for any or all of these uses which in common rely on long stems. The confused nature of the site stratigraphy means it is not possible to be specific with respect to the thatching material used to construct the dwelling, but nevertheless the circumstantial evidence does allow confident speculation.

Remains of bracken (*Pteridium aquilinum*) were prolific throughout the site. Bracken makes an excellent thatching material, surviving *c*.20 years before it needs to be replaced. Only heather (*Calluna vulgaris* (L.) Hull) outlasts it on Skye (Rymer 1976). This was long enough for the short tenancies of the old Western Isles crofts, and realistically is likely to be as long as a crannog could last without needing some refurbishment. In this sense bracken would have made a perfectly satisfactory thatch. Reeds (*Phragmites australis* (Cav.) Trin. ex Steud.) and great fen-sedge (*Cladium mariscus* (L.) Pohl) are generally accepted as the best thatching material, but remains are entirely absent from the Oakbank samples examined. Reeds do grow in Perthshire today, albeit at some distance from the site, but great fen-sedge is not common anywhere in Scotland (Perring & Walters 1976). Differential preservation of the caryopses (seeds) at Oakbank is recognised as a possibility (Hall 1986) but discounted in the presence of more immediately available alternatives, and the absence of any evidence of culm (stem) material whatsoever. Considering the size of the site and the range of sampling areas, at least some would have been expected, had it been there.

Rymer (1976) indicates two methods of thatching with bracken. The first, and more ancient, involves cutting at the base of tall, mature rachis (stems) in the late summer, when maximum length had been achieved but before they became brittle, then stripping them free of fronds (leaves). Bundles of rachis would then be used in the same manner as reeds or straw, leaving a plentiful supply of fronds for flooring or bedding material. The second method of thatching with bracken was common in the last 200 years, whereby the entire plants were uprooted in late summer, including the small bulbous underground rhizomes. The plants were then treated in the same manner as before, but in this thatch only the rhizomes were exposed to the elements. A modern reconstruction of this is reported in the refurbishment of the Jean McAlpine Inn at Aberfoyle (Harrison 1994). However, this method effectively removes the plants from the area, and it is clear that the ancient method of harvesting the fronds without the rhizome would be a more satisfactory way of utilising this natural resource in a sustainable manner (Rymer 1976). The evidence from finds of parallel aggregations of stripped bracken rachis in some deposits at Oakbank (Miller 1997) indicates it is highly probable that bracken was used as a thatching material. No rhizomes were found in any samples, suggesting management of the resource for recurrent use.

Bracken is highly likely to have been used for byre and household flooring at Oakbank as well as thatch, as finds of pinnae (individual leaves of the frond, which are more absorbent than straw) were abundant on the site (Rymer 1976). Flooring material would have been renewed regularly as required. As with the oak and alder timbers, tannin leaching from the abundant bracken remains on the site has assisted in the preservation of the site as a whole. Bracken has been recovered frequently in flooring or bedding contexts on archaeological sites (e.g. medieval Perth, Robinson 1987) and was used as bedding at the Roman site of Vindolanda (Seaward 1976) and in Fortingall village near Oakbank until fairly recently (Rymer 1976). Bracken fronds could also have been used together with mosses for wind proofing the walls of the crannog.

Although bracken is most likely to have formed the main thatch, other plants may have been used in conjunction. Long-stemmed rushes including soft/compact rush (*Juncus effusus/ conglomeratus* L.) and jointed/sharp-flowered rush (*J. articulatus* L./*acutiflorus* Ehrh ex Hoffm.) have been found consistently on the site. These taxa inhabit similar places, are equally common, and have identical growth habits. They would have been collected for similar purposes. It would take a phenomenal amount of rushes to make satisfactory thatch, but they could supplement or repair an existing thatch. This would be most useful in the winter or spring months, because rush stems are long at these times even when bracken is short or wintering underground, and straw or hay is not available. However, the primary use for the long stemmed rushes at Oakbank was probably to cover the floor on a recurrent basis, and for the manufacture of rush oil lamps. Rushes make a particularly resilient floor covering, and were frequently used in medieval towns as floor coverings, often sweetened with wild flowers such as meadowsweet (*Filipendula ulmaria* (L.) Maxim.). They were suggested for this at York (Hall 1986), and have been found together with meadowsweet in Oakbank samples (Miller 1997).

Straw from cereal processing can also be used for thatching (Hall 1986), but at Oakbank the incidence of low growing cornfield weeds are such as to suggest reaping was carried out low on the stem (Miller *et al.* 1998). This phenomenon rules out straw thatch, because the act of threshing breaks the culm. Straw intended for this purpose in the past was commonly hand picked at ear height, and reaped separately later. At Oakbank, straw remains were only very noticeable in samples, which had chaff and wild species interpreted as byre fodder. Meadow hay is also a possibility, but at Oakbank the evidence would suggest this was kept for fodder (Miller 1997).

## First aid

High numbers of seeds of selfheal (*Prunella vulgaris* L.) (**colour plate 9**) were found consistently in many samples representative of domestic scatter. Selfheal is a weed of waste grassland, and could be interpreted as a crop contaminant. However, numbers of its seeds were often conspicuously higher than those of other potential crop contaminants, which would tend to suggest purposeful collection of the plant. The dried flowering parts of this common herb were once used in folk medicine as an antiseptic and to stem blood from domestic accidents (Stuart 1989), which gave rise to one of its vernacular names, *'the carpenter's herb'*. Although there is no direct evidence, it is possible that selfheal may have been collected to treat the cuts and abrasions which would have happened frequently during woodworking or other domestic activities.

## Utilisation of mosses

At Oakbank Crannog, remains of 12 species of mosses commonly utilised by people recurred in many occupation deposits (Miller *et al.* 1998), including most especially *Neckera complanata* and *Hylocomium splendens*. Of the taxa useful to man found, 11 were pleurocarpous (weft-forming) mosses which form dense, flattened mats over rocks and trees in damp shady areas. Their shape contrasts with the acrocarpous (tussock-forming) species, which have an upright growth habit and domes of leafy stems.

Growth habit as much as size determined selection for specific human purposes in antiquity. The large wefts were useful for numerous packing and wiping applications, and could be easily ripped up in handfuls without the problem of adherent soil often found with the small acrocarpous mosses. The uses for mosses in antiquity were prolific. The dense springy morphology of the larger weft-forming mosses made them ideal for a variety of uses including weather-proofing walls and cracks in the floor or roof, and improving comfort in bedding. Keller (1866) reports some of the large weft species being used for these purposes in the Neolithic Swiss lake dwellings, including *Antitrichia curtipendula* (Hedw.) Brid., and *Neckera complanata*. These species were also found at Oakbank. The presence in some abundance of *Neckera complanata* and *Hylocomium splendens* in all areas of the Oakbank crannog site suggests the possibility of these mosses being especially favoured for general purposes. Other potential uses for weft-forming mosses include all sorts of small-scale packing activities, including insulating boots or padding tool handles. The unique discovery of a Mesolithic flint flake with a padded handle of *Hylocomium brevirostre* (Brid.) B., S. & G. from the River Bann (photographed in Dickson 1973, plate 21) probably reflects a frequency of use only guessed at before this fortunate preservation.

The weft-forming mosses have also been used for a wide variety of wiping duties including cleaning pots and for toilet purposes. Mosses are well known from latrine fills (e.g. Hall 1986; Dickson 1986; Dickson & Brough 1989; Robinson 1987; Hall & Kenward 1990; Kenward & Hall 1995) and their application in a toilet capacity must have been commonplace. Other wiping/absorptive functions of the larger mosses are as bandages and babies' nappies. The weft-forming species are preferable to the tussock types here too, with the notable exception of bog moss (*Sphagnum*) species, a few leaves of which were found at Oakbank samples. The bog mosses are particularly useful for wound dressings, nappies, or any purpose requiring intensive absorption due to their phenomenal properties of fluid retention and acidifying effects, which inhibit bacterial growth. The genus has been used in recent wars as emergency field dressings, and clumps of leafy stems may have been used with selfheal to staunch blood flow in household accidents.

The largest of the tussock mosses had their own particular uses in antiquity for rope and small item weaving. *Polytrichum commune* Hedw. is well known in the fossil record in this respect, as photographed in Dickson (1973) in the form of caulking rope. There is no evidence for moss rope at Oakbank, but a bundle of birch spray was found, together with remains of heather, flax (*Linum usitatissimum* L.) and nettle (*Urtica dioica* L.), and the use of these taxa for rope or twine may have been preferred.

## Conclusions

The study of plant remains from the crannog at Oakbank indicates that the entire dwelling was built from plant materials, as summarised in **Table 1**. The selection of wood species for construction timbers in the building reflects a sound knowledge of the properties of different types of wood as well as the availability of each kind of tree. Alder and oak were the preferred taxa for the upright piles and timber platform because of the working properties and durability of the wood of these types of tree. The structure was held together with wooden dowels, at least some of which were oak, selected for strength. Carved household utensils and implements were most frequently alder, including plates, a canoe paddle and a butter dish. Coppiced hazel wood and some birch were used to make hurdle walls and partitions. Birch and alder charcoal were utilised most frequently for burning, along with lesser amounts of other taxa, and pine tapers were used for some kindling at least.

Roofing thatch was probably bracken, although other materials may also have been used to a lesser extent. Rope to bind the thatch may have been made from birch twigs or heather stems, with nettle or flax fibres possibly used for applications requiring finer twine. Floors were covered with bracken, rushes and possibly wild flowers and hay or straw, and rushes may also have formed the wicks of oil lamps. Small wood shavings or chips from structural repairs are likely to have been scattered on the floors to absorb liquid or increase comfort. Weft-forming mosses were used for a variety of packing and wiping applications, including insulating the walls. Bracken may also have been used for this. Selfheal was probably collected for use with bog moss as dressings for minor wounds resultant from woodworking and other household accidents.

A great deal of effort went into the construction of Oakbank Crannog, which suggests that it may have been a high status dwelling. Certainly, evidence of a successful arable and pastoral economy and remains of exotic traded foods such as spelt wheat and opium poppy, together with the highly ornate alder bowl found, would indicate that this was not the home of a poor family. However, the evidence also demonstrates the great understanding that the people who built and lived in this dwelling had of their environment. Their sympathetic use and sustained management of wild resources meant that it was possible for the site at Oakbank to be inhabited regularly over a period of some 400 years. This period may even have been longer, since the boulder capping over the organic mound protected the fragile remains on which all the studies have been made. It is ironic that the only use of stone on the whole site was for this latest consolidation phase, no further evidence of which has survived.

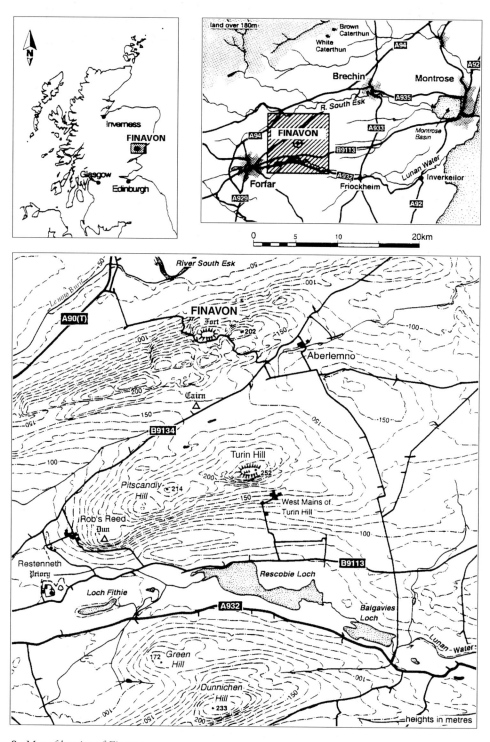

**9**  *Map of location of Finavon*

# 5 The oblong fort at Finavon, Angus
## an example of the over-reliance on the appliance of science?

*Derek Alexander*

## Introduction

This report presents the results of survey work undertaken on Finavon Hill over four days in March 1999 as part of the University of Edinburgh's Angus and South Aberdeenshire Field School. Finavon Hill is located approximately 6.5km north-east of Forfar and 1.5km south-west of Aberlemno in central Angus (NO55NW 32; NO 506 556) (**9**). It has open views to the north and north-east, overlooking the confluence of the Lemno Burn and the River South Esk. The fortified summits of the Caterthuns (Dunwell & Strachan forthcoming) are visible 14km to the north-east while the enclosures on Turin Hill can be seen 2km to the south-east (Alexander & Ralston 1999).

Finavon Hill is a ridge of Devonian Lower Old Red Sandstone conglomerate aligned south-west to north-east (**9 & 10**). The south-eastern side of the hill is formed by a steep cliff line which rises from 175m OD at the modern road to the summit at 252m OD. The northern slope of the hill, by contrast, is much gentler and has no cliff lines. There are a number of conglomerate bedrock outcrops on the summit along the top of the cliff line. The vegetation on the hill is mainly rough grass and is used for grazing both cattle and sheep.

The objectives of the survey were to produce a plan of the archaeological features on Finavon Hill in order to identify and assess the nature and extent of any threats affecting the archaeological remains. In addition, the intention of the survey was to teach undergraduate students a range of appropriate survey techniques.

## Previous work

The archaeological features on Finavon Hill are marked on the first edition Ordnance Survey map (**11a**), which was surveyed in 1861 and published in 1865. This shows the oblong shape of the fort with a depression marked as a 'well' at the western end. In addition the fort is also labelled as being vitrified. A track is marked on the map as running up to the south-western end of the fort but is not shown as cutting through the northern side as is depicted on a subsequent plan drawn by David Christison (**11b**) at the end of the nineteenth century (1900, 99, illus 50). The latter showed the depression at the western end of the fort and another smaller depression towards the eastern end. In addition, it also mapped a T-shaped outwork attached to the eastern end of the fort. To accompany his plan Christison provided a profile down the length of the fort.

**10** *Aerial photograph of Finavon Hill. Copyright: Jim Bone*

In addition to the early maps and plans of the site there are some detailed descriptions. The Statistical Account (1791-99, vol. XIII), in the entry for Oathlaw parish, describes the site as follows:

> On the top of the hill are the remains of an old castle: the formation of the whole of it is yet visible. Its dimensions are 137 yards in length, and 37 in breadth, nearly in the form of a parallelogram. The foundation seems to have been without mortar. The ruins discover something like vitriable stones, and plainly appear to have undergone the action of fire . . . There are evident marks of a well on the west end of it. (OSA 1791-1799, 579-580).

The other detailed accounts of the site can be found in Warden's volumes on Angus (Warden 1885 Vol I, 43-46 and Vol V, 473) of which the second is worth quoting at length:

> A Brechin man who visited the Hill of Finhaven in 1812, and again in 1846, 'says the prettiest part of the vitrified stones had been removed in the interval, but vitrification was still to be found round all the walls at different depths. The vitrification generally goes down the centre of the wall from the top, leaving the loose stones to slope off on each side to the base but vitrification terminates at different depths and does not reach the base. The stones of the walls are principally small, flat free stones. Though the site of the fort was examined very minutely, no charcoal could be found, but in some of the vitrified stones a black substance like animal matter was found, having the appearance of snuff. The greatest curiosity at Finhaven is the well on the west side of the ring, of great depth, funnel-shaped, with walls rising higher than those of the ring (or oval) itself, and separated from the ring by a wall.

The next published plans of Finavon were by Professor Gordon Childe (**11c**) of the University of Edinburgh, after he undertook extensive excavations on the hillfort in 1933-4 (Childe 1935, 50 illus 2; 1936, 347 fig. 5). The ramparts are more clearly defined than on Christison's plan and the slope of the ground inside and outside the fort is indicated by contours at 10ft (3m) intervals. There are portions of the rampart line, which have been left blank, without hachures, on Childe's plan – most notably on either side of the trackway through the site. These are some of the areas which had been affected by quarrying. The excavations showed that the wall was faced both internally and externally and was up to 6m wide. The internal face survived to 3.6m high while

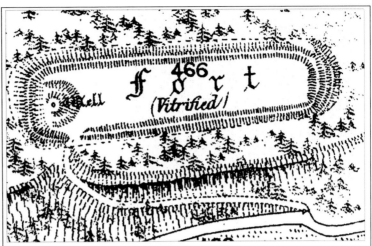

a) Ordnance Survey 1st. Edition 1865

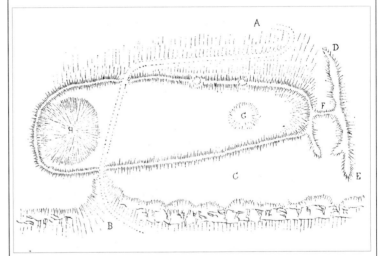

b) Christison's Plan 1900

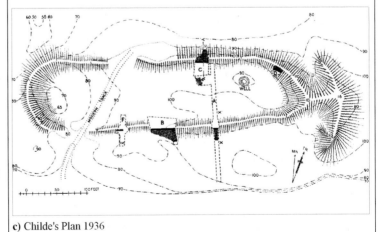

c) Childe's Plan 1936

**11** *Previous plans*:
a) reproduced with permission of the Trustees of the National Library of Scotland, b) after Christison 1900, 99, illus 50, c) after Childe 1936 347, fig. 5

the external one was around 4.8m. Excavation also revealed the remains of possible structures against the inner side of the north wall. The artefactual evidence was relatively undiagnostic with sherds of plain, gritty pottery, stone whorls, some flints, an iron ring and a thick jet ring (NMAS Accession No's. AO 104, BE 480, HH 386-416).

Following Childe's work on the site, two small trenches were excavated by Euan MacKie in 1966 to obtain samples for radiocarbon dates (MacKie 1969 & 1976). Further dating work was subsequently undertaken on the vitrified wall-core using both thermoluminesence (Sanderson *et al.* 1988) and archaeomagnetic dating techniques (Gentles 1989 & 1993). The survey was undertaken partly to provide a framework for these dating exercises and partly to understand how the features visible on the ground today relate to earlier descriptions of and interventions on the site.

## Field survey results

### General

The new plan of Finavon Hill (**12**) confirmed the general elongated outline of the fort and its outwork at the eastern end as had been shown on a number of the earlier plans. However, the difference is that the level of detail on the earlier plans is restricted and does not wholly represent the site as it appears on the ground. In particular the site has been subject to a number of activities, which have severely affected its present form and condition, and therefore have an impact on the interpretation of the field remains (**colour plate 10**).

### Fort

The fort is *c.*155m long by *c.*55m wide, from the outer margin of wall tumble (**12**). There is a T-shaped outwork at the eastern end. As described by Childe, the southern side of the fort sits back at least 20m from the cliff edge. In addition, the western end has been extended to incorporate a natural depression, although this is likely to have been modified and it is difficult to tell which gradients here are natural or man-made. In both cases the apparent disregard for the natural topography as a line for the ramparts surely indicates that the practical need for a defensive position was not the *a priori* reason behind the construction of the fort. Indeed the need to obtain an oblong shape, despite the topographic variations, suggests that this may have been as much an issue in the minds of the builders. It is also possible that the inclusion of the natural hollow at the western end may have been of some significance, perhaps as a location for a well, similar to that which survives towards the eastern end of the fort.

The depression in which this latter well is situated is *c.*10m in diameter at the top and is funnel-shaped reducing to *c.*5-6m in diameter at the top of the well itself. When excavated, the well was found to be *c.*6.5m deep and was cut down into the bedrock. The base of the well measured 1.6m by 1.5m. Childe suggested that because the well did not fill up with water that it had been a disappointment to its builders who had then filled it in (Childe 1935, 70). It is perhaps more likely that it was used as a cistern for storing water collected at the surface rather than a well – perhaps it was originally lined with clay. Certainly, the lowest 3.6m of the fill consisted of a red clayey soil and some large stones. Above this layer was a thick deposit of stone with earth between from which fragmentary remains of a human skull were recovered. Apart

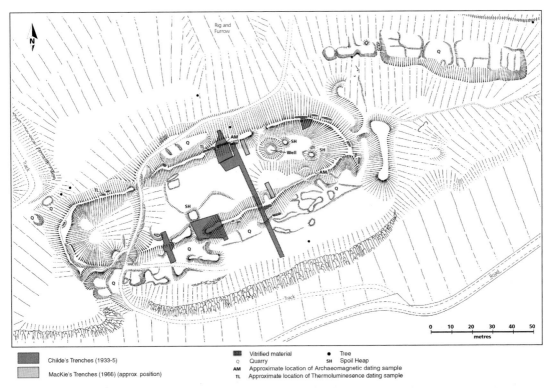

Childe's Trenches (1933-5)

MacKie's Trenches (1966) (approx. position)

▦ Vitrified material     ● Tree
Q Quarry     SH Spoil Heap
AM Approximate location of Archaeomagnetic dating sample
TL Approximate location of Thermoluminesence dating sample

**12** *1999 Survey plan of the hillfort on Finavon Hill*

from a few sherds of coarse pottery and other fragments of bone no other artefacts were recovered from the fill of the well. Given the presence of the skull fragment, it is possible that the well represented a focus for ritual activity and deposition.

Childe suggested that the entrance to the fort may have been located somewhere on the line of the trackway through the site (Childe 1936, 349) and although this may be correct the possibility that there was no entrance through the wall must also be considered, as other oblong forts, such as the Tap o'Noth, Aberdeenshire, are apparently gateless. It is possible that access was gained to these sites by climbing over the wall, perhaps on a purpose-built stair or track incorporated into the wall construction. Alternatively, the entrance may have been so narrow that once it collapsed its position was no longer apparent.

### Quarries and trackway

The fort and its immediate surroundings have been subject to a great deal of quarrying which has had a profound effect on the nature of the archaeological remains and can be very confusing especially around the periphery (**12**).

One of the most obvious signs of the later activity on the site is the presence of the trackway that runs up the southern side of the hill and crosses the fort, above the hollow at the western end before descending the northern face of the hill. This trackway clearly cuts through the collapse of both the southern and the northern ramparts. In the interior of the fort the track is slightly terraced into the hill-slope. The precise date of the construction of the track remains unknown although its southern portion appears on the first edition OS map of 1865. It is likely to have been associated with the quarrying activity rather than with felling of the forestry on the hill as suggested by Childe (1936, 50). A short length of track branches off the main route across the hill and provides access to the southern terrace.

From the map evidence it is likely that the quarrying on the hill took place prior to the mid-nineteenth century. Childe located the stem of a clay pipe on the subsoil beside a gap in the inner face (in Trench F) of the southern rampart and attributed it to the activity of workmen in the nineteenth century (Childe 1936, 348). Three main areas of quarrying can be identified on the hill: the entire southern side of the southern rampart; a small section into the exterior off the northern rampart; and an extensive set along the north-eastern face of the hill outside the fort.

The southern side of the south rampart has been heavily mutilated by quarrying to such an extenet that almost nothing must survive of the foundation courses of the wall. This explains the unusual sections, which were recorded by both Childe and MacKie through the rampart, which showed that the crest of the bank as it now survives actually sits inside the line of the inner face of the wall. In fact MacKie did not locate the inner wall face. The quarrying has left such an even face that it could be easily mistaken for the collapse of the rampart, although the very low internal slope of the surviving bank compared to the northern rampart perhaps gives it away. The quarrying is possibly most noticeable at the eastern and western ends of the southern rampart. At the eastern end it is clearly cut into the corner of the rampart as loose tumble is exposed. At the western end, where the trackway has been cut through the rampart, there are also extensive areas of quarrying, which too have removed large portions of the defences. The situation is not made any clearer by the dumping of spoil, for example down the south-eastern side of the hollow, and the numerous sheep tracks that cross the features.

On the northern side of the fort a large quarry has been cut into the external face of the rampart to the south of the track. This quarry is c.25m long, east to west, by 10m wide, and its base, 22m long by 5m wide, is almost level. Some of the material from this quarry may have been used to construct the trackway, which leads into it from the north-east and continues to the south-west. To the south-west where the track turns and cuts through the rampart are the remains of a small quarry scoop on the eastern side.

The best-defined sets of quarries are those on the north-eastern flank of the hill outside the area of the hillfort. These consist of a large elongated set of quarry scoops c.70m long by up to 18m wide and by a smaller set, to the north-west, 25m long by c.7m wide. The larger set displays a number of terraces and ridges running across the breadth of the quarry, which may represent ledges in the underlying bedrock. The smaller set has what appears to be a slight trackway running into it from the north. An area of rig-and-furrow lies on the northern slope of the hill.

### Excavation trenches and spoil heaps

In addition to the quarries, archaeological excavation work has left its mark on the remains of Finavon (**12**). When visited in August 1999 these trench locations were more readily apparent than earlier in the year by virtue of most having a dense growth of nettles. When looked for, some trench positions do become apparent and in many cases they are also marked by a higher concentration of loose stones. Most of the recorded excavation trenches can therefore be accounted for. However, there are two features on the inside of the fort to the east of the trackway, and at the foot of both the north and south ramparts, which are not so easily explained. These look similar in many ways to the other excavation trenches. The one to the north-west of Childe's trench F may be related to that work but there are no records of the feature on the north side of the fort.

There are three main spoil heaps within the interior of the fort that appear to be the material uncovered during the archaeological excavations on the site. There is one at the foot of the eastern rampart, one to the east of the well and one to the north-west of Childe's trench B. The low spread bank around the lip of the well may also be a direct result of archaeological excavation.

## Erosion

One of the aims of the survey was to identify and record any damage to the archaeological remains on Finavon Hill. Although in general the state of preservation of the features can be described as stable there are a number of small areas of active erosion. The areas affected by the quarrying and the excavations are the most unstable and most prone to erosion. Particularly noticeable is the loose stone-work in what was Childe's trench D and in the eastern end of the main quarry along the southern rampart. Animal activity on the site appears to be relatively restricted although there are a large number of mole-hills on the southern external terrace. Burrowing animals do not appear to be too much of a problem on the ramparts, probably because of their high stone content. However, the northern end of the outwork appears to be heavily burrowed as does the soil immediately above the western end of the cliff edge.

# Dating

## Radiocarbon dating

Dr Euan MacKie then of the Hunterian Museum, University of Glasgow, excavated two trenches against the inner face of both the north and south ramparts in 1966 with the aim of recovering samples of charcoal for radiocarbon dating (**12** & **13**). The excavations inside the southern rampart confirmed the sequence of deposits located by Childe. Immediately above the brownish-pink gravelly subsoil, close to the wall there was a layer of carbonised planks from which a radiocarbon date was obtained (GaK-1224). MacKie suggested these could be the remains of a wooden floor of a structure built against the wall or part of a wooden walkway. Above and between these planks was a black occupation layer (200mm thick at the southern end and 50mm thick at the northern end). A radiocarbon date was obtained for charcoal from this layer (GaK-1223). The occupation deposit was covered by tumble, which had collapsed inwards from the wall. Charcoal from within the wall tumble produced a radiocarbon date (GaK-1222). MacKie's trenches did not locate any remains of the wall faces and it is possible that the later quarrying activity on the site (discussed above) had removed these and the core of the wall along the vast majority of the southern side of the fort.

The following dates (**Table 2**) were obtained and calibrated following Stuiver and Kra 1986 and OxCalv 2.18.

However, Spriggs and Anderson (1993) have reservations about the accuracy of many GaK dates measured in the 1970s and 80s. Patrick Ashmore has recently suggested

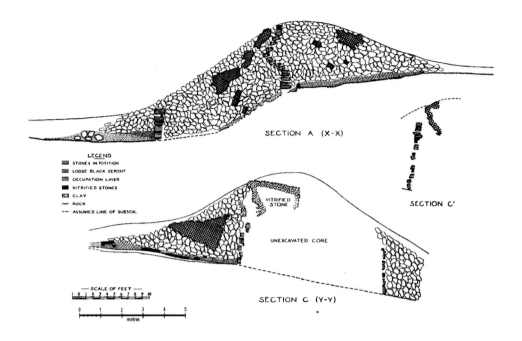

**a)** Childe's Sections 1936

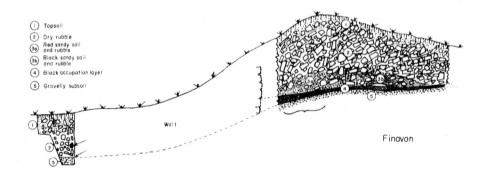

**b)** MacKie's Section 1976   ( scale not known )

**13**  *Sections through wall*: a) Childe 1936, b) MacKie 1976

(Ashmore *et al.* forthcoming) that the error ranges for these dates should be increased to take account of the inaccuracy and the following results (**Table 3**) are obtained by observing his recommendations.

## Thermoluminescence dating

Thermoluminescence (TL) dating is based on the principle that some minerals will absorb background radiation from their surrounding environment, which provided the annual dose remains constant, will accumulate and can be measured. When a material containing mineral components is fired, or heated, the accumulated radiation is given off as light and the radiation level of the sample returns to zero. Thus when pottery, or in this case rock, is fired the radiation starts to accumulate again at a steady rate from the day it was fired. To be able to determine the rate of the annual dose background measurements must be taken from where the sample was recovered, when the sample to be dated is heated in the laboratory.

Thermoluminescence (TL) dating was carried out of the vitrified material from the site (Sanderson *et al.* 1988) in an attempt to check the chronology put forward by MacKie (1969, 1976). In particular they wanted to check the interpretation that vitrified forts were the result of a particular type of construction of timber-laced rampart, belonging to a specific cultural tradition, from the Iron Age (Sanderson *et al.* 1988, 307). However as outlined above the quality of the radiocarbon dating of its walls when calibrated in fact produce very long chronological ranges covering the whole of the first millennium BC and into the start of the first millennium AD.

The samples were taken from the two cores drilled using a 80mm diamond coring rig in 1984. The cores were 0.3–0.5m long and were taken from massive blocks of vitrification at two points on the northern rampart (Sanderson pers. comm.): one at the western end and the other slightly east of centre (**12**). The samples used for dating were taken at different depths down the cores to check that the method was not affected by the depth of the deposits. The following results (**Table 4**) were obtained (Sanderson *et al.* 1988, 312).

These dates provide a mean date of 1340BP giving a range of 640 AD ± 70, 130 (*ibid.*, 315), significantly more recent than the radiocarbon dates.

## Archaeomagnetic dating

Another technique that has been applied to dating vitrified material in Scotland is archaeo-magnetic dating and once again Finavon was chosen as an example (Gentles 1993). Archaeomagnetic (AM) dating is based on the fact that the earth's magnetic field has changed in direction and strength through time and that often materials that have been burnt will retain a signal of this at the time they were fired. To obtain a date it is necessary to compare the results against the levels of the earth's magnetic field as it has changed over time. Gentles undertook a study of six vitrified sites in Scotland as part of his PhD research. The samples from Finavon (Gentles 1989, 109; 1993) were taken by digging small trenches and exposing vitrified material in the northern and southern rampart (**12**). A mean of at least seven samples produced a date with a 95 per cent confidence of between *c.*180 – 90 BC (Gentles pers. comm., 1989, 1993).

## Conclusions

The University of Edinburgh Archaeology Department's Field School survey has produced a more detailed plan of the archaeological features on the summit of Finavon Hill than was previously available. In particular it has highlighted the amount of damage caused to the site by quarrying activity, probably culminating in the first half of the nineteenth century. The condition of most of the site can be considered presently as stable.

In presenting the results of the survey work it was felt that it would also be useful to synthesise the results of the various dating techniques, which have been applied to the site. Even with the plethora of scientific techniques that have been deployed the date of the fort must remain a matter of debate. The radiocarbon dates suggest that structures in the interior of the fort were constructed in the first millennium BC. The archaeomagnetic dates and the thermoluminescence dates appear to contradict each other over the destruction of the site and the vitrification of the wall core. The AM dates indicate that this happened in the last two centuries BC while the TL dates suggest a date in the mid-first millennium AD.

Unfortunately this lack of consistency amongst the various techniques has meant that different authors chose the dates, which best suit their theories. Armit in his recent review of the Iron Age prefers to see Finavon as belonging to the first millennium BC and having been destroyed and abandoned by the time of the Roman advance (Armit 1997, 108). In contrast Ritchie used the thermoluminesence dates to argue for an early historic use of the site (Ritchie 1995, 8) perhaps linked both to the Pictish symbol stones at Aberlemno and to the related early church site at Aikenhatt to the north of Finavon fort at the confluence of the Lemno Burn and the South Esk. The artefacts however are generally undiagnostic and cannot be used for dating the site. However, the lack of Roman period artefacts, so common elsewhere in Angus (on the souterrain sites for example) is perhaps telling. Indeed the lack of even later material dating to the Early Historic period may also be important although the artefactual remains can often be as undiagnostic as the Iron Age material, apart from imports such as E-ware which are rare in eastern Scotland.

The author is not qualified to provide a critical review of the science behind each dating technique and there have undoubtedly been advances since they were applied to Finavon; however, this case study must strike a note of caution into all archaeologists studying the Iron Age in Scotland. It is perhaps surprising that a set of sites, which appear so morphologically similar as these oblong forts, and have also been relatively extensively examined, still remain to be tied down chronologically. Archaeologists studying hillforts in Scotland rely heavily on scientific dating techniques but also need to be aware of the limitations of these methods and to avoid over-reliance on the application of science. If the date range for oblong forts is to be investigated further perhaps scientific dating techniques should be used in conjunction with extensive excavation of a site where there is a degree of time-depth and sequence visible in the surface remains. Such a site could well be found on Turin Hill which only lies *c.*2km south-east of Finavon and where an apparent oblong fort is preceded by a bivallate enclosure, and replaced by at least one circular homestead (Alexander & Ralston 1999).

# 6 Mid-first millennium BC settlement in the Atlantic West?

*Simon Gilmour*

## Introduction

Several recent excavations have recovered remains of radiocarbon-dated structures of the mid-first millennium BC. A brief resume of the current evidence is followed by tentative interpretations of what is still a very small database of information. However, there are some interesting implications for the evidence presented that should be addressed in the future. It is suggested here that two main possibilities exist: that the relatively small buildings which occupy this period represent specific, possibly seasonal, locations in an economic landscape or that they represent the standard dwelling of the period in question. Both require further analysis for support, but also need explanations in terms of their environmental and cultural context. The similarities to, and differences from, other building forms are analysed and suggest dramatic differentiation in the architectural tradition of the area.

## Simple Atlantic roundhouses

Early to mid-first millennium BC northern Scotland is marked by the construction of a class of monument known as the simple Atlantic roundhouse (Armit 1991; 1996; Mercer 1985; 1996; Hedges 1987i, ii, iii). Thick-walled drystone roundhouses have been excavated at Pierowall (Sharples 1984), Bu (Hedges 1987i, **14a**), Quanterness (Renfrew 1979, **14c**), Tofts Ness (Dockrill 1988), St Boniface (Lowe 1998, **14e**) and Cnoc Stanger, Caithness (Mercer 1996). Further sites are known in the landscape of Caithness but remain unexcavated (Mercer 1980; 1981; 1985). The very ephemeral remains of a possible simple Atlantic roundhouse were recovered during excavations at the Howe in Orkney (Phase 5, **14b**), and assigned an early to mid-first millennium calBC date (Ballin Smith 1994, 38). These structures are relatively thick-walled and monumental compared to similarly early buildings at Clickhimin, Shetland (Hamilton 1968) and the earlier 'Late Bronze Age' settlement at Jarlshof (Hamilton 1956, 18). The latter developed into a second 'Late Bronze Age' settlement incorporating roundhouses with radial divisions (*op. cit,* 32). Several sites such as Skaill Site 5, on Orkney, Sumburgh, on Shetland, and perhaps Liddle, on South Ronaldsay (Buteaux 1997, 255), have oval structures with cellular compartments in the wall. The sites at Skaill Site 5 and Bu both underwent a sequence of development including the thickening of the walls, suggesting the reinforcement of permanence on the same site over time.

This is also illustrated at the Howe where a large simple Atlantic roundhouse was replaced by complex Atlantic roundhouses on the same site, and settlement continued to the end of the first millennium calAD. A similar horizon of construction is unrecorded in the Western Isles, and this is significant since it means that the knowledge to build large upstanding monumental round-

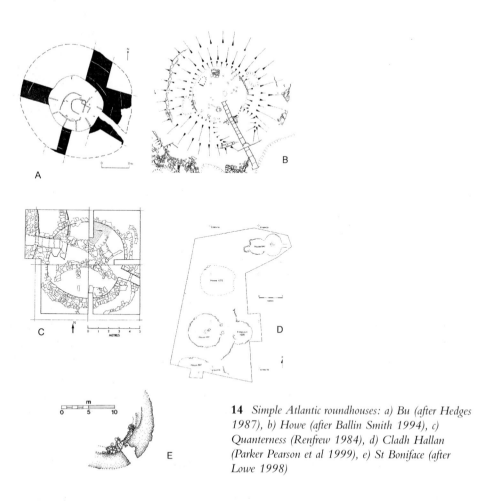

**14** *Simple Atlantic roundhouses: a) Bu (after Hedges 1987), b) Howe (after Ballin Smith 1994), c) Quanterness (Renfrew 1984), d) Cladh Hallan (Parker Pearson et al 1999), e) St Boniface (after Lowe 1998)*

houses was either lacking or immaterial during the early to mid-first millennium BC. Without such precursors the construction of complex Atlantic roundhouses must therefore be introduced to the area. In Argyll there is a suggestion that simple Atlantic roundhouses may exist among the poorly-defined mass of heterogenic 'duns' (Gilmour & Henderson forthcoming). Rahoy is an early site of this type (Childe & Thorneycroft 1938; Gilmour 1994, 77, **15a**). In view of the lack of evidence to the contrary these simple walled roundhouses are generally considered to be single storey buildings and may represent the development of distinct social hierarchies.

The development from simple Atlantic roundhouse to complex Atlantic roundhouse suggested by the Orkney evidence, and particularly the Howe (**colour plates 4** & **5**), is yet to be conclusively proven as applicable elsewhere. Sites such as Clickhimin, Shetland (Hamilton 1968; Fojut 1998, 35), Langwell, Sutherland (Nisbet 1996; **15b**), and Crosskirk, Caithness (Fairhurst 1984; **15c**), argue that a similar early development of complex Atlantic roundhouses could be relevant here too. The complex Atlantic roundhouse at Scatness is dated prior to the first century calBC, on the basis of dates from a secondary or even tertiary structure abutting the main roundhouse (Dockrill *et al.* 2000, 9). The excavations at Cnoc Stanger in Caithness (Mercer 1996) produced a sequence of structures the closest yet to simple Atlantic roundhouses

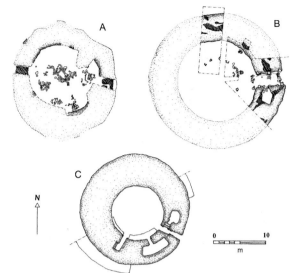

**15** *Vitrified Atlantic roundhouses and Crosskirk broch: a) Rahoy (after Childe and Thornicroft 1938), b) Langwell (after Nisbet 1996), c) Crosskirk (after Fairhurst 1984)*

in the Northern mainland. These presumably precede the early complex Atlantic roundhouses, for example Crosskirk, and also add to the growing body of evidence for a pan-North Atlantic development sequence. Further unexcavated examples have been suggested for Caithness, often sitting on raised areas of land, and uniquely present in groups of more than one (Mercer 1981). The indications are therefore that the first millennium BC in northern Scotland is dominated by the development of large monumental roundhouses, and that the mid-first millennium is an approximate period of change where simple forms evolve into more complex architecture.

## Early Iron Age non-monumental structures

Under the Atlantic roundhouse at Dun Bharabhat, hearth material was dated to between the ninth and sixth centuries calBC (**Table 5**) (Harding & Dixon 2000). Unfortunately, there are no building remains associated with this date but the deposits run under the inner wall of the Atlantic roundhouse suggesting a slightly larger internal area at least and presumably much less substantial walling. Several other excavations in the Atlantic west have recovered early material generally associated with relatively small, revetted structures that may be analogous to the ephemeral structure at Bharabhat.

Radiocarbon dates for the unpublished sites at Baleshare and Hornish Point (Armit 1991, 211-212; Barber *et al.* 1989) calibrate to the mid-first millennium calBC but unfortunately a lack of full publication means their contextual information is difficult to assess and the use of marine shell makes their calibration and interpretation problematic. The structure at Hornish Point is a small irregular building with radial partitions revetted into a 1500m$^2$ area of midden and other structures on the north coast of South Uist. A series of four pits was cut into earlier deposits and overlain by occupation material and in one case a radial pier of the structure. Within these pits were the dismembered remains of an adolescent male accompanied in three of the pits by animal remains (Barber *et al.* 1989, 774-775). The radiocarbon dates came from material above and below the pits.

At Eilean Olabhat on North Uist, recent radiocarbon dates from organic residues on pottery have placed the site between the fifth and third centuries calBC (Ian Armit and Ewan Campbell pers. comm.). The site's early phases comprise an oval building with later piers lining the south-eastern entrance and leading to a central triangular area of paving (**16d**). This latter appears to split the interior 5m by 4m space into three unpaved areas that may be further divided by cobbling to the north-east and a collapsed stone pier to the south. In the earlier phase it is possible that wooden partitions performed the same function (**16b**).

A mid-first millennium calBC date has been obtained for a similar oval structure at Coile a'Ghasgain on Skye (Armit 1996, 104). The entrance to this structure has also been lengthened, albeit by an increase in wall width or 'hornwork' rather than internal piers, and also faces south-east (**16a**). Unfortunately, the single radiocarbon date has a very wide variation across almost the entire first millennium calBC (**Table 5**). The diameter of 5.2m is comparable to Eilean Olabhat and both may have utilised wooden posts to support an organic roof. Although Eilean Olabhat has no central hearth in its second and best-preserved phase, its earlier phase was comparable in layout and incorporated an arched or 'horseshoe-shaped' hearth: the hearth at Coile a'Ghasgain is also arched in shape.

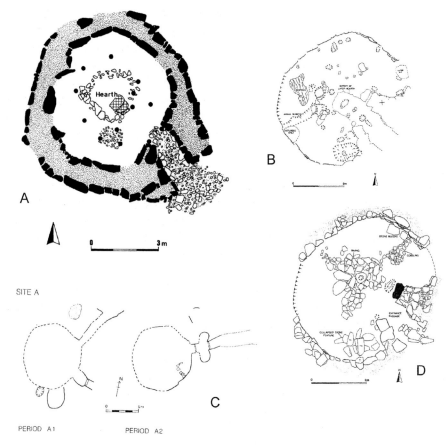

**16** *Non-monumental roundhouses: a) Choile a' Chasgain (Armit 1996), b) Eilean Olabhat Phase 1 (Armit 1996), c) Sollas Site A phasing (Cambell 1991), d) Eilean Olabhat Phases 2 (Armit 1996)*

Recent excavations at the eroding site of Ceann nan Clachan, North Uist, revealed a possible early to middle Iron Age oval structure underlying a series of multiphase constructions (Armit and Braby 1996). Unfortunately, these later constructions meant the underlying oval building was severely truncated. However, it appears to have been built using large basal stones perhaps with a superstructure of turf (Ian Armit pers. comm.). There was a drain in the centre of the building and burnt mound debris began to accumulate around the structure. Although no material was recovered securely stratified within the earth fill due to the later re-use of the site, sherds of incised decorated pottery have been found on the beach and may have eroded from this building. The combination of this pottery style, the large boulder architecture and the burnt mound debris strongly suggests this is an early building, probably dating to the early to mid-first millennium BC.

Excavations by the author and Michael Church on a series of structures on the Uig peninsula, west of the Bhaltos peninsula on Lewis, have recovered two sites, relevant to the Atlantic Iron Age, but each of very different character. An Dunan, near Uig Sands (Church and Gilmour 1999), is reasonably well dated to between 400 calBC and 100 calBC (**Table 5**) and represents a ritual island site associated with human cremation. The building was a small sub-rectangular structure with a west facing entrance and a large central hearth area. Deposits from this hearth may have been dumped from elsewhere and included cremated human bone, incised and applied decorated pottery and quartzite pebbles. The walls of the building were constructed from a low outer wall or rough stonework revetted on the interior by large orthostats and may have had a superstructure of turf or other organic material. A similar construction might be envisaged for the small double-chambered structure revetted into a Neolithic cairn at Unival, North Uist (Scott 1947). This site produced relatively coarse pottery with fingernail decorated rims and furrows below the rim compared to early phases at Jarlshof (*op. cit.* 4–5) suggesting an early date for this structure. Early first millennium calBC sites at Howe and Quanterness in the north were also located on the remains of Neolithic cairns and this may support the early Iron Age interpretation of Unival suggested here.

Guinnerso, on the west coast of Lewis in the middle of the peat 'blacklands' of the Uig peninsula, has revealed a sequence of small buildings underlying medieval constructions (Church and Gilmour 1999). Within the upper of the underlying buildings was pottery with globular profiles, upright and everted rims and applied and incised geometric decoration. The style of decoration is poorly executed compared to that found on the Dun Bharabhat pottery and preliminary examination suggests that the incised designs are not paralleled at Cnip wheelhouse either (Ian Armit pers. comm.; Anne MacSween pers. comm.). Excavations are incomplete but there is a visible sequence of buildings probably dating to the Iron Age incorporating an upper structure with an east facing entrance passage 1m long (Church and Gilmour 1999; forthcoming). It is possible that the differences in pottery from that discovered at the nearby sites of Cnip, Loch na Beirgh and Dun Bharabhat may imply an earlier date for this pottery at Guinnerso since succeeding wares are probably more refined in their decoration.

Alternatively, these differences could simply reflect the difference in structure type, location and presumed function. The overall dimensions of the upper building are somewhat smaller than Eilean Olabhat or Coile a'Ghasgain but several structural similarities do exist. The entrance to the later phase has been elongated by the addition of external 'hornworks', as at Coile a'Ghasgain, and all the visible structures have been revetted into earlier material, the lowest butting onto bedrock like Eilean Olabhat. The upper building at least has a multiphase rectangular central hearth.

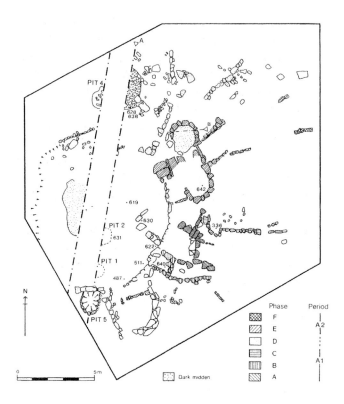

**17** *Sollas Site A.*
Campbell 1991

A pollen diagram from Loch Ruadh Guinnerso indicated that this locale had been open and probably marginal since the beginning of the Holocene (Flitcroft 1997). The structure at Coile a'Ghasgain is *'in a fairly marginal inland valley setting'* (Armit 1996, 103). Eilean Olabhat is located on a promontory jutting into Loch Olabhat surrounded by marshy peat bog (Armit 1997, 899), although it is perhaps less marginal owing to the nearby presence of several Atlantic roundhouses and wheelhouses in the Vallay area. However, these latter are more coastal in their outlook and the loch is within rough grazing and invisible from any round-house site. Dun Bharabhat was also very close to other Atlantic roundhouses and wheel-houses, although its location in an upland loch surrounded by peat bogs is similar. Given the generally poor Iron Age environmental conditions, perhaps comparable to today's climate, it is possible that without recent demographic pressure and technology the area around Eilean Olabhat and Dun Bharabhat would have been considered marginal in the Iron Age. It is also possible (especially considering the lack of a hearth in the later phase at Eilean Olabhat) that this is a site uninhabited for at least part of the year (probably winter). The location of Coile a'Ghasgain and Guinnerso also suggests they are transhumance sites.

Sollas Site A was an 8m by 9m roughly circular structure, or series of structures, investigated during rescue excavations of the nearby wheelhouse in 1957 by R.J.C. Atkinson (Campbell 1991, **17**). Campbell considers the site to have two main phases (A1 and A2) and suggests it is dated to the first or second centuries AD, albeit perhaps prior to the wheelhouse (*op. cit.* 168, **16c**). However, Campbell also acknowledges that the earlier phases of the site are very poorly preserved and Atkinson had suggested at least six phases. The dating is based on a radiocarbon assay from the final deposits (*infra*) and the presence of a piece of Egyptian Blue pigment from period A2 (*op. cit.* 124, 164) considered to have arrived after the Roman invasion of Britain. However, it is in fact possible that this pigment was in use in Britain from the late Bronze Age (Henderson 1991; Needham and Bimson 1988) and there are strong comparisons between the presumably mixed Sollas Site A pottery and the pottery from the well-dated An Dunan site (**18 – 22**).

Note, for example, the preponderance of upright or slightly incurving or flaring rims, and the generally upright profiles of the sections as well as the relatively poor execution of incised linework. There are also distinctive decorative traits such as the applied roundels with slashed decoration (**18**, 340; **20a** and **21b**) and the twisted cord impression applied cordons (**19**, 341 and **21f**). Similar comparisons are possible between the impressed rims (**18**, 365 & 350 and **22b**). These suggest that the assemblages are comparable and that a 400calBC to 100calBC date is also applicable to at least some of the Sollas Site A material. Recent radiocarbon dating of pottery residues from this site (**Table 5**) has suggested a rather later date but there may be some problem with these dates due to the circumstances of deposition, post-deposition processes and the methodology employed in their dating (Campbell, this volume). A single charcoal date from A2 suggests a date around the second century calAD but this is from the final layers when the site could have developed into a wheelhouse (Ewan Campbell pers. comm.).

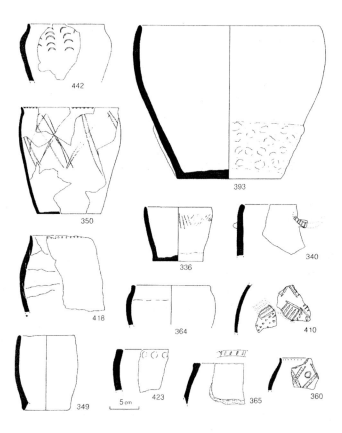

**18** *Sollas Site A pottery.*
Campbell 1991

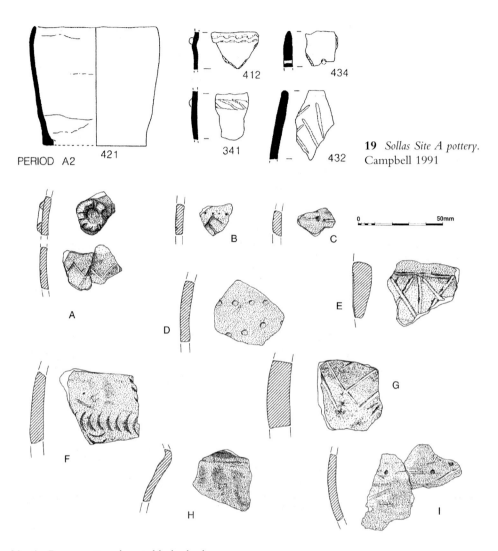

**19** *Sollas Site A pottery.* Campbell 1991

**20** *An Dunan pottery decorated body sherds*

The dates from the nearby Site B wheelhouse pottery residues are similarly several centuries later than the bone and charcoal ages and archaeomagnetic date, which suggest a first- or second-century calAD date for the wheelhouse on Site B (Campbell 1991, 141). If this same problem exists with the Site A material then these residue dates could similarly be backdated by a couple of centuries, placing them well into the period defined by the An Dunan dating, and supporting the conclusion that this is an earlier building than Site B. Interestingly, Site A also shares several structural similarities with the sites at Coile a'Ghasgain, Guinnerso and Eilean Olabhat, including their revetted nature, elongated entrances facing south-east and north-east, and possible radial partitioning. Except for the single charcoal date from this structure, the evidence appears to favour an earlier pre-Roman Iron Age date range in the second half of the first millennium calBC for the earlier phases.

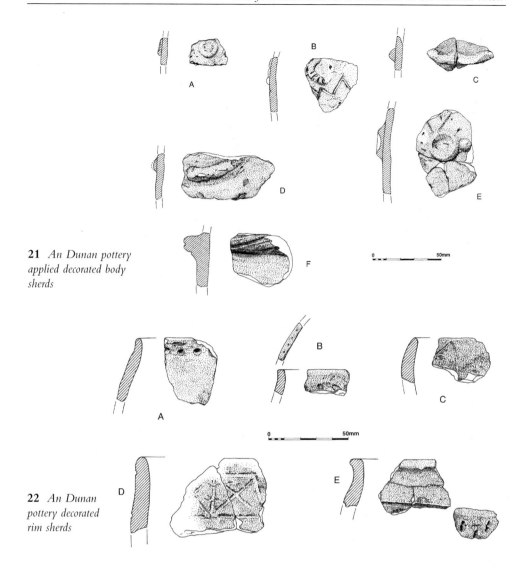

**21** *An Dunan pottery applied decorated body sherds*

**22** *An Dunan pottery decorated rim sherds*

## Discussion

It is possible to interpret the current evidence for the Iron Age in the Outer Hebrides in a very detailed manner, allowing a discussion of possible settlement patterns and their changes and continuity. Several structures exist in the west that can be dated through pottery styles and decoration (Guinnerso, Sollas Site A, Eilean Olabhat), radiocarbon dating (An Dunan, Eilean Olabhat, Hornish Point) and stratigraphic association or constructional technique (Ceann nan Clachan) to a period around the middle of the first millennium BC, perhaps continuing into the later first millennium BC. These structures are at least superficially similar in form and layout and may include the radial division of internal space. How these buildings relate to the complex Atlantic roundhouses is a matter of debate; we currently have only one site, Dun Bharabhat, excavated to basal levels and this only has *terminus ante quem* and *terminus post quem* dates.

However, the pottery at Dun Bharabhat compares well with the earliest Loch na Beirgh, Cnip and Sollas Site B material, which is later, and thus these small sites could represent earlier structures. Alternatively, differences in function across the sites would introduce differences in the assemblages, including perhaps pottery decoration. More work is currently underway to compare these assemblages and continued excavations at Loch na Beirgh would eventually produce a very well-defined chronology for the development of the massive complex Atlantic roundhouse.

An Dunan has pottery comparable to the Sollas Site A assemblage which could also date to this same period. Forms at An Dunan, such as relatively straight-sided vessels with applied slash decorated roundels and impressed decoration, are associated with crude incised decoration and a penannular shale bracelet (Burgess *et al.* 1997). The latter artefact would not be out of place in a first millennium BC context (Fraser Hunter pers. comm.) and the site has been radiocarbon dated between *circa* 400 calBC and 100 calBC. This is important because it is almost certainly a building relating to ritual and religion, incorporating human and animal cremations and votive deposition. It cannot therefore be compared directly with secular domestic or transhumance sites, but may for the first time provide detailed information on the mortuary record of the first millennium BC Iron Age in this area. A later Iron Age burial from Galson, West Lewis, not only suggests changes in the treatment of the dead but included a pot apparently made especially for the burial (Johnson forthcoming). This might support the idea that varying pottery styles and decoration could reflect functional and status differences between sites rather than strictly chronological distinctions.

### Early settlement sites?

The evidence of the pottery and the plausible early dates of these non-monumental structures could suggest that these sites are chronological predecessors to the complex Atlantic roundhouses in the Outer Hebrides. If this is the case they would be comparable to simple Atlantic roundhouses discovered in northern Scotland, but up till recently no simple Atlantic roundhouse had been claimed for the Western Isles (Armit 1990, 55; 1992). However, excavations in South Uist have now uncovered a series of large circular and oval buildings with thick turf and stone walls dating to the late Bronze Age or early Iron Age (Parker Pearson *et. al* 1999). It is possible these are comparable to the multiple simple Atlantic roundhouses discovered in Caithness (*supra*). A possible simple Atlantic roundhouse may also be lying beneath the wheelhouse at Ben Tangaval, Alt Chrisal, Barra (Pouncet 2000) but it is impossible to evaluate due to poor preservation. If these structures can really be compared with the monumental drystone roundhouses in the north then here is evidence for a possible tradition of early simple Atlantic roundhouses in the Western Isles.

Non-monumental sites such as the material under Dun Bharabhat, or the two sigma dating of Coile a'Ghasgain, could be at least partially contemporary with these Atlantic roundhouses. However, if the turf-walled roundhouses are not considered to be comparable with simple Atlantic roundhouses then the sample of non-monumental structures so far discovered would be the progenitors of a sudden and fully-developed series of large monumental buildings with complex and sophisticated architecture. There is none of the gradual development evidenced in the northern Scottish archaeological record. Structures excavated around their basal levels such as Dun Vulan and Bharabhat do not appear to have an earlier monumental simple Atlantic roundhouse under them, nor even sequential developments of complex Atlantic roundhouses. Similar arguments could be suggested for the majority of visible structures such as Carloway,

Dun Loch an Duna in Bragar, Dun Borranish in Uig and so on, although none of these have been fully excavated. Sites in the north, by comparison, such as the Howe, Clickhimin and Jarlshof, have reasonably clear evidence for earlier roundhouse structures.

It may therefore be necessary to explain the sudden introduction of complex Atlantic round-houses into an area with no previous evidence of similar constructions. The easiest suggestion is a migration of ideas (or people) from the north into the Western Isles. However, similar devel-opments may have been occurring in Argyll during the first millennium BC that may include the construction of simple Atlantic roundhouses (Gilmour 1994). If so then Argyll would also be a possible origin point for the complex architecture seen in the Outer Hebrides, perhaps transmitted through close contacts developed to provide the Western Isles with the timber necessary for the construction and furnishing of complex Atlantic roundhouses. Environmental evidence from various areas of mainland Argyll suggests possible woodland management around the mid- to late first millennium BC (Nichols 1967; Rhodes *et al.* 1992). Indeed, the relative wall-base percentages increase from Argyll into the Western Isles and then into the north (Gilmour forthcoming a & b), suggesting increasing monumentality from one area to the next. However, numerous aspects of the indigenous material culture and architecture continue into the construction of complex Atlantic roundhouses in the Western Isles. Radial division of space may be continued, although only through analogy to Atlantic roundhouses elsewhere.

The main evidence for continuation is the pottery assemblage; not only does decorated pottery continue to be made but the incised and applied styles continue and develop. Similar decoration is rare on northern pottery and, although some decorated wares have been recovered from Argyll, the majority of excavations seem to produce little or no pottery at all. This deco-ration and pottery style is probably indigenous to the Western Isles from the first millennium BC and continues until the early centuries AD, presumably indicating that the sites were occupied by locals and not incomers. It is thus much more likely that only the idea spread, indi-cating close contacts at this time, perhaps including the movement of specialist 'architects'. The development of complex Atlantic roundhouses in the Western Isles, at a period roughly contemporary with other areas, therefore reflects wider social changes albeit with distinctly local effects and may be related to changes in patterns of inheritance (Armit this volume). Is it possible given the general lack of simple Atlantic roundhouses in the Western Isles that these sites represent the normal settlement of the early to mid-first millennium BC? Could their preservation in relatively poor environmental locations suggest a more dispersed population that subsequently focused on the coastal zone?

## *Atlantic roundhouse landscapes?*

Alternatively, it is possible, given the dating of complex Atlantic roundhouses to the mid- to late-first millennium calBC (Gilmour forthcoming a & b; Armit this volume), that at least some are contemporary with Atlantic roundhouses in the Western Isles. Construction of monumental roundhouses might reflect the development of the clientship system in the area, allowing much greater differentiation of social position, or at least the outward expression of these differences. Society may have become more stable, allowing communal effort to be expended on the construction of individual houses and homes. The statement made by these structures in relation to the surrounding landscape indicates a more secure tenureship of the land and a projection of control over an economic base. The comparisons between the late Bronze Age/early Iron Age

South Uist roundhouses (Marshall *et al.* 1999) and the Caithness simple Atlantic roundhouses (Mercer 1996; 1980; 1981; 1985) suggests perhaps a similar background, with local development into complex Atlantic roundhouses. It is possible that the relatively insubstantial construction of the South Uist 'simple Atlantic roundhouses', incorporating turf walls, is the reason why so few have been discovered, and may be comparable to the ephemeral structure under Dun Bharabhat.

What stands out about the small and revetted early structures when compared to the Atlantic roundhouses is their total lack of visible monumentality. They are less regular and symmetrical than the more strictly defined circular roundhouses with massive walls. If they are contemporary with Atlantic roundhouses, they are almost certainly functionally ancillary. Whether they represent the domestic structures of the lower classes in this context is debatable, although the distinct marginality of two (Guinnerso and Coile a'Ghasgain), the possibility of the same for the others, and their lack of evidence for long-term occupation, would seem to argue for temporary use by people living elsewhere. They may have been functionally specific sites within the Atlantic roundhouse settlement pattern, again reflecting the secure tenureship of land outside the immediate vicinity of the domestic structures. The excavated sites at Eilean Olabhat, Sollas Site A and Hornish Point all incorporated pits cut into the floors before use, a practice which was to become more prevalent in later periods, such as at Sollas Site B (Campbell 1991). Perhaps these were special buildings, or perhaps the pits are regular occurrences on all sites of the Iron Age.

Dunan Ruadh complex Atlantic roundhouse produced at least one pit in possible primary deposits (John Pouncet and Patrick Foster pers. comm.) and another was discovered within the Atlantic roundhouse at Bharabhat although probably relating to the secondary phase contemporary with wheelhouses (Harding and Dixon 2000, 17). Hornish Point included the burial of a young boy, deliberately dismembered and placed in pits under the floor, which has been argued as being different from the usual, presumably votive, deposition of animal bone (Barber *et al.* 1989). Yet animal bone was incorporated in some of the pits and could signify that although different this act was still related to general ritual practice; for example, cremated human and animal bone was recovered from An Dunan. Again a lack of primary Atlantic roundhouse deposits frustrates our interpretation and discussion of these issues.

## Conclusion

If these seasonal sites were contemporary with the permanently occupied Atlantic round-houses, it would support a relatively early date for the construction of large monumental roundhouses in the Western Isles. The discovery of simple Atlantic roundhouses in South Uist (if that is what they are) suggests a pan-Atlantic Scottish phenomenon of development culminating in the complex Atlantic roundhouses of the mid- to late-first millennium BC. The location and nature of the mid-first millennium BC sites discussed here strongly argues against their use as permanent domestic occupation and suggests they are ancillary to Atlantic roundhouse structures. However, only detailed analysis and dating of the different assemblages and their associated structures will enable the investigation of the various suggestions presented in this paper. It is obvious however, that we are now able to move towards more complex and detailed analysis of the first millennium BC settlement of Atlantic Scotland, as begun by Euan MacKie several decades earlier.

# 7  The archaeological and archaeobotanical implications of a destruction layer in Dun Bharabhat, Lewis

*M.J. Church*

## Introduction

Dr. Euan MacKie is not immediately associated with archaeobotany. However, one of his many major publications, *Dun Mor Vaul: An Iron Age broch on Tiree* (MacKie 1974) contained one of the first modern archaeobotanical reports in Atlantic Scotland (Renfrew 1974), analysing a cache of burnt six-row barley (*Hordeum vulgare* L.) Research across the region has since confirmed six-row barley as the staple cereal crop of the Iron Age and earlier (Boyd 1988; Dickson & Dickson 2000).

The 25 years since the publication of Dun Mor Vaul have seen Atlantic Scotland at the forefront of environmental archaeological research in Britain. A number of long-term inter-disciplinary research campaigns have been undertaken, with strong emphasis on palaeoenvi-ronmental and palaeoeconomic reconstruction. These campaigns have focused on single settlement complexes and their immediate environs (e.g. Howe, Ballin Smith 1994 (**colour plate 5**); Old Scatness, Nicholson & Dockrill 1998) and wider regional investigations (e.g. SEARCH in the Western Isles, Gilbertson *et al.* 1996). Archaeobotany, the study of the human/plant interaction of the past (van Zeist *et al.* 1991), has played a key role in recon-structing the way human groups viewed, managed and used the plant resource within these research campaigns (cf. Bond & Hunter 1987; Dickson 1994; Boardman 1995; Holden & Boardman 1998; Smith 1999).

Dun Bharabhat, a complex Atlantic roundhouse in a small loch in the Bhaltos Peninsula, West Lewis, was excavated between 1985-7 as part of the wider research campaign of the University of Edinburgh, the Calanais Archaeological Research Project (CARP, Harding 2000). This paper outlines the archaeological and archaeobotanical implications of a destruc-tion layer in the secondary occupation of the roundhouse. These implications are then discussed with regard to the regional context of the Atlantic Scottish Iron Age.

## The site

The first research campaign of CARP saw excavation of three Iron Age sites on the Bhaltos Peninsula on the west coast of Lewis (**4**). At the time of excavation the sites were seen to represent the main Iron Age settlement forms common throughout the Western Isles (Harding & Armit 1990): an 'island dun' at Dun Bharabhat (Harding & Dixon 2000), a 'broch' at Loch na Beirgh (Harding & Gilmour 2000) and a wheelhouse and cellular complex at Traigh Cnip (Armit 1996) Excavations at the three sites initially characterised the form and date of the structures with the eventual aim of comparing their structural, artefactual and ecofactual sequences to create an integrated socio-economic model for the area (cf. Ceron-Carrasco *et al.* 2001).

Dun Bharabhat is located in one of the small lochs dotted throughout the hilly interior of the peninsula. The present loch catchment area comprises a *Calluna* rich heathland (Pankhurst & Mullin 1994) and bare rock, suitable for rough grazing. The Holocene vegetation history has been reconstructed through a pollen profile taken from the loch sediments and detrital mud (Lomax & Edwards 2000). At approximately 3700 14C BP (at the start of the Bronze Age), a major loss of relatively mixed woodland occurred, with a rapid spread of heathland taxa and evidence of arable and pastoral activity within the area. Erosional disturbance increased through the late Bronze Age and Iron Age, presumably as a direct result of the islet occupation and associated settlement. A small rise in arboreal taxa, including Scots Pine (*Pinus sylvestris* L.), oak (*Quercus* sp.) and alder (*Alnus* sp.) occurred during the mid to late Iron Age. This tree pollen may be secondarily derived from erosion of the surrounding soil (*ibid.*, 111), or may represent woodland regeneration in the form of a localised copse or small extent of woodland within the catchment.

The excavations concentrated on the roundhouse interior and an adjacent structure that had slumped into the loch and therefore required underwater investigation. Initial clearance of the rubble demonstrated that the roundhouse wall was double-skinned with intra-mural galleries (**23**), identifying the site as a complex Atlantic roundhouse (after Armit 1992). The terrestrial structural sequence begins with ephemeral early Iron Age activity, before the construction of the complex Atlantic roundhouse. This, in turn, was modified to form a simple cellular unit, which used the interior of the roundhouse and a remodelled gallery. Radiocarbon dating of timbers in a destruction layer of the secondary occupation indicates the roundhouse was occupied within the second half of the first millennium BC (see below for further discussion).

This destruction layer was readily identified during excavation and comprised thick deposits of interleaved orange ash, substantial fragments of charred timber and bands of carbonised material. Burnt bone and pottery were found throughout the horizon that covered nearly all of the internal space of the secondary occupation (Harding & Dixon 2000, 20). Only *judgement* samples were taken (Jones M, 1991), including representative fragments of the charred timber and a single bulk sample of carbonised material (*C.169*) immediately overlying and interspersed with the timber. On analysis, *C.169* was rich in barley straw (Church 2000; see below). The most likely explanation for this horizon is the remains of a conflagration of the roof and organic superstructure. The timber fragments, some up to 0.6m in length, were radially orientated, the configuration expected for collapsed roof timbers (Gordon Thomas pers. comm.). It is likely that the barley straw represents part of the roofing thatch. The orange ash stems from the burning of peat or turf (Peters *et al.* 2001), representing a further component of the roof material or flooring material burnt by the conflagration in a situation similar to that observed at Scalloway (Carter 1998).

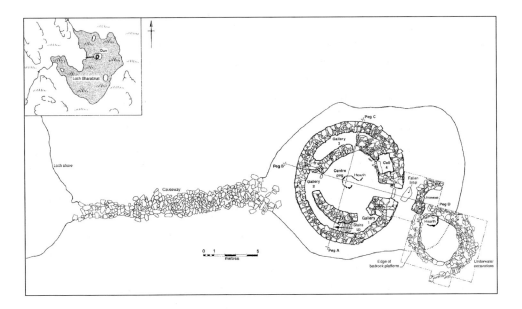

**23** *Plan of principal features of Dun Bharabhat, Lewis*

## The dating of the event

Radiocarbon dates from two separate charred timbers were obtained from the secondary occupation destruction layer (**Table 6**). When calibrated using OxCal (Version 3.5, Bronk-Ramsey, 2000 based on atmospheric data from Stuiver *et al.* 1998) the dates do not extend later than the first century AD and could encompass a much earlier evaluation. These dates have important implications for the chronology of Iron Age settlement in the region. Firstly they have been used to demonstrate early secondary occupation of Atlantic roundhouses. More significantly, some researchers have seen these dates, in conjunction with the other date from the pre-roundhouse level, bracketing the construction and occupation of the complex Atlantic roundhouse to the mid to late first millennium BC (Armit 1996 117; Harding & Dixon 2000, 26-7; Gilmour 2001). This represents a considerably earlier date than the conventional assignment of these structures to the end of the first millennium BC and first millennium AD (cf. MacKie 1971; Parker-Pearson & Sharples 1999 355-360). However, a number of problems exist for this early dating. Firstly, three radiocarbon dates is a small number from which a site sequence can be proposed, let alone an important component of a revised framework for the region, a fact acknowledged by the excavators (Harding & Dixon 2000, 26). Also, none of the dates are directly associated with the primary occupation of the roundhouse. However, this is a factor of the availability of sufficient material for the bulk radiocarbon dating employed a decade ago. Modern advances in radiocarbon dating mean AMS dating of cereal grain recovered from the primary occupation of the roundhouse (Church 2000, 130) could provide more definitive dating.

The second major problem involves the material dated. The pre-roundhouse date came from a single piece of unidentified timber, whilst the two later dates again came from single pieces of timber, presumably of either Scots Pine (*Pinus sylvestris* L.) or spruce (*Picea* sp.) judging by the identifications made of comparable timber samples (see below). Whilst avoiding the problems of bulk dating through the use of single entities (cf. Ashmore 1999) the use of these timbers raises other problems. Firstly timber would have been a very valued resource in the area by the Iron Age. It can be envisaged that timber would be kept for as long as possible, with perhaps forms of curatorship of timber involving re-use over several generations. More significantly, the age ranges of the pine and spruce were at least 95 and 75 years respectively but none of these ring-counts represented the total age of the tree from heartwood to bark (Church 2000, 126-127). Furthermore, the spruce must have been driftwood (see below) and may have been spent many years since within the Atlantic, especially if derived from Siberia via the Arctic (Dickson 1992). Therefore single entity dating of these timbers is not dating the point of conflagration. It is instead dating an accumulation of annual growth rings of trees that could have been over 100 years old and died many decades before their final incorporation into the superstructure of the secondary occupation. This means the actual conflagration could have occurred at least a century or so later than indicated by the radiocarbon dates. Therefore a significant chronological adjustment in the context of Atlantic roundhouse development may be required.

## The nature of the conflagration

Destruction deposits are usually implicitly assumed to be the result of an accident. However, at Dun Bharabhat it is probable that the secondary structure was allowed to burn. This is suggested through the nature of the deposits; the timbers and straw thatch would have been carbonised through slow burning over a number of hours within reduced atmospheric conditions, a situation most likely to have occurred within a mound of collapsed roofing and structural material. Timber would have been a very valued resource (Ceron-Carrasco *et al.* 2001) so it seems unlikely that no effort would have been made to save as much wood as possible if accidental firing of the structure occurred. Of course, if the firing was an act of aggression then the occupants may have been killed or had fled and so could not put out the fire, allowing the debris to smoulder for days. An alternative hypothesis is that the conflagration was a deliberate act of closure incorporating conspicuous consumption of a valued resource, as the final act in the 'life cycle' of the secondary occupation building. Indeed, no further occupation of the roundhouse interior occurred after the conflagration, though activity continued elsewhere on the islet and external underwater cell. This concept of a 'life cycle' for structures is beginning to emerge with evidence for structured deposition at foundation levels of buildings at a range of sites (Parker-Pearson and Sharples 1999; Sharples 2001). These include the 'ritual' pits underlying the primary floor levels at the wheelhouse at Sollas (Campbell 1991) and one of the 'figure-of-eight' houses at Bostadh (Neighbour & Burgess 1997). Also, a thick peat horizon was uncovered at the foundations of the cellular buildings at Loch na Beirgh (Harding and Gilmour 2000), perhaps indicating a metaphoric link to the moorland zone, an important economic hinterland for the inhabitants of the structures.

## Archaeobotanical implications

The detailed analysis of the archaeobotanical material from the destruction layer has already been outlined (Church 2000). All the plant macrofossils, from the thatch to the burnt timber, were very well preserved. For example, the degree of preservation for all the grain from the barley thatch (*C.169*) was compared to grain from a number of other archaeobotanical assemblages from Lewis (**Table 7**), using indices formulated by Hubbard (1990). Over 65 per cent of the grain from *C.169* lay within the two best preservation classes, indicating near perfect preservation, whereas generally over 50 per cent of the grain from the other assemblages lay within the two worst preservation classes, indicating severe degradation of the grain. This allowed much more detailed identification to be made for *C.169* than is usually possible for material derived from the occupation levels from Atlantic Scottish sites. The excellent preservation stems from the carbonisation process that occurred during the conflagration of the roof. The roof, if left to burn, would eventually have collapsed inwards, providing excellent conditions for slow carbonisation of plant material at a relatively low heat, within a reducing atmosphere (G. Thomas, pers. comm). Experimental work by Boardman and Jones (1990) has shown that these conditions produce the best preservation, in terms of density, condition and the range of plant parts, many of which (the chaff, culms and seeds) would be destroyed in higher temperatures.

The destruction level is also important in terms of its archaeobotanical taphonomy, as we can confidently relate the assemblages to specific sets of plant remains. For example, the burnt timbers were certainly used as structural components, whilst the cereal rich *C.169* has been interpreted as a barley thatch, though it may represent bedding, flooring or stored straw within the loft or roof of the structure. The key issue is the relative lack of mixing with other plant material from human behavioural episodes of discard (Jones G, 1991). This mixing is an unquantifiable process that represents the biggest interpretative problem of archaeobotanical assemblages stemming from carbonisation in the domestic hearths of Atlantic Scotland (Church & Peters 2001). Analysis of individual components and lenses of material from destruction levels therefore avoids this taphonomic problem, so a more confident and detailed analysis of issues such as timber procurement and arable agriculture is possible.

### Timber

Five hand-retrieved samples were taken of the burnt timber. *C.169* also contained fragments of burnt timber. The timber comprised Scots Pine (*Pinus sylvestris* L.) and spruce (*Picea* sp.), with small amounts of birch (*Betula* sp.), ling heather (*Calluna vulgaris* L. Hull) and rootwood of indeterminate taxa. The timber was in excellent condition allowing identification of most fragments, including ring counts. The birch and ling displayed comparatively low ring counts, with the highest counts being 16 and 8 respectively. Also, all the fragments were of roundwood suggesting that small branches and twigs were present within the roof, perhaps as furnishings such as heather rope or birch wattle. Both these taxa would have been available locally (Lomax & Edwards 2000). The pine seems to have been of a greater age than the spruce, with the highest counts being 95 and 75 respectively. Further morphological characteristics provide information on the nature and origin of the timber. Several of the spruce fragments contained bore holes, indicating the use of driftwood (Malmros 1994; Taylor

1999). This seems to be the likely source for the spruce, as the taxon was non-native to the British Isles during the Iron Age. The timber could have drifted from North America or even Siberia, having first been transported through the Arctic (Dickson 1992). The pine did not exhibit any sign of boreholes and bark fragments were recovered from *C.169*. Also, the ring pattern from the larger pine fragments was very narrow, which suggests the tree was growing in stressed conditions. This evidence, coupled with the presence of Scots Pine pollen in the contemporary subzone from the loch core (*ibid.*, 2000), points to the use of locally-derived timber. Therefore the procurement strategies for timber were both opportunistic, in terms of the driftwood, and also potentially managed, in the case of the locally-derived pine.

## Thatch

As stated above, *C.169* contained a high density of very well-preserved carbonised cereal plant macrofossils (**Table 8**). Much of the plant material was derived from cereal straw including nodes, bases and thousands of culm fragments. The assemblage was therefore interpreted as a possible fragment of thatch. The straw crop seems to be a mix of six-row hulled barley (*Hordeum vulgare* var. *vulgare* L.) and two-row hulled barley (*Hordeum distichum* var. *vulgare* L.). From the proportions of the rachis fragments, 73 per cent of the assemblage was six-row with 27 per cent two-row. Also, in two-row barley only symmetric grain is produced whereas six-row barley produces asymmetric and symmetric grain in a ratio of 2:1. Hence, the ratio of 1.4:1 within *C.169* confirms a mix of six-row and two-row barley, with the six-row species dominant. The identification of two-row barley is surprisingly rare within the Atlantic Scottish Iron Age. This is partly because of the relative rarity in survival of those features (sterile lateral spikelet and rachis internode) which are used to differentiate the species, but also may suggest sophisticated management of the arable resource through selective cultivation of specific species and variants for different functions. For example, the presence of two-row barley in the thatch may represent particular qualities the straw from this species exhibit. Conversely, six-row barley may have been preferred for consumption, as it would have provided a greater grain yield per hectare. Some of this six-row barley would have become carbonised in the domestic hearths, mostly through 'graddening' (Fenton 1978) and cooking accidents, which subsequently became incorporated into ash spreads, floors and middens. It is these remains that comprise much of the archaeobotanical assemblages across Atlantic Scotland, potentially creating a bias towards a perceived monoculture of six-row barley in the region during most of the Iron Age.

The crop seems to have been harvested by uprooting, due to the high number of culm bases of both cereals and smaller monocotyledons and weed associations with low lying plants, such as violets (*Viola* sp.) The straw would have been removed early in the crop-processing, in the threshing stage for example. This is confirmed by the ratio between the culm bases and the basal rachises (4.6:1), which shows that most of the ears were separated from the straw prior to its use as thatch. Hence, an estimate can be made of approximately 80 per cent efficiency for the separation of the ear from the straw during early crop-processing.

The presence of wild taxa within the straw relates largely to weed contamination of the crop. Heather furnishings, such as rope or twine, can explain the limited presence of heathland taxa, such as *Erica/Calluna* spp. The remaining taxa are all common weeds of cultivation and dry grassland. The presence of Chickweed (*Stellaria media* L. Vill.) indicates relatively nitrogenous soil conditions, presumably enhanced through the addition of animal manure and seaweed to the soil. Several of the species, including Ray's knotgrass (*Polygonum oxyspermum* Meyer & Bunge ex Ledeb.), Bulbous buttercup (*Ranunculus bulbosus* L.) and Wild turnip (*Brassica rapa* L.) have strong associations with machair grassland (Pankhurst & Mullin 1994). This evidence, coupled with a second series of pollen sequences from Loch na Beirgh (Lomax 1997), points to the cultivation of the barley crop occurring largely within the machair grassland behind Traigh na Beirgh (**4**). The presence of Wild turnip within samples from the occupation levels in Dun Bharabhat and the later phases at Cnip and Loch na Beirgh may also point to the repeated use of the machair as the primary environment for arable cultivation (Church 2000; Ceron-Carrasco *et al.* 2001).

## Other sites in Atlantic Scotland

The destruction layer from Dun Bharabhat demonstrates the increased level of archaeological and archaeobotanical interpretation which is possible from conflagrations. A review of the literature relating to the Atlantic Scottish Iron Age highlights the surprising infrequency of such deposits (**Table 9**). This is probably a product of a number of factors including archaeological recognition, climatic constraints, and site formation and erosion processes.

The conflagration at Scalloway (Sharples 1998) marked the end of the primary occupation of the complex Atlantic roundhouse. It was recognised archaeologically through the widespread evidence of interleaved ash and charcoal. Soil micromorphological analysis (Carter 1998) suggested that this 'red ash layer' represented not the remains of the roof as first thought but rather the burnt remains of the organic floor material built up during the final period of occupation. The roof material itself was thought to have either burnt away completely or been removed, as a deliberate action or as a product of the re-occupation.

The extensive excavations at the Howe, Orkney (Ballin Smith 1994) (**colour plate 4**) uncovered the highest frequency of conflagrations at a single site. Fires occurred in both secondary occupation levels within the broch and also at different points of the middle Iron Age external occupation. Detailed sampling and archaeobotanical analysis (Dickson 1994) of these conflagrations provided a wealth of information on the plant materials used in the structure. Little explanation is given for the cause of the fires except for the conflagration in the rampart cells of the north-west building. This may represent a deliberate firing of the cell roofs as part of a closure episode, for the fire was prevented from spreading into the main house and the cells then fell out of use for the remainder of the period.

Turning to the Western Isles, recent excavations at Bornais, South Uist (Sharples 2000) have revealed a conflagration horizon of a probable wheelhouse, which was replaced by a rectilinear structure. Archaeobotanical research, including the analysis of several burnt timber planks, is ongoing. Further structural information was also recovered at the excavations at Loch na Beirgh, Lewis (Harding & Gilmour 2000), preserved by the waterlogged conditions of the lowest levels of the Cellular Period (second-fourth centuries cal AD) rather than carbonisation (see below).

Research in the Inner Hebrides has also produced two sites with conflagrations, both excavated by Mackie. At Dun Mor Vaul, Tiree (MacKie 1974) excavations revealed ephemeral evidence of a conflagration of an early Iron Age structure underlying the main complex Atlantic roundhouse, including a cache of burnt barley grain (Renfrew 1974) and an *in situ* carbonised post. The conflagration at Dun Ardtreck is much more substantial, with a thick layer of charcoal and ash across much of the site interpreted as a major structural fire (MacKie forthcoming). The partial excavation of a 'vitrified dun' at Langwell in Sutherland also revealed the extensive remains of a major structural fire, including what appear to be several radially orientated roofing timbers (Nisbet 1995).

A number of important points are raised by this brief review. Firstly, there is a recurring theme in the way that these fires signal the end, or perhaps the beginning, of a period of occupation on the site. Many of these conflagration deposits are followed by a period of abandonment, sometimes signalling the final major archaeological episode on the site, as at Dun Bharabhat and Langwell. The other sites that continue to be occupied or re-occupied at a later date all display major structural or spatial re-organisation, for example at Scalloway, Bornais and the Howe, Orkney. The conflagration could also mark a deliberate action to clear or 'cleanse' the site prior to re-occupation. Therefore, these conflagrations, no matter what their cause, mark major changes in the way these sites are used, viewed or lived in by their occupants i.e. an episode of closure or re-birth in the life-history of the structure.

As argued above, it is probable that timber within these deposits was specifically chosen for some form of structural component of the building. This provides information on the type of tree or shrub used and its likely source within the wider economic landscape. The issue of timber procurement is seen as an important economic consideration throughout Iron Age Atlantic Scotland (Fojut 2001), with some researchers viewing timber availability as a possible stimulus for social and structural change (cf. wheelhouses Armit 1992, 1996). The identifications made of timber from a variety of site types from the middle Iron Age through to the late Iron Age show that timber procurement was based upon the gathering of driftwood, such as spruce (*Picea* sp.), and the use of smaller timbers of species that could have been obtained locally, such as willow (*Salix* sp.) and hazel (*Corylus* sp.). Indeed, it has been argued from the preliminary analysis of hazel wattle-work from Loch na Beirgh that the remains stemmed from a local, coppiced woodland (Church forthcoming). This pattern of procurement does not require large-scale trade networks of timber and the consequent trade deficits would result in an island – mainland axis. However, none of the evidence directly relates to the superstructure of the Atlantic roundhouse, the monument theoretically requiring the greatest volume of timber. Instead the evidence is derived from a wheelhouse (Bornais) and smaller cellular units within 1) the shell of abandoned round-houses (e.g. Dun Bharabhat) or 2) external buildings to the roundhouses at their time of occu-pation (e.g. Howe). Hence, timber procurement within the middle Iron Age (the *floruit* of complex Atlantic roundhouses) may have required a trade in timber. The likely presence of *in situ* substantial timber remains from the primary and secondary roundhouses at Loch na Beirgh represents an unique opportunity to address this important issue in detail. Other site types, such as vitrified forts (e.g. Rahoy, Argyll, Childe & Thorneycroft 1938) and waterlogged sites, such as the external structure at Dun Bharabhat, are also important site types to address this question of timber procurement.

Conflagration deposits provide a valuable resource for future research into the human/plant relationship in Atlantic Scotland. For example, Dickson provided very detailed identifications from the Howe, Orkney from the five conflagration levels on the site, which now rest in the site archive. Amongst these are a number of samples with direct weed associations with the barley thatch that would allow estimations of the position of the arable component within the wider landscape. As argued above, this is generally not possible because of the inherent taphonomic problems within Atlantic Scotland's archaeobotany (Church & Peters 2001). Further comparison between the different phases, both qualitative and quantitative, could highlight issues of continuity or change. Re-analysis could also occur onsite, with the opening of old excavation trenches followed by detailed sampling at sites with little archaeobotanical analysis, as part of their final publication (e.g. Langwell). This detailed sampling would include the use of techniques with a proven ability to answer questions pertinent to understanding these conflagration deposits, such as soil micromorphology (Carter 1998), mineral magnetism (Batt & Dockrill 1998; Peters *et al.* 2000, 2001) and archaeobotany (Dickson 1994; Church 2000).

## Conclusion

This paper has outlined the archaeological and archaeobotanical implications from a conflagration at the end of the secondary occupation of Dun Bharabhat, Lewis. This analysis and review of other similar deposits has highlighted the importance of conflagration deposits to the archaeobotany of the Atlantic Scottish Iron Age. Three key conclusions can be drawn from this analysis and review, as follows:

While it is difficult to identify the mechanism and nature of the conflagration from the available evidence, it is important to consider the alternative hypotheses of aggression and deliberate episodes in the life history of the building, as well as the usual interpretation of accidental firing.

Analysis of individual components and lenses of material from destruction levels avoids the problems of taphonomic mixing, characteristic of most archaeobotanical assemblages from the region. More confident and detailed analysis of issues such as timber procurement and arable agriculture should be possible.

The identifications made of timber from a variety of site types from the middle Iron Age through to the late Iron Age show that timber procurement was based upon the gathering of driftwood, such as spruce (*Picea* sp.), and the use of smaller timbers of species that could have been obtained locally, such as willow (*Salix* sp.) and hazel (*Corylus* sp.). Complex trade networks for timber procurement need not be invoked, although the evidence stems from smaller cellular units rather than larger structures, such as the Atlantic roundhouses.

# 8  The souterrains of Skye

*Roger Miket*

## Introduction

Fieldwork and excavation on Skye over the last decade have substantially enlarged the number of known souterrains, as well as enriching the quality of our information about them. Against a general Scottish background, an inventory of 31 sites on the island informs a discussion of their characteristics and context. The first part of this paper considers some aspects of Scottish souterrains in general before focusing upon the characteristics of those on Skye in particular, accompanied by an inventory.

## The Scottish context for the souterrains of Skye

> There are feveral little ftone houfes, built underground, call'd Earth-houfes, which ferv'd to hide a few People and their Goods in time of War; the Entry to them was on the Sea or River-fide: there is one of them in the Village Lachsay and another in Camftinvag.
>
> Martin Martin 1716, 154

Souterrains hold a respectable position in Scottish antiquarian literature, taking their place alongside chambered cairns, brochs and duns, as one of the earliest structural forms to be distinguished, examined and recorded by early travellers. The above account by Martin Martin referring to two souterrains on Skye is one of the earliest in an age that took delight in historical enquiry; but it is also a description, and to many of his day and later, an explanation of their purpose.

Since Martin wrote, a more rigorous and analytical assessment of the class has developed. Yet, in common with so much of the 'monumentality' that has come down to us from an antiquarian age, souterrains have continued to be regarded as 'artefacts' in isolation, with analysis focusing upon their distribution, architectural form, associations and chronology, at the expense of their context. The abandonment of such simplistic explanations of their purpose, as advanced by Martin and his near-contemporaries, has left a vacuum, which over a century of scholarship has failed adequately to fill. Nevertheless, the questions posed and the methods employed in attempting to resolve them have become increasingly sophisticated, even if the answers have remained obstinately elusive. Additional discoveries and excavation have certainly enriched our understanding of the society that built them, bringing about subtle, but significant, shifts in our perception of Iron Age society in Scotland as a whole. Recognition of the role of many as adjuncts to substantial surface structures, for example, clearly underlines the current need for a wide-ranging review of the class, which might focus upon their context within the settlements and structures rather than consider them as distinctive entities in isolation.

## Distribution

Souterrains have a wide distribution (**24**), but one with a major concentration on the Atlantic seaboard and its immediate hinterland. Although Brittany (Giot 1979), Cornwall (Christie 1979; Cooke 1993) and Ireland (Warner 1979, 1980) all share this generalised architectural form with Scotland, its characteristics in each region reveal geographically discrete traditions, so that the souterrains of one area are unlikely to be confused with those of another. In this respect, while the sea might offer both a highway and a boundary, it is the latter which impresses.

Well over 400 souterrain sites have been identified in Scotland, although the characteristically subterranean aspect of the majority must make such a figure a meaningless indicator of the number originally built. As with the chambered tombs of an earlier age which were also encased

**24** *Distribution of souterrains in Scotland*

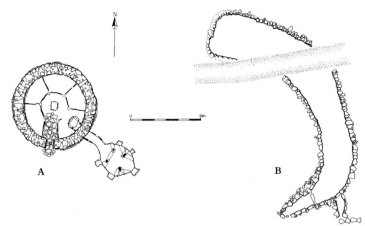

**25** *Souterrains: Rennibister, Orkney (after Ritchie 1995) and Newmill, Perthshire (after Watkins 1981b)*

within soil and stone, the potential for survival is high and doubtless many await discovery. This has usually arisen by chance, most commonly through the collapse of lintels, or through activities resulting from agricultural activity. Within Scotland the principal distribution extends northwards from the Ardnamurchan peninsular (including the isles of Coll and Tiree), to include the Western Hebrides, Sutherland, Caithness, the Northern Isles, and Ross and Cromarty, before continuing down the eastern side of Scotland to embrace Grampian, Tayside and Fife. Elsewhere souterrains are sparse, although an interesting 'southern' group, which may represent a late stage in the series, occurs in Lothian and the Borders (Welfare 1984). The most south-easterly of the Scottish souterrains, the only example found south of the present Anglo-Scottish border, lay at Milfield in north Northumberland (Jobey 1975).

## Architecture

Scottish souterrains demonstrate considerable regional variation in terms of size, design and form of construction (Wainwright 1953; 1963; Welfare 1984). For example, the substantial curved and paved galleries of Angus that can run for distances in excess of 40m and widen markedly at their inner end are especially distinctive. By contrast, those of Sutherland and Aberdeenshire are significantly smaller, whereas the galleries of those in Orkney and Shetland invariably lead to a small chamber which, but for their pillared supports, would be more reminiscent of the mortuary architecture of an earlier age (**25**).

As early as the 1860s it was suggested that materials other than stone might have been used for the main structural elements of sidewalls and roof-lintels (Jervise 1870, 473-4). Although stone might be preferred for its durability, the availability of suitable local materials dictated whether a souterrain was constructed partially or entirely of stone, with timber offering a viable alternative. The susceptibility of wood to decay and the corresponding collapse has rendered identification of timber-built forms difficult. However, in recent years aerial photography and chance encounters during excavation have plainly demonstrated the presence of galleries in areas where wood was plentiful and suitable building stone scarce (Maxwell 1987; Watkins 1981a, 1981b; Armit 1999, 582). In the absence of aerial photographic evidence, all that may remain of a timber-lined souterrain is the earth-filled gully to challenge an excavator's skills (e.g. Auchlishie, Angus, Dick 1996, 12; see also Armit 1999, 582 & Alexander 2000, 18-26). In the case of just such a gully at Cyderhall, Sutherland, the excavator was fortunate in discovering a series of paired posts along its length, a feature duplicated in an adjacent partially stone-lined cutting, which allowed the feature to be interpreted as a timber-lined souterrain with a timber roof (Pollack 1992, 152-5).

As their name implies, the majority of souterrains have been built entirely underground, with no trace of the line of the gallery visible at the surface. However it has been suggested that in some instances the discrete nature of souterrains might have been overstated, and that the course of the gallery might have been visible on the surface. There is certainly no compelling reason (other than for that of simple convenience) why the course of a gallery should be concealed anymore than its entrances, which in many instances are evidently not situated with a view to concealment. Such a situation would only present problems should the mounded projection at the surface covering the main structure have presented an obstacle to surface traffic, or upon interpretations, which considers souterrains in terms of secrecy and refuge. That the course of the souterrain might have been traceable at the surface had been remarked upon by Wainwright, who, on the basis of his work at Carlungie and Ardestie, stated that 'we know that in Angus a souterrain usually protruded well above the level of the ground' (Wainwright 1963, 14).

Unfortunately some have taken this further, to the extent of postulating that the gallery itself might have stood exposed to the elements. At Newmill, for example, rather than accepting that simply the timber equivalent of horizontal stone lintels once rested upon side-walls, the excavator proposed the more complex solution of an exposed gabled roof frame (Watkins 1981b, 195-6). The difficulties of maintaining an even ridge-line and the change in roof-angle required to cap a building of diminishing width is challenging enough, without the added difficulties of constructing the roof to follow the tight curve imposed by the gallery (see for example Hope-Taylor 1962, 16). Other claims, such as the proposition that a roof with such an increased catchment area would substantially waterproof the souterrain, stand unproven, as they do not appear to have been critical requirements of the souterrains elsewhere.

Apart from such illusory claims (which will be shown to run counter to the purpose of the souterrain), it is not contentious that souterrains either wholly or in part might rise above the *natural* surface; indeed many lie in just such situations, inserted within man-made features such as the earthen banks of hillforts or within middens. However, even in these situations it is plain that the gallery was not exposed, but was encased within a built-up surface or contained within a structure is not contentious; misunderstanding about this has led to a climate of thinking in which the importance of the soil casing is diminished, and with this is lost the very qualities that this cladding brings to the souterrain. As will be demonstrated, this insulated casing was critical to the souterrains purpose, just as it was to the icehouses of a later age.

By their nature, souterrains are essentially 'embedded galleries', this encasement being the integral and unifying characteristic of all known examples, irrespective of regional variation. Indeed, as the subterranean examples demonstrate, the considerable restrictions imposed architecturally in terms of useable space for the degree of effort expended only become understandable in terms of the aims that the builders were trying to achieve: aims which required that the gallery be, if not truly 'subterranean', then at least 'encased', whether as in the case of the souterrain inserted into the Knowe of Rowiegar, an Orkney-Cromarty stalled cairn (Henshall 1963, 214-5), or contained within the stone walls of surface-built homesteads (e.g. Fairhurst & Taylor 1971; see *infra*).

Though this feature of 'embeddedness' serves to help define the souterrains as a group, there is a danger of overlooking the point that the main structural components exist within a wide range of contemporary Iron Age structures. As galleries in their own right, they share many of the characteristics of other constructions. Though many of the galleries leading to wheelhouse interiors are short, others are lengthier constructions, and in that guise offer the potential for confusion with what we call souterrains (e.g. Campbell 1991,123; Young 1955, 87-8 & fig. 3). Better known however are the curved, stone-lintelled galleries so characteristic of broch architecture, which, it may be noted, are similarly contained within the thickness of a wall.

The second factor mitigating their distinctiveness is that multiple examples within domestic settlement contexts are well attested from aerial photography, a factor which must inform future interpretations. Their incidence highlights the pressing desirability of the total excavation of such sites.

## Some contexts

Since the late nineteenth century, there has been increased understanding of the relationship between souterrains and surface structures. Modern archaeological illustrations which portray an underground souterrain running away from beneath a round timber house now occasion little remark (Anderson 1883, 305; RCAHMS 1911, nos 318, 327 and 328). Often souterrains lie adjacent to the house, but occasionally they are found incorporated within the 'thickened' wall skins of structures. The distribution of the latter within Scotland is widespread (Small 1967, 227 & fig. 3; Fairhurst & Taylor 1974, 86-7, 92-3; Hingley *et al.* 1997, 447), perhaps echoing the substantial 'passageway' noted within the outer and inner walls of certain categories of ring-ditch house extending from Angus through south-east Scotland, to the English Border (Reynolds 1982, 48-54; RCAHMS 1994, 62, 71-3, and O'Sullivan *forthcoming*). The *floruit* of ring-ditch house is believed to lie around the middle centuries of the first millennium BC (Hill 1984, 12). It has been suggested that these 'passages' may have functioned as cattle-stalls (Jobey and Tait 1966, 14), an echo of Wainwright's suggestion that the souterrain at Carlungie I may have functioned as a shelter for stock (Wainwright 1963, 127-8). There is however, no evidence in either case that this was so and consequently the hypothesis has not won widespread acceptance (e.g. Watkins 1981b, 197).

## Chronology

The relationship proposed between souterrains and certain ring-ditch houses, together with the dates from sites such as Suisgill, and Cyderhall in Sutherland (Barclay 1985, 194; Pollock 1992, 159), suggests their emergence soon after the middle of the first millennium BC. Their main floruit however occurred around the centuries either side of the BC/AD divide. In the case of the southern souterrains, the re-use of dressed Roman stonework at Shirva, Newstead I, and Crichton Mains points to construction no earlier than the last quarter of the second century AD (Welfare 1984, 313-14). Unlike Ireland, where souterrains continued to be constructed throughout the first millennium AD (Warner 1979; Williams 1985, 69-80), there is little evidence to show the construction of new souterrains in Scotland after the third century AD. The creation of the curved passage inserted within the south-east quadrant of the broch tower at Beirgh, Lewis, dated to sometime between the mid-third and mid-fifth centuries AD, makes this currently one of the latest securely dated gallery constructions (Harding & Gilmour 2000, 78). In the case of the southern souterrains Armit has developed an idea first proposed by Macinnes over a decade earlier (Macinnes, 1984, 245; Armit 1999, 577-596). This suggests that not only were no new souterrains built after the third century AD but it was the very moment when they were being purposefully demolished wholesale. This, it is argued, was either a direct result of the historically attested Roman military intervention in the latter half of the second century, or part of the general social upheaval attendant upon the loss of whatever grain market may have existed prior to the Roman military's withdrawal to the Hadrianic frontier in the latter half of the third century AD.

Thereafter, the situation is a confusing one, for many souterrains clearly had a life well beyond that date. The discovery of Scandinavian objects, such as the stone bearing 'Runic Letters' said to have been found within the souterrain at Cos Ceumach, Sutherland (SMR NC90NW 3), the spearhead and net-sinkers from within Taigh an t-Sithiche, St Kilda (Stell & Harman 1988, 48-9; SMR NF19NW 7), and the craggan vessels from within Sithean an Altair Vallay, North Uist (Beveridge 1911, 118-21) all indicate re-use by a later age, perhaps as no more than a convenient place for the disposal of domestic refuse. Objects most frequently recovered include pottery, quernstone fragments and animal bones. Human remains have been found within souterrains, although the circumstances of deposition are rarely clear (Hedges 1987, i, 29; Marwick 1927).

## Function

Whatever the truth of Wainwright's observation that not all souterrains were necessarily constructed with the same purpose in mind (1963, 13), three centuries of observation and excavation have failed to confirm even one of the many possibilities. Rejecting the more fanciful interpretations of souterrains, such as hiding places for ships' oars, or 'pigmies kirks', explanations have favoured one of three principal interpretations; their use as dwellings or refuges in times of danger, their use as cellars for storage, and their use as places of religious importance.

### Dwellings and refuges
Until well into the nineteenth century it was believed by many that the earlier inhabitants of Scotland were a race of small people, whose 'elfin darts' (flint arrowheads) were to be found in many a gentleman's 'cabinet of curiosities'. Indigenous descriptive terms, such as *eird-hoos* (Lowland Scots: earth-house) and *tigh-fo-thalaimh* (Gaelic: house underground), gave vivid expression to the idea of the souterrain as an underground home for the 'earlier aborigines'. This was strengthened by those excavations which retrieved from their interiors items of domestic utility (e.g. pottery and quernstones) and what were believed to have been 'fireplaces'. Given situations of social upheaval the use of some souterrains and caves for shelter is

highly probable. Two of the souterrains at Clova, Kildrummy, Aberdeenshire (SMR NJ41NE 1), were found to contain fireplaces, and were known to have been inhabited within the last 200 years (Mitchel 1912).

That most souterrains were on the small side for use as dwellings did not pass unnoticed. As early as 1549, in describing what may have been a souterrain on Lewis, Dean Munro noted, 'It is sa little that ane man may scairscelie stand uprichtlie in it efter he has gane in on his kneis' (Munro 1549), and in the mid-nineteenth century such critical reasoning led many to reject the dwelling hypothesis altogether. In 1869, for example, Dr John Stuart perceived that 'having no opening for light or ventilation, they could scarcely have been used as a permanent dwelling' (Stuart 1869, 25). Once it was demonstrated that some souterrains appeared to be linked to surface buildings, it was but a short step to wonder that if both were contemporary and the more likely dwelling was the hut-circle, what then was the souterrain? From the latter half of the nineteenth century the term 'souterrain' replaced the earlier terms.

For those who, like Munro, were unhappy to regard souterrains as places of permanent residence, there was nevertheless scope for regarding them as places for 'concealment in perilous times', a role for which they seemed particularly suited, given their apparent remoteness from habitation and their concealed nature. While excavation repeatedly reveals the illusory nature of their 'remoteness', the idea of a souterrain as a temporary refuge in times of danger has persisted into the present, and has only recently fallen out of favour. What might offer discrete and safe refuge in an open landscape does not hold the same significance within a settlement, and consequently it is time to reject any lingering notions that purposeful concealment played any part in their creation. As shown below, in the case of those at Tungadale (*9*) and Kilvaxter (*30*), the entrances were always clearly visible. Indeed, there is nothing to suggest that attempts were made to hide those in any of the Skye examples.

## Storage

Support for the idea of souterrains as places for safeguarding products and perhaps possessions has grown with the increased recognition of their role within settlement, and their, often intimate, relationship with individual buildings. While it is reasonable to regard some of the roomier souterrains as store-houses, the small size, layout and cramped interiors of the majority has led many to question their ability to fulfil such a role. If space alone were required, alternative forms of construction, offering far more spacious interiors for storage, and for considerably less effort, could have been considered. Consequently, some other influential factor must have operated, the identification of which might offer some clue as to their function. The gallery-style characterising souterrains only recommends itself when the nature of the materials available are combined with the requirement that either the structure should be wholly encased, or where there are limitations upon the use of other forms of roof-construction (e.g. corbelling). In this case the width of the gallery is determined by the length of the available lintels. Under such restrictions, options for the creation of storage space are naturally circumscribed making the narrow gallery, with all its inherent disadvantages, the only viable option (Wainwright, 1963, 15).

While the recognition of a context for souterrains amidst settlements of surface buildings has tipped the balance of probability as to their function more firmly towards that of store-houses, what was stored within remains uncertain. The unsuitability of souterrains for sheltering livestock (particularly where the interior has impediments such as steps) has already been noted. Some have considered the possibility of souterrains functioning as underground granaries (e.g. Watkins 1984, 73 and Armit 2000, 583), but it is difficult to reconcile these complicated, highly humid (often 75 per cent +) labour-intensive constructions which offer such limited returns of space for the effort involved, with such a concept. Moreover, there were plainly better alternatives.

It is significant that the objects found within souterrains have given no clear answer as to their function. From a Hebridean perspective where, until recently, communities had few possessions, it is difficult to regard souterrains as stores for 'possessions' as opposed to 'goods'. The purposeful creation of dark, frost-free, cool, damp and potentially stable environments might rather suggest the storage of organic material. This would imply a dynamic role for souterrains, one in which they offer conditions conducive both to the maintenance and, perhaps, the maturing of their contents (Fox 1964, 151-2; Pearce 1981, 111). It is usually held that their builders were of a society that measured wealth by livestock. Following the wide-scale abandonment of much upland settlement at the close of the previous millennium, vast expanses of upland landscape were potentially available for pastoral agriculture. It is precisely in such an economic context that transhumance, and that 'summering' of stock (later to be known from its Scandinavian form as 'shieling') might be expected to play a significant part in building up stores for the winter months. This is especially evident in the case of dairying, which was practised to a degree capable of producing surpluses which required storage strategies. The recovery of 'bog-butter' reveals one storage strategy, which was clearly both considerable in scale and widespread throughout the Highland and Hebridean areas. For Skye, the records show no less than six separate discoveries of 'bog-butter' deposits sufficient to indicate widespread practice at a time contemporary with that of souterrain construction.[1]

By their nature bogs offered cool, stable and anaerobic conditions which might be used to advantage in preserving produce. However, the use of bogs was not entirely free of risk and inconvenience. For example, in an open landscape security was likely to be poor, with the possibility of theft from marked locations, and difficulties in relocating unmarked ones. As the bog was unlikely to be the place of end-use, recovery and transport will have been necessary when supplies were required.

It is reasonable to ask, as perhaps many did at the time, whether bogs were really ideal storage areas. Was it not possible to create an effective cold store which might, like the 'Highland Pantries' of a later age, prolong the life of their contents, while at the same time offer the added benefits of greater security and more convenient access. Certainly the relationship of the souterrain at Tungadale to the domestic living area might bear profitable comparison with that of these later Highland 'pantries' or cold store larders.[2]

If bogs and cold marshy places were important for the preservation of certain commodities in the Hebrides and Highlands, what options were open to those culturally similar communities in other parts of North Britain without such ready access to them as natural larders? It is here where the conditions which appear to have been common to all souterrains come closest towards satisfying the criteria necessary for the storage of dairy produce and other perishable materials. It is amidst the potentially richer arable acres of south-eastern Scotland where souterrain densities are highest, and the recovery of animal remains reveals a significant level of pastoral/dairy activity. Perceived difficulties, such as access to the different types of commodities stored within these narrow linear passageways diminish if, as suggested above, they are the result of an annual harvest to be used, and replenished on an annual basis.

If the interpretation of souterrains as seasonal storehouses for perishable produce were correct, this would account for the paucity of the evidence relating to their use. As with any abandoned warehouse, the probability of its contents surviving intact is small. In this respect, the recovery of hemp and flax from the floor of the souterrain at Cyderhall, Sutherland (considered by the excavator as perhaps indicative of its storage either as a material in its own right or in the form of sacks), is likely to be significant (Pollock 1992, 158).

*Religious role*

While it is reasonable to speculate that the purpose of souterrains may have been entirely ceremonial there has been little in support of such a belief. For example, the Scottish examples do not adhere to a particular cosmological orientation, as is suggested for the Cornish fogous (Cooke 1993, 207-15). Paradoxically, the very ambiguity inherent in what may or may not be claimed as evidence for ritual activity, has in itself excited a tendency to over-emphasis. This is particularly true of those constructions that incorporate what have been regarded as, 'significant stones' such as blocks of Roman masonry, or cup and ring marked rocks (e.g. Hingley 1992, 29). In the case of the Roman masonry, there is nothing to show that the souterrain builders of Crichton Mains understood their stonework as anything other than raw material.

By contrast, the incidence of discovery of cup, and cup and ring marked rocks at souterrain sites does require more consideration. Stones bearing cups, and cup-and-rings, either singly or in groups, have been recovered from 15 souterrain sites.[3] In some cases the physical relationship is tenuous. Most stones were built into sidewalls, or were found upon lintels or pinning-stones. That some stones lie near the entrance *may* indicate a chosen position, but one that is difficult to interpret. Others are lost to view entirely, e.g. Ruthven. Extensive speculation (see Bradley, 1997) has brought us little closer to an understanding of their purpose. Even accepting the currently consensual view that these stones represent, in some unfathomable way, an expression of religious belief, their origin lies in the Neolithic and arguments for continuity into the Bronze Age is in itself contentious (Burgess 1991, 21-6). There is nothing to show that their incorporation into structures of Iron Age date arose out of anything other than curiosity.

Less readily explicable are those idiosyncrasies which recur to such a high degree as to put their occurrence well beyond the realms of chance. The tendency for galleries to curve and frequently enlarge towards the inner terminal, and the preference for the entrances of many to lie close by a water source (very typical of those on Skye) are examples. Much might be deduced from the potential of souterrains for storage, as well as analysis of their volumetric capacity.

## Souterrains on Skye

> Sneaking out of those dark burrows one might see a crowd of rollicking Pictish children after a stormy night like fairies emerging from a Sithean [Fairy knoll] in order to scamper about the doors of the brighter huts above.
>
> Lamont, Strath in Isle of Skye. 1913, 9.

In 1716 Martin Martin noted two souterrains in Skye. Two centuries later the Royal Commission recorded details of 14 sites (1928, 148-9). This has risen through fieldwork over the last decade to a total of some 31 sites (including contentious examples). Despite this, any comparative analysis has to recognise the bias in the present data. This includes the loss of certain sites and thereby, the opportunity to re-evaluate them. It is a matter of recent historical record that in at least five instances souterrains have been purposefully in-filled and their entrances blocked, so as not to present a danger to stock or children. Such considerations might well have operated in earlier times (see Armit 1999, 583-6).

Of those available for re-examination, there is an almost repetitive consistency in their current condition. In the majority of cases, the souterrain is earth-fast, with only part of its structure visible. Usually this consists of stretches of the wall-heads flanking the earth-filled gallery, visible through the removal or collapse of the lintels. Generally, there is little to show the form of either the entrance or the terminal; and where the gallery remains accessible, it usually reveals no more than a view of an unevenly in-filled interior.

The historical record for these souterrains rarely consists of more than a brief acknowledgement of their existence; that for the souterrain at Carn nam Bodach (*23*) is exceptional. Only two souterrains have been excavated. In 1987 Tungadale (*9*) was examined in advance of afforestation, and this led to a wider consideration of those on Skye in general. This, in its turn, resulted in a search for additional examples, the production of plans and section drawings, where appropriate, of other souterrains, some useful sampling of the souterrain at Alt na Cille (*16*) as well as some minor measures of conservation, such as the removal of modern infill from within 'Uamh na Ramh', Raasay (*21*). The second excavation, that at Kilvaxter (*30*), is currently in progress.

## Distribution

The distribution and location of recorded souterrains on Skye (**26**) reveals a preference for areas of potential cultivation (brown forest soils, humic gleys and podsols), which are found on the undulating lowland slopes and terraces, as well as the less moderately inclined slopes encountered on the glen sides. A similar attraction to such soils has been remarked upon in the case of other Iron Age sites (MacSween, 1985, map 11).

Many souterrains sit comfortably alongside relict fields, as if to imply some lengthy tradition of agricultural activity, but the observed relationship is complex. In the 50 years between 1780 and 1830, the population of the island almost doubled from around 12,000 to just under 23,000 souls. This rise, together with an imposed policy of resettlement on marginal land, significantly extended the area of cultivated land in the later eighteenth and early nineteenth centuries, and it is adjacent to these intakes that many of the souterrains are found. That this island may well have experienced similar ebbs and flows in more remote periods is a question for future research, and the presence of souterrains in these more marginal locations could well be significant in this context (e.g. Inventory nos *2, 5, 8, 9, 14, 16, 17, 23, 27, 28 & 29*) The appearance on marginal land of some categories of site more familiar on arable ground might be taken to indicate areas of formerly cultivated land. Similarly, in a localised context the soil map fails to reflect those small-scale *assarts* which appear as a flash of emerald against the duller background vegetation.

The distribution of souterrains is weighted towards the northern half of the island, with over 87 per cent of sites lying north of a line drawn from Carbost to Sligachan. Until as

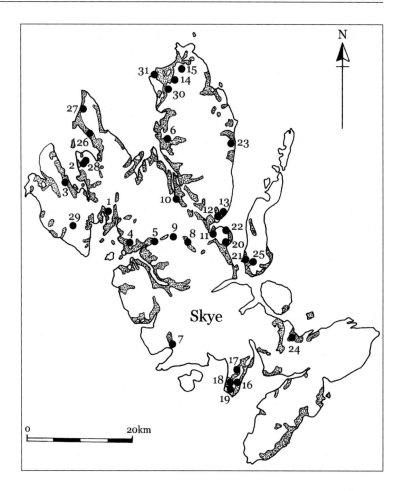

**26** *Distribution of souterrains on Skye*

recently as 1981, the only souterrain recorded south of this line was that at Broadford (*24*), and the evident bias invited comparison with a similar weighting to the northern half of the island in the distribution of brochs (MacSween, 1985, map 4). The addition of sites in Strath (*16-19*) and south-west Bracadale (*7*) offers limited redress. Notable omissions in the distribution pattern are particularly evident along the south-east coast of Sleat where hut-circles and enclosures are known to exist. However, the southern half of Skye possesses only 31 per cent of the island's total arable potential and discoveries reflect this. Staffin, and zones around Lochs Harport, Snizort and Greshornish apparently lack souterrains, although there seems no real reason why they might not contribute some examples in the future.

## Architecture
Architecturally, the souterrains of Skye exhibit features entirely consistent with the galleried form current within the Atlantic tradition.

## Roofs
Only when the foundation trench had achieved its final length and the sidewalls had been built to their wall-head height was the structure was ready to receive its roof capping. Basalt

87

slabs form the predominant roofing material, in some cases (e.g. Kilvaxter, *30*) carried from quarries over 1km distant. Few lintels are over 2m in length, demonstrating that this was the optimum length beyond which the chances of cracking and collapse increased greatly. The length of lintels was the critical factor governing the width of the gallery below. Where the width of the gallery varied, great care was taken to ensure a reasonably safe overlap with the sidewalls: rarely was less than 0.1m tolerated. At 'Uamh na Rambh', Raasay (*21*) the builders apparently experienced difficulties in obtaining lintels of sufficient length to bridge the natural cleft that formed the gallery. It was precisely at this point that lintel collapse occurred. Similarly, at Tungadale (*9*) the two lintels that collapsed inwards were found to be only marginally longer than the gallery they bridged. By contrast, it was the very fissile nature of the columnar basalt at Kilvaxter (*30*), which ensured the failure of some of the lintels, which fell in sharp splinters onto the gallery floor.

Lintels were lain alongside one another along the whole length of the gallery, the builders minimising the gap between them as far as possible. The overlap between those at Kilvaxter (*30*) shows that work progressed in a down-slope direction, working from the inner terminal towards the entrance. Once in place the spaces between the butt-ends of the lintels and the natural sides of the cutting were packed with large stones to prevent lateral movement.

Where a wider gap than usual occurred between two lintels, such as where the gallery changed direction and the lintels followed the curve, they might be plugged with large stones. Once the lintels were in place, the interstices between were invariably packed by small stones, to reduce the incidence of percolation of the covering soil into the void below. At Kilvaxter (*30*), a small cup-marked stone had apparently attracted the builders' interest and was incorporated in a prominent position face-up as a pinning stone; however, it was hidden once the earth covering was in place.

## Side-walls

Three souterrains are formed from natural clefts covered with lintelled slabs. At Alt na Cille (*16*), some further quarrying was necessary to circumnavigate a basalt dyke and it was this unexpected obstacle which resulted in the atypical reversed Z-plan of the passage. Both there and at 'Uamh na Ramh' Raasay (*21*), the cleft in the vertical rock face produced a cave-like entrance at ground level, rather than a descent. In both souterrains and perhaps also at Broadford (*21*), the underpinning of the lintels was necessary to compensate for irregularities in the upper rock surface in order to produce a relatively even wall-head.

Where discernible, the sidewalls of roughly coursed basalt were raised within trenches excavated into sub-strata as varied as clay, gravel, shale and basalt. Frequently the uneven and irregular nature of the natural rock surface resulted in considerable variation in the height of the passageway floor, in marked contrast to the effort expended on ensuring that the roof was relatively level.

The sidewalls of the galleries occasionally demonstrate no greater care in their construction than that invested in the walls of contemporary surface buildings. Occasionally larger stones were used, as in the orthostats set upright in the sidewalls of Tungadale (*9*). Of the handful of galleries where the relationship between the wall and the floor is visible an almost negligent attitude is evident on the part of the original builders in ensuring that the lower courses were securely founded. At Claigan 1 (*2*) and Tungadale (*9*), and Kilvaxter (*30*), the footings of the lower courses are sometimes found to 'float' above the level of the gallery floor, upon upstands of unexcavated natural subsoil. Their appearance is regarded as a critical clue as to the method of construction of some galleries.

The first stage of activity in constructing a souterrain presumably consisted of marking out its course (perhaps by stripping away its turf). At Kilvaxter (*30*), spade-cuttings into the natural subsoil, which continue the line of the gallery a short distance beyond its actual terminal, seem to indicate the removal of turf and surface soil for a souterrain slightly longer than was actually built. The question is whether the trench within which the walls were to be raised was cut in one single operation before wall construction commenced, or whether work progressed in stages.

It is suggested that the trench was not excavated in its entirety before walling was introduced, but rather that the gallery passage (minus its roof) was built in stages, and that once each section or length had been cut (in most cases) to floor level, the side-walls were introduced. This interpretation would regard these upstands of natural face incorporated within the side-walls as marking the break between the different stages of work, for in continuing the line of the gallery the builders would be confined within the line of the constructed gallery rather than the 'foundation trench'. While the original width of the gallery would be easy to re-establish at a higher level, there does not always seem to have been investment in cutting back the natural face at lower levels. The reasons for this are difficult to determine, though the indications from Kilvaxter (*30*) could suggest that in some cases it might arise when the upper courses of completed walling had drifted a little over what was to be excavated next. Rather than remove these upper courses to allow construction from the base, the builders used the subsoil to build from a little higher up. This model would see souterrains as constructions built in sections and would account for the sharp profile of the 'foundation trench' despite the often soft subsoil in which they are set, and also explain the 'segmental' form of some galleries.

## Gallery dimensions (**Table 10**)

The length of the gallery of seven souterrains is known with some certainty, while information is available for the minimum extent of seven others. This shows the Skye souterrains to have been rather lengthy constructions, with the shortest complete souterrain at around 8m (Tungadale), and longest at 27m (Broadford).

In practice, the length of a gallery emphasises its narrowness, which is conditional upon the optimum length of a lintel (see above). However, the usual width of a gallery on Skye is in the order of 0.7–0.8m, although this may extend to *c.*1m (see table above) and their height rarely exceeds *c.*1.7m. This adds further to the potential physical discomfort experienced in the souterrains. Nevertheless, the use of techniques such as corbelling the top of the sidewalls inwards to carry the lintels to allow a slightly wider gallery below is common to many Skye souterrains. This reveals the subtle relationship between the constraints of the materials to hand and the abilities of the builders to maximise space without lengthening the gallery.

## Recesses

Recesses have been recorded in the sidewalls of five souterrains. There are as many as three at Tungadale (*9*); all sit in the south wall, take the form of relatively shallow recesses of little more than 0.5m in depth and extend the full height of the side-wall. They are not so evenly spaced as to appear convenient for holding lamps to light the interior, although the darkness within the souterrains would certainly have demanded lamps or torches. Two lie in close proximity near the entrance, and none lie within the innermost half of the souterrain. That at Camustianavaig (*20*) was *c*.0.85m wide, and opposite the presumed entrance. That at Carn nam Bodach (*23*) was, from its description, more in the nature of an aumbry inset within the wall above the floor level. At Lachasay (*14*), the 'recess' in the south wall is little more than a shallow curve, though the depth of that in the north wall (1m minimum) might indicate something more substantial, possibly in the nature of a satellite gallery. Their purpose is unclear.

## Satellite Galleries

Only at Lachasay (*14*), and Kilvaxter (*30*) is there the hint of satellite galleries. At Kilvaxter the satellite gallery opposite the entrance is only *c*.1.4m long. This feature suggests that the primary gallery was somehow insufficient to fully satisfy the requirements of the souterrain builders and it might indicate a need for a more specialised space. Alternatively, it could have resulted from factors which placed limits upon the length of the primary gallery, or simply reflect a method of increasing the souterrain's capacity for additional space.

## Floors

Where the interiors are accessible, the accumulated debris obscures the original floor surfaces and their analysis. At Alt na Cille (*16*) (**colour plate 11**) and 'Uamh na Ramh' (*21*), the floor was hard natural bedrock, but at Tungadale (*9*) the bedrock floor was rotten and broken. It is reported that the floor of Carn nam Bodachd (*23*) was a 'blue clay' and that at Kilvaxter (*30*) appears to consist of some cobbling on a subsoil of clay and crushed rock.

## Entrances (**Table 10**)

With the possible exception of Uamh na Ramh (*21*) and Kilvaxter (*30*), all Skye souterrains were provided with a single entrance, invariably sited at the down-slope end of the structure. The entrances to seven of the souterrains lie in the bank-side of a stream and in five additional instances a stream lies within a few metres of the entrance. This relationship cannot be coincidental and reinforces a long-standing axiom that proximity to water was important.[4]

The clear association of some souterrains with the remains of surface structures (*infra*) leaves the question open as to whether access could have been gained from the interiors of these buildings. At present, only Tungadale (*9*) demonstrates this unequivocally. The large doorway here is comparable not only with those observed in the interior walls of certain circular home-steads noted above, but also with those found within brochs, giving access to galleries and cells. Like them, it was plainly a bold architectural feature, emphasised by the way in which the accumulation of occupation layers which built up within the main dwelling were kept clear of the area immediately fronting the souterrain doorway by a low walled revetment. This 'sunken' approach to the doorway leading into the souterrain must have presented a significantly visible element within the building, making concealment of the entrance impossible. Although no evidence of any door fitting was discovered, the stairwell appears to have been designed to allow a door in a wooden frame to open outwards into the living area.

## Terminals and chambers (**Table 10**)

Information is available on the terminals of 12 of the 31 souterrains, and this allows two forms to be identified. In five instances there is an abrupt butt-end, but in seven the gallery appears to lead directly to a circular chamber. At Claigan 1 (*2*), and Totaig (*3*), the circular chamber is inferred from the pronounced circular depression marking what appears to be the end of the gallery, but elsewhere the situation is clearer. The chambers are generally of between 1.5 – 3m in diameter and between 1.5 – 2m in height. Where the chamber is wider than might safely be bridged with lintels, the roof appears to have been corbelled, a feature that is best preserved at At Tigh Talamhain, Lachasay (*14*). The nineteenth-century record of the chamber at Vatten (*1*) is a puzzling anomaly as it most closely describes a wheelhouse, a form of construction not found on Skye (Clerk, 1845, 446).

## Volumetric Capacity

It is only possible to calculate the volumetric capacity of four of the souterrains. Two of the four are souterrains formed from natural clefts where the builders have had little control over dimensions, which were largely laid down in geological times. Moreover, at Alt na Cille (*16*) the presence of an intrusive dyke considerably reduces the relatively high internal volume of *c.*35 cubic metres. By contrast, Tungadale (*9*) has a volumetric content of 18 cubic metres and Kilvaxter (*30*) 27 cubic metres. In the case of the latter, it is worth noting that to achieve this space over 66 cubic metres of compacted glacial clay had first to be removed before some 40 tons of quarried stonework could be raised within the trench.

## Context

The majority of souterrains on Skye are 'subterranean' in the sense that they have been constructed below the natural ground surface, with no suggestion that the line of the passageway was visible at the surface. Some of the souterrains have a physical association with the degraded remains of surface structures but their chronological relationship is unclear. In the case of 'Uamh na Ramh', Raasay (*21*) and Tigh Talamhain, Lachasay (*14*), the surface structures lie adjacent to the souterrain entrance; while at Ullinish (*4*), Glen Bracadale (*5*) and Alt na Cille (*16*), they straddle the souterrain terminal. The possible souterrains at Penduin (*6*) and Camus Mor (*29*) are quite clearly related to substantial structures of unquestionably prehistoric date.

Tungadale (*9*) is the only souterrain that is demonstrably contemporary with an adjacent building (**colour plate 12**). The sub-rectangular homestead lay at right-angles to the hill-slope into which it was partially terraced. There was no outer wall on the up-slope side, although within the building the inner wall presented a normal vertical face. Between this and the hill-slope outside, there was a dense stone packing encasing the gallery some 8m in length, which could only be entered from the living area within the building (**30**). Its form stood in startling contrast to contemporary circular forms in the area.

The implications of establishing the presence of rectangular homesteads within the Iron Age landscape of Skye, where the tradition has long been held to have been one of circular forms, are evident. Such surprises are compounded by the difficulties in isolating other, similar, Iron Age buildings from a landscape littered with rectangular buildings of later ages. Yet as fieldwork carried out since the discovery of Tungadale reveals, this form of homestead is not unique e.g. Greshornish Point (NG 3456 5601). The characteristics common to this type include:

An entrance in the (leeward) end wall.
A slight expansion in the thickness of the wall at the end where the doorway lies.
A plan whose length is proportional to its breadth in the ratio of 3:1.
The presence of a gallery or cell within the wall thickness on the up-slope side of the building.

## Orientation (**Table 10**)

Of the 17 cases where the orientation of the gallery is known, seven are aligned east-west (41 per cent), three north-south (18 per cent), two north-west to south-east (12 per cent), and five north-east to south-west (29 per cent). From this sample, it appears that orientation was dictated solely by local circumstances. Moreover, all the souterrain passages, with the exception of those at Claigan 1 (*2*) and Uamh na Ramh (*21*) are curved. The reasons for this curvature, which is often slight and with the majority favouring a 'sunwise' or clockwise direction, is unknown. At Alt na Cille (*16*), the souterrain changes course twice to curve in both directions, though this is explicable from the special circumstances of the geology.

## Chronology

Artefactual material has been recovered from six souterrains, but in two instances the finds are missing. Broadford souterrain (*23*) produced some cinders, sheep bones and a quern, while at Cuillin Cottage (*7*), pottery, flint, bone and shell were recovered, only to be subsequently discarded by the crofter. At Alt na Cille (*16*) a fragment of an annular pottery loom-weight was recovered from the floor-silt (**colour plate 13**). At both Tungadale (*9*) and Carn nam Bodach (*23*), plain and decorated pottery of later Iron Age type was recovered (**31-33** & **37**). In addition to the pottery, the latter site also produced the bones of horse, ox, red deer and pig, as well as numerous limpet shells. Kilvaxter (*30*) is currently under excavation, but has already produced later Iron Age pottery and stone artefacts.

There are radiocarbon dates (**Table 11**) from only two sites: Tungadale (*9*) and Alt na Cille (*16*). Those from the Tungadale homestead intimate that there is a 95 per cent probability that it was constructed sometime in the second – third century BC, while those from Alt na Cille (*16*), suggest it would have been in use around the middle of the second century AD (dates from Kilvaxter (*30*) are awaited).

## Later activity

In reporting the discovery of Carn nam Bodach (*23*), Callander (1914) remarked upon a 'small Latin cross' painted upon one of the lintels, together with two other red markings nearby, and conceivably suggests that this site may have been accessible and in use during the Early Christian era. This accords with the wider picture, which intimates that souterrains remained a familiar feature long after the purpose for which they had been constructed had been forgotten. In the Hebrides, the persistent attraction of settlement to a particular location was always likely to involve some re-use of earlier structures. Such a rich quarry of lintels for doorways and window-heads explains why so many souterrains adjacent to later settlement have had these stripped, leaving only the projecting heads of the sidewalls to reveal their presence. Neither is there any reason why subsequent generations should not have discovered new uses for these ancient relics: uses in which concealment in times of danger might well have jostled with the more prosaic use as 'potato store' or rubbish pit.

## An inventory of souterrains on Skye (26) (Table 12)

### 1. Roskill [Vatten], Duirinish (souterrain) NG 2805 4483

In 1845 the Reverend Archibald Clerk described in some detail, a souterrain:

> situated on the farm of Vatten, having its entrance in the face of a very precipitous bank, overhanging a deep ravine. The door, or more appropriately fox-hole, is completely covered over with heather and moss, so that its existence would never be suspected even after a minute's examination of the bank. A passage about three feet in height, and near the same breadth, roofed by stones laid on as lintels, leads inwards to the distance of sixty or seventy feet, when it appears to have opened into a central room of considerable extent, arched over with stone, and from four to five feet in height. Off this room, several narrow galleries branch off in various directions, but to what extent has never been ascertained, as it is difficult and even dangerous to explore them until they be opened from above, and free air admitted into them.

> Clerk, 1845, 336

The description suggests a souterrain different from the others on the island and more reminiscent of a wheelhouse, a type of structure not yet encountered on Skye.

The position of the souterrain is unknown and Clerk's description offers only a general location somewhere on the gently sloping terrace south of the ravine occupied by the Roskill river. It is said to lie 'barely 200 yards NE of Rosgill School'. Access to this area is from the minor road immediately south of its junction with the A863, and along a farm track between Roskill School and the river. 120m along this track is a ruined enclosure with associated buildings. Within the north-eastern extremity of this enclosure is a shallow depression which may mark a point of subsidence into the underground structure. Local tradition places the entrance in the bank of the ravine some 15m to the south-east.

*Clerk 1845, 336; RCAHMS 1928, 165 no.533; Gillies 1920-70, 24. SMR NG24SE 2*

### 2. Claigan 1, Duirinish (souterrain) NG 2380 5392 (27)

The line of a gallery is visible as a broad linear hollow with some protruding stonework, in gently rising ground immediately north-east of where the trackway from the B road to Claigan turns to the south-east.

The souterrain is orientated south-west to north-east. Flanking the line of the gallery on both sides are parallel linear mounds of upcast, presumably the result of quarrying the lintel-stones. Thereafter lintel stones rest upon drystone walling, flanking a straight and narrow gallery (0.75m – 0.65m), which is at least 23m long. On either side of the gallery are small recesses. The floor is blanketed in boulder clay, which rises to fill the souterrain at a distance of 4.55m from the first lintel. This point coincides with a field dyke at the surface, beyond which a narrow linear depression leads to a circular hollow, some 14m short of a second field-dyke to the north-east. This may indicate the position of a terminal chamber.

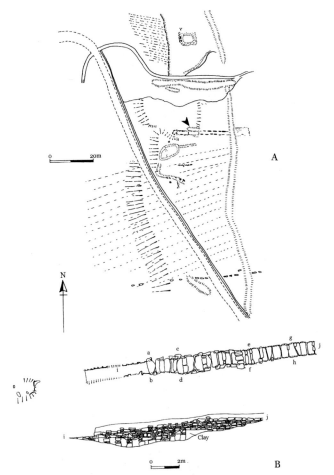

*27  Claigan 1 souterrain in relation to surface structures **A**, plan and section **B***

At its western end the souterrain runs beneath a rectangular stone building, which is overlain by later structures with adjacent enclosures possibly post medieval period in date. *Clerk 1845, 336; RCAHM, 1928, 164-5, no. 527; Gillies 1920-70, 24. SMR NG25SW 2*

## 3. Totaig, Duirinish (souterrain) NG 2027 5007
The gallery is orientated east-west, and though its length is unclear, it possibly terminated in a chamber. It is situated behind a stable 20m east of a stream and some 400m north-east of Colbost schoolhouse. The entrance is said to have been from the riverbank.
*RCAHMS 1928, 164. no. 534; Gillies 1920-70, 26. SMR NG25SW 3*

## 4. Ullinish, Bracadale (souterrain and rectangular building) NG 3333 3851 (28)
The souterrain had only recently been discovered in digging out a fox, when Donald MacQueen showed this 'specimen of the houses of the Aborigines' to Boswell and Johnson in September 1773. Johnson responded that more skill was required to build a souterrain than the adjacent building, capping this comment with the observation that a souterrain could be an adjunct to a house and not a dwelling in its own right:

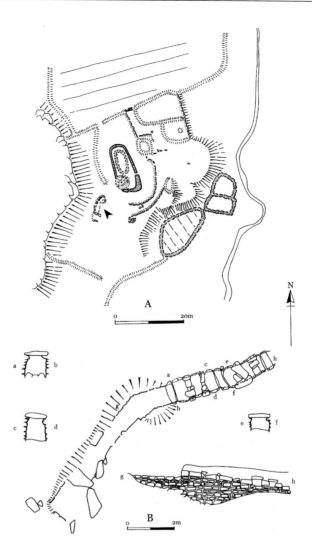

**28** *Ullinish souterrain
in relation to surface
structures* ***A****, plan and
sections* ***B***

From the dun, (Dun Beag, Struan.) we were conducted to another place of
security, a cave carried a great way under ground, which had been discovered by
digging a fox. These caves, of which many have been found, and many probably
remain concealed, are formed, I believe, commonly by taking advantage of a
hollow, where banks or rocks rise on either side. If no such place can be found,
the ground must be cut away. The walls are made by piling stones against the
earth, on either side. It is then roofed by larger stones laid across the cavern, which
therefore cannot be wide. Over the roof, turfs were placed, and the grass was
suffered to grow; and the mouth was concealed by bushes, or some other cover.

These caves were represented to us as the cabins of the first rude inhabitants
of which, however, I am by no means persuaded. This was so low, that no man
could stand upright in it. By their construction, they are all so narrow, that two
can never pass along them together, and being subterraneous, they must always
be damp. They are not the work of an age much ruder than the present; for
they are formed with as much art as the construction of a common hut

95

requires. I imagine them to have been places only of occasional use, in which the islander, upon a sudden alarm hid his utensils, or his cloaths, and perhaps sometimes his wife and children.

This cave we entered, but could not proceed the whole length, and went away without knowing how far it was carried. For this omission, we shall be blamed, as we perhaps have blamed other travellers; but the day was rainy, and the ground was damp. We had with us neither spades nor pick axes, and if love of ease surmounted our desire of knowledge, the offence has not the invidiousness of singularity.

Johnson 1775

The souterrain is predominantly orientated south-west to north-east, is of dry-stone construction and has a minimum length of 13m. It lies in the midst of later settlement activity on the site, including buildings and yard enclosures.

The original entrance is badly mutilated, although the depression marking its course is visible as a stone lined hollow, curving eastwards for *c*.6.9m until the first capping stone is reached. The present access lies near the mid-point of its original length. Here the passage is 0.9m wide and 0.6m high. Earth and stone debris covers the floor, which slopes down from the point of entry to allow a maximum height of 1.1m. The souterrain here is orientated 60 degrees east of north. In places the capstones are carried on a corbelled course of stones, which lie as much as 0.6 – 0.7m inside the wall-line. The gallery continues for a distance of 5.8m, where it coincides with the south-west wall of the rectangular structure on the ground surface. A hollow at this point marks a relatively recent disturbance, possibly that associated with the digging out of the fox.

The souterrain is located due west of the junction between the Ullinish road and the A863 on the Knock Ullinish promontory. Contained between two field-dykes climbing the eastern side of the promontory, and situated above a stream, are the remains of a small circular structure with an adjacent, larger rectangular building to the south. The north-west corner of the building has been largely quarried away, but a few metres west of its south-western corner lies the present opening to the souterrain.

*Johnson 1775, 84-5; Boswell 1786, 300-1; MacLeod 1792, 249; RCAHMS 1928, 148 no. 496; Gillies 1920-70. SMR NG33NW 2.*

## 5. Glen Bracadale, Bracadale (souterrain and rectangular structure) NG 3826 3896 (**29**)

In 1792 it was recorded that, 'A subterranean cavern or grotto, artificially built with stones within the top, laid over with earth so that it cannot be seen till a person is close at the entry, which is narrow and difficult of access. It is believed that all these subterranean caverns were used as places of shelter or concealment in perilous times' (Macleod 1792, 249).

The course of the souterrain can be traced northwards over a distance of 9m to 12.2m. The depression has a width of *c*.1m and rises with the slope to curve gently to the north-west. Upcast to either side reflects quarrying of the lintels, and only in the mid-length of the passage do capstones remain *in situ*; two lengths of four capstones, each covering a gallery 0.7m in width, for a distance of 1.5m. They rest upon a rough drystone walling derived from local volcanic rocks.

1.3km east of Amer, the valley floor below Beinn Steilg opens into a broad undulating embayment *c*.100m OD. Some 27m due north of a small stream lie two ruined enclosures and remains from a substantial post-medieval settlement. The gallery runs below a rectangular structure. The northern bank of the stream is marked by a revetment of boulders, broken just

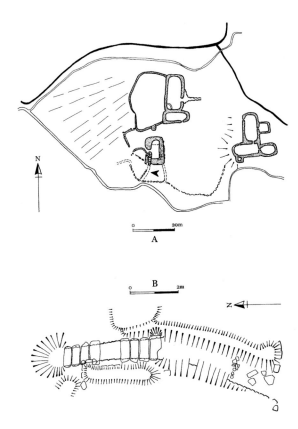

**29** *Glen Bracadale souterrain in relation to surface structures* **A**, *and plan* **B**

at that point where the linear hollow of the souterrain opens onto the stream from the north. *RCAHMS 1928, 148, no. 145; Gillies 1920-70, 26. SMR NG33NE 4.*

## 6. Penduin, Snizort (?souterrain, hillfort and roundhouse) NG 3882 5770

The crest of the hill is defined by the degraded remnants of a defensive stone wall 2 – 4.5m in width, standing 2m high at the south-west, and enclosing an area 60m by 28m. On a lower terrace to the south-east, and some 9m from the inner wall, four large stones set on edge may indicate a crude *'chevaux-de-frise'*. The entrance to the hillfort lies near the middle of the east side, 1.4m wide.

Just within the defences on the south-west lies a clearly-defined substantial circular structure, 2m high and enclosing an area with a diameter of 10.5m. A sunken passage, 1m wide and 8.2m long, connects this enclosure with a corbelled oval cell 6m long, built against the inner face of the defences. The gallery appearance and its characteristics suggest it may be a souterrain. To the south are indications of one or more hut circles.

It is located on the flat-topped oval summit of Dun near Penduin some 300m north-east of the ruined house of Penduin. *SMR NG35NE 2*

## 7. Cuillin Cottage, Glen Brittle, Bracadale (souterrain) NG 411 205

Located by the shore at Glen Brittle is a curving gallery of dry-stone construction *c.*1m high and set into clean, wind-blown sand. It was discovered during ploughing in 1982. Fragments of pottery, flint, bone and shell were noted by the farmer's son amidst upcast from a partial emptying of the gallery, but these were not retained. There is now no surface trace of the structure, although some of the lintel stones might be incorporated into a nearby stack-base. *SMR NG42SW 8*

### 8. Glenmore, Portree (souterrain) NG 4285 4055

The site is located close to the Skriag Burn below Glenmore where it is met by a rough cart-track converging from the south. Recent improved drainage and a realignment of the burn at this point have caused considerable damage to surface features, including rig and furrow and a rectangular stone structure. Some 7m to the east of the latter and 8m from the bank of the stream lie the badly mutilated remains of the souterrain.

Only a short section of the inner face of the north wall of a gallery is visible, standing to a height of 1m. A lintel lies fallen at its base, and other lintels have been cast up to the north-east. A general east-west alignment for the gallery can only be inferred from the debris, with a possible original passage width of around 0.7m.

What may have been other souterrains have been reported at Glenmore but are said to have been filled in. Their locations are unknown. *RCAHMS 1928, 185, no. 589. SMR NG44NW 2*

### 9. Tungadale Bracadale (souterrain and rectangular homestead) NG 4076 4006 (30)

A sub-rectangular stone and earth-built homestead, *c*.11 by 4m with a contemporary souterrain, lies with its long-axis set at right-angles to the hill-slope into which it was recessed. Its entrance is in the centre of the narrow east wall. A lintelled gallery 10.8m long and *c*.1m high

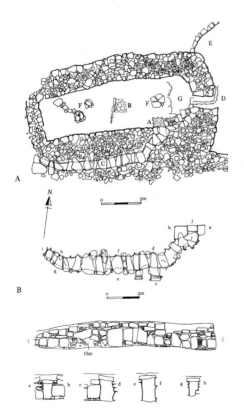

**30** *Tungadale homestead **A**, and souterrain with plan and sections **B**. A – step down onto entrance platform, B – hearth, C – souterrain passage, D – drain from souterrain and homestead interior, E – cobbled courtyard, F – post pads, G – area kept clear of interior build-up, to allow homestead door to open inwards and maintain a maximum height at the doorway*

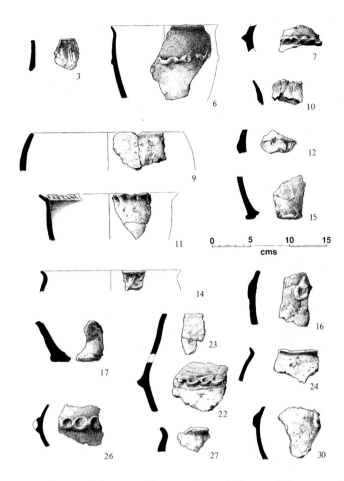

**31** *Tungadale pottery nos 3–30*

was located within the thickness of the wall, between the interior wall-face and the natural hill-slope. It ran parallel with the inner wall face and was enclosed within the rubble of the wall core. Its width between the large upright slabs forming its sides was 0.7 – 0.9m. The far end of the gallery narrowed to a ragged termination below the point where the wall of the building turned away from the hill-slope.

The interior of the homestead appears to have been for domestic habitation with remnant benches in the eastern half of the building and a central hearth. Mid-way between the entrance and the hearth, a lintelled entrance in the south wall (1m high and 0.7m wide) gave access to the souterrain. Within the entrance, the gallery curved sharply before assuming its course within the thickness of the homestead wall. Three substantial recesses were built within the outer wall (i.e. that furthest away from the interior of the building). The first lay just within the entrance on the left-hand side. Its dimensions were 0.7 by 0.4 by 1.10m high. The second lay 3m from the entrance with dimensions of 0.48 by 0.5m and was 0.9m high. The third lay 0.47m west of the second. It measured 0.25 by 0.4 by 0.9m. The latter two were capped with flagstones independently of the main passage roof. A drain had been inserted into the floor of the souterrain, leading out through the souterrain entrance, beneath the main occupation area, to an external cobbled yard *via* the main entrance passage.

The accumulation of occupational debris on the floor of the homestead resulted in the floor levels being cut back for a distance of about 1m from the homestead wall, edged with

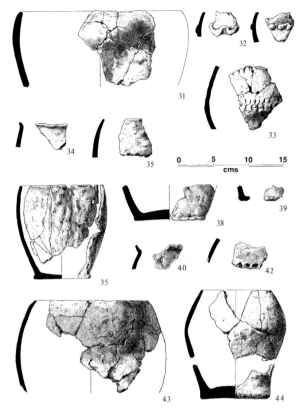

**32** *Tungadale pottery nos 31-44*

a stone revetment to prevent the soil from spilling into the souterrain. This work produced an obvious stepped hollow within the living space that could not readily be concealed from the view of anyone within the building.

A circular 'shieling-type' building was built subsequently within the ruins of the homestead. It had a well-built inner wall-face, short entrance passageway and two floor levels each with a hearth. Radiocarbon dates and a small fourteenth-century bronze mirror case recovered from the passageway confirm a thirteenth- to fourteenth-century date for this later building. Sometime within the eighteenth or nineteenth century two rectangular stone buildings were built a few metres to the east. The finds from the excavation are in *Dualchas*, Skye & Lochalsh Museums Service, Highland Council (Accn. No. 1990.10 (**31-3**)).

The site lies on the north-facing crest of a small knoll above the flood plain of the Abhainn an Acha-Leathan, at the east end of Loch Duagrich. The site was excavated in 1988, prior to nearby planting of sitka spruce and lodgepole pine. Today the site is laid out for display, with access by foot from Totarder, Glen Bracadale (walking *via* site No.5 Glen Bracadale).
*RCAHMS 1928, 148-9 no. 497; Armit 1996, 131-3, 241; Ritchie and Harman 1996, 29. SMR NG44SW 1*

## 10. Cnoc Sianta, Snizort (souterrain) NG 430 475

Donald Gillies noted a souterrain midway between Carbost School House and the township of Peiness, but added no further detail. A search of the area noted a linear hollow, some 9.8m in long, 3m wide and 1.2m deep just within the plantation at NG 4277 4725, and adjacent to the fence-line marching with the road. Although the width is greater than that of a souterrain,

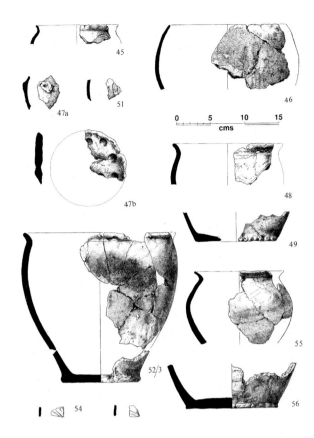

**33** *Tungadale pottery nos 45-56*

there are clear indications of coursed stonework along the eastern side, and it is just conceivable that the hollow represents a souterrain now quarried out and largely destroyed.
*Gillies 1920-70, 29.*

## 11. Heatherfield, Portree (souterrain) NG 4821 4167

Discovered sometime *ante* 1928 while hoeing potatoes, this souterrain was partially opened but then re-filled. The entrance is said to have been set in a west-facing bank of alluvium at the rear of a croft-house. The bank has recently been modified and no trace of the entrance is visible in this position. Some 10m to the south-east is a linear depression *c.*1.5m in width which curves gently west to north-east. It is traceable for a distance of 5m.
*RCAHMS 1928, 185 no. 587; Gillies 1920-70, 29. SMR NG44SE 8*

## 12. Bile 1, Portree (Souterrain) NG 495 444

There is record of a souterrain lying within a ploughed field below Torvaig and above the chapel at Bile. The site has not been located.
*RCAHMS 1928, 185 no. 590. SMR NG44SE 9*

## 13. Bile 2, Portree (souterrain) NG 49 44

A souterrain is reported to lie on Bile cliff. It has not been located.
*RCAHMS 1928 185 no. 591. SMR NG44SE 10*

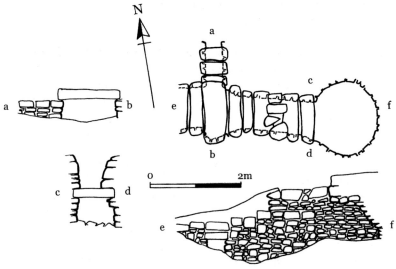

**34** *Lachasay souterrain*

*14. Tigh Talamhain, Lachasay, Kilmuir (souterrain and building) NG 4146 7124 (34)*
The 'earth-house' was first noted by Martin Martin (1716, 154). A second, early record of the souterrain is provided by Matthew Stobie, who in the 1770s carried out a detailed land survey of the MacDonald estates. A note on the original map in the Clan Donald Centre, Armadale, records, 'At A Tytalbra [Tigh Talamhain = earth-house] the . . . of a large house below ground inhabited in times of war'.

The line of a gallery, now robbed of its lintels, is marked by a well-defined hollow between 1.5 – 2m in width, rising with the slope for a distance of 11m. Within this hollow, the wall-head formerly supporting the robbed lintels is visible, revealing a gallery 0.9m wide. From here the lintels remain in position, covering a passage of random rubble construction, which continues for a little over 3m before opening out into a corbelled eastern chamber 1.6m in diameter. Before reaching this chamber the interior swells slightly on its southern side, coincidental with a satellite gallery in the north wall, 0.4m in width. This gallery was traced for 1.2m, beyond which it was choked with soil. The lower levels of the corbelled chamber are filled with collapsed debris.

Today access to the souterrain is through the roof of the corbelled chamber onto a floor of collapsed debris. The lintels of the gallery where they meet the chamber are in an unusual 'stepped' arrangement, before running westwards from it (see plan). Just west of the gallery termination the lintels are stepped upwards. The odd arrangement of the third lintel resting upon lintels 2 and 4 is only explicable in terms of a more even weight distribution of the backing to create an aperture, such as might allow access (or viewing) into the corbelled chamber.

Some 3km south of Duntulm the landscape broadens out into an undulating valley drained to the north by the Abhainn Sneosdal. Traces of post-medieval settlement abound and due east of the larger of these dwellings, at Lachasay, a cluster of structures representing several periods occupies the eastern bank of the Abhainn Sneosdal. The most recent is the remains of house with byre and kale yard to the north, and sheep enclosure to the south. About 9m south-east of the house lies the souterrain.

*Martin, 1716, 154; RCAHMS 1928, 175-6, no. 556; Gillies 1920-70, 23. SMR NG47SW 5*

## 15. Kilmaluag, Kilmuir (fort & souterrain) NG 41705 73227

This was first noted in 1979, when it was described as:

> An earth house has been noted on the hillside below the rocky summit of Carn Urugag. The passage oriented ENE for *c*.3m, curves NE for another metre and terminates in a circular chamber, *c*.0.5m in diameter. The entrance is *c*.0.65m wide; an exposed roofing stone is *c*. 8cm thick; the chamber is ruined but the passage is practically intact.
>
> Davies & Bunce 1979

The gallery was originally 8.8m long of which only the middle 4.5m remains lintelled. The entrance opens directly onto the steep hill-slope just below the encircling wall. Though almost all the facing stonework of the encasing wall has gone, the gallery appears to lie at an angle across its line. No lintels remain over the initial 3m of the passage but from the first intact lintel it angles north-eastwards. Ten lintels with pinning stones remain *in situ*, resting upon reasonably coursed stone walls set into the scree. The width of the gallery is 0.7m below the lintels. Earth has filled the gallery-way to a depth of 0.18m from the underside of the lintels.

Lintels are absent at the eastern end where the gallery appears to terminate in natural rock. To the north however, a lintelled 'creep', 0.35m in length, gives access to a small, unroofed chamber measuring 1m in length and 0.6m in width.

The souterrain is found at the northern end of the Trotternish Ridge, where the ground descends in a series of broken steps to a more gently rolling landscape, before rising again at The Aird to overlook the Minch. The western lower slopes are interspersed with crag formations that have left extensive pockets of broken rock and scree debris. A broken rock formation lies at Carn Urugag on the eastern side of the small glen known as the Bealach Uachdarach. At the most prominent free-standing rock formation is a substantial detached boss of broken rock, rising some 21m above the saddle which connects it to the parent mass to the south. Just below its crown, there is a narrow platform, bordered with what was once a substantial wall, indicating the site of a previously unrecorded defended platform enclosed within a defensive wall. The souterrain lies on the southern edge of the platform, and in a position which puts it in intimate relationship with the defensive wall.
*Davies and Bunce 1979,17. SMR NG47SW 16.*

## 16. Alt na Cille, Strath (souterrain and structures) NG 5395 1417 (**35**)

This is a rock-cut souterrain with an entrance, 1m wide, 0.84m high and 2m in depth, lintelled by two sandstone capstones. In plan it is a reversed Z 11.5m long, though for most of its length the lintels rest directly upon bedrock. In two places it has been necessary to raise the height of the souterrain roof above the rock by introducing low walling: firstly at the centre bar of the Z, where the floor rises at a 35° angle, and secondly at the inner end of the souterrain, where it rises into the overlying soil.

The change in direction producing the unusual Z shape was due to an intrusive dyke of basalt encountered by the builders. It is possible that the rock cleft which became the entrance existed before work began, as this souterrain is inordinately large for one from Skye. Only after the dyke was encountered was it realised that a realignment of the souterrain would be necessary. This obstacle need not have affected the intended position of the terminus, for the gallery was subsequently realigned. However, the gentle curve assumed in the earlier stage betrays the intention of a more gently curving course, confounded by the basalt intrusion.

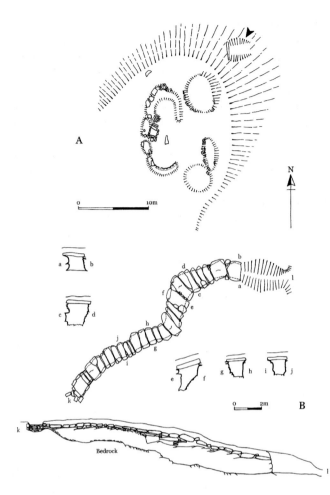

**35** *Allt na Cille souterrain in relation to surface features **A**, plan and sections **B***

The internal height ranges from 1.4m at the entrance to 1.8m where the V-shaped floor rises at a 35° angle. The roof in its final stages lies at a height of *c*.0.88m above a floor rising at *c*.10°, and terminating at a simple butt-end. At this point lintels have subsequently been removed or collapsed. The souterrain terminates beneath a sub-rectangular earth and stone structure at the surface. The structure measures internally *c*.10m north-south by 4m east-west. Indications of either the quarry for the capstones, or a ruinous second souterrain, lie 300m to the west of the souterrain at NG 5370 1420.

Sample excavation within the gallery at its inner, western, end produced a fragment of a clay loom-weight (**colour plate 13**) and charcoal from the souterrain floor. Paleobotanical material from the flooring included alder (*Alnus*), hazel (*Corylus*), willow (*salix*), hulled six-row barley (*hordeum vulgare var. vulgare*), pale persicaria (*persicaria lapathifolia*) and chickweed (*stellaria media*). Radiocarbon assay was obtained from this material.

The souterrain is located above the lower slopes between Drinan and Glasnacille. West of a point where the track from the east crosses the Alt na Cille and diverts southwards, a deserted dwelling stands amidst relict rig and furrow. Behind this is a field dyke shrouded in light birch woodland, above which the slope increases. At a distance of some 5m from this dyke, and some 15m to the north-east of a small stream, an artificial cutting 3m long and 2.2m (max.) wide leads to the mouth of the souterrain.

## 17. Alt a Ghoirtein, Elgol, Strath (souterrain/natural cave) NG 5308 1513

On the southern slopes of the saddle linking Ben Cleat and Ben Meabost a promontory marks the confluence of two streams. Extensive traces of rig and furrow cultivation encircle the site, which is a natural cave with structural modifications. Remains of dwellings lie some 150m to the east where a modern water-tank stands.

At the eastern edge of the promontory is the entrance to the cave, the opening narrowed to 0.7m in width by the construction of a blocking-wall to the west. A short downward incline opens into a chamber *c.*7m long (north-south) and 3m wide, with an earth and rock-debris floor containing recent midden material. To the west is a second gallery of similar dimensions. The two galleries are linked by a third, originally *c.*2m wide, but reduced to *c.*1m through the construction of a wall projecting from the south wall of the cave. Access to the inner gallery is currently restricted due to floor debris.

The galleries underlie an oval enclosure some 13.5m east-west by 11m north-south. The earth and stone perimeter is of variable width and height, broken on the western side. It contains a reed-filled hollow.

## 18. Elgol 1, Strath (souterrain) NG 5287 1460

There are local reports of a souterrain at the position given, although nothing is visible today.

## 19. Elgol 2, Strath (souterrain) NG 529 147

This is said to lie in front of the Post Office but was filled in 'some years ago'. There are no further details.

## 20. Camustianavaig, Portree (souterrain) NG 5095 3495

On an outcrop on a moderately steep and broken hill-slope east of Camustianavaig are the ruins of rectangular houses, which have been incorporated into a sheep fank. Within the angle formed between the south-western corner of the fank and the modern fence line lies the souterrain first noted by Martin in 1716.

The entrance at present is from the west, where a shallow depression 0.75m wide reveals an opening into the gallery. This probably preserves the original line of entry (rather than breaching a side-recess), as is suggested from the orientation of capstones, which are set at right-angles to the present approach. Beneath the first capstone, the gallery turns at an angle of 80° to run northwards for *c.*4m. Thereafter it appears to turn eastwards towards the line of the fank wall. Here the interior is filled with soil, almost to the level of the capstones. These rest upon a combination of basalt outcrop and dry-stone walling to cover a gallery 0.9m wide. A shallow recess in the eastern wall, some 0.85m wide lies opposite the western approach. *Martin 1716,154; RCAHMS 1928, 185 no. 588; Gillies 1920-70, 29. SMR NG53NW 8*

## 21. 'Uamh na Ramh' Raasay, Portree (souterrain & building?) NG 5492 3639 (36)

Both Boswell and Johnson supply information concerning a souterrain near Raasay House. While Boswell's description is the more detailed, Johnson's is included for confounding with sense, yet another ingenious local belief as to their purpose.

> A little from the shore, westward [of Raasay House pier], is a kind of subterranean house. There has been a natural fissure, or separation of the rock, running towards the sea, which has been roofed over with long stones, and above them turf has been laid. In that place the inhabitants used to keep their oars.
>
> Boswell 1786. 255

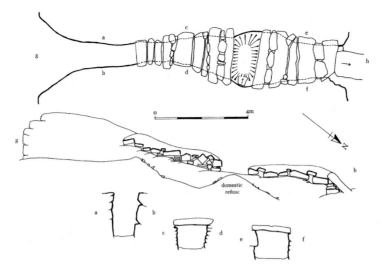

**36** *'Uamh na Ramh' souterrain, Raasay*

> There is still a cavity near the house called the oar cave, in which the seamen, after one of these piratical expeditions, used as tradition tells us, to hide their oars. This hollow was near the sea, that nothing so necessary might be far to be fetched and it was secret, that enemies if they landed, could find nothing. Yet it is not very evident of what use it was to hide their oars from those, who, if they were masters of the coast, could take away their boats.
>
> Johnson 1775, 77

To this day the souterrain is known locally as 'Uamh na Ramh', 'The Cave of Oars'.

In addition, Nicolson (1950) records how, when the Hanoverian troops landed to fire the newly-built home of the MacLeods of Raasay, the family hid their valuables within the cave.

The souterrain was formed by placing lintels over a natural fissure in bedrock. As the eighteenth-century accounts make plain, the souterrain was considered a local curiosity, receiving the occasional visitor. Recently, it became a convenient place to dispose of modern domestic refuse. In 1990 *Dualchas*, Skye and Lochalsh Museums Service and the Raasay Heritage Society removed the recent debris, which was found to lie directly upon the rock floor of the gallery, thereby revealing something of its structure and form.

The gallery is 13m long, although the initial 4.5m are unlintelled. It is aligned south-east to north-west and is irregular in width ranging from *c*.0.8m to a maximum of 2.4m at mid-length. For most of its length the gallery is *c*.1m high. At its northern end this reduces dramatically, terminating in what originally must have been a stone end-wall. This has now been partially removed to allow an exit at the rear of the rock outcrop. It is not possible to determine whether an entrance originally existed at this end of the souterrain, but its length was determined by the depth of the rock outcrop and its fissure, though the latter may well have been modified by the souterrain-builders. The floor slopes down steeply from south to north, a feature which, given the unroofed nature of the initial approach, must have made for a wet interior, however well drained from its northern end.

The site lies at a point where the roadway approaching Raasay House from the south intersects with the short entrance to the former Post Office (just to the north of the Raasay Hotel), close to a low stone wall on the western side of the road. Steps introduced recently allow access onto a gently westward-sloping grassed area with a substantial rock outcrop on

the northern side. The souterrain entrance is visible as a substantial cleft in the rock face.
*Boswell 1786, 255; Johnson 1775, 77; Nicolson 1950, 79. SMR NG55NW 7.*

## 22. Udairn, Portree (souterrain) NG 5142

A souterrain recorded at Udairn below Ben Tianavaig and at the entrance to Portree harbour
has not been relocated.
*RCAHMS, 1928, 185 no. 586. SMR NG54SW 1*

## 23. Carn nam Bodach, Portree (souterrain) NG 512 552 (37)

The souterrain was built *c.*17m to the west of the present road. In July 1913 it was both
discovered and damaged in extracting gravel for a realignment of the Portree to Staffin road.
Thereafter it appears to have been completely destroyed (Callander 1914).

Callander records that a gallery with sidewalls of random rubble construction sloped
downwards in a southerly direction, then curved slightly to the south-west. This gallery, with
a minimum length of 9.7m, apparently opened into a chamber, although Callander does
distinguish this 'chamber' from the gallery. The chamber is said to have been 10.3m long,
1.2–1.6m high, with a width of 1.1m narrowing to 0.6m near its butt-end. A recess had been
formed in the east wall 3.4m from the terminal and 0.36m above the floor. It was 0.26m high
and measured 0.36 by 0.3m.

The floor was of blue clay throughout, with the final 2.7m reddened by burning. Animal
bones were recovered from the floor in both the passage and 'chamber' but pottery was found
in the chamber alone. The animal bones represent horse, ox, pig and red deer. Shells of the
common limpet (*Patella vulgata*) were also recovered. Particularly remarkable is the description of
a 'small Latin cross' about 48mm in length painted in red on one of the lintels. Two other red
markings of indeterminate character were noted adjacent to this. The few vessels represented are

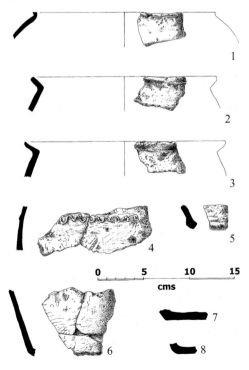

**37** *Carn nam Bodach, Portree, pottery*
*Illustration: Caitlin Evans*

predominantly plain jars with everted rims, apart from one vessel, which carries a wavy cordon decoration. They are in the Hunterian Museum, University of Glasgow (Accn No. B.1914.528). *Callander 1914, 200-5; Gillies 1920-70, 20-22. SMR NG55NW 4.*

### 24. Broadford, Strath (souterrain) NG 650 230

The souterrain has not been rediscovered, and the 1841 account in *The Gentleman's Magazine* by 'J.W.B', following its discovery and examination by Dr Sutherland, provides the basis for all subsequent accounts. The entrance width was about 1.15m, with a gallery 'capacious enough to admit a person on all fours' extending seawards for about 29m. It terminated in a circular chamber, 'which might have contained four persons crowded close together', containing some sheep-bones, a few cinders and a quern (lost). The sidewalls of the gallery are said to have been corbelled to support the capstones.

A natural cleft capped with lintels was discovered during ploughing at Goirtean nan h-uamha ('the field of the cave') 'a few years' *ante* 1839. Lamont states that it lay on the right bank of the Alt-a-Bhrachaidh behind the manse at Church Park, Broadford.
*The Gentleman's Magazine, 1841 part 1. 36-7; The Gentleman's Magazine Library, Archaeology, Pt 1, 1886, 175-6; Lamont 1913, 9-10 and 165; RCAHMS 1928, 215, no. 677; Gillies 1920-70, 29. SMR NG62SW 15.*

### 25. Suishnish, (Raasay) Portree (souterrain) NG 5555 3485

A little to the south of Suishnish House is an erd-house, beautifully chiselled out of the Jurassic shales and lintelled with the local granite.

Nicolson 1950, 83.

Lying on an east-facing slope amongst the ruinous structures of the deserted settlement of Suishnish are the ruinous remains of a small souterrain. The collapsed entrance faces to the east and opens onto a small hollow containing a burn. A shallow sink 5m to the west of the entrance may indicate the line of the gallery.
*Nicolson 1950,83; MacCulloch 1905, 229.*

### 26. Hallin Park, (Waternish) Duirinish (souterrain) NG 2490 5862

In 1986 while ploughing within the south-western enclosure at Hallin Park, a capstone was dislodged revealing a souterrain. This was seen by several local people before it was covered up again as they did not want it brought to a wider attention.
*Pers. comm. Capt MacLeod, Upper Halistra, Waternish. June 1990. SMR NG25NW 7.*

### 27. Trumpan Beag, (Waternish) Duirinish (souterrain) NG 2315 6244

A 'sub-rectangular' depression measuring 5.3m from NE to SW by 1.5m transversely and 0.2m in depth runs SW from a gap in an arc of bank. The linear depression is similar to that at the end of the of the known souterrain at Clagan [see Inventory No. 2]. Turf over an area of 1.2m by 0.4m was lifted across the depression to reveal poorly consolidated rubble, and a pot-boiler broken into three pieces. At a depth of 0.2m lay a lintel stone covering a void. At this point the turf was relaid. (SMR NG33NE 4)

During field survey of the Waternish peninsular, the Royal Commission on the Ancient and Historical Monuments of Scotland recorded what was interpreted as a possible souterrain, on the west-south-west side of slight knoll straddled by a rectangular building of earth and stone construction and a field bank.
*SMR NG33NE 4.*

### 28. Claigan 2, Duirinish (souterrain) NG 239 541

This is reportedly orientated north-east to south-west, with a gallery 7.7m long and 1.2m wide, which is said to terminate in a circular chamber *c*.3m in diameter, enclosing a smaller structure 1.5m in diameter.

A souterrain lying some 250m north-east of that at Claigan has been recorded but not located. *Davies and Calder 1978.*

### 29. Ollisdal, Duirinish (souterrain?) Centred NG 221 401

A possible souterrain was located in the upper reaches of Glen Ollisdal, set into the south-west facing slope of Coire Mor. It is reputed to lie on the western bank of the middle tributary of the stream, close by the small waterfall, but has not been located. *Pers. comm. Paul Rosher, 'Grainal', Dunvegan.*

### 30. Kilvaxter, Kilmuir (souterrain) NG 3899 6960 (38)

This souterrain was discovered in April 2000, when a lintel collapsed. At present, excavation is in progress to make the monument publicly accessible; therefore the information given here is limited and interim in nature.

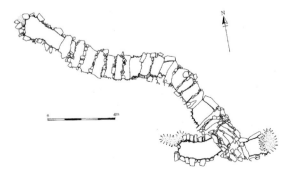

**38** *Kilvaxter souterrain from the east, September 2000 and plan.*
Photo: Paul Booth

North of Uig Bay the landscape is one of gentle and strong slopes broken by rocky outcrops, The souterrain lies within the north-eastern quadrant of a small stone-wall enclosed field which was previously ploughed. Within 10m north of the souterrain lie the remains of a degraded, but prominent, circular homestead.

The souterrain lies on the eastern, leeward, slope of a ridge with its simple butt-ended terminal lying just below the crest. It runs for a distance of some 17m in a sinuous course from north-north-west to south-south-east, partially following the contour, and constructed to respect the adjacent homestead.

The sidewalls are constructed of random rubble (local basalt and water-worn 'flags') and support massive lintels *c*.1.8m in length. The lintels were fixed in place by stones jammed between their butt-ends and the natural clay side. These edges were luted with clay, to prevent water-penetration, and stones were driven into the interstices between the lintels to hinder earth trickling down into the interior. One such pinning stone carries a single cup-mark. The lintels were then covered in soil to level the ground surface, using the spoil from cutting the souterrain trench.

The gallery attains a maximum height of 1.6m from its rotted bedrock floor to the underside of the lintels where the main gallery meets the satellite gallery. The lintels are set at right-angles to the line of the main gallery and are supported upon cross-lintels at either side. Elsewhere the lintels rest upon the wall-heads which, in some instances, are corbelled inwards. The short satellite passage rises up the slope, its lintels raised to a higher level than those of the main gallery, which varies in width from 0.75m to *c*.1m.

Contemporary with the souterrain is a well cobbled and kerbed 'yard' running down-slope from the foot of the bank in which the souterrain is constructed. A cup-marked stone is associated with the kerbing. Another three cup-marked stones have been found in the vicinity, none in direct association with the souterrain.

The site also exhibits medieval and post-medieval occupation. The former is represented by a platform of large boulders associated with a small mid-thirteenth-century coin hoard, and the latter by a post-medieval settlement of houses and byres.

### *31. Borneskitaig, Kilmuir (possible souterrain & homestead?) NG 3692 7047*

A substantial stone platform overlooks the bay at Camus Ban and the former loch of St Columba from the lower northern slope of Knockhoe. It has a commanding outlook of the surrounding landscape to the north and west. At its greatest diameter (18.7m), its skirt of large blocks and inner features cumulatively indicate a monument of some architectural and chronological complexity with prehistoric origins and subsequent historic activity. Lying on the perimeter of the platform at the north-north-east side is a single large lintel with indications of a hollow beneath. Beyond this is a rubble-filled depression, some 1.4m wide, running north-north-eastwards away from the platform. The rubble continues in linear fashion for a total distance of 18.5m.

It is difficult to disentangle the structural elements, although the overall form is reminiscent of the situation at Penduin (6). Examination of the linear feature approaching the monument would, in all probability, reveal it to have been either the entrance to a surface building or a souterrain.

# 9 The wheelhouse

*Iain Crawford*

## Introduction

This study is intended to be a complete compendium of current structural evidence and associated factors to initiate a wheelhouse database. Wheelhouse information has long seemed enigmatic, contradictory and unfocused, and is a poor relation, if collateral, of broch studies. However, pottery comparison has been a major consideration of both. The intention here is to attempt to give wheelhouse studies an independent status by an holistic presentation of the *structural characteristics* as now known, together with a commentary on distribution, and a consideration of, and conjecture on, the vexed questions of function and ritual. Also examined is the surprisingly abrupt terminus of wheelhouse use, as distinct from re-use, accentuated by closely confirmatory radiocarbon determinations in some number.

## Wheelhouse approaches

The method used in this study has been to list all wheelhouses, numbered *1–62*, in terms of the criteria cited for this study and to tabulate them according to their significant or distinctive features, of which 51 have been identified (**Tables 13** & **14**). This quantitive assessment is associated with a qualitative approach to evaluating the calibre of the individual wheelhouses and any work undertaken on them. Also addressed are exterior factors such as 'neighbouring' structures and wheelhouse/late Iron Age ground horizons. Finally there are new features including recent discoveries, incorporated as part of the standard feature key: these include internal guttering, cultivation, ritual and burial, none of which have been observed before. Selected for inclusion in this list were all planned and academically accepted wheelhouses, and all examples of surviving elements of what could be presumed to have been such. The criteria used were: late Iron Age dating indications associated with a curve of drystone walling showing at least two radial piers (these criteria have been adhered to barely without exception). The registered numbers refer to individual structures consecutively within sites. A comprehensive distribution map was also deemed essential to determine the total geographical extent of wheelhouses, and the focus of this investigation (**39**). This study, then, describes the wheelhouse on the basis of its parts, and is also an exercise in source evaluation.

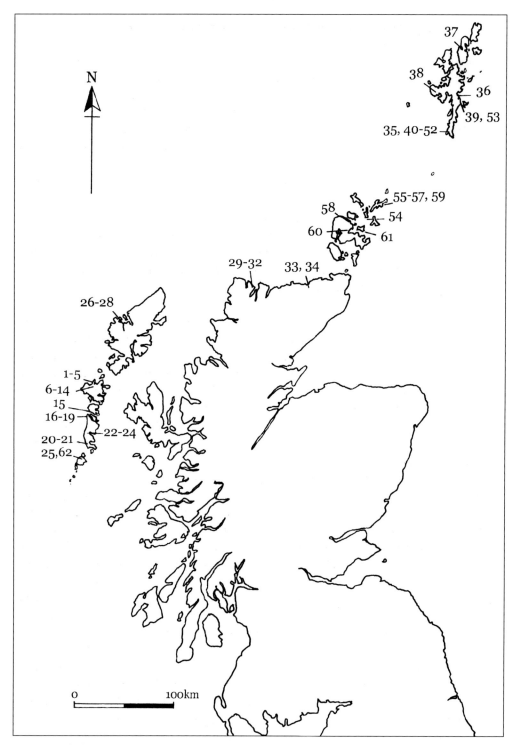

**39** *Map of wheelhouse distribution in Scotland.* I. Crawford

# The wheelhouse and the history of its investigation

Wheelhouse investigation has a long if patchy pedigree. The encompassing mounds were conspicuous and attracted the enthusiastic attention of the leisured classes from the middle of the nineteenth century and the early part of the twentieth century. For the west coast comment is recorded from 1855 when C. Gordon (possibly of the proprietorial family in South Uist) opened a mound on the west shore 'nearly level with the sea'. He made a verbal report of his findings to Sir Henry Dryden when in London, but no location is recorded and the site cannot now be identified. In *Sailing Directions for the West Coast* the comment was made 'these blocks (piers) radiate like the spokes of a wheel', and thus was born the 'nickname' wheelhouse.

In itself this illustrates the weakness of traditional archaeological taxonomy: wheelhouses are neither wheels nor perhaps houses. To make matters worse there is such a thing as a wheelhouse, the casing or housing of a mill wheel. However, long-term usage over a century and a half dictates a resigned persistence. Further attempts at terminology seem futile and no more accurate. As Lethbridge (1952) remarked 'I find the term "aisled round-house" less descriptive and more ponderous'.

In fact, there seems little likelihood that the original wheelhouse builders intended any such thing as an aisle. It must be common ground that they intended a curved colonnade and the so-called aisle is purely fortuitous. The piers are surely the drystone equivalent of a column, a point emphasised in Shetland where incorporated orthostats produce an uncanny resemblance to pillars. If the term wheelhouse is a persistent archaism for, say, 'radial-piered drystone walled circles', it is on balance best to continue this. As for the interesting, if inaccurate and conjectural, work of Captain Thomas (1869) and the naval surveyors of the 1860s around Usinish (see *22* & *23*, **Table 13**), it must be said to have laid the foundations for the subject.

Further developments were less satisfactory. In the summer of 1906 the Middlequarter, North Uist cattleherd 'carefully excavated a series of four underground chambers' (Beveridge 1911, 121). These were in fact four of the bays/cells between the piers of the Middlequarter wheelhouse excavated by Beveridge later in 1906 and by Atkinson in 1956-7. This site, excellently written up some 35 years after the field work by Campbell (1991) and named by him Sollas (*5*) (on the basis of erroneous information supplied), was quite one of the best surviving of its class. That the site should have been first fossicked in by the township herd and then by the proprietor Erskine Beveridge was a tragedy and Atkinson's achievements despite this prior mutilation must be seen as quite remarkable. In 1931-2 Callander arranged for Beveridge's results to see a posthumus light of day. No further work took place until the post-war years.

In the Northern Isles a rather different pattern unfolded. Despite the activities of over-enthusiastic proprietors there where the baling out of brochs was a favourite pastime, a number of committed research workers followed up these recreations. The work of Dryden, Traill, Petrie and Farrar, for example, was comparable with standards elsewhere and merits being rated as research. Work in the Northern Isles was strangely skewed by the apparent absence of recognisable wheelhouses in Orkney (see below). The proclivity, especially in Shetland, for inserting wheelhouses like parasites within brochs (a circumstance unknown in the Western Isles) also masked the situation in early years. In the west of Scotland, contrastingly, there were excavations of purely wheelhouse sites. On the north mainland coast no such excavations ever occurred (**39**).

In the period between the Wars, developments progressed quite well in international terms in Shetland. The Ministry of Works' purchases at Jarlshof (*42 – 45*) in 1925, formerly a proprietorial target, later marked a crucial turning point for archaeology generally in Scotland and for wheelhouse studies in particular. From then on substantial professional archaeological research took place in the north, at Gurness (*58*) in the 1930s (RCAHMS 1946), and by Curle at Jarlshof in 1931-5 with major archaeological sequences established, including wheelhouses. This circumstance was without parallel in the Western Isles where no work was done. There was a conflict between national and regional interests, a reflection too of the cognate contrast between a northern region of massive well-preserved multi-phase sites which the Ministry of Works saw as of paramount importance and for which there was, and is, generally no parallel in the west.

After the Second World War the state-organised and state-funded large projects in Orkney and Shetland were resumed and expanded: Hamilton (1956) worked on Jarlshof between 1949 and 1951, and on Clickhimin (1968) (*36*) between 1953 and 1957. This work has been the basis for more recent follow-up investigations at a number of sites, some currently proceeding such as Old Scatness (*46 – 52*) (for a discussion of these sites, see below). Again, the wheelhouses are submerged in complexes of later and earlier buildings which, while providing excellent contexts, have in themselves inevitably engendered moderate if not severe damage, compounding the effect of erosion on what are so frequently coastal sites (**Table 13** *Site condition*).

Meantime in the 'neglected' West, work devolved on 'private' professional individual enterprise, on emergency salvage crises and more recently on university training operations. Nevertheless, as Euan MacKie (1965) has remarked for the West and for individual wheelhouse work, the first work of its kind up to modern standards was conducted by Sir Lindsay Scott on North Uist at Clettraval (*9*) in 1946-8. This was followed in 1951-2 by Lethbridge at Kilpheder (*21*), by Scott again at the Allasdale on Barra (*25*) in 1951-2, followed up by Young (1953) and then by the rocket range pre-construction 'team enterprise' in particular at A'Ceardach Mhor, West Geirinish (*17*) (Young & Richardson 1960), and by Fairhurst in 1956 at A'Ceardach Bheag (*18 & 19*) actually at Drimore (Fairhurst 1971).

The most productive site was, as already mentioned, the major undertaking at Middlequarter named inaccurately Sollas (Gae. *Solas*) (*5*), by Atkinson in 1957 (Campbell 1991). To refer again to MacKie's remark above, if Clettraval represents a new level of product then Sollas is the high point, at least at salvage or rescue excavation level. There was then a positive flurry of activity in the 1950s occasioned in many cases by Vere Gordon Childe's extramural teaching in London and of course by proposed military intrusion. It is something of an irony that the Royal Artillery guided missile practice range was eventually so severely cut back that, with the possible exception of West Geirinish, none of the sites funded need have been excavated, in emergency terms.

By contrast to the 1950s, the 1960s and 1970s saw very little archaeological activity of any sort except at the Udal, North Uist where four wheelhouse horizons were recorded (*1, 2, 3 & 4*) (Crawford in general), and a Public Schools Research Expedition worked at Usinish.

Euan MacKie (1969) flew the martial banner of late Iron Age studies throughout from every broch he excavated but not at wheelhouses. In the Northern Isles Anna Ritchie and others were active on late Iron Age/Pictish and Norse sites where no wheelhouses were in evidence.

## The distribution of wheelhouses

It would seem appropriate to recognise the actual distribution of these 62 monuments, as one of the few aspects of them that engenders little debate, though the general picture is surprising. The map (**39**) shows a remarkably confined and limited distribution in general Scottish terms, yet even within that there are distinct provinces. Geographically, there are the four well-defined sub-regions of the Western Isles, the North mainland coast (Sutherland and Caithness), Orkney and Shetland. As discussed below, wheelhouses fall into four groups distinct from one another, yet with uniformity within each group. Another remarkable observation is that almost 50 per cent of wheelhouses are found in just two parishes: 16 in Dunrossness, Shetland and 13 in Solas, North Uist (no. 4 is omitted as an old ground horizon only). Solas is both a parish with many wheelhouses as stated and also a township, which iron-ically has none at all! Obviously this startling pattern must have major significance in terms of the origins and development of wheelhouses.

The quantity and localisation of wheelhouses are extraordinary in general archaeological terms. It is rare indeed to encounter any monument about which we may have close to a total estimate of numbers. In addition to the 62 cited examples there are a few probable sites as well as some eroded or even demolished before the nineteenth century. In the machair areas of the Western Isles, shore-face erosion has damaged sites severely and must have wiped out a few others, given that the last two millennia have seen rising sea levels of two metres or more. It is by no means impossible that a few wheelhouses remain buried and undiscovered. It is along the north coastal region of Sutherland and Caithness that the best prospects for further discoveries lie. That region has been very neglected in terms of archaeological fieldwork and there have been no wheelhouse excavations despite the presence of numerous substantial wags along the eastern part of the coast, especially in the Latheron district, which may well contain such sites.

In Orkney and Shetland the profusion of discoveries cannot be at an end though as elsewhere fortuitous exposures are unpredictable. One of the editors of this festschrift deserves credit for spotting that a silage pit being machine-opened at Ward Hill, Shetland (*41*) contained the inimitable wheelhouse indications (Smith 1988). Another recent discovery was made in a remote part of Grimsay, North Uist at Bagh Nam Fheadaig (*15*) and excavated between 1994-7 (Hethersall & Tyre 2000).

Today with the amount of professional and amateur fieldwalking it must be highly unlikely that results will be forthcoming from adjacent regions like Wester Ross or Eastern Sutherland. It is suggested that there could be *c.* five wheelhouses awaiting identification in each of the regions cited above. There could be an ultimate total of say 90–100 buildings. It is something of a relevation that we can probably count on having on record approximately 60 per cent of a total monument type and a surprisingly accurate outline of scope and scale.

# Wheelhouse evaluation

The table of structural details (**Table 13**) has been designed to be not just a necessary catalogue for the benefit of future workers but an evaluation exercise suitable for any studies that are as uneven in quality as archaeological sources usually are.

The distribution map (**39**) shows the site coverage ordered by number sequence commencing in the Western Isles, that being where the so-called 'classic type' is found and indeed is almost entirely confined, with the exception of those such as Jarlshof. Within the Isles the Udal (*1–4*) and Sollas (Middlequarter) (*5*) were chosen as the starting points and to a certain extent the models from which all other examples follow. This is because these two neighbouring sites, only 1.8km apart on the Machair Leathann, are much the most productive in fine structural detail in most respects, as the simplistic points crediting system highlights. The numbering continues south through the Isles and then takes in Lewis. The North Scottish coastal strip is then covered from west to east, next Shetland from north to south and finally Orkney, which is last because it presents peculiar problems better handled separately from the rest.

A method of awarding points has been adopted to roughly quantify a site's physical attributes and indicate its comparative calibre: this simply entails giving a point per feature recorded in pursuit of the qualitative approach. Two points have been awarded where there has been research motivation, salvage excavation receives one point and recreational clearance receives none. Severe erosion and/or other major damage is recorded as -1. The maximum possible site 'score' would be 43.

The Udal sites were chosen as a yardstick because they were discovered during a purely research operation: the late Iron Age being part of a much larger suite of deposits. The results of the points system are shown on the bottom line of the table (**Table 13**). For example, Udal S A (*1*) receives 27 points, Udal S B (*2*) 26 points and Udal S C (*3*) 16 points. A total for the sites, avoiding duplication of results and including (*4*), amounts to 38 points. Sollas (*5*) is very much the cream of the salvage efforts, rating 24 points. The Udal complex and Sollas verge on the identical and between them virtually cover the list of features, with the exception of the new phenomena such as drip courses and the exterior contemporaneous features. The discrepancy is so great between these two sites and the remaining 60 as to make the latter's contribution confined more or less to making up the numbers and the distribution.

This perhaps is not entirely fair to the four next highest ranked sites Clettraval (*9*) with 21 points, Jarlshof 1 (*42*) with 18, Jarlshof 2 (*43*) with 19 and Kilpheder (*21*) with 18, which are all moderately informative. Where the Machair Leathan sites score heavily is in floor lifting, which has rarely been carried out, and in both cases reveals complex pit systems, which can only reflect ritual complications. As with Sollas, the Udal S A (*1*) builders commenced with the digging of a drift platform into a machair ridge and the excavation of huge 'bathtub-shaped' pits, which were immediately back filled with clean sand. In the life of both wheelhouses dozens of small pits were dug and packed with tightly fitting animal inhumations. These were mostly the bones of peri-foetal lambs at the Udal S A (*1*) (Legge pers. comm. and Crawford in prep.). These two sites cover what must be close to comprehensive accounts of wheelhouse culture: structurally, ritually and agriculturally, with the certainty that ritual function was fundamental to both construction and use. The failure of almost all other excavators to lift floors has effectively obscured these matters, though what Scott could have retrieved in the shallow soil profiles of Clettraval, or any other worker given these conditions, is most problematic.

## Excavation details

While the two prime loci (*1 – 4* and *5*) give the known range of details in themselves, it is still pertinent to validate the general wheelhouse profile to be proposed by analysing the frequency of feature records across the whole spectrum of sites. The first four categories of *Excavation details* on **Table 13** provide the evaluation of the site as source. There are 32 sites with a research rating; however, 11 of these are nineteenth-century work, which though having research motivations are hopelessly out of date more than a century later (Nos *35, 39 & 53 – 61*) (i.e. Goudie 1872). Three, Clettraval (*9*), Kilpheder (*21*) and Allasdale (*25*) represent old-fashioned dilettantism, in particular the attempts to graft on post-Medieval structures which have no stratigraphic integrity, so that despite ratings of 19, 18 and 14 they are considered to be second-class sources.

The four Udal sites classify as only a single source for these purposes as do the four wheel-houses at Jarlshof (*42 – 45*) and the seven at Old Scatness (*46 – 52*). Clickhimin (*36*) is frag-mentary due to meddling and barely qualifies as research. Eilean Maleit (*6*) also scarcely ranks as research as the bulk of the return is from a previous Beveridge 'recreational' investigation. The re-excavation in recent times (Armit 1998a) achieved negligible results and the site makes virtually no contribution to a wheelhouse corpus. Only a handful of the excavations therefore represents serious modern research sources, in contrast to the numerous opportu-nities suggested.

Relevant salvage operations have been few. As remarked above, Sollas (*5*) rated at 24 is much the most outstanding of these and is a rare excellent example of how salvage and research need not be mutually exclusive. The remainder of the rocket range projects, West Geirinish (*17*) and Drimore I with Drimore II (*18 & 19*), were competently handled within the inevitable time limits. Their scores of 13, 17 and 10 represent a fair return given the circumstances, which included the impossibility of concluding. Work by the AOC unit revealed a vestigial site at the Hornish (*16*) (Barber 1989), although limited interim informa-tion is available, a score of 4 seems, subject to revision, appropriate. Historic Scotland's retrieval work on the shore face erosion of Cnip (*26 & 27*) is very recent (Armit 1988b and 1996). At present, 12 and 7 points are registered based on current evidence. Brough Head (*40*) was part of a coastal erosion rescue programme and again adverse circumstances limit the rating to 11. In severely depleted circumstances salvage can only achieve remnant returns. Excavation at Bayanne (*37*) is ongoing (Moore and Wilson 1997) and therefore the score is presently a nominal 6.

Recreation or illicit fossicking accounts for ten of the list (*6–8, 10–15 & 28*), nine of them in North Uist. In 11 further cases no action has ever been taken but all are discernible wheelhouse ruins.

## Constructional details

### Double walling

It has been said by previous authorities (Beveridge & Callander 1931) that wheelhouses were usually subterranean and reconstructions on this theme have appeared in publications (Beith 1997, and HMSO). However, this is not entirely the case. There are 20 wheelhouses (37 per cent of those for which there are adequate returns, and not discounting the broch insertions, for which see below) with double-faced walls and thus entirely, or for the major part, free-standing. These are numbers *2, 3, 6–9, 22–23, 30–32, 35, 38, 42–45 & 54.*

### Single walling

By contrast 34 examples (63 per cent) have a revetted facing to a hollow or dug-out drift into an old dune or ridge, except of course for the entranceway. They are numbers *1–3, 6, 10–22, 26, 27, 33, 34, 37, 43, 45–47, 49–52 & 55–57.* No conclusion seems obvious from this except to observe that the builders adapted their tactics according to the local physical relief. The semi-subterranean factor has little relevance beyond that. It occurs at the Udal throughout the Medieval period and as late as the seventeenth century. Local descriptions, rather than place names as such, have done much to engender the subterranean view. Examples like Tigh Talamhanta (earth house) and Wag (uamhag = cave-like) among others are widespread and, except as a signal to field workers, of little consequence. There is no evidence for the wholly subterranean, which must depend on overall roofing.

### Broch inserts

The differentiation alluded to above between wheelhouse regions is nowhere more evident than in the opportunistic 'reuse' of brochs. Unknown in the West or the north Mainland, the effective slighting of these forts is not uncommon and looks to have significant historical implications. There are 10 examples out of the total of 26 wheelhouses in the Northern Isles. This means a surprising 38 per cent of wheelhouses are located within brochs with nine more instances clustering round them, indicating 72 per cent are in close association. What is striking about these various infringements is that they both destroy the brochs' defensive integrity and show, in all these cases at least, that wheelhouses are later than brochs (see also Wainwright 1962).

### Piers

Piers are at once the most striking and diagnostic of wheelhouse attributes. Their occurrence within any building is of course quite closely linked to the overall diameter (see below), which varies between extremes of 4 and 13m. They differ markedly in design and do so regionally (see the 6 types listed in **Table 13**). In the Western Isles 'classics', the piers are drystone blocks 1.2–1.5m long and *c.*0.4m wide standing some 1m free of the main wall face, thus leaving a passage of that dimension. This passage is what has been referred to as the 'aisle' (type i). This could be described as the standard arrangement in that 24 examples out of the 27 in the Western Isles are thus, with an additional eight in the east. In many of these 32 cases the aisle has been blocked so that the pier face abuts onto the main wall (type ii). *Ad hoc* rubble may be used or, by contrast, an extension was so carefully laid as for the junction to be barely discernible.

Type iii involves the bonding of the pier to the wall, irrespective of lintels, which seems to be a Northern Isles technique. There is only one possible Western Isles example of this at Foshigarry A (*12*) but here Beveridge's drawing is ambiguous (Beveridge & Callander 1931). A further form of bonding (type iv) occurs eight times and this is where one or other of the doorway piers is thickened, forming part of the general door assemblage, possibly to counterpoise the door or gate itself. Seven are of this type in the Western Isles, with only one, Howmae (*57*), elsewhere. Another Northern Isles factor mainly seen in plan is the triangular pier (type v). This seems generally, as at Jarlshof (*42 & 43*), to have been bonded into the wall. There are 12 cases of this, two (*10 & 12*), are schematic Beveridge plans and perhaps should be viewed with caution. Exclusive to the North coast and in the Northern Isles is the use of orthostats (type vi) both as facing stones and as sole constituents. In these regions, 25 out of 33 of the examples are constructed so. These are remarkable structures, and especially at Jarlshof bear an uncanny resemblance to pillars. In north coast examples the orthostats are set 'edge on' to the buildings' centre. Piers then show much variation with distinct regional differences, but presumably a common function.

## Diameter

The principal factor in wheelhouse size is diameter, although this is not obvious in the irregular shapes of Orkney, and even elsewhere the circle wall is not always perfect. The dimensions recorded in **Table 13** are the largest. In 59 examples the breadth is listed, exactly where possible, but frequently as an approximation where no excavation has occurred. A drawing interpretation where only a curved arc survives must be regarded with caution as concerns perfect circularity as this can be an optimistic assumption. For 'intact' buildings an average diameter is taken from the reading variants of drystone dyking faces. The range is considerable, extending from 4 to 11.5m and perhaps justifying nominal size categories of Large, Medium and Small. The Foshigarry B (*13*) figure of 11.9m results from drawing out from a 'three piered arc' and may not be reliable. The spread among the above categories taking arbitrary divisions of Large as 9–11.5m, Medium as 7–9m, and Small as 4–7m gives corresponding groupings of 18, 24 and 16. This range of sizes is distributed fairly evenly through the regions. If there is significance in this it is not immediately apparent.

## Radiocarbon dates

The late Iron Age dating of these monuments is not in doubt and as stated above, the comparative evidence of very distinctive pottery was a major criterion for selection. When Euan MacKie (1969) wrote on radiocarbon dates and the Scottish Iron Age 30 years ago there were no wheelhouse dates at all. Now radiocarbon determinations are in reasonable supply from sites *2, 3, 4, 5* and *40* (**Table 15**) and more are expected from the Udal *1,* Cnip *26, 27,* from Bayanne *37* and from the Old Scatness multiple site *46–52* (**colour plates 21** & **22**). The pattern is distinct, and the table gives the technical details of calibration and variation. A condensed impression taking the median dates gives the following run from 25 BC to AD 380. These 13 dates show remarkable uniformity indicating a wheelhouse *floruit* around the late second century to early third century AD.

This consorts well with the remnant magnetic date for Sollas (*5*) of *c.*AD 50 (**Table 15**). Further confirmation of this early first millennium AD calendar estimates comes from the presence of late third-century Roman pottery in an unambiguously terminal context (**Table 16**). Later 'pivotal dates' from the sealing levels of the earliest medieval horizons on the Udal N of AD 336 & 448 are reliable confirmation of a *terminus ante quem*. What is missing from this picture is earlier dating i.e. pre-wheelhouse returns. Late Bronze Age levels at the Udal S B (*2*) centre on 600 BC (determinations are awaited for (*1*) where the stratigraphic and comparative evidence is early). The Hornish (*16*) results (centring provisionally on 410 & 335 BC) for a certainly pre-wheelhouse horizon bring the prospect of a *terminus post quem* closer.

## Pottery dating

Pottery as the principal comparative dating element is present at 48 sites and is well defined in copious literature. Of the remaining 14 sites most are unexcavated. The presence of late Roman pottery (late third-century grey ware) in a definite post-wheelhouse horizon suggests an approximation to terminal dating at the Udal S B (*2*), as does Rhenish pottery at Clickhimin. Roman glass and coin imports also corroborate the dating range (**Tables 15-17**).

## Archaeomagnetic dating

Remnant magnetism has proved of very limited value as a dating technique until quite recently but the Uist return of AD 1–100 fits well into the present date range suggested above (**Tables 15-17**). In a recent revival of the technique, sampled hearths at Old Scatness 5 (*46*) give a date range for a Pictish house sealing the wheelhouse of AD 650–800.

## Lintels

Lintels could be described as indispensable adjuncts to wheelhouse sites, but unfortunately the same is also true of souterrains. This has inevitably been the source of much confusion to field workers in the identification of sites (see Miket, this volume). A mound bestrewn with 1–2m long lintels could be either a wheelhouse or a souterrain and occasionally both. Lintels have always been at a premium even into the twentieth century AD and are always a relatively scarce commodity in areas lacking good building stone. To any succeeding opportunist the relatively vast quantities of these long stones totalling up to 40 per wheelhouse or tunnel would be irresistible. Lintels are of course the crucial component of the Greek arch, which bridges the cells and passageways and stabilises the whole wheelhouse form. There are 19 sites which still retain this vital arch while some 14 show evidence of it in ruin.

## Hearths

Approximately 28 hearths survive but the evidence is enigmatic and the total relatively small. The symmetrical situation of a hearth setting in the centre of a wheelhouse would seem to be the expected primary arrangement, as at Sollas (*5*). However, while 26 sites have central hearths, there are 22 without any at all. This poses the question of the status of hearths, whether primary or secondary, and the function of the buildings. Fires after all could be predicted as the first act of new occupiers. It is worth remarking that in the case of Udal S A (*1*), which is possibly very early, no amount of careful excavation produced a fireplace despite an abundance of ash. The matter has some bearing on the problems of the function of wheelhouses and of their roofing.

## Tanks or sinks

The so-called tanks or sinks, set into the floor of wheelhouses, are not common except in North Uist where there are eight out of a total of 13 sites, the remainder being located at Jarlshof and Mousa, with three in Orkney. Their purpose is obscure.

## Twin wheelhouses

This survey suggests that 'twinning' of wheelhouses was a positive arrangement where buildings were not merely conjoined by chance but deliberately respected each other's presence. Hamilton has used the graphic term 'spliced' for the Jarlshof pair (*42 & 43*) but there are eight more examples. These are *18/19, 26/27, 31/32, 56/57*, with *2/3, 33/34, 47/49*, and *50/51*. This constitutes nearly 30 per cent of the total survey and must have its own significance, an assertion emphasised by the fact that the first four pairings above have communicating doors.

## Founding pits

The rarity of some of the listed features (**Table 13**) reflects more restrictions of investigation technique or of time available for excavation, than definite absence. Floors, which completely conceal the pits that constitute the major ritual element present, have, as emphasised above, very rarely been lifted. Only at three sites has this been accomplished, *1, 2 & 5*. The earliest horizon in *1 & 5* and probably in *2* shows the digging of an arc of giant pits (up to 1.6m long), which seem to have immediately been backfilled with sterile sand. 'Founding pits' seems an appropriate term.

## Entrances

Long, splayed entrance passages, up to 8m in length, with revetment faces only, are another apparent rarity. They are present in only five cases, at *1, 5, 7, 18* and *21*. All of these are in Uist and, except for *7*, are recent discoveries. In the published reconstructions referred to above these passages are given roofs, which is quite out of the question given the walls' light revetment quality. These 'funnels' suggest animal management whether it be agricultural or the lead-in to ritual slaughter.

## Satellite cells

The term satellite has been applied to 'lean-to' structures appended to main wheelhouse walls usually with a doorway to the main enclosure. These can take the form of small circular cells no more than 3m in diameter or up to 8m long, almost sub-rectangular shapes, clinging to the wheelhouse outline. There are six of the latter, numbers *2, 5, 6, 8 & 25* in the Western Isles with one (*50*) in Shetland. They must have an appreciable significance especially in examples *2* (**40**) (**colour plate 14**) and *50*, which resemble miniature wheelhouses. While religious imaging is risky these two near-identical structures, each with three piers, are reminiscent of side chapels. Example *2*, the satellite to the Udal S B, has so much detail as to make it a critical model for wheelhouses in general and as such is discussed again below.

## Aumbries

Aumbries resemble large wall cupboards and any other purpose they may have had is not obvious. The 21 recorded examples are spread evenly across the regions. There may well

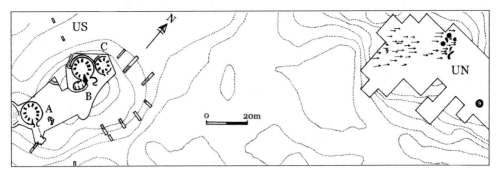

**40** *Plan of the Udal wheelhouses.* I. Crawford

have been many more but any reduction of the wheelhouse wall height to below 1m is likely to have eliminated most. Nevertheless they would seem to be an essential of the wheelhouse repertoire.

## Door 'guard' cells

'Guard' cells is perhaps a misnomer, as no other signs of potential fortification exist. Dodgshon's (1981) terming of wheelhouses as fortlets is wholly inappropriate. There are 15 instances where these small arcades or cells *c.*3m in diameter front onto the doorway passages, sometimes in opposed pairs. Some minor measure of gate control seems likely, emphasised by the draw bolt shafts shown (see below). This feature is well distributed and is probably diagnostic.

## Corbelling

Corbelling is a critical feature of wheelhouse architecture and the source of much controversy in terms of its implications for roofing. There can now be no doubt from excavation observation that piers were the basis for lintel arches that in turn acted as springing for corbelling for the roofing of cells or bays. From Captain Thomas's initial observations over a century ago at Usinish (*22 & 23*) through to recent evidence at Cnip (*26 & 27*) corbelling is a most notable characteristic of wheelhouses. Pier corbelling survives in 16 cases, most impressively at Jarlshof (*42 & 43*). Wall corbelling is much less common, as it is observed in only 10 cases. The surviving degree of elevation is critical here, but does it lead to a form of overall roofing or not? This has always been a crucial question.

## Bay kerbs

Bay or cell kerbs may be described fairly as universal, appearing more or less intact on 29 plans. They clearly form one of the five stone rings that are the basic blueprint for a wheelhouse plan. These concentric rings are: innermost the drip course, then the bay kerbing, then the pier back faces, the inner main wall face, and where present the outer wall. Invariably kerbs lie across the mouths of bays set just back from the piers' inner face. They clearly revet compartments with a specific usage (see bay 'bowl' pits below). Kerbs seem to be an essential component of the wheelhouse, but where they are missing from the records there seems likely to have been stone robbing or defective observation. The important point about them is that they revet the split-level situation where bay floors are a step up from the central floor.

## Drip courses and gutters

There has been a seminal recent discovery, which sheds light, all too necessarily, on the roofing question. Wheelhouses were clearly afflicted with a severe drainage problem (see also Covered drains below). While this problem is understandable on shallow upland soils, as at Clettraval (9), it makes, at first sight, little sense on machair sites where sand drains easily. There is, however, a specific machair hazard in that falling eaves water produces wall base scour which if allowed to persist brings down drystone walls. The remedy devised was a ground level guttering or drip course.

There is completely convincing evidence of a drip course at the Udal S A (1) where a single course of flat 'stepping stones' fronts the bays, and the kerbs, in an arc, link the inner faces of the piers. The technique appears to have been refined when the later Udal S B (2) wheelhouse and its satellite were erected. The stones were erected in a chevron formation like an uncovered drain. There is evidence here to suggest that these are not drains in the conventional sense, as they are more like soakaways, though these as such would tend to displace some sand. In fact they are soak 'ins' or soak *in situ*, whereby there is in effect temporary puddling but no sand displacement. It is of overwhelming importance to stress that these water constraint systems are internal and must therefore have had corresponding eaves.

## Aeolianite deposits

The roofing giveaway is at Udal S A (1) where a thick coating of aeolianite encrusted the drip course. This represents heavy persistent dripping, which caused the build up of this nascent sandstone below eaves *inter alia*. This is quite a well-known phenomenon in itself and forms on firm surfaces under the eaves of semi-permanent site huts. In natural circumstances in coileagan (sand bunkers) in the machair it is formed by turf edge drip, and is known in Coll as 'dune rock'. The importance of this evidence is that it is a firm statement that Udal wheelhouses 1 & 2 were roofless except above the bays. Close examination of other reports shows that water splash control was probably present though unrecorded because it was unrecognised as such on seven other research sites: *9, 19, 21, 25, 42* and *45*.

## Animal burials

The multiplicity of animal burials revealed when floors are taken up is startling and promises to be a major study at the Udal (1 – 2) as at Sollas (5) where the quantity of material is unparalleled except at West Geirinish (17). Legge, who worked at the sites and on the bone, has commented (pers. comm.) that the most common content of these inhumations is peri-foetal lamb. This tends to highlight the proposition already suspected, that these buildings were primarily, if not solely, ritual/religious in purpose.

## Bay 'bowl' pits

These dished hollows or basins fully occupy the bay interior precluding its further use and would definitely have tended to destabilise the adjacent piers. For these reasons they must be adjudged to have been backfilled quickly. They seem to be important if little recognised phenomena. At the Udal they are present in all wheelhouse sites but especially in Udal S A (*1*) where there are ten, one for every bay. Pits are also recorded for Sollas (*5*) and Kilpheder (*21*) making a total of five sites. The likelihood of many more having been unobserved at other sites seems strong.

## Covered drains

Seventeen covered drains occur at sites distributed through the regions. They point to a recurrent problem (see above) but only at Allasdale (*25*) do water control devices, drains and drip courses occur together.

## Peripheral postholes

A unique discovery at the Udal sites (*1 – 2*) was a ring of postholes numbering originally as many as 22 in each case, sited concentric with the main stone walling of the wheelhouse and apparently just preceding its construction. Former holes may be a better term for they are evidenced by what might be called 'extraction cores'. Packer stones stood in small cones indicating, it is concluded, deliberate extraction. This would have been essential as they are incompatible, when *in situ*, with the succeeding use of the wheelhouse. Whether these represent a constructional device used to mark out the wheelhouse or are evidence of ritual has not been concluded.

## Obelisks

At five of the Western Isles sites obelisks or menhirs were erected. They can only be ritual in intent. In particular, at the satellite cell of Udal S B (*2*) a fine water-rolled columnar boulder was carefully erected with packing stones and looks markedly phallic (**colour plate 14**).

## Plaster/mortar

A most notable if not precocious feature of 15 sites is the presence of a striking red and black *wet* mortar. This was employed as a binder in pier courses but also applied as a wash. McCullagh (Carter *et al.* 1995) has suggested an aesthetic purpose, and this impression was reinforced at the Udal S A where the material was widely spread. It may be worth remarking that in the presumed stygian darkness of a roofed wheelhouse there could be little appreciation of this decorative effect.

## Putlog holes

There is a slight scatter of evidence for putlog holes and scarcements associated with wheelhouses but these features are not entirely convincing. In the Northern Isles, where wheelhouses have been inserted into brochs there is an ambiguity as to which structure these features belong.

## Paving

Paving is commonplace, appearing at 25 sites, although its appearance can be curiously patchy within any one building. It is usually distributed among cells but there is rarely coverage of the main enceinte, with the exception of Clettraval (*9*). Paving is not strictly necessary on machair sites where a tamped smooth floor surface is readily obtained, but it is commoner in the Northern Isles where suitable slabbing is more readily recovered. It is a feature of Jarlshof A (*45*), while at Old Scatness all seven buildings (*46–52*) have total stone coverage.

## Door draw bolt shafts

As suggested above (see Door cells) there was some regard for door keeping and at six wheelhouses bolt shafts survived. In the cases of Udal S A (*1*) and Sollas (*5*) there was evidence for massive shaft holes 2.5m long, features associated usually with forts.

## Later insertions

In view of the discussion below as to 'alternative' occupation sites in this phase of the late Iron Age, indications of contemporary structures to wheelhouses are crucial. However, that evidence is very slight. In the Western Isles insertions and squatter building is evident only at Udal S A (*1*) and West Geirinish (*17*) where incomplete curvilinear walls appear to be contemporary with adjacent wheelhouses or indeed inserted within them. This is a serious problem for those who discount wheelhouse habitation.

# External structures

It is inevitable, with work closely focused on a single monument, that information as the above tends to be confined to a pathology of the type outlined. What then of the world outside the wheelhouse?

## Broch and souterrains associations

The composition of the wheelhouse *per se* has been detailed above, but what about its immediate cultural associations and the contemporary environment. Where does it actually fit in the late Iron Age of the Highlands and Islands? The period is distinguished by two further major monuments, brochs and souterrains, and all three present a common problem in terms of the near absence of related habitation sites: the farming units where most of the population presumably lived. In the Northern Isles, brochs precede wheelhouses in a seemingly inevitable intimacy and in the Western Isles some souterrains at least succeed them. (In Skye they are given a wider dating range, see Miket this volume.) There are 19 Northern instances of wheelhouse/broch association but in the West there is no single instance! In a completely contrasting pattern there are eight associated souterrains in the West and only one elsewhere (nine, if Hamilton's passageway houses at Jarlshof are accepted as such). In the case of the souterrain at the Udal S B (*2*) the stratigraphic and dating evidence is wholly convincing. Here the builders cut through the wheelhouse double wall, and the souterrain emerged within an *ad hoc* 'squatter chamber' contained by revetting wheelhouse rubble and reusing its doorway.

Wheelhouses were obviously sitting targets for incoming politico-social change as the brochs had been before them (see above). What is remarkable is the uneven pattern of these associations across the regions.

## Other structures

Evidence and dating for contemporary (non-wheelhouse) building is disappointingly slight, especially in the Western Isles. The proximity of minor building can be claimed at the Udal S (*1–2*) and at West Geirinish (*17*) where incomplete curvilinear walls relate to adjacent wheelhouses. The best prospect to date has been Sollas A, some 70m south-west of the main complex B (*5*), where curves of stone wall may be contemporary with the main monument, but are tantalisingly short of being interpretable. At Clettraval (*9*) and the Allasdale (*25*) extensive enclosures and rectilinear 'outbuildings' were claimed as Iron Age without any comparative, stratigraphic or artefactual record, being merely proximate. These structures look post-wheelhouse and indeed may well be post-medieval. By contrast, in the Northern Isles some of the site mounds show dense subsidiary buildings clustering around wheelhouse remains e.g. at Gurness (*58*) and most noticeably at Scatness (*48–52*). There are 33 sites showing at least elements of this.

## Landscape

Excavators have very rarely been presented with old ground horizons of the period or the opportunities or funding to explore such. The removal of post-Iron Age levels at the Udal N (*4*), revealed a field system with a series of cremation platforms intercalated with seasonal ploughing episodes. These stone platforms had plentiful late Iron Age pottery in their makeup, which also included bone samples giving a radiocarbon median date of *c*.AD 55 (**Table 15**). At the Udal S the 20m gap between wheelhouses *1* and *2* revealed the intervening old ground horizon *in extenso*. Remains of timber enclosures and small huts also survived. Hence something of an extramural *embarras de richesse* could be recorded.

## Discussion and conclusions

The table (**Table 13**) and the above commentary define the physiognomy of the wheelhouse as currently known. Collectively this corpus of minutiae describes a monument that has to be regarded as a highly idiosyncratic example of conspicuous construction and demonstrates an extravagant use of material (stone). All this would be a prescription elsewhere for a ritual identification, and it now seems likely that the prevalence of animal and perhaps human sacrifice confirms it here. There is a clear, if intricate, uniformity of design that extends with some local variation throughout the extraordinary distribution of the monument, which stretches in a 550km crescent from Barra to Yell. It is a distribution that at first sight expresses a preference for fertile habitats and hence an agricultural purpose. Closer inspection does not sustain this view. Clettraval (*9*) and the Uist east coast sites (*22–24*) and Loch nam Fheadaig, Grimay (*15*), are far from propitious for arable farming while Tigh na Fhearnain (*29*) at *c*.300m elevation is bleak in the extreme (Noel Fojut pers. comm.). There must have been agriculture in the wider vicinity, as at the Udal N (*4*), broken querns are embodied in wheelhouse walling and the sacrifices must represent stock rearing. As remarked, the cognate settlements have yet to be located. The use of timber for housing may be the explanation for this apparent vacuum.

It has been estimated above that close to 60 per cent of sites may have survived and this must represent a surprising lack of demolition or overbuild until modern times: a suggestion here perhaps of respecting the sacred. However, demographic studies show that machair settlement in the later first Millennium AD migrates inland to the black soil/shell sand conjunction, which also accounts for the high preservation of Iron Age structures, and wheel-houses in particular, in the Western Isles at least.

Returning to the theme of structural variation, firstly there is size. The diameters range from 4 – 11m. These are extreme differences (considering that farming units conform fairly closely at most periods to a standard dimension), and argue against agriculture. There are regional differences; the Western Isles are the home of the classic 'wheel' with its drystone piers or 'spokes'; the north coast, as observed to date, has orthostats employed as whole piers, while Shetland has orthostatic facing to its drystone piers. Orkney is an anomaly in that uniformity is not present. It could indeed be argued that there are no wheelhouses at all on Orkney, and this paper, while stretching a point perhaps in including the eight sites listed, would see them as motley derivatives if just conforming to the definitive criteria offered earlier. The marked predilection for insertion within pre-existing brochs in the Northern Isles has no counterpart in the West, which is yet another inconclusive enigma.

The amount of dating evidence (**Tables 15-17**) is encouraging with 19 items in toto which show a neat conformity around a central focus in the second century AD. This much is not enigmatic but incontrovertible.

As stated at the outset this paper has been concerned to catalogue the currently available constructional data old and new. What are wheelhouses in the light of present improved information? That question answered exhaustively, a standard procedure with any monument; would pose three further questions. Firstly what were they for, secondly what were their origins, and finally had they a future? As regards function, two cognate factors invite consideration, firstly use: whether religious or habitational, or both; and secondly, roofing of the central 'theatre'. Associated with the thought is: no roof then no residential or agricultural function. Shortly before he died R.B.K. Stevenson engaged this author in a debate on the subject of wheelhouse function. Reluctantly he found himself forced by his encyclopaedic knowledge of the Scottish Iron Age (*inter alia*), to accept them as of ritual character. His last hope of an alternative was that the cellular houses at the Udal N, figure-of-eights, were contemporary with the wheelhouses on the Udal S. Stratigraphically this was impossible. Stevenson's conclusion was that only religion could be in question.

There is a distinctly religious aura to wheelhouses. Captain Thomas saw them as very reminiscent of Gujerati temples he had known (Thomas 1869). To the anthropologist there is a characteristically extravagant architecture apparently designed for display rather than any domestic purpose. To an architect or an engineer the immediate impression is of heavy load bearing galleries. Unless these supportive arrangements are pure exhibitionism, they must have propped a second gallery, for which there is no evidence, or just possibly a platform for the only other mass available: an audience. To summarise there is a massiveness or monu-mentality here that is normally associated with fortifications, churches or amphitheatres. The former is out of the question.

An historian's view of the prehistoric pattern detailed above would be that a religious cult evidenced by a unique architectural style, sacrifices, and apparently dysfunctional in settlement terms, spread across the north-west Atlantic fringes in the first three centuries AD. The boundary of the distribution is surprisingly precise, suggesting a political frontier. There is no evidence for a future for the tradition after *c.*AD 350. Special pleading needs to be deployed to see the figure-of-eight houses of the following period as derived.

Much more remarkably, there is no evidence as to origins of the wheelhouse. There are no proto-wheelhouses. The only indication is the timber framework under Udal S A but this looks just pre-contemporaneous to the stone version. It seems inescapable that both ideas and builders came from outside. It is scarcely envisaged that wheelhouses sprang into being fully-fledged, nor their rituals for that matter. There is only one possible source at this time, the neighbouring Roman super-power. It is intriguing (perhaps deceptively so) that the wheel-house *flourit* coincides so closely with the arrival and spread of Christianity in Scotland, and likewise the Roman army, its vehicle. These sites qualify, at least illustratively, to be termed *arenas*, or *amphitheatres*, metaphorically speaking.

Campbell (1991) has commented on the Roman proximity in the closing passages of his Sollas report 'This is not to suggest that wheelhouses in general were a development of the Roman period'. Exactly the opposite is argued here. Campbell would cast doubt on any profound social effect resulting from the Roman's transient presence on the outlying Hebrides. This tends to imply a remoteness that may be illusory. The Allasdale wheelhouse (*25*) is only some 125 miles (200km) from the nearest Roman station on the Firth of Clyde, at Lurg Moor, and there is of course a simple, if longer, sea passage. Macinnes has indicated that Scotland was not so peripheral to Britannia. Fitzpatrick's insights into the Claudian contact with Orkney develop the theme more locally. Campbell tends to contradict himself when he writes of the physical manifestation of political and social alliances, which could have had significant effects on native societies. Following Barrett (1981) this suggestion seems entirely consonant with the argument advanced here. The late Iron Age in the Atlantic approaches was arguably not so closed a complex as has been assumed.

Wheelhouses exhibit a sophistication that is neither indigenous nor *sui generis*: they look borrowed not home bred.

**1** *Euan MacKie at Old Scatness.*
Photo: B. Ballin Smith

**2** *Euan MacKie (right, with scarf) at Lang Cairn,
Dumbarton.* Muir Photo: Alex Morrison

**3** *Euan MacKie (with tie) on the Lipari Islands 1961.*
Photo: Iain Crawford

**4** *The broch tower at Howe, Orkney.* Photo: B. Ballin Smith

**5** *The broch and settlement at Howe, Orkney.* Photo: B. Ballin Smith

**6** *The reconstructed Oakbank Crannog.* Photo: J. Miller

**7** *Structural timbers at Oakbank Crannog.* Photo: J. Miller

**8** *Woodland carr.* Photo: J. Miller

**9** *Selfheal.* Photo: J. Miller

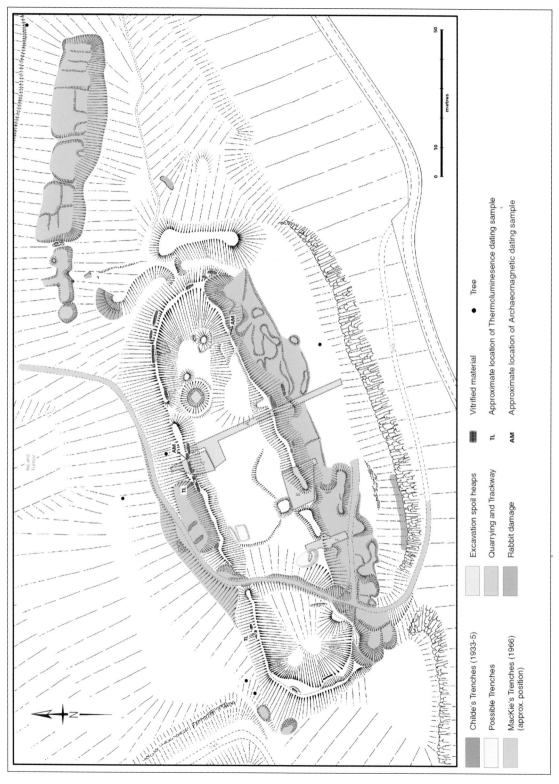

**Legend:**

Childe's Trenches (1933-5)

Possible Trenches

MacKie's Trenches (1966)
(approx. position)

Excavation spoil heaps

Quarrying and Trackway

Rabbit damage

Vitrified material

TL   Approximate location of Thermoluminesence dating sample

AM   Approximate location of Archaeomagnetic dating sample

•   Tree

Rig and Furrow

metres
0   10   50

**10**   *Colour coded map of Finavon Fort*

**11** *Interior of Allt na Cille souterrain.* Photo: R. Miket

**12** *The sub-rectangular homestead, Tungdale.* Photo: R. Miket

**13** *Allt na Cille loom weight.* Photo: R. Miket

**14** *The Udal S B satellite building. Note the grey phallic stone right of the central figure and the doorway to the main wheelhouse at the far right.* Photo: I. Crawford

**15** *Supposed Viking grave at Rubha Langannis, Canna.* Photo: J. Hunter

**16** *Exploratory excavation showing likely Columban foundation on Canna.*
Photo: J. Hunter

**17** *Remain of monastic foundation at Sgor nam Ban-naomha, Canna*
Photo: J. Hunter

**18** *Dun Beag broch near Struan, Skye.*
Crown Copyright: reproduced courtesy of Historic Scotland

**19** *The early Iron Age roundhouse excavated in Mound 11, Tofts Ness, Sanday, Orkney.*
Crown Copyright: Historic Scotland

**20** *The early Iron Age roundhouse, Tofts Ness, Sanday, Orkney.*
Crown Copyright: Historic Scotland

**21** *Old Scatness broch, roundhouse and wheelhouses.* Photo: S. Dockrill

**22** *Old Scatness broch, roundhouse and wheelhouses.* Photo: S. Dockrill

**23** *The remaining stonework of the broch with the excavated well.* Photo: B. Ballin Smith

**24** *The eroding promontory north of the broch with structures visible beneath the turf.*
Photo: B. Ballin Smith

**25** *Detail of the eroding structures in the promontory north of the broch.* Photo: B. Ballin Smith

**26** *Eroding wall with paving and other features between the broch and the ditch.* Photo: B. Ballin Smith

**27** *Structures revealed in the promontory south of the broch.* Photo: B. Ballin Smith

**28**  *Castletown oval brooch IL 221.*
Copyright: Trustees of the National Museums of Scotland

**29**  *Excavation of the crannog at Dumbuck: watercolour by William Donnelly.*
Crown Copyright: Royal Commission on the Ancient and Historical
Monuments of Scotland

# THE ROMANS AT NEWSTEAD, MELROSE.
### A CHARIOT RACE (2nd Century).

*From a Water Colour by Geo. Hope Tait*

Mercury urged the charioteers
That tore up the sacred ground,
And the Eildons echoed the merry cheers
Of a Roman victor crowned !

TRIMONTIUM.

SP·QR

The Romans fought and the Romans played,
And the Tweed went singing by,
And oft in the glade a Pictish maid
Would watch their chariots fly.

**30** *A postcard printed at the time of the excavations by James Curle and preserved in one of Curle's notebooks.* Crown Copyright: Royal Commission on the Ancient and Historical Monuments of Scotland

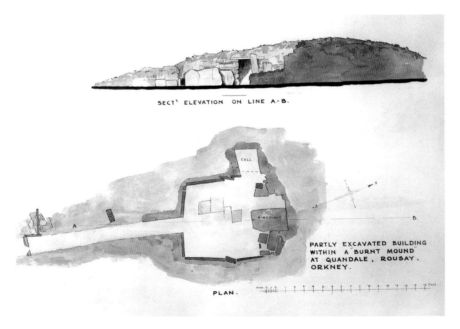

SECT' ELEVATION ON LINE A-B.

PARTLY EXCAVATED BUILDING WITHIN A BURNT MOUND AT QUANDALE, ROUSAY, ORKNEY.

PLAN.

**31** *Burnt Mound at Quandale, Rousay, Orkney, from the portfolio prepared by David Wilson for Walter Grant and now preserved in the Orkney Archive.* Crown Copyright: Royal Commission on the Ancient and Historical Monuments of Scotland

# 10  Saints and sinners
## The archaeology of the late Iron Age in the Western Isles

*J.R. Hunter*

## Background

The later Iron Age in northern Scotland is a period which traditionally extends from the decline of brochs: the perceived end of monumental architecture, marker of sociological change, and main focus of Euan MacKie's contribution to Scottish archaeology, through to the dramatic beginnings of the Viking Age which offered a new cultural infusion and language. The intervening half millennium, effectively sandwiched between two distinctive forces has, until recently, been a less fashionable area of study in the Western Isles. It has an uncomfortable inheritance, which to any new student of the period might seem to rely overly on the recorded wanderings of holy men, and on the discovery of antiquities from eroded dunes handed in by excited tourists. The aim of this paper is to provide a less emotive view of the material evidence and to outline some key elements of the period, particularly in relation to the effects of the early Church (**41**).

In the Western Isles the period is host to several different influences: Picts to the north and north-west; growing Irish contact already visible in the ceramic record from the middle Iron Age; the onset of Christian missions and monasticism (including influences from Northumbria creeping in post-Whitby by the end of the seventh century), and a consolidated Kingdom of Dal Riata in the south-east. Cultural diversity and ambiguity are inevitable and are often manifest in the archaeological record as difficulties of stratigraphic definition and as absence of structural continuity. There are also problems of defining diagnostic remains, particularly of pottery sequences (e.g. Topping 1987; Lane 1990). Happily, however, no longer viewed as a 'dark age', the period is slowly becoming better understood, and its outline can be sketched out against the somewhat misty political geography of the time (e.g. Armit 1990a; Foster 1996; Gilmour 2000). Much more is now known of contemporary settlement, particularly of cellular buildings, of agriculture and craft, of burials and of perceived hierarchies, although there is less tangible evidence for the Christian missions which tend to dominate the documentary history of the time, or of the nature, extent and impact of the Norse settlement which followed.

The extremes of the period are not open to exact dating and also have regional characteristics. The shift of settlement away from brochs is perceived as gradual and not closely datable, and has also been skewed by the misconception that many structures lying within the shadow of brochs were later enveloped settlements rather than buildings contemporary with the brochs themselves (e.g. Hedges 1990). Even these have been subject to the dangerous

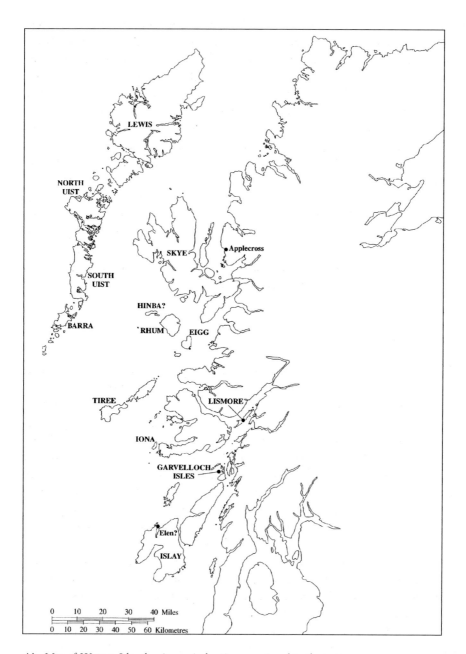

**41** *Map of Western Isles showing main locations mentioned in the text*

assertions of structural morphology, which saw cellular buildings as the precursors of rectangular buildings, now fortunately discarded as a cultural and chronological indicator (Armit 1991, 204). As further proof, excavations at Bornish have produced buildings of both Iron Age and Norse periods which fail to conform to expected structural stereotypes (Sharples 1997); there is also evidence from Kilpheder, South Uist, where Norse buildings took on a distinctly regional flavour with the use of sunken or revetted features (Brennand *et al.* 1998; Sharples and Parker Pearson 1999, fig. 7). In any event, the date of the incoming Scandinavians has no single fixed point, tending to hang on documented plundering in the late part of the eighth century. There is the additional problem of attempting archaeological distinction between the chronology of Viking contact and the chronology of Viking settlement. Thus the period is not one of exact definitions: the terminals are necessarily imprecise and the material culture can often only be outlined in broad terms. Even the beginnings of the period inherit the umbrella term 'Atlantic roundhouse' to cover a range of morphologically similar structures which defy closer definition (Armit 1990b). In contrast, however, is the ironic precision of the occasional documentary reference detailing selected saintly movements and noteworthy Viking atrocities to the exact year.

## Secular archaeology

The period as a whole has been the subject of various approaches, many of which have viewed the Western Isles simply as the geographical context for early Christianity, drawing together a range of historical and hagiographical sources and interpreting the relationships between secular and ecclesiastical power-mongers. Field archaeology has been an underused component, except at Iona itself which has been investigated by a distinguished list of worthies (see O'Sullivan 1998) and which has enabled a more rigorous view of monastic economics to take place. By contrast the role of field archaeology in the understanding of secular settlement has been more progressive (see Armit 1990a; 1996), stemming from Beveridge's antiquarian activities through to the last decade of more intensive area study, notably on Lewis, on the Bhaltos peninsula (e.g. Armit 1994), which has provided a wealth of new data from sites such as Cnip and Loch na Berie, and at Bostadh Beach where important new structural remains have been discovered (Neighbour 2001), as well as on North Uist, at Eilean Olabhat (Armit *et al.* forthcoming). These presumably represent the type of population centre that Christianity, fed by the Ionan mission, would serve but for which no infrastructure is yet evident (**42**). On the basis of interpreted early Christian cemeteries at sites such as Galson, Lewis (Neighbour *et al*, forthcoming) these missions met with some success. Nevertheless, the first dimly seen relationship between Church and population occurs only later in the Norse period where the distribution of *cill* chapels may reflect elements of some otherwise unproven population spread.

The character of pre-Norse settlement is one of small cellular buildings, often irregularly devised, but sufficiently numerous to be recognisable as architectural forms in their own right (Armit 1990c, 65) and with sufficient morphological parallels in the Northern Isles to suggest common stock. These similarities are unsurprising considering that the Northern Isles and the outer Western Isles are ostensibly Pictish by this time, whereas the inner Western Isles

**42** *Post-wheelhouse cellular building at Cnip, Lewis.* After Armit

looked politically to Dal Riata. However, structural similarity is not fully supported by other evidence: the location of Pictish symbol stones places little emphasis on the outer isles (Foster 1996, fig. 47); few of the Celtic placenames of the Western Isles are likely to be pre-Norse (Harding 1990, 14); and the distribution of *pit-* names, traditionally a key to Pictish settlement concentrations, moves no further west than Glen Elg to the east of Skye (Whittington 1975, fig. 1). These differences are greater than those which might be explained by regional diversity alone. To complicate matters, placename studies in the Western Isles run the additional problem of foundering through extensive and geographically selective replacement, by Norse and Scottish influences, and by a later Gaelic resurgence in the Middle Ages. Gilmour, however, argues that the morphological change to cellular forms is more fundamentally based, and may include an Irish parameter, possibly representing 'a more coherent political structure' for which the cellular building was somehow an architectural expression (2000, 163). His model is supported by evidence for trading and contact. It may, indirectly, presuppose an underlying Christian element.

Some sites are ascribed to the pre-Norse period by a process of elimination, because their cultural diagnostics are neither broch-like nor Viking in character. Therefore in the stratigraphic way of things they belong to this rather undefined period, particularly within earlier excavated sites, for example at A'Cheardach Mhor where the structural remains lie sandwiched stratigraphically between better recognised features (Young & Richardson 1960, 159). Ardnave, Islay, a site with a very specific economic contribution to make, provides a similar problem with hearths and enclosure walling representing the final phase in an Iron Age sequence. The site appears uncharacteristic of the earlier Iron Age and subsequent Norse periods but is not more closely datable (Ritchie & Welfare 1983). There are also sites on Barra, multi-cellular buildings which fail to fall within any other obvious chronological category (Branigan & Foster 1995, 45; fig. 3.10) and which may end up in this broadly-defined period of structures by a process of elimination.

Absence of strong diagnostic features might also be extended to graves where there is an inevitable tendency to allocate such burials to a late Iron Age no-man's land, for example Cnoc Aingil, Islay (Ritchie and Ritchie 1975, 208) which was dated to the mid-first millennium by analogy with a Caithness example. Pottery sequences offer little support and despite various working successes on the pottery of Iona, Topping was obliged to concede that the western prehistoric sequences were 'clearly more complex than has been generally recognised' (1985, 208). Lane identifies some of the problems: handmade wares persisting into the nineteenth century; the lack of major stratified collections; and the difficulties in understanding the significance of grasswares. There is strength in Lane's confirmation of long-held views of pottery links with Ireland, already postulated from Iona (Lane & Campbell 1988, 208-212), and of the ceramic separation between the north Hebrides and the area of Dal Riatian territory to the south (Lane 1990, 127). The consensus is that there is clearly no single overall pottery seriation and little in the way of a yardstick to help classify groups of unstratified material blown free from sand, although some local sequences are now being identified on South Uist (Sharples & Parker Pearson 1999, 46). At Mangersta on Lewis material eroded from a dune face included both pottery and Norse metalwork (Carson 1976), and on Coll and Tiree unstratified pottery (especially grass-marked/tempered wares) has presented a difficult basis for interpreting the likely periods of eroding settlements (see also Crawford 1997).

To some extent Viking studies in the Western Isles serve to endorse many of these difficulties and have been comprehensively reviewed (see Graham Campbell and Batey 1998). Until recently (and with notable exceptions) research design has been countered by serendipity due to the unpredictable but well-attested natural movement of sand. It is a period which has traditionally relied heavily on unstratified finds, many from the last century and collated by Grieg in his 1940 corpus. One of the critical features has been the source integrity of the Norse material of which a considerable proportion is open to some doubt including, for example, some long-standing 'Norse' graves on Canna, which have appeared on distribution maps. One in particular at Rubha Langannis (**colour plate 15**), argued as a Norse grave by analogy with Norwegian examples by Sommerfelt and by the cist-like similarity to graves of the Kiloran Bay type (1984, 235), is now legally scheduled as such. Alcock has argued that it is not a Norse grave, instead offering the interpretation of structural foundations for this and similar remains on the island (1983). Geophysical survey and keyhole excavations in 1994 demonstrated that one hillside example (not scheduled) seemed not to be a burial: the earth had been cleared to bedrock and the infilling was natural and sterile without any anthropogenic material (Hunter 1994). Similar inland features on Barra, described as 'enlarged cists', have been interpreted, among other things, as corpse platforms, although not of the Viking period (Branigan & Foster 1995, figs 3.11 and 176).

The Commission's 1984 Inventory of Islay, Jura, Colonsay and Oronsay, for example, identifies some 11 individual graves with almost a similar number being questionable. All but one of these were recovered from sand dune contexts as the result of erosion or chance finds rather than from organised research-orientated excavation, a feature which characterises the validity of the database but which is rarely emphasised when lists of Norse finds in the Western Isles are trotted out (but see Graham Campbell and Batey 1998, Chapter 5). Typical examples include 'loose' grave finds possibly of occupation origin on Islay (Gordon 1990), tortoise brooch fragments picked up on Harris, a gold arm ring found by divers in the Sound of Jura, bridal mounts washed out of a sand midden on Lewis and items handed over to an Austrian Countess on Skye because she was known to be interested in antiquities (Graham-Campbell 1975; 1983; 1986 and 1982 respectively), not to mention the salvage of a burial on Uig, Lewis under the auspices of forensic examination (Welander *et al.* 1987). This was undertaken hurriedly, in the words of the excavators due to 'the unconcealed interest of holiday makers' (*ibid.* 153). The same site, at Cnip, has since revealed other burials, excavated under more controlled conditions, and attests to a major Viking Age cemetery (Cowie *et al.* 1993; Dunwell *et al.* 1995). To this picture we can add the discovery, on this occasion by systematic fieldwork, of a cist burial at Machrins, Colonsay on the same island as the much vaunted glamour grave at Kiloran Bay. In likely association lay circular or part-circular structures dated to around AD 800, possibly used seasonally, with useful ecofactual data (Ritchie 1981).

Structural remains of the Viking period itself, or of the interface period which leads into it, are still comparatively rare. The earlier excavated domestic dwelling at Drimore on South Uist (Maclaren 1974) has no obvious local predecessor, contemporary or successor, although this may be a consequence of the relatively small area opened. Elsewhere, the Udal, North Uist is the only excavated site to have shown continuous settlement from the Iron Age through to the Middle Ages; it does so in a manner which, the excavator argues, overcomes the dislocation of continuity and chronology that has traditionally plagued the subject (Crawford & Switsur 1977, 124). The site sees Iron Age polycellular structures emerging with increasing sophistication into the ninth century where they become superimposed by rectangular structures of the Viking Age. The circumstances of this are described as 'very sudden' and 'strongly suggest violence' (*ibid.* 24), but are at odds with findings in the Northern Isles where evidence at Birsay, Buckquoy, Pool and Skaill points towards more peaceful assimilation of cultures (Hunter 1997). Results of survey and preliminary excavations have suggested that this also appears to be the case in the machair at Kilpheder and at Bornish, South Uist where groups of mounds indicate continuity of occupation, demonstrating localised settlement shift around a traditional focus (Sharples & Parker Pearson 1999). Discontinuity appears to occur not with the arrival of the Vikings, but somewhat later after the islands had been incorporated into the Scottish kingdom (*ibid.* 48). Ironically, exploration of two reputed Norse burial grounds in the Bornish vicinity proved fruitless. Given the thin local soil cover, it was proposed that cemeteries may have been located in the deeper sand promontories, since eroded or washed away completely. Conversely, in the Bhaltos area in Lewis, despite the relative density of Norse graves and placenames in the vicinity, the location of associated

Norse settlement persistently defies identification (Armit 1994, 82f). The extent of continuity through from the earlier Iron Age is still to be fully identified.

Research by Cox (1989) and by the Alcocks (1980) has demonstrated the difficulties of trying to apply placename modelling to resolve problems of settlement and settlement continuity. There are, however, a number of features worthy of comment: the propensity towards Scandinavian names in the outer isles, particularly in Lewis; a decreasing frequency of Scandinavian names from north to south in the inner isles; and a particular density of names applied to both settlements and natural features on Islay. There is useful scope for analysis in Nicolaisen's early assertion that *stadir* names preceded *setr* names in the Norse settlement process (1969, 17), the former being particularly abundant in Lewis and in the north part of Skye. He identified a different distribution for *bolstadr* (outlying farm) and also for *dalr* (valley), which interestingly includes the former Dal Riatan territory and which might be viewed as representing areas of contact as opposed to denser settlement. Despite later modification, elements of the argument are still maintained (*ibid.* 1989). Even in diluted form the argument suggests a Scandinavian density which, with some exceptions, is northern and peripheral rather than evenly weighted, although there is little in the archaeological record other than pottery distribution to support it (Graham Campbell & Batey 1998, fig. 3.5).

## Ecclesiastical archaeology

The history of the region, both secular and ecclesiastical, is undoubtedly warped by the strength of the Columban tradition from the later part of the sixth century. Adamnan's biography of Columba is probably one of the more biased of contemporary sources (Sharpe 1995), but is one cited most frequently and must carry some of the blame for Iona being perceived as a 'cultural transit camp' (Smyth 1984, 79). The foundation on Iona was both political and pastoral in its focus on Dal Riata and spawned a scatter of monasteries and religious houses ranging between the extremes of Loch Awe (Cella Diuni) and Skye. Their pastoral function (or lack of it) has been the subject of discussion (e.g. Clancy & Markus 1995, 23f) and has been summarised by Foster as part of a wider review (1997). Further afield, and out with areas of political sanction, Iona's voice was more muted.

On Iona itself the land appears to have been cultivated throughout the Iron Age, although Adamnan makes no mention of an earlier lay population. The nature of monastic lifestyle, its organisation and aestheticism, has been documented fully elsewhere (e.g. RCHAMS 1982, 44f; Barber 1981, 364-66) and need not be recounted here, save to emphasise the relatively sophisticated economy identified from plaggen soils deliberately introduced and supplemented by kitchen waste (Shiel 1988), the likelihood of horizontal milling (O'Sullivan 1994a), the variety of diet from both domestic and wild species (Barber 1981, 315ff), and the nature of contact abroad evidenced not only from north African pottery, but also from the large collection of later carved stones showing influences from Ireland, Northumbria and the Mediterranean (e.g. RCAHMS 1982; Robertson 1975; Smyth 1984, 126). It is clear too that the structural evidence (such as it is) is distinct from what little is known of secular counterparts, for example in timber, or in O'Sullivan's eighth- to twelfth-century unicameral church with clay-bonded masonry and with lime mortar on inner and outer faces (1994b, 332). Adamnan complements this with at least one vivid account of the transportation of timber across from Mull (Sharpe 1995, *Cap* 46) as well as a comprehensive description of buildings and materials, a description confirmed by Barber whose Brugelesque vision of 'huts or wattle and daub and larger wooden buildings' frequented by monks some 'well shod and others in soleless stockings' was based on primary material evidence (1981, 366).

Iona's geographical position and growing reputation consolidated the transit route between Ireland and the Scottish west coast, already developed in the earlier Iron Age, now becoming a recognised passage for career saints in the making, notably Brendan, Cormac, Maelrubai, and Donnan, each in the words of Adamnan, 'seeking a desert in the ocean' (Sharpe 1995, *Cap* 6). By the end of the seventh century, and in most cases well before, the monastic network was extended (**41**): to Applecross; to Rhum; to the three centres on Tiree – Artchain, Bledach and Mag Luinge; to the Garvelloch Isles (RCAHMS 1984, no. 354); to Lismore; to the unlocated centres of Elen; to Hinba (possibly on Canna or Jura); and to Eigg where Donnan the founder may have received less than full support from Dal Riata and therefore less later historical acclaim (Smyth 1984, 110). The fact that many Donnain dedications appear to belong to the north and west Hebrides rather than to the south and east may further reflect a geographical division based on political foundations and a different patronage from the one which sponsored Columba. Columba's network was shrewdly sited both for political expedience and for facilitating eastward movement to achieve ultimate conversion of the Pictish kingdom based near Inverness. There is good reason to see Columba less perhaps as the incognito warlord that Smyth suggests (*ibid.*, 99), and more as a strategist providing an important link between secular and ecclesiastical power bases.

On the ground, however, and using the list of early religious foundations compiled by Cowan and Easson (1976) the evidence is harder to find beyond Iona itself which has been well investigated. Applecross shows later ecclesiastical development but mostly in the form of sculpture; the site has been affected by forestry work although the remains of an oval enclosure are traceable (Thomas 1971, 41). Despite a peppering of cross-marked stones, there is less than satisfactory evidence for the three reputed sites on Tiree: Archain is recorded as showing 'no visible remains' and is believed to be 'mistakenly identified' (RCAHMS 1980, no. 259), Bledach is unlocated, and Mag Luinge is tentatively associated with the former site and burial ground of Soroby (*ibid.*, no.327) where the last traces were removed during the first half of the nineteenth century. An alternative site of early Christian activity might be found at Ceann a' Mhara where there is topographical evidence for an enclosure, chapel and associated structures (RCAHMS 1980, no. 325). On the Garvelloch Isles where the location can probably be identified from later (?Norse) remains, a full record has been made showing the multiplicity of buildings and arrangements (RCAHMS 1984, no. 354), and a likely site has been identified for Lismore (MacDonald 1973) but no further work has occurred. The monastery at Elen has been possibly identified with Nave Island on Islay (RCAHMS 1984, no. 383) lying below a medieval chapel. The foundation on Rhum remains unlocated, and on Eigg targeted investigation was unsuccessful in identifying Donnan's church, vallum and reputed grave (Macdonald 1973).

This leaves Hinba, possibly on Jura according to some sources (RCHAMS 1984, 27; no. 331) in a location altered by later ecclesiastical activity or, as Campbell considers (1984 5f), on the island of Canna in the location of the standing cross at A' Chill which depicts Hiberno-Norse characteristics (RCAHMS 1928, no. 678). The site, formerly the 'main town' on the island until the clearances of 1851, is recorded as having contained a small derelict chapel, burial ground and some 20 domestic structures all of which were used to provide building material for the sheep dyke which encompasses that part of the island. Records tell how local worthies rescued the best-carved stones and hid them in the ground. Geophysical survey on the island has been used to identify a rectangular structure measuring *c*.20 by 6m whose central axis was aligned to the standing cross and which appeared to be circumscribed by a boundary wall. The deployment of a narrow trench (**colour plate 16**) not only confirmed the existence of the walling, but also the ecclesiastical nature of the structure by virtue of imported building materials and disturbed burials, the existence of earlier flooring and, possibly most interesting of all, the presence of an underlying burial cairn (presumably pagan). The graveyard boundary had been rebuilt, probably in the fourteenth century according to the pottery, which would be in keeping with the size and character of the associated building. The location is clearly a burial site of some antiquity. The pagan origin, the earlier medieval floors and the adjacent ninth-century standing cross, indicate a degree of continuity encompassing the early spread of monasticism from Iona.

These are just the recorded foundations according to Adamnan and others. Further examples clearly existed, on North Rona, Annait on Skye (RCHAMS 1928, no. 499) despite its problems of interpretation, and possibly also Loch Chaluim Chille in Kilmuir (*ibid.*, no. 535), in a system which seems to have had little in the way of territorial organisation other than constraints imposed by the prevailing political climate. According to models proposed for contemporary Ireland, the nature and size of the individual establishments and the extent to which each was expected to undertake pastoral mission seem likely to have varied (for discussion see Foster 1997). There are, for example, those foundations which may not have been considered noteworthy – to use the Commission's phrase 'shadowy Irish missionaries working independently of Iona' (1982, 45), possibly identified by *papa* names. It is interesting that of the nine *papa* names in the west seven lie in the outer isles and only two (on Skye and Rum) to the east (Macdonald 1977, 28). Additionally, there are those establishments of relatively late foundation, or even those too politically sensitive for Adamnan's purpose, lying out with Dal Riata: two contenders here might include Howmore on South Uist (RCAMHS 1928, no. 367) and Cille-bharra on Barra (*ibid.*, no. 436). Other variables include the issue of dedications and the complex processes by which traditionally strong Celtic names might be reasserted; these may explain some of the Columban dedications in the outer isles.

Reference to the Commission volumes, particularly the 1984 *Inventory* for Islay, Jura, Colonsay and Oronsay, illustrates all too well the difficulty of dating ecclesiastical monuments by typology, carved stone and stray memorial. There are, for example, the *cill* sites, of which there are over a dozen on Islay alone, consisting of burial grounds and small chapels, traditionally argued to run into the twelfth century and reflect the geography of Norse settlement. However, the profusion is such that some at least may have earlier origins, although whatever patterning survives is opaque and attempts to extrapolate it back in time, notably by Professor Cant (1984), demonstrate the difficulties. Some later sites also contain tantalisingly early sculpture, at Kildalton and Kilnave on Islay, with distinctive art-historical links to eighth-century Iona (RCAHMS 1984, 29). Two early crosses on St Kilda, one found in a cleit roof and one in a cottage wall, also point to the early origins of chapels last recorded in the island during the nineteenth century (Harman 1977). Many of these sites will never be resolved without excavation, for example Sgor nam Ban-naomha (place of the holy women; **colour plate 17**) on Canna, which emerges through the ferns during the winter and possesses all the trappings of classic Celtic monasticism (RCAHMS 1928, no. 679; Macdonald 1973). Some have even been lost: the site of Cill Donnain on South Uist which was unrecorded in the 1928 Inventory was 'rediscovered' on an island promontory by the Sheffield SEARCH group and shows vallum, central chapel and outer sites with associated structures. Dating however can only be by analogy with the twelfth century according to parallels with bicameral churches in the Northern Isles (Fleming & Woolf 1992, 342).

Considering their historical and cultural impact, many of these early foundations remain remarkably intangible partly through the later development of the same site, partly through the profusion of later church building and the retention of characteristic layouts, and partly because their location may be uncertain. Other detrimental elements almost certainly include factors of Viking activity although this may be overstated. There is a world of difference between the early cut-throat, beer-vomiting heroes to which Smyth alludes (1984, 142) who savaged the population of the Hebrides according to the pages of the *Orkneyinga Saga*, and those who later tilled the soils and sheltered under the broadening umbrella of Christianity. The graveyard at Iona continued in use throughout the Norse period and there is now much argument suggesting that the monastery retained its status throughout the period of Scandinavian incursions (Veitch 1997; Jennings 1998), although the main monastic population was forced to move to Kells in the early ninth century. Olaf Curaran, former King of Dublin, made it his retirement home in 980 a short time before Olaf Trygvasson proclaimed Christianity the official religion. This not only legitimised the growth and organisation of chapel building, but also denied archaeologists the ability to date a Norse grave beyond the end of the tenth century.

The whole concept of a Christian landscape still finds reluctant support although one of the key elements, the nature of land taken or given by secular power for monastic purpose, is now more widely recognised. Alcock has already identified the targeting of prime land (1987, 90) and Lamb has shown how best-quality land may have been a prerequisite for major monastic foundation (1995), an argument which he has explored further with the Petrine dedications in Orkney and Shetland. It may well be that investigation should now be directed towards factors of economics rather than to chasing deserts in the ocean, and that monastic archaeology, its effect on local society, and its reflection of population infrastructure should be pushed higher up the list of research priorities. Although the Western Isles are now much more in the mainstream of archaeological research the period still tends to divide the innocent lay population, the Christian, and Viking in a discrete way reflecting study traditions in the three respective interests. The role of the Church in particular, its organisation in pre-Norse times as well as in Norse times, remains substantially conjectural. The period is one of profound social change; it has neither chronological nor geographical consistency; and its optimum understanding will only emerge from the integration of the various themes, not in their continued separation.

# 11  The Western Isles pottery sequence

*Ewan Campbell*

## Introduction

Recent work, both excavation and scientific dating, is helping to clarify the sequence of pottery in the Western Isles. This paper will concentrate on the southern part of the *'Long Island'*, from Barra to North Uist, and cover the last three millennia of pottery development. This is largely an interim statement, as much work is in progress, both in this area, particularly by the Sheffield/Cardiff universities SEARCH project, and in the northern part of the Isles, with the Edinburgh University projects in Lewis and North Uist.

As is well known, the Western isles have a tradition of hand-built pottery that is continuous from the Neolithic to the twentieth century, in contrast to most other areas of western Britain where long periods were aceramic (Lane 1990). The study of the pottery sequence has been controversial, particularly over the typological sequence in the Iron Age and its chronology, for example the date of the middle Iron Age 'Clettraval' style (Young 1966; MacKie 1974; Topping 1987; Lane 1990; Armit 1991 and Campbell 1991). Part of the problem is the unique difficulty of dating in the Hebridean environment, where the lack of charcoal, the use of old peat, marine reservoir effects and lack of coinage combine to rule out many conventional methods of independent dating of deposits. More recently recognised problems of taphonomy, residuality and stratigraphic interpretation in the machair environment compound the issue. This paper was stimulated by a programme of AMS dating of charred food residues, which attempted to circumvent some of these problems by direct dating of pottery vessels (Campbell 2000 and Campbell *et al.* forthcoming).

The pottery of Hebridean sites is also difficult to study for more mundane reasons. The fabric of almost all vessels is formed from glacial clays composed of much-decayed Lewisian gneiss and minerals derived from these metamorphic rocks, which comprise the bedrock over almost all the Isles. However, there are great variations in colour and temper density which can cause the unwary to erect a multitude of fabric types which have no real validity, merely reflecting that the bedrock is very variable in its mineralogy over very short distances, or the result of irregular firing in clamp kilns. The number of sherds is also an issue. The Post-Roman levels at the Udal produced about 40,000 sherds (Lane 1990, 117) and the broch at Dun Vulan 19,000 (Parker Pearson & Sharples 1999, 199). Many of these sherds are, however, plain body sherds and it is often difficult to reconstruct vessel profiles due to the fragmentation of the poorly-fired wares. The wheelhouse at Sollas was unusual in that although there were only 3,000 sherds, more complete profiles could be reconstructed than, for example, at

Dun Vulan because there were pits containing fairly complete vessels. Although the basic fabric is rock-tempered, varying amounts of organic material can be incorporated. On some sites such as Sollas organic temper appears to be chronologically significant (Campbell 1991, illus 13), but at the Udal North Hill it is not (Lane 1983). One further problem is a continuing confusion in the region between grass-marked pottery (characteristic of Norse assemblages) and grass-tempered pottery, and the fact that some of the grass used in tempering is very fine *Festuca* sp. grasses (Campbell 1991, 150), which the uninitiated can fail to recognise. This makes it difficult to cross-compare assemblages as it can be uncertain whether similar terms are being used in fabric descriptions on different sites.

Despite these problems, it has become apparent with recent excavations that there is an identifiable sequence of pottery forms in the area, an outline of which is presented below.

## Late Bronze Age

The excavations in South Uist at Cladh Hallan have provided the first detailed study of a late Bronze Age settlement in the area. A series of roundhouses, with one having at least eight phases of flooring, enable an excellent sequence to be determined. The pottery consists of simple upright jars with an inturned upper profile. There are a variety of rim forms, and it has been suggested that there is a sequence from T-shaped rims in the lowest levels, through flat-topped to rounded and thickened rims in the latest levels (Marshall *et al.* 1999, 3). This preliminary sequence will need to be ratified by full publication, but the important point is that the vessel form stays fairly constant throughout the sequence, and there is a lack of decoration. There are problems with the dating due to the calibration problems in the early Iron Age, but a series of radiocarbon dates indicate a start to the settlement around the turn of the second millennium BC, and the latest levels somewhere in the middle of the first millennium BC.

## Early Iron Age

The beginning of the Iron Age sequence is best seen at the Eilean Olabhat site in North Uist (Armit *et al.* forthcoming). Here there is a stone-built roundhouse with a modified entrance flanked by piers, which seems to be an early stage in the development of the characteristic middle Iron Age wheelhouse. The pottery associated with the early phases (Phases I and II) differs from that at Cladh Hallan, and some of the forms are so far unique. The main form still appears to be a simple bucket shape, but it is much squatter in the only complete profile which can be reconstructed. There are a variety of rims, including slightly out-splayed forms. Unusual constructional features include vessels with unsmoothed inner coil surfaces, and vessels with the impression of coarse woven grass matting on the base. Most significantly, however, by Phase II there is the first appearance of decoration. This includes fingermarking below the rim, applied thick cordons, and coarse incised chevrons. There is also an unusual applied ring with circular impressions. These types of decoration are clearly predecessors of the more accomplished schemes of the middle Iron Age, but coarser and more roughly executed. Dating of charred food residues on the interiors of some vessels indicate a fourth-century BC date for these phases (Campbell *et al.* forthcoming).

This site is important as it is one of the few that appear to date to this period. Most of the Eilean Olabhat vessels are thicker than middle Iron Age examples, but the fabric is generally similar. One exception is a few sherds in very coarse rock-tempered fabric, similar to the fabric of 'Dunagoil ware' found principally in pre-broch and primary levels at Dun Mor Vaul (MacKie 1974, fig. 21), and other sites such as Dunadd (Lane & Campbell 2000, 105). Although the early dating of the sequence at Dun Mor Vaul has been questioned (Lane 1990, 113), there does seem to be a horizon of use of this type of fabric in the middle first millennium BC in the Western Isles, even if the fabric may be diachronic over wider areas, such as eastern and southern Scotland (Lane 1990, 112). The fabric is found at Dun Vulan in a pre-broch level with a *terminus post quem* of eighth/fifth century BC (AA-22916; 2435 ± 50 BP) and sealed by a level with second-first-century BC dates (Parker Pearson & Sharples 1999, 58, 210); in a context dated to the fourth century BC at Eilean Olabhat (Ox-A 6949: 2205 ± 50 BP); and in levels (Phase IA) dated to the fourth/third century BC (GU-2464: 2280 ± 50 BP) at Dunadd (Lane & Campbell 2000, 84). It may be that this very coarse pottery is a distinctive early Iron Age fabric in the Western Isles, which along with the beginnings of decoration on thick vessels, will help to identify sites of this period.

## Middle Iron Age

Much of the controversy over Iron Age assemblages has been over the variety of middle Iron Age types, as these provide the main body of distinctive forms. The wheelhouses at Sollas was one of the best dated middle Iron Age sites (Campbell 1991), and now has a series of new AMS dates on charred food remains to extend the sequence of dates originally obtained (Campbell *et al.* forthcoming). The sequence worked out at Sollas confirmed Alison Young's earlier (Young & Richardson 1960) sequence of incised vessels with 'weak rims' to sharply everted rims with channelled and arcaded decoration, and finally plain vessels with long flaring rims. The original Sollas report suggested that the emergence of the sharply everted rim dated to the first-second centuries AD (Campbell 1991, 168). The new dates show that the earlier structure, wheelhouse A, was abandoned around the second century AD, and presumably the new structure of wheelhouse B was constructed at this time. The complete lack of everted rim pottery on site A confirms the late introduction of this style. At Dun Vulan, a second or third century AD date was suggested, though some material occurs in levels dated to the first/second centuries (Parker Pearson & Sharples 1998, 210). The phase of decorated middle Iron Age pottery (Sollas types A-C), which predates everted rim ware at Sollas, therefore dates to the centuries around the first millennium BC/AD boundary and probably emerged gradually from the early Iron Age forms of the fourth/third century BC. The one Type D vessel from Sollas (Campbell 1991, illus. 15: 442) probably dates to this early/middle transition phase and is from the earliest context on the site.

Although there is one example of a double-cordoned vessel at Sollas, all the other pottery is of decorated middle Iron Age types, so it is not possible to date the end of the decorated sequence here. There are some late dates from the site amongst the AMS determinations, but there are technical problems with the process of dating charred food residues, which suggest that these cannot be relied on, as they may be younger than their true age.

## Late Iron Age

The late Iron Age house at Bornais Mound 1 provides a key link in the sequence from middle to late Iron Age in South Uist. Here the pottery is all undecorated apart from cordons, and the basics forms are double-cordoned or plain flaring rim types (sometimes referred to as Dun Cueir ware). Dates bracket the second (final) phase of occupation to between the third/fourth and fifth/sixth centuries AD (Sharples 2000, 25). The only other reliable dates for this type of pottery come from the Phase 3 deposits at Eilean Olabhat. Here, the charred food remains of a vessel date to the fifth/sixth centuries AD (Ox-A 6946: 1575 ± 45; Ox-A 6947: 1590 ± 50 BP). A range of fourth to sixth centuries AD seems likely, confining the decorated pottery of the everted rim phase to the second and third centuries AD.

The last part of the late Iron Age is exemplified by the sequence at the Udal North Hill. The only form in the pre-Norse levels is the Plain Style of Lane (1983; 1990), which includes flaring rim and straight-side bucket forms which remain unchanged until the postulated Norse levels. The published dates suggest a range from the third/fourth century to the eighth/ninth, but the dates are unreliable because of the very large standard deviations (Lane 1990, 120). The lack of cordons suggests that the earliest levels post-date the Eilean Olabhat Phase 3 and Bornais Mound 1 sequences, and a start date for the North Hill sequence before the sixth century AD seems unlikely.

## Norse

The general categorization of Norse pottery has been outlined by Lane (1990, 122-3), but there are problems with the dating of the sequence. At the Udal there is a transition from Plain Style pottery to an entirely new suite of forms including platters, flat-bottomed bowls and cups. The date of this transition is problematic, but the single radiocarbon date and a decorated strap end could suggest a tenth-century start to the 'Norse' tradition. The disc-shaped platters seem to be skeumorphs of bakestones, which are characteristic of Late Norse sites in the Northern Isles and Scandinavia (Graham-Campbell & Batey 1998, 223). Unless one argues that the stone parallels are in fact skeumorphs of the pottery platters, this early dating at the Udal is a problem. At the recently-excavated Norse house at Cille Pheadair, South Uist, the earliest levels did not contain platters but they do appear in levels with imported Wiltshire pottery of the late eleventh or twelfth century and are still present at the end of the settlement in the thirteenth century (Brennand *et al.* 1998). The lack of platters in the early layers may be due to many factors, but it seems that the distinctive platters may continue quite late into the medieval sequence and may be a feature of later Norse levels. At Bornais Mound 2, platters were again found with imported twelfth-century pottery in the secondary floor of the Norse house (Sharples 2000, 18).

## Medieval to modern

This is perhaps the most obscure period in Hebridean pottery studies, but a few recent excavations have helped to establish a sketchy outline chronology and sequence of development. At the

Udal, Lane noted the appearance of spare incised and impressed decoration in the Late Norse sequence, continuing on into the medieval sequence, which was not studied by him. In the final structures at Eilean Olabhat (Phase 4) there are some distinctive small bag-shaped jars with impressed decoration on the top of the rim and the upright neck. Small hollow bones appear to have been used for this. These are in a hard, black fabric, which is more highly fired than Iron Age/Norse wares. There is no dating for this assemblage, but similar vessels with stabbing and impressed decoration have also turned up on Barra shieling sites (Campbell forthcoming), and in field walking on medieval sites in south Uist (Parker Pearson pers. comm.). Related forms, with a different pattern of decoration, are present in the lowest levels at Breachacha Castle, Coll, which date to the fifteenth/sixteenth century (Turner & Dunbar 1970, fig. 13, nos. I.1, I.2). There seems to be a pattern emerging in which the Late Norse vessel forms with rounded bottoms give way to globular forms that continue to be the main form up till the end of production in the twentieth century. This author suggests the transition took place around the fourteenth century and lasted perhaps until the sixteenth century. In South Uist it is associated with the major settlement shift from the machair location of the prehistoric/Norse period, to the blacklands sites of the medieval and later periods (Sharples & Parker Pearson 1999, 59). One excavated site in North Uist, which is of significance, is the post-medieval settlement at Druim nan Dearcag (Armit 1997). Here there were small globular vessels with upright necks, but no decoration. The occupation was dated to the sixteenth/seventh centuries on the basis of imported glazed pottery, and perhaps indicates that decoration was dying out by that period.

There are few clues as to later developments that culminated in the craggans of the nineteenth century, which were recorded and collected by tourists and antiquarians (Cheape 1993). These crude, often lopsided globular jars with tall necks occur in a variety of sizes, but many are larger than the small medieval forms. One vessel from near Stornoway contained a seventeenth-century coin hoard (Cheape 1993, fig. 8). These vessels have a distinctive uneven surface, with their thickness formed by thumbing the clay, but they are as hard fired as the medieval examples. Similar wares have been found in profusion at the site of Dun Eistan, Lewis (Harry pers. comm.), which has associations with a Clan Morrison centre in the sixteenth/seventeenth centuries. It is difficult to see a progression in form through the post-medieval period given that there are so few dated examples. Occasional decoration of incised or impressed form occurs, but the vessels are mainly plain.

## Conclusion

This brief survey is an account of work in progress and by no means a definitive statement. The illustration (**43**) shows a rough outline of the proposed sequence of the more distinctive forms, but it should be noted that there are many simple forms, often bucket-shaped, which are frequently not identifiable to any period. Often it is the fabric which gives clues as to the date, not in terms of the clay body and inclusions, which are generally similar throughout the sequence, but in the surface finish and mode of construction. It should also be noted that the sequence given here does not necessarily apply to other areas of the Hebrides. Similar wares to Sollas Type Ax have recently been found in St Kilda on a site with middle Iron Age dates (R. Will pers. comm.), but the pottery is much thicker and cruder than on North Uist. To the

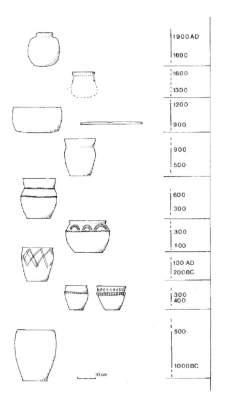

| | |
|---|---|
| 1900 AD | |
| 1600 | |
| 1600 | |
| 1300 | |
| 1200 | |
| 900 | |
| 900 | |
| 500 | |
| 600 | |
| 300 | |
| 300 | |
| 100 | |
| 100 AD | |
| 200 BC | |
| 300 | |
| 400 | |
| 500 | |
| 1000 BC | |

10 cm

**43** *Proposed outline of pottery sequence in Western Isles. Forms are schematic and roughly to scale*

north, the important site at Bereigh, Riof, on Lewis (Harding & Gilmour 2000) is in the process of publication and will establish a middle/late Iron Age sequence in this area. To the south, the island of Gunna has produced imported fifteenth-century medieval pottery in association with handmade wares (H. James pers. comm.) and study of this assemblage may help to establish if the southern Hebridean sequence can be tied into the northern one. At present, it is not even clear whether there are diachronic features within the region of the Uists, or even temporal or functional differences between neighbouring sites. The variety of decorative forms, particularly in the middle Iron Age where some features seem to be peculiar to individual sites, suggests that generalisations about stylistic development may be difficult to sustain.

The establishment of a basic sequence of pottery types is very much a traditional approach to pottery studies, but it is essential to the study of any area. It is perhaps surprising that this outline is the first to be attempted for an area of Britain that has been studied for over 100 years, but the peculiar nature of the pottery assemblages there make any study frustratingly difficult. It is sometimes impossible to be sure if a small assemblage is Iron Age, medieval or post-medieval, undermining the confidence of both the excavator and the pottery specialist in the ceramic evidence (cf. Topping 1986, 127-8). It is hoped this preliminary outline will help to redress the balance in favour of the pottery.

# 12  Dun Beag

## and the role of pottery in interpretations of the Hebridean Iron Age

*Ann MacSween*

## Introduction

The artefactual record of the Hebridean Iron Age, despite its rich and varied nature, has seldom been central to recent interpretations (Sharples forthcoming; Smith forthcoming). Instead, research has focused primarily on the structural record (Armit & Ralston 1997, 170). In particular, assemblages from old excavations are often disregarded by researchers because they are perceived to be incompatible with more recently-excavated material and unsuitable for sustaining wider discussions. The result is that many of these assemblages are used by researchers only to provide examples of comparative material.

Using the pottery assemblage from the broch of Dun Beag, Skye (**colour plate 18**) as a case study, this paper concludes that while the vagaries of old excavation techniques undoubtedly hinder the interpretation of some aspects of the material record, our present methodologies are also detrimental to its wider interpretation. In spite of much active research over the last few decades there remain significant gaps in our understanding of the ceramic record and consequently in its use in interpretations of the Hebridean Iron Age.

At a recent conference on aspects of the Iron Age in Scotland (Circular Arguments: the Archaeology of Roundhouses, University of Glasgow, October 1999), Euan MacKie drew attention to the lack of good artefactual sequences for the period, and called for this to be addressed. This paper is offered to encourage more detailed recording and more critical analysis of coarse pottery, both during the excavation and post-excavation of sites in the Hebrides, with the aim of providing the information base necessary to tackle some of the questions pertinent to our understanding of the archaeology of that area.

## Dun Beag: The site and its finds

Dun Beag in Skye was excavated by Countess Vincent Baillet de Latour between 1914 and 1920. The finds were presented to the National Museums of Scotland and published by the new Keeper of Archaeology, J.G. Callander, in the following year (Callander 1921). The report includes this account, which illustrates something of the scale and technique of the excavations (*ibid.* 110-111):

> During the course of the operations . . . the inner court as well as two small cells, a staircase, and the greater part of a gallery, all within the thickness of the wall, were cleared out; also a section of the outer face of the wall on the southern arc, which was obscured by fallen stones, was laid bare . . . About two hundred tons of stone and earth had to be removed, and, as all the soil was sifted through the fingers, extraordinary patience and perseverance were required to complete the work.

Although the excavations produced a rich material assemblage, the antiquarian methods used established few meaningful contextual relationships. That said the care taken in the retrieval of the artefacts is demonstrated by the recovery of small objects such as glass and wire beads. The artefacts are described in varying levels of detail in Callander's publication (*ibid.*, 120-31).

Callander argued for two periods of occupation. From the stratigraphy he noted that:

> Many layers of red peat ash were found throughout the interior at various levels, with many fragments of rude, hand-made pottery, broken rotary querns, and food refuse in the shape of occasional animal bones and shells. A regular network of drains occurred at various levels, and the hollow parts of the floor were brought up to the level of the outcrop of rock by a slab pavement on the southern half of the court . . . The divisional wall and the drains seem to be of a very late date, as the greater bulk of the pottery and nearly all the relics were found at the lowest level, some being found under the paving. (*ibid.*, 117)

While accepting that remodelling of the broch made it difficult to assign specific artefact groups to specific periods, Callander concluded, from analogy with other sites and from the stratigraphy recorded by the Countess, that a variety of objects were recognisable as 'broch relics' and could be assigned to the early centuries of the first millennium AD. These included grooved pebbles, spindle whorls, a stone cup, crucibles and a glass armlet fragment. A bronze buckle and ring were assigned to 'a race different from the original native broch dwellers, which appeared in Scotland in much later times', with the gold ring considered to be indicative of Viking influence. The coins were thought to derive from later visits or occupations of the site between the twelfth and eighteenth centuries (*ibid.*, 127). Callander found great difficulty in assigning dates to some object groups, especially the pottery, and the bronze pins. He stated that only by 'correlating them with other contemporary objects of which the period is known' (*ibid.*, 130), could any useful relationship be ascertained.

## Reanalysis of the pottery

The result of the 80 years of research carried out since the publication of Dun Beag is a large corpus of new structural and artefactual information for the Hebridean Iron Age as well as a number of synthetic works (e.g. Harding 1990; Armit 1991, 1996; Hingley 1992; Lane 1990; Ritchie 1997). It was perhaps not unrealistic, therefore, to suppose that reassessment of the Dun Beag pottery within the context of recent work would allow new insight into the date of the pottery and the nature of the assemblage.

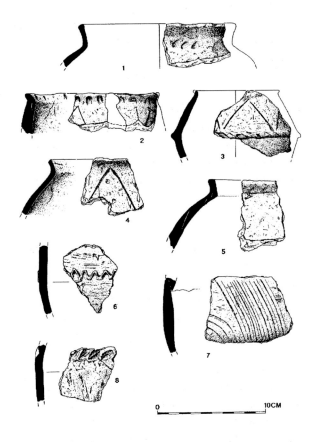

**44** *Pottery from Dun Beag: undecorated sherds (1, 2, 5); incised applied band with incised decoration above (3); incised decoration (4); applied decoration (6); wiped decoration (7); impressed decoration (8)*

Callander concluded that some of the Dun Beag sherds represented craggans of comparatively recent date, while the majority, especially those showing 'ornamental patterns', probably belonged to the 'broch period'.

Reanalysis of the 100 sherds or so in the museum collection shows that the assemblage comprises mainly rims, decorated body sherds and bases, indicating some selection in what was kept because this fraction of a typical Hebridean assemblage usually accounts for less than 10 per cent of the total recovery. (A selection of the sherds is illustrated in **44** and **45**.) Where morphology can be determined, the decorated pottery is all from vessels with everted rims. A variety of decorative techniques and motifs was used – applied dimpled bosses, zigzags and cordons (some decorated with incisions); incised geometric designs including infilled triangles; incised stabs in rows; and wiping in a circular pattern. Where position on the vessel can be determined, decoration is confined to the area between the shoulder and the neck, although two base interiors are 'decorated' with fingertip impressions. Some of these elements can be paralleled in assemblages from other Hebridean Iron Age sites including Dun an Iardhard, Skye (MacLeod 1915); Dun Flodigarry, Skye (Martlew 1985); Cnip, Lewis (Armit, forthcoming); Sollas, North Uist (Campbell 1991); Dun Vulan, South Uist (Parker-

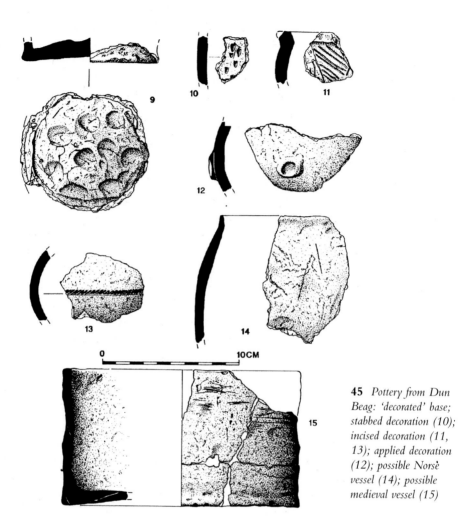

**45** *Pottery from Dun Beag: 'decorated' base; stabbed decoration (10); incised decoration (11, 13); applied decoration (12); possible Norse vessel (14); possible medieval vessel (15)*

Pearson & Sharples 1999); and Balelone, North Uist (Barber forthcoming).

The generally accepted typological sequence for the Iron Age of the West Coast is as follows:

• pottery with slightly inverted rims, sometimes with a row of impressed decoration
• the addition of pottery with slightly everted rims and the predominance of impressed and incised decoration
• the introduction of sharply everted rims and an increase in the range of decoration with the addition of applied motifs and channelled patterns
• the introduction of vessels with longer necks and a decrease in the range of decorative motifs, with applied cordons being most common (see Campbell, this volume **43**).

There is, however, no generally accepted absolute chronology for the sequence.

On comparison with the Cnip pottery (Armit & MacSween forthcoming), the Dun Beag material may date to between 100 BC and AD 200 (from preliminary analysis of the radiocarbon dates from that site). However, this assumes a parallelism in the evolution and development of sequences across the island groups. Comparison of material from sites which have produced large assemblages shows that this may not be the case. For example, comparison of pottery from Sollas (Campbell 1991), Dun Vulan (Parker Pearson & Sharples 1999) and Cnip (MacSween forthcoming) indicates that although the overall characteristics are similar, the sequences cannot be replicated from site to site.

Interestingly, while the majority of vessels in the Dun Beag assemblage are of Iron Age date, some of the undecorated pottery could be of later date. There are, for example, a couple of squat, undecorated 'jars' which are uncharacteristic of Iron Age assemblages of the area (e.g. **45**, 15). Their diameters decrease very slightly at the waist, from which point they rise straight to the rim. The possibility of a medieval date for these vessels should remain open (Andrea Smith, pers. comm.). Similarly shaped jars are, for example, known in Scottish East Coast White Gritty Wares of thirteenth to fourteenth-century date (e.g. McCarthy & Brooks 1988, 213, fig. 116 no. 555; 217, fig. 118 no. 580). Nor should the possibility of a Norse date for some of the pottery be discounted (e.g. the thin-walled vessel represented in **45**, 14). Despite attempts to characterise fabrics (e.g. Lane 1990), the lack of an accepted fabric-based sequence for Hebridean pottery continues to hinder the dating of undecorated material (see Campbell, this volume). No craggans of more recent date were identified in the re-examination of the assemblage.

## Discussion

Reanalysis of the Dun Beag pottery provided limited new information – a date range can now be suggested for the broch pottery and the possibility that some of the pottery is of Norse or medieval date was raised. However, reanalysis did highlight gaps in our understanding of the record, and consequently in our ability to progress interpretation of the evidence for the area. It is not yet possible, for example, to discuss whether:

- certain types of decoration or vessel are restricted to certain site types, that is, if all the pottery types are found on brochs, duns, hut circles and wheelhouses at all points in the sequence
- the same types of decoration are introduced throughout the islands at the same time
- some islands have some pottery types, but not others
- the pottery of the islands is similar to the pottery of the adjacent mainland
- the new styles of decoration represent gradual changes or sudden introductions.

It would appear that many aspects of our interpretations of the pottery of the Hebrides have, then, not progressed significantly since the publication of Dun Beag, 80 years ago. This lack of success in tackling wider issues seems to stem largely from the limitations of the available data. Three areas in particular need to be tackled:

• reassessment of the chronological sequence for the ceramics of the Hebridean Iron Age
• characterisation of later material
• more detailed consideration of fabric and technology in determining the nature of changes in the record.

## Reassessment of the chronological sequence for the ceramics of the Hebridean Iron Age

While syntheses of the available data such as Lane (1990) and Campbell (this volume) provide useful overviews, it is argued here that what is needed is a detailed critical re-examination. In constructing a key sequence for the area only securely stratified material should be used. This would help to iron out the 'major flaws in the current classification and chronology of the Iron Age pottery' identified by Lane (1990). It is suggested that dates should be weighted: Category One for dates for the material itself, for example a radiocarbon date for a residue adhering to a sherd; Category Two for associated material in a primary context; Category Three for associated material where there is the possibility of mixing. The key sequence for the area would comprise only dates for Category One – Category Two and Category Three material and information from 'relative' sequences would be added at a 'lower' level. Much work remains to be done on radiocarbon dating itself, for example to determine the significance of the 'marine reservoir effect' on dates from shells from the area (see Barber forthcoming for a discussion).

Construction of a ceramic sequence for the Hebrides must become an excavation priority, with samples collected for the purpose of artefact research. Sampling for collection of material specifically to date the deposition of pottery or to retrieve a large enough sample to construct a reliable sequence should be considered where practical. The success of this approach was demonstrated at Upper Scalloway, Shetland, where extra sampling was carried out to retrieve a statistically valid sample of pottery from the later phases of the midden (Sharples 1998, 91). Advances in dating techniques offer the potential to date individual objects. AMS, for example, has been successfully applied to the dating of pottery residues (see Campbell, this volume). The dating of material to progress the understanding of the ceramic sequence should become an integral element of project designs when excavating in the area.

## More critical examination of contextual information

### Use of key sequences
More critical examination of contextual information should be carried out. There is a general desire to assign all contexts, and therefore objects, to a definitive phase of a site, the phases usually being based on structural information. Often specialists are furnished with a list of contexts attributed to structural phases, which is used as a framework on which to base the pottery analysis. This approach tends to 'flatten out' chronological differences, as was highlighted in the analysis of the pottery from Cnip, Lewis. Here, secondary deposition made it difficult to identify a pottery sequence – analysis of the total assemblage by structural phase

indicated that there was no change in the pottery being used throughout the life of the site. When 'key' contexts (those thought from the stratigraphy to be primary contexts) were extracted and reanalysed, however, a clear sequence did emerge (Armit & MacSween forthcoming). If this approach is used, however, the results should make clear the criteria on which the selection was based, and a complete data set made available for reanalysis.

## Construction of a ceramics narrative

A more time-consuming but critical approach is to construct a ceramics narrative (see for example, MacSween 2001). In a ceramics narrative, the pottery from each context is described in detail with particular attention being paid to the size and abrasion of the sherds, the relative quantities of each fabric and sherd to vessel ratios. Detailed examination of this information in conjunction with stratigraphic information, results of environmental analysis and data for other artefact groups is useful in analysing the nature of a deposit. The existence of abraded sherds with a low sherd to vessel ration might, for example, indicate that material from an earlier midden was used to backfill a structure, and if the fabrics were different to adjoining contexts this would further strengthen the argument. When the analysis is complete, informed decisions can then be taken as to which contexts are appropriate to use in constructing the ceramic sequence for the site. This approach could be extended to the reanalysis of pottery from museum collections, where context information is available.

## Characterisation of later pottery

Medieval and later handthrown pottery from the area is difficult to characterise (Lane & Cowie 1997). In the Western Isles pottery was being made on the domestic hearth until the beginning of the twentieth century (Cheape 1988). At the later end of the sequence, much of the pottery appears to have comprised globular vessels with everted rims. This pottery needs to be analysed, perhaps from a technological point of view, to determine whether it can be differentiated on technological grounds – fabric, method of forming the vessel, surface finish, etc. More work is also required on the identification of medieval handthrown vessels. Assemblages from sites where there is the possibility of medieval reoccupation should be scanned by a specialist in medieval pottery for identification of, for example, local handthrown copies of wheelthrown vessels.

There should be more detailed consideration of fabric and technology in determining the nature of change in the record. Characterisation of coarse pottery from Scotland by analysis of the composition of fabrics has been attempted in some studies, e.g. by Neutron Activation Analysis of pottery from the Western Isles (Topping 1986) and by Inductively Coupled Plasma Spectrometry and x-ray fluorescence analysis of pottery from Orkney (MacSween 1990 & 1995). The conclusion from these studies was that the results of the trace element analyses of coarse pottery are not easily related to the fabric groups identified by eye. As Rye (1981, 27) has noted:

> The classificatory and control devices used by potters in the past have usually been far less precise than our facilities for analysing their results. Materials that vary widely according to our physical and chemical measurements may have been considered identical or interchangeable.

In analysing coarse pottery assemblages, then, fabric groups should be kept as general as possible: it is more useful initially to designate fabric groups to reflect additions which might have affected the technology of the pottery than to record minute variations. Specific questions can then be tackled with more detailed analysis. The usefulness of this approach was demonstrated in analysis of the pottery from the multi-period site of Kebister, Shetland, where four main fabrics were identified. When the distribution of these fabrics was plotted they were found to be concentrated in different areas of the site, with chronological variation the most likely explanation (Dalland & MacSween 1999).

Once the major fabric groups have been identified by eye, thin section analysis can be used to achieve more detailed descriptions of the clays and tempers and to determine whether the pottery could have been produced from local clays or if it is more likely that the clay or temper, or the pottery itself, was imported to the site. This information can then be used in conjunction with typological analysis to look at the nature of change in an assemblage. Do the identified points of change in a sequence indicate gradual or sudden change? Changes in, for example, fabric, surface finish, vessel shape and decoration simultaneously could indicate a new group of inhabitants on a site, whereas if decoration changes but fabric remains the same, this might indicate the adoption of new styles of pottery by the existing inhabitants.

Once this type of analysis has been carried out for individual sites, a regional picture can be built up and questioned. It would be interesting to determine, for example, if the identified points of change, such as that from everted rims to vessels with longer necks, reflect gradual or abrupt change, if they are restricted to areas of the Atlantic region, or more widespread. We have little idea how much variation in the ceramic sequence there is within and between areas. Detailed studies of several sites in one area would be useful in building up regional pictures.

At present there are too few excavated and fully published sites to answer many of these questions, but an overall research agenda and an agreed methodology, as called for by Haselgrove *et al.* (2001, 15-17) should be established to allow consistent recording of data for ease of comparison.

## Conclusions

Reanalysis of the pottery from Dun Beag provided limited new information, and the problems encountered in attempting to reanalyse the material are reflected in the minimal contribution of artefact assemblages to site interpretations and regional syntheses. It is suggested that a major problem in progressing the construction of a ceramic sequence for the Iron Age of the Hebrides is the lack of critical review of the available data and the low priority that construction of a ceramic sequence for the area has in most excavation strategies. Detailed analysis of contextual information from both old and recent excavations, collection of material specifically for construction of a ceramic sequence, improvements in the identification of medieval and later handthrown pottery, and advances in methods of fabric analysis to better understand the nature of change on individual sites are seen as essential in the construction of a well-dated ceramic sequence for the Hebrides.

# 13  Brochs, economy and power

*Stephen J. Dockrill*

## Introduction

Brochs, through their archaeological visibility, have been a focus for investigation, study and debate in the later part of the nineteenth and throughout the twentieth century. Interpretations have ranged from defensive refuges, watchtowers/signal stations, forts and farms. Even today their definition, origin, and function are still able to arouse fierce debate.

This paper seeks to understand the role of the Northern Isles broch within Iron Age society, by examining the economic potential of the arable component of the brochs' agricultural resource base. The economies of two sites, Tofts Ness, Sanday, Orkney (an early Iron Age roundhouse) and Old Scatness, Shetland (a multi-period settlement mound containing a broch) (**46**), are used to construct a social-economic model for the Broch Period.

The integration of scientific techniques with the archaeology of the 1990s has provided a greater understanding of the apparent relationship between the broch at Old Scatness and its associated arable land. The focus of this study is formed by the brochs of the south Mainland of Shetland (which include Old Scatness). A number of these sites are foci for extramural settlement beyond the broch tower and are located in arguably the most fertile part of Shetland. These factors may be used to suggest that some of the South Mainland sites such as Old Scatness, Jarlshof and East Shore are atypical of many of the Shetland brochs and parallel a number of the Orcadian brochs. However, many elements of this discussion are transferable to other Shetland broch sites.

Although brochs are highly visible monuments in the archaeological record, our full understanding of their economic role in the Iron Age society of northern Scotland and the Western and Northern Isles is still limited. In part this is due to the large number of monuments investigated by antiquarians in the nineteenth century and archaeologists in the early twentieth century without the support of modern scientific methods and sampling strategies. Recent rescue excavations such as those at Scalloway (Sharples 1998), Howe (**colour plates 4** & **5**) (Ballin Smith 1994) and research investigations at Dun Vulan (Parker Pearson *et al.* 1996) have helped both to elucidate the full archaeological potential of these monuments and to shape the research agenda for Old Scatness, South Mainland, Shetland (**46** & **47**). Research excavations (Phase 1 1995-1997 and Phase 2 1998-2000) by the author within an heritage project managed by the Shetland Amenity Trust at Old Scatness are providing new contextual information on both the broch period, and on the succeeding occupation phases spanning the late Iron Age to the Viking period (Dockrill 1998).

The Old Scatness site is significant as its stratigraphic sequences parallel the broch and post-broch components of the site of Jarlshof (**47**) less than a mile away, excavated between

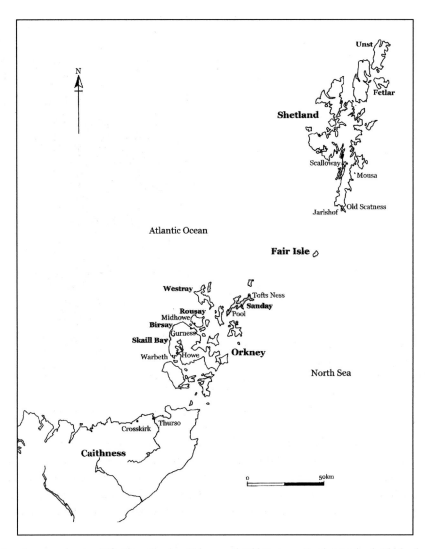

**46** *Location map showing Tofts Ness, Sanday, Orkney and Old Scatness, South Mainland, Shetland*

1897 and 1952 and published in 1956 by John Hamilton (1956). Although excavated without today's recording and sampling methodologies, Jarlshof is still central to research of the later prehistoric and Norse settlements of the Northern Isles. The lack of systematic sampling for environmental and economic reconstruction and scientific dating at Jarlshof is being remedied by the integrated scientific research agenda of the Old Scatness project. Central to Phase 2 (1998-2000) of the Old Scatness research programme is a full understanding of the role of the broch in Iron Age society. It is hoped that the Scatness data will be able to add significantly to our understanding of the issues of social hierarchies and the centralised control of the economic resource proposed by this paper.

The theoretical model outlined in this paper suggests an economic interpretation for the broch and attempts to provide an understanding of the contemporary Iron Age society within which it functioned. The broch in this model for southern Shetland is seen simply as representing

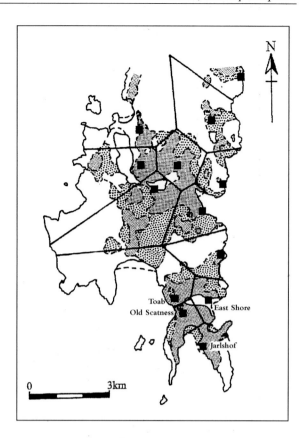

**47** *Broch distribution (squares) with arable land (dense shading/grey) and land of arable potential (course).* This illustration is based on that produced by Fojut 1982 and amended with the discovery of Toab in 1998

a dwelling with multiple floors and defensive/status characteristics acting as focus for a small community perhaps of village proportions (this supporting group may be centralised within an extramural settlement or perhaps dispersed). The issue of intensive agriculture and reliance on barley, which is central to the model, is not in itself new. Childe identified their importance to the broch communities in his 1944 Rhind lectures. He advocated for the 'Celtic' Iron Age an:

> ' . . . intensified agriculture with an increased reliance on cereal foods' and added that ' . . . among the broch-builders tillage was evidently a primary interest . . . '
>
> Childe 1946, 82

New evidence (discussed below) for infield management, however, has provided a fresh understanding for the cultivation of six-row barley in the broch period. Barley cultivated within an 'infield system' is perceived in this theoretical model as representing a significant storable element of the available mixed subsistence resource.

## A case for settlement continuity?

Although the broch has been equated with incoming populations (Childe 1935, 204), recent archaeological work suggests that brochs were built by established communities (Fojut 1982,

155

56). Archaeological evidence for three South Mainland broch sites (**47**): Jarlshof (Hamilton 1956), East Shore (Carter *et al*, 1995) and Old Scatness (Dockrill 1998) (**colour plates 21 & 22**), all suggest a case of settlement continuity with evidence for both earlier and later occupation sequences at each of these sites.

The following questions arise: Why were these sites the focus for settlement over such long time spans? Was it just their geographical location and proximity to resources that provided such sustained viability?

One reason for such continuity in settlement focus may be the high value of the manured infields surrounding early settlements (discussed in detail below). Fojut, in his research, focused on the dense distribution of brochs present in the South Mainland (to which must be added that of Toab (**47**), discovered in 1998 by the Shetland Amenity Trust's survey of the landscape surrounding Old Scatness) and suggested that these might be equated with the high arable resource potential in perhaps the most favourable area of Shetland for arable cultivation (Fojut 1982, 46).

## A model for a pre-broch economy: Tofts Ness, Sanday, Orkney

Before the broch period is explored in depth it is necessary to understand the economic evidence for the agriculture of the preceding early Iron Age period in the Northern Isles. Excavation from 1985-8 of a prehistoric settlement mound containing an early Iron Age (mid-first millennium BC) roundhouse structure at Tofts Ness, Sanday, Orkney (**46**) produced good-quality palaeoeconomic data (Dockrill 1993). Bond has identified hulled six-row barley as being the focus for arable cultivation from the Neolithic to the site's abandonment through sand movements in the early Iron Age (Bond in Dockrill *et al.* 1994, 130). Soil samples taken from contexts within the bounds of both the 'site' and the surrounding landscape provided the base material for an interdisciplinary research programme. This revealed clear evidence for manured infield cultivation (**48**) and so provided evidence for an understanding of arable land management strategies from the Neolithic through to the abandonment of the site (Dockrill *et al.* 1994; Dockrill & Simpson 1994; Simpson *et al.* 1998). A complex mixture of materials including ash, carbonised plant remains (including seaweed), grassy turf derived from a podsolised source and chemical signatures suggesting human faecal material, have been identified within these buried soils (Simpson *et al.* 1998). It is interesting that human, rather than cattle manure was being utilised within this management strategy, but it may be explained by the importance of cattle manure as a fuel source on Sanday, an island without a natural peat source. These soils represent some of the earliest examples of 'plaggen' soils in Northern Europe. During the later part of the stratigraphic sequence the battle to maintain fertility and structure to support intensive infield cultivation was hampered by sand movements. The resulting increased sand content of the arable soils contemporary with the early Iron Age roundhouse rendered them more susceptible to wind erosion, though the high levels of organic material within the soil matrix would have helped to counter this threat by binding the soils structure (*ibid.*). Even in what may be determined as inhospitable marginal zones great effort appears to have been made first to establish and then to maintain infield areas in order to return repeated high yields of six-row barley (Dockrill 1993, 161).

**48** *Early Iron Age ard cultivation of an amended sandy infield soil (the sand component representing an extensive movement of sand by wind) cutting a dark anthropogenic soil spanning the Neolithic through to the Late Bronze Age.* Crown Copyright

The pre-broch picture suggested here is a progression from an economic model developed for the Tofts Ness roundhouse Structure 5 (Dockrill 1993). Tofts Ness, Structure 5, may be regarded as a low-status building (**colour plate 19**), on marginal land occupied as a homestead for a single family. The archaeological evidence indicates a mixed resource base of barley cultivation, animal husbandry (cattle, sheep and some pig in small numbers) and hunting and gathering (fishing, fowling and exploitation of the seashore). An analysis of the archaeological evidence and the energy requirements for a family group suggests that the long-term viability of the settlement was dependent on high barley yields grown in the infield area (*ibid.*). Intensive cultivation and management of a manured 'infield' area of one hectare might produce a grain return as high as 30:1 (Dockrill 1993, 155).

This view is reinforced by more recent archaeological research into the management strategies for infield cultivation from sites in Shetland, including the multi-period settlement mound containing the Old Scatness broch. The relict field systems associated with the many visible prehistoric house sites in Shetland attest to the importance of the infield in prehistory. Abandonment of many of these sites, such as the Scord of Brouster (Whittle 1986, 149), can be associated with the poorer climatic conditions of the Bronze Age, when the fight against podsolisation and peat growth was lost. Positive evidence for managed and curated prehistoric infields has been identified by the joint Bradford University/Shetland Amenity survey and excavation project investigating the archaeological development of the South Nesting area of Shetland (Dockrill & Simpson 1994; Dockrill *et al.* 1998, 81). In the south of Shetland, at

Old Scatness, excavation of primary soils dating to the late Neolithic/early Bronze Age (based on artefacts and an OSL date of 44461195 BP) reveal an ard cultivated soil with a high ash content with some domestic waste (Simpson *et al.* 1998b).

The economic evidence from a number of pre-broch settlements in both Orkney and Shetland suggests that six-row barley provides the calorific 'backbone' within a mixed subsistence economy providing the settlement with the potential for long-term viability. In times of crop failure the diversity of the mixed resource base provides a short-term safety net (Bond 1994). The long settlement spans seen in the archaeological record at sites such as Tofts Ness attest to the success of this system in the marginal conditions associated with the Northern Isles. Six-row barley in this mixed resource system provides a storable source of energy. Crop surpluses may be kept over as insurance against either low yields or crop failure. The accumulating evidence from Northern Isles sites suggests that this form of intensive arable agriculture has its origins within the Neolithic period and continues into the Iron Age. Although the brochs' arable resource has been discussed in depth by Fojut (1982), little has been done in the way of examining the contemporary arable fields.

The following research question needs to be asked: does intensive infield management survive the broch and post-broch periods or is there a move to larger field systems?

## Infields and the Old Scatness Iron Age

Preliminary research on arable soils associated with the Iron Age settlement phases at Old Scatness strongly supports the continuation for the intensive management of the infield. There is evidence for expansion but this appears later and seems associated with the Norse period: further work is required to define accurately this chronology. Preliminary research has provided Optically Stimulated Thermoluminesence (OSL) dating evidence for a sequence of soil and windblown sand events (Burbidge forthcoming). Within this sequence soils dating to the middle and later Iron Age have been identified and their stratigraphic/soil micromorphological characterisation sequence have been traced to other stratigraphic sequences within the infield area. These Iron Age soils show the continued use of domestic waste, with animal manure becoming an integral part of the amendment strategies (Simpson *et al.* 1998b). An increased intensity in cultivation is also strongly suggested by the micromorphological data, with silty clay pedofeatures becoming a common characteristic of these thin sections. This evidence provides a convincing case for the continuity of infield practice; however there also appears to be a case for intensification, illustrated by the increased use of animal manure and the evidence for greater levels of cultivation. Based on the data gathered so far at Old Scatness there appears to be little evidence to support a move from intensive infield cultivation to larger field cultivation during the broch period. In such a scenario higher yields would require greater acreage under cultivation and these would both receive less input of midden material as well as having a lower intensity of cultivation. This evidence supports rather then contradicts Fojut's (1982) discussions on arable potentials providing greater potential for both sustainablility and viability to a number of his broch sites.

# Brochs: the power base for the elite

The emergence of a 'visible' social elite in the Iron Age might be suggested by the substantial roundhouse form or proto-broch at Bu on Orkney, dating to the mid-first millennium BC (Hedges 1983) and contemporary with the much smaller roundhouse form of Tofts Ness (**colour plate 20**), discussed above (Dockrill 1993, 136). Evidence of an elite social class within the broch period can be suggested by the form of the broch itself, which combines defensive qualities with an elaborate roundhouse structure symbolically re-enforcing the social status of the occupier. Although these monuments suggest a focus of power for an elite the numbers and close distribution of monuments do not suggest a social ranking of chiefdoms or great warlords, but rather a more localised elite in line with the broch as a defended high-status farmstead or Hingley's (1992, 24-5) 'substantial houses'.

The power base of the broch 'elite' in this model is defined as being the centralised control and storage of the economic resource. The social structure behind such a system has been suggested by John Barrett as being that of clientage. Clientage is defined in this context as being:

> the relationship of patronage, repaid by dues, between individuals of distinct and unquestionable status, a relationship of benefit between client and master by which the reality of exploitation remains concealed.
>
> 1982, 215

Clientage is seen by Nieke (1990, 140-2) as representing an underpinning to Iron Age society whereby reciprocal relationships between individuals of different social positions provided both economic and social security to the lower orders. This social system, Barrett suggests, evolved from the relationships of 'power, domination, conflict and inheritance'. Central to this argument are the themes of marriage and external alliances. Barrett also identifies the dangers of looking at the economy of a single site rather than trying to understand the interaction of sites through a time depth and suggests a social system where 'claims of inheritance, kinship and social debt' might have run in conflict with the grazing, arable and sea shore resource' (Barrett 1982, 214).

In the model presented, a social hierarchy based on clientage, the power of an 'elite' would be reinforced by the control of the economic resource. Barrett has produced a framework in which we could see economic competition and the need for defence, together with a potentially complicated network of social relationships within Iron Age society. Central to the argument made here is the significance of the arable resource within the economy of the Iron Age. The association of the broch with this arable resource was made by Anderson as early as 1881. Anderson describes the broch as follows:

> they are therefore the defensive strongholds of a population located upon the arable lands . . . against such oft-recurring but transient dangers to the cultivators and to the produce of their soil there could be no more effective system of defence than a multitude of safes . . .
>
> Anderson, 1883, 205

The model supports these earlier views that barley continues to be of vital importance within the mixed subsistence economy as argued by the author above for the earlier prehistoric period. One major factor for its importance is that it provides an important storable energy source. Any surpluses from one year to another can effectively be banked for the following year, allowing an effective mechanism for the accumulation and control of wealth (Dockrill 1998, 77). Central control of grain surplus would provide some insurance against inter-annual fluctuations in yields. This in turn would provide a high degree of stability to an economy subject to the marginality present in the Northern Isles and the risks encountered by the longer growing season dictated by their latitude. Such economic stability derived from this central storage model would effectively reinforce and strengthen the hold of patron over client.

Storage is an important consideration within this model and the requirement for supporting archaeological evidence within this hypothesis for central storage presents a potential problem. One possible solution is the utilisation of an upper storey of the broch as a secure central store. Access using the intramural stairway might be seen as a potential difficulty. This could be eased by having some form of trap door system to facilitate easy movement of bulky items. The upper floors of the broch have the potential for providing both a protective and a dry environment for the central storage of grain and other items of economic value. Smoke filtering through from hearths on lower floors might also have a protective curing effect, aiding preservation. This might be seen as developing from the usage of the internal space within the conical roofs of earlier roundhouse structures such as Tofts Ness. Use of the roof space provides a probable candidate for a storage area in which grain (together with dried and cured meat, fish and possibly fodder such as hay) could be successfully stored (Dockrill forthcoming). Armit argues that another and larger roundhouse structure at Kilphedir, Sutherland, could have had an upper floor supported by the inner wall and an internal ring of posts (Armit 1997, 29). An illustrative interpretation of this structure by Armit and Braby suggests that this space may have been utilised for storage (Armit 1997, 30) (**2**). The presence of pier supports and a scarcement ledge within a post-broch structure at Scatness might suggest functional continuity of roof space for storage (Dockrill 1998, 70).

This model has concentrated on barley but other aspects of central economic control reinforcing such social hierarchical relationships are possible. The control of breeding stock would foster a client/patron hierarchy. For example, maintenance of bulls for breeding would be economically costly for smaller or dependant households, needing the provision of extra energy requirements in terms of summer grazing and winter fodder (Dockrill 1993, 143). Such resources would be readily available within the controlled economy suggested for the broch elite. Apart from the agricultural economy it is possible to infer similar centralised controls and wealth redistribution for other materials. It is perhaps significant that recent excavations such as Howe, Scalloway and Old Scatness (**colour plates 5 & 21**) have indicated that these sites have within their broch or post-broch phase evidence for metalworking. McDonnell argues that the ' . . . iron smith underpins many crafts and skills, not least warfare...' (1998, 159). In examining the evidence McDonnell provides a convincing example for patronage and status, with the smith representing a status craft working within the core of the settlement area.

This model suggests that the broch elite would facilitate through central control the procurement of surplus that may be exchanged for material (or other forms of economic) wealth as well as acting as a reserve buffer for times of stress. The broch itself would act as a symbolic and practical centre of power and protection from either an adjacent or remote threat. Such a model would be advantageous in terms of both economic success and security to the supporting population following a period of contraction from secondary, less viable, marginal upland zones. The emergence of the broch, it is suggested, would also see the development of a dependant group who by client-based exchange would contribute both labour services and economic resources to this system. Controlled centralisation of economic wealth and powers of redistribution would then reinforce the position of an elite class within a social hierarchy. Redistribution of the economic resource would foster both patronage and client-based relationships with the supporting population (Dockrill 1998, 77). Such centralisation of economic wealth provides a mechanism at one level for exchange or trade and at another for tax or tribute that might be required by the unknown social hierarchy above the broch elite.

## The need for supporting evidence

At present much of this model is based on conjecture, and needs supporting evidence from the archaeological record. If grain is considered as a material asset representing economic wealth, evidence for central storage and control is required. Gordon Childe in his review of the Celtic Iron Age identifies the 'heavy consumption of corn' from the numbers of querns found from Iron Age Brochs sites (Childe 1946, 82). Both Childe and Armit discuss the uptake of the rotary quern in the Iron Age, identifying its superiority over the conventional saddle quern (Childe 1946, 82; Armit 1990, 70). Technologically, the rotary quern might be seen as representing an artefact associated with resource centralisation able significantly to increase grain-processing efficiency (Bond pers. comm.).

Evidence from the late usage of the Orcadian broch of Howe suggests barley processing within the broch tower itself. Grain parching as well as grinding is interpreted by the late Camilla Dickson by the survival of carbonised ears of barley, a kiln structure and a quern (Dickson in Ballin Smith 1994, 130). Does this evidence represent a normal domestic activity or more specialised activity? Ballin Smith in her discussion of the archaeological structural and depositional evidence suggests that a number of activities were occurring on the ground floor level of the broch in this late phase, suggesting perhaps specialised usage. These activities include pottery manufacture and stone working (Ballin Smith 1994, 76-7). Burnt ears of barley appeared to have been deliberately spread over the central area and Ballin Smith suggests that these accidentally caught alight setting the whole of the inner circle on fire. This evidence is difficult to interpret, but it would seem to be indicative of some form of central processing.

If the storage function for upper floor levels of the broch is to be advocated, then firm supporting archaeological evidence is required. Such evidence for the storage of grain in the Northern Isles is difficult to ascertain from the archaeological record. In addition many early sites were excavated in the infancy of archaeology as a scientific discipline and the quality of recording of many excavated sites is extremely poor. The most recently excavated evidence from Shetland is the broch of Scalloway, which although outside of the South Mainland area may be used to support this discussion. Here scientific sampling and analysis have provided an important insight into the formation processes. Micromorphological analysis of surviving burnt floor and ash deposits adjacent to the inner broch wall indicate an organic rich surface, with earthworm activity sealed by ash from an intense fire associated with a large quantity of carbonised barley (Sharples 1998, 31). In a discussion of agricultural practice based on the carbonised plant remains Holden comments that:

> During the fire the floor deposits were mixed with material contained in the broch superstructure. It would seem likely that, rather than being part of the floor, the grain was stored at a higher level, and that it fell and spread over the surface of the floor during the course of the fire. (Holden 1988, 126).

Holden is unable to estimate the number of grains that were not carbonised and were ashed in the fire but remarks that the 10,000 barley grains from 200 litres of sample 'represents a substantial store'. Holden suggests that such bulk storage is likely 'only where cereals were being traded or given in the form of rent or tribute' (*ibid.*).

Evidence then is emerging from recent archaeological investigations in the Northern Isles, which might be used to support the hypothesis for controlled and centralised storage of barley.

## Conclusions

This paper has concentrated on barley as providing a bankable form of wealth and the associated infields whose management was essential if high yields were to be maintained over time. Barley is seen as being a significant part of the mixed resource base exploited during the broch period. It would seem likely that control and power by the broch elite would have extended over a wide spectrum of other activities, such as that suggested by McDonnell for metalwork (1998). At present the available evidence for the arable economy of the broch period in the Northern Isles is still restricted due to the limitations of excavation work and sampling on many of the brochs investigated during the earlier part of this century. The presence of carbonised barley on a number of broch sites together with the introduction of the rotary quern is suggested here as representing a continued dependence on the arable resource.

A full understanding of the complete economic resource base is required in order to understand these issues fully. Excavation at Old Scatness (**colour plate 22**), supported by an extensive and integrated sampling policy, is providing the opportunity to examine in detail both the utilisation of the available economic resources and the examination of the management of contemporary field systems. Despite the atypical nature of Old Scatness, the apparent continued use of an infield arable system in the broch period is transferable to more marginal locations. In such locations this system has the potential to return high yields annually. Central and controlled storage is seen as advantageous in providing economic stability in marginal locations where a combination of surplus and economic diversity may mitigate against potential famine in adverse growing seasons. Such an economic strategy as outlined in the above model would reinforce a client/patron relationship as well as being a means of securing wealth for trade or tribute. The model presented above provides a framework by which we can now start to understand these complicated linkages of broch, economy and power.

# 14 The relentless pursuit of the sea

## Breckness, an eroding Orcadian Broch

*Beverley Ballin Smith*

## Introduction

Along the exposed western seaboard of Orkney, directly facing the Atlantic Ocean, are the remains of several coastal brochs, one of which, Breckness, is the subject of this paper. These Iron Age sites are not just confined to the mainland, or to the west coast, but can be found throughout the Northern and Western Isles and along the north coastal regions of Scotland. They are particularly vulnerable to continuous coastal erosion, and the recently recognised phenomenon of global warming, may be intensifying the attritional effects of wind and sea. The balance between removal and preservation indicates the vulnerability of archaeological sites of all periods and the information they contain.

While this paper highlights the plight of brochs with their complex stratigraphy and massive walls protruding from cliffs they are also the dramatic expression of coastal erosion in the North of Scotland. They lie as partially-hidden reminders of times past, with what has disappeared and what still remains being largely unknown. Erosion is of particular concern in areas of internationally recognised archaeological heritage especially where brochs are monumental or visible landmarks and where information can be eradicated overnight with the power of one storm. Modern erosion of these sites highlights other difficulties including the exposure of features, such as broch wells, which can be accessible but with potentially dangerous consequences, and the possibilities of undercut cliffs with intact stratigraphy above. Health and safety issues are a matter for all, but for the archaeologist these sites are often the most difficult of situations.

By reviewing the events that have occurred at Breckness Broch this paper highlights the fact that coastal erosion on a substantial scale is by no means a new event. The application of appropriate methods of evaluation and monitoring at this site demonstrates a significant enhancement in information recovery, in spite of the steady erosion of the 'archive'.

## The setting and the problems

Gales mainly occur on Orkney during the winter months, but this pattern is not exclusive. Prevailing winds affecting the west coast originate in the south to west quadrant of the compass (Berry 1985, 22) but when combined with spring equinoxes and high tides, the devastation wrought on the more vulnerable low coastal cliffs and the prehistoric settlement

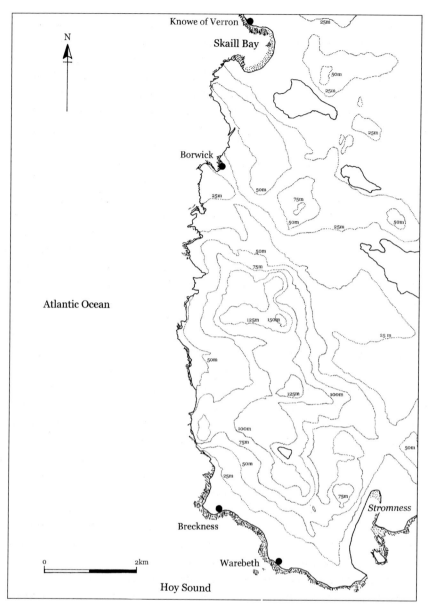

**49** *Map of the location of the west coast Orcadian Mainland brochs*

they bear can be at its most severe. During the winter and spring storms of 1992-3 at least 4m of cliff edge was lost in the area to the immediate south of the Broch of Breckness (Ballin Smith & Ballin, 1993, 105).

Erosion of prehistoric coastal settlements may have been occurring since their inception. However, the current problem concerns not just the loss of the cultural heritage, but the rate of that loss. It is evident from nineteenth-century publications (see Laing below) that coastal erosion was recognised earlier, but no systematic search of historical and climatic data and documentary evidence from an archaeological perspective has taken place. The compilation of information from weather and storm reports, diaries, photographs and written accounts may prove a valuable tool with which to evaluate critically the threat to coastal sites.

The effects of coastal erosion are well attested at other Iron Age sites on Orkney (Lowe 1998), including the brochs of Gurness and Midhowe. These settlements lie either side of Eynhallow Sound, which separates the Orkney Mainland from the island of Rousay. The deepening and widening of geos (natural rock clefts and sea inlets) and the natural breakage of extensive areas of flagstone by the sea has removed buildings and defensive features from both sites, clearly identified by analysis of their surviving settlement patterns. Erosion probably began as soon as these brochs were constructed but it is the degree and the effect of the erosion which are important. Additional factors such as the collapse of structures and the effects of rabbit burrowing will also have affected the rate of destruction and removal of sites, but statistical analysis of this is rare or non-existent. Erosion cannot be considered as simply a modern phenomenon, as the evidence at Breckness attests (see below). Here, historical documentation is important in the accurate assessment of loss over time. The force and the intensity of erosion is a phenomenon that we are aware of, but as archaeologists we are not adequately equipped to manage the consequences.

The Middle Old Red Sandstones of Orkney form the main geology and landscape characteristics of the islands. However, where they are exposed on the west coast they are in the form of Stromness Flagstones, which are highly laminated. These laminations can be so fine that the fragments of individual beds may be broken by hand from the low cliffs they form. The thin beds of soft rock are easily shattered by the impact of wind, the force of salt spray and tides, and diurnal fluctuations in temperature. The combination of wet-dry and warm-cold can break up the flagstone into small fragments of rock within a short time as has been noted by the author at an exposed quarry site close to Breckness and during archaeological excavations on the islands. The characteristics of the bedrock resource, which attracted settlement in prehistory and in the Iron Age in particular, are the same characteristics, which now threaten those settlements.

Along the west coast of Orkney from Stromness to the Bay of Skaill, approximately 12km in a direct line, are four known brochs (**46** & **49**). These are Warebeth, lying below the cemetery at Stromness; Breckness, situated below the ruins of the bishop's house of the same name at Outertown, north of Stromness; further north are the more complete but partly excavated ruins of the Broch of Borwick which lies south of Skaill Bay; and to the immediate north of Skaill Bay is the Knowe of Verron. Each has suffered the effects of coastal erosion in the distant past but recent damage was recorded most noticeably at Warebeth in the 1980s (Bell & Dickson 1989), when part of the broch and its well were exposed after storm damage. During the 2001-2 winter, storm erosion of the coast was noted as continuing to affect the Broch of Borwick as well as the World Heritage Site of Skara Brae (*The Times*, February 18, 2002). During the 1990s a series of high tides coinciding with the spring and autumn equinoxes and predominantly strong westerly winds exposed new archaeological features at the Broch of Breckness. These features were recorded and in one instance excavated for the retrieval of information and finds, prior to the next storm (see below).

The historical value of the brochs of Warebeth and Breckness is increased by the medieval and ecclesiastical activities which later focussed upon them. The use of coastal and inland sites of former prehistoric activity for monasteries, churches and burial grounds is not unusual on Orkney where many Iron Age settlements were taken over by the early Christian church (Lowe 1998). Both Breckness and Warebeth have been used for the burial of the dead, the former in early medieval times while the latter is still active as the town cemetery.

What remains of the four sites from Stromness to Skaill are the partially surviving ruins of middle Iron Age settlements. The Knowe of Verron, situated beside a geo, is most probably a broch but was only identified as a possible settlement in Hedges' three-volume work on the brochs of Orkney (Hedges 1987, pt 3, 51). It is a grass-covered mound with eroding midden deposits (RCAHMS 1946, 254). Borwick is the most recognisable broch settlement of the four. Its prominent broch tower walls and single entrance are clearly visible due to late nine-teenth-century excavations by the landowner of the Sandwick and Breckness estates, Mr W.G.T. Watt. With its back to the sea the broch sits on what is now a diminishing defensive promontory. External earthworks and remains of buildings indicate a great structural complexity and chronological depth of which the broch seems to represent the most prominent component. Breckness is distinguished by the presence of a remaining arc of broch wall and features of contemporary and later settlement with medieval burials exposed in the cliff face. Little if anything can presently be seen of Warebeth but as reported on numerous occasions, evidence of artefacts and settlement features has been found during grave digging. Laing and Petrie investigated the site in 1866 and although no traces of the broch tower were visible, they were certain that the site was that of a broch. In 1980 part of the entrance to the broch was recorded in the eroded cliff section (Laing 1867-68; Bell & Dickson 1989).

The effects of coastal erosion can also be identified in the exposure of middens and of arte-factual and ecofactual evidence at these sites. Easily recognised 'artefacts' such as human skulls and bones constantly trickling from higher levels of later occupation are often found amongst the features of the Breckness cliffs, and fragments of pottery vessels are not uncommon eroding out of the cliffs below Borwick Broch. These may often alert the museum curator or the archaeologist to the erosional threat in the first instance. But what of less easily recognised material such as stone artefacts lying amongst beach stones with a tendency to be removed from the site by the next high tide? Artefacts such as these, and less robust ecofacts with a tendency to disintegrate in the humid, salt-laden atmosphere, are easily lost from the archaeological record of these sites and with them goes part of the settlement story. This problem could be partially resolved by regular monitoring of coastal sites by archaeologists with a wide range of observa-tional skills in structural and artefactual evidence (see below).

## Breckness Broch

*The recent past and the erosion of the broch*
Samuel Laing in 1866-7 in his published account of the age of brochs in Orkney and Caithness describes for the first time the position and condition of the Broch of Breckness:

> At Breckness, near Stromness, part of a burg remains in the face of the cliff, the rest having been carried away by the action of the sea. The curvature of the remaining wall shows that this burg has been originally a circle of 44 feet inner diameter, and the thickness of the wall is 12 feet, so that the outer diameter has been 68 feet. Of this about 15 feet only remain, and upwards of 50 feet have been carried away. Now, the burg stands on solid sandstone rock, and it is apparent that before 50 feet of the

rock were wasted away here, the point of Breckness must have extended at least 50 feet farther out, and probably more. The minimum time, therefore, that can have elapsed since the building of this burg must be sufficient to allow for the wasting away of 50 feet of a shore line consisting of solid sandstone cliffs of the height of 30 or 40 feet, in a locality where no perceptible change has taken place in the memory of the existing generation. Those who know the slow rate at which a solid rocky coast is wasted away, must feel that such facts as are exhibited by the section of the burg and cliff at Breckness are altogether incompatible with any theory that assigns the origin of burgs to a recent period. (p.63-4)

The illustration accompanying this account (**50**) shows the broch (burg) in a state that is still recognisable today. In the intervening 136 years the ends of the broch wall have become less distinct but are still visible (**colour plate 23**) and the remaining portion of the interior wall face of the broch is still extant, but not as tall as the engraving suggests. What is most noticeable is the erosion of the base of the broch and the retreat of the small headland to its immediate north.

To return to Laing:

if we knew the rate of retreat of such a line of rocky coast, we could fix the minimum limit of the age of the burg. Unfortunately, there are no data from which I could venture to assign any precise rate of waste of such a cliff as that of Breckness, but there can be no doubt it is extremely slow. Many castles exist, perched on precipitous rocks overhanging the sea, where we can prove from historical records that no very sensible change has taken place for centuries.

I may add that the burg at Breckness is not exposed to the full force of the Atlantic, being partly sheltered from the west by the point of Breckness, and that the rock is a very hard and homogenous sandstone of the Devonian formation. (p.65).

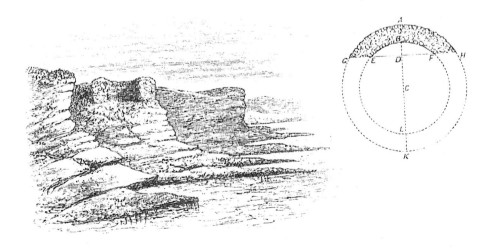

**50** *Copy of Laing's 1866/67 illustration of the ruins of Breckness with an estimate of how much of the broch tower survived*

167

The understanding of the geological situation is now quite different, and the rate of cliff removal has altered significantly over recent decades. It is unclear whether active periods of erosion have been followed by significant phases of inactivity and water-land stability. However, as can be measured from recent 1:10,000 Ordnance Survey maps of the area (Sheet HY 10/20 Stromness, 1979) the expanse of skerries exposed at low water from the base of the Breckness cliffs to Hoy Sound measures as much as 120m. These, obviously harder, rocks which lie beneath the softer rocks of the cliffs can perhaps be viewed as indicating the extent of the coastline in former periods. Could the seaward edge of the skerries suggest a late prehistoric coastline? Whether this could be borne out by scientific investigation is, however, beyond the scope of this paper. The coastal erosion of Orkney has been much discussed in environmental circles where it has been stated that:

> . . . the actual retreat of the coast in these exposed situations is not easy to measure, but the absence of the seaward facing half of the brochs at Borwick, Sandwick (Knowe of Verron) and Breckness and the almost total disappearance of that at Stromness Kirkyard suggest that it has been . . . 8-13 m in these places.
>
> Berry 1985, 47

Whatever the truth and significance of the erosional situation, part of an Iron Age broch lies in the cliffs below the sixteenth-century bishop's palace at Breckness with its earlier chapel and burial ground (Orkney Name Book 1880). Where not exposed, stonework is often covered by maritime vegetation. The ends of the surviving arc of broch walling are still visible but the structural remains now give the impression of a slowly crumbling settlement gradually falling into the sea. The situation is not helped by the intrusion of rabbits and nesting fulmars. The remaining arc of the tower and the survival of interior stratigraphy as indicated by Laing (**50**) suggests that a major erosional event may have taken place before the mid-nineteenth century, causing a breach of the broch wall and its removal along with a large section of cliff on which it sat. A picture of the still largely intact broch at Borwick perched on the cliff edge may have been the situation at Breckness 200 or more years ago. Whether by cataclysmic removal, or wear over time, such destruction may nevertheless provide the archaeologist with opportunities for the recovery of valuable information which otherwise would be denied.

## Rescue of the broch well

The accessibility of Breckness Broch for study and monitoring has been demonstrated by this author and others since 1985 (Smith 1985; Smith and Lorimer 1987). The methodology employed has been a visual examination combined, where achievable, with a more detailed analysis of the cliff profile, identification and recognition of features in the cliff face, collection of artefactual and ecofactual evidence where eroded out of the section, a photographic record (usually overlapping photographs), and note taking. In addition, cliff top inspection has also been carried out where possible. It was, however, in 1992 during general monitoring that an underground feature (**51 & 52**) was discovered to be eroding from the base of the cliff in front of, and below, the surviving arc of wall and internal stratigraphy of the broch tower. It lay just above the high water mark. Comparison of photographs taken in March 1992 with those of the previous summer suggested that approximately 1m of cliff and bedrock had been

**51** *Breckness cliffs below the sixteenth-century Bishop's House. The spoil on the beach indicated the location of the well. Stonework of the broch and associated buildings can be seen in the cliff*

**52** *The well seen in the cliff section in 1992*

removed by the winter storms: along the coastline to the south the erosion had been more severe (see above). The feature was identified as a well while to the north of the broch the enclosing ditch to the settlement became visible for the first time.

Four factors guided the subsequent archaeological excavation of the well. It was unclear what stratigraphy remained *in situ* in the feature because of the undercutting and removal of deposits by the sea and slumping of stratigraphy from the centre of the broch above; the survival of intact environmental samples, which could be used for radiocarbon dating, remained a possibility. Health and safety were important considerations especially given the survival of the intact well at Stromness cemetery broch, and the final aim was to preserve the archaeological record of the feature before it was taken by the next storm (which occurred on 24 July 1993).

The well (**52**) was accessible directly from the beach. Two sides of the feature protruded from the cliff and it was possible to excavate the fill by hand from the south-east corner, which had been removed by the sea. The excavation was confined to the fill, which lay within walls cut through bedrock. The turf and topsoil above the well had been contoured and partly removed by the sea but where they overhung they were cut back for safety reasons and to expose any surviving stratigraphy.

The access to the well had been from the south-east, where steps cut into the bedrock had been largely removed by the winter storms. During the removal of the slumped earth and rubble fill from the well, which had originated from the stratigraphy within the broch interior, it was seen that its roof, comprising stone slabs, had collapsed inwards from the south-east. This had possibly occurred during the occupation of the settlement. Deposits of slumped hearth material adhering to the capping stones indicated that part of the broch floor had subsided into the well when its roof collapsed. The well cavity was filled with rubble and masonry, interpreted as primarily deriving from its access and the deposits above. It is unknown whether the collapse of the well roof was solely the result of its structural failure, or was due to some event within the broch itself. Whatever the cause, no indication of further occupation above the well fill was noted and no attempt had been made by the occupiers of the broch to clean out the well or repair its roof. A paper by W.G.T. Watt in 1905, suggests that the broch had never been excavated in antiquity in spite of the exposure of its walls, and no finds had been recovered from it.

The well chamber was a parallelogram, which measured 1.7 by 2.6m and lay beneath the broch tower floor. Its north-western corner cut through approximately 2m of soft laminated bedrock. The amount of stone in its fill and the survival of a small patch of masonry above its north wall suggest that not only was the bedrock built up in places, but that the roof of the well may have been partly corbelled. A large slab, interpreted as an almost intact roofing slab measuring 0.9 by 0.9m, was found in the fill (**53**). One edge had been straightened by chipping and two opposing notches were cut near one end. It is conceivable that the well opening was reduced in size by corbelling to permit covering by one or two large flagstones.

Traces of extensive burning in the south-western corner of the well suggest that fire was used to excavate the bedrock. On its base was a 50mm thick deposit of flat beach stones, which rested on a layer of clean redeposited clayey subsoil. The preparation of this floor possibly allowed it to function as a filter for the well water. The floor sloped from east to west but remains of the foot of the well in the south-east had already been removed by the storms. Although the lowest deposits were damp, no water was found in its base during the excavation.

*53  The well in the cliff face after excavation with the surviving roof slab leaning against the well wall*

## Finds from the well

From within the fill of the feature a number of finds were located and samples were collected. These included eight ceramic body sherds from as many as seven different vessels, of probably middle Iron Age date. There were in addition three bone points, borers or gouges, formed from antler and a sheep bone. Three sandstone artefacts included a small pot lid less than 80mm in diameter, a cobble tool with ground and facetted ends, possibly used as a rubber, and another cobble tool with pounded and flaked ends, which may have been used as a hammer. There were also a small number of marine shells, crustacean fragments and a small sample of charcoal.

The well fill contained 381 animal and fish bones in a very good state of preservation. They included bones of domestic species (cattle, sheep, pig, red deer, dog and cat), wild mammals (fox, seal and rabbit), a number of bird species including domestic fowl, and fish. Analysis of the material suggests that whole carcasses of sheep were introduced within the well while it was still accessible. Other bones may have derived from the floor of the broch or are later intrusions (Catherine Smith undertook the identification of the bone).

## The Iron Age ditch

In 1993 a previously unrecorded ditch was found enclosing the settlement. Its flat-bottomed profile was clearly visible in the newly cut cliff section *c.*27m west of the well. The vegetation and turf cover of the cliff had been washed away to reveal the complete ditch profile, which was recorded photographically (**54**). The base of the ditch was cut through bedrock to a depth of 1m with a width of approximately 2m. The upper part of the ditch was much wider and appeared stepped to its base. The mixed fill comprised clayey soil with large and small stones that appeared to have been tipped in from the east. Two ceramic body sherds were found within the exposed fill.

171

**54** *The broch ditch seen in section in the eroding cliff, 1992*

Immediately north of the ditch and lying outside the settlement is a small U-shaped depression of unknown purpose with minimum dimensions of 0.3 x 0.5m. It was cut into the bedrock and filled with stone and clayey soil.

### Other structures in the cliff

From the ditch leading out to the headland north and west of the broch is evidence of more prehistoric buildings including walling and cist- or tank-like structures of thin-bedded sandstone (**colour plate 24**). These included one with large capping slab. The smaller has a slabbed base and is associated with surrounding stonework (**colour plate 25**). These features have not been recorded in detail and there is no dating evidence for them. Although erosion has been less severe here since 1993, the clarity of the structures in 2000 suggests that continued exposure is a threat to their survival.

Between the ditch and the broch wall a number of other structures visible in 2002 were quite overgrown in 1997. A double-faced wall of at least 11 courses prominently protrudes from the cliff (**colour plate 26**). Associated with it to its immediate north are two areas of paving, one at its base, with collapses and tumble from at least one other wall. This area may represent the remains of an external structure or structures to the broch tower. Monitoring between 1997 and 2000 revealed little impact on this area from erosion.

The centre of the broch and its visible walling has also altered little since 1993, but the most noticeable threat is that of rabbit burrowing, which has disturbed stratigraphy and walls in this area. The well, lying beneath the remains of the broch, and the stratigraphically earlier deposits of midden and stonework to the south have also remained largely unchanged since 1997. Exposure of these deposits and the lack of turf covering indicates that they are vulnerable to both wind and water erosion. Occasional fragments of middle Iron Age pottery sherds and bone artefacts have been found here.

The most notable change in this area has occurred on the small headland lying immediately south of the broch. Continuous horizons of prehistoric midden and stonework emanating from the broch cumulate on this headland which has seen the removal of as much as 1m of cliff edge between 1997 and 2000. Where the cliff was previously vertical, it is now stepped and much of the known archaeology has altered beyond recognition. An upright stone with associated walling seen in 1997 had been completely removed by 2000 and new stonework had become visible lying immediately below the turf on the top of the headland (**colour plate 27**). Active erosion of this point could be seen in the amount of loose stone, turf damage and undercut deposits. In previous years, additional structural features including walls, paving and another slab-sided 'drain' were noted following the headland to the south and east where the archaeological deposits gradually peter out. This area was not recorded in 2000.

## Summary results from Breckness

The monitoring of this one Iron Age site since 1986 has revealed a complex archaeological record, which is subject to periodic alteration by marine, aerial and faunal damage. The deposits containing archaeological material extend for a couple of hundred metres either side of the broch tower and represent remains from pre-broch to post-broch events. Evidence of medieval features noted in the bishop's house and the earlier chapel and graveyard (**55**) are at present limited to occasional human remains eroding out of the top of the cliff section above the broch stonework (Smith and Lorimer 1987 and archive report by Lorimer).

From Laing's description of Breckness there have been significant changes to the coastline even though the centre of the broch is still visible, albeit in a reduced condition. The headland to the south has most noticeably altered and the ever-changing evidence of structures indicates the persistent removal of the cliff edge and its archaeological heritage by high-energy environmental events. What is problematic is the inaccessibility of many of the archaeological structures for more detailed recording and sampling purposes, and the lack of characterisation and understanding of them for the greater knowledge of the settlement complex as a whole.

The single excavation of the well has highlighted a little of the story of the broch. Environmental evidence indicates the occurrence of animal carcasses in a feature which may have become redundant during the life of the settlement. However, these events have yet to be dated. The situation may be similar to one found at Howe during the early Iron Age or Phase 4 (Ballin Smith 1994) where red deer carcasses were thrown into a well just outside the settlement. Although the Breckness feature is interpreted as a well, there is no confirmatory evidence to suggest it functioned as one. Underground Iron Age features with steps leading to a dry chamber are not uncommon on Orkney (Card & Downes 2001).

What is also of interest at this site is perhaps not so much the depth of archaeological deposits but its linear expanse across the cliffs from the broch at the centre (**55**). There are few recognised features under the turf and back from the cliff top, except those associated with medieval ecclesiastical remains. How far inland the prehistoric settlement evidence survives is presently unknown as is the extent of medieval activity. Geophysical prospection could yield much valuable information to aid the understanding of this site and inform future monitoring procedures.

The processes of erosion are also little researched and are not documented with any accuracy. The evidence from monitoring the site over the last decade indicates that erosion is erratic with little patterning in the behaviour of winds and waves. There are many variable factors such as wind speed and direction, height of tides, equinoxes, geology, the durability of the bedrock, the stability of the overlying archaeological remains and that of the vegetative cover, and effects of animals and birds. Erosion can attack one part of the site in particular and be reduced at others dependent on wind direction. The re-recognition of a strip of

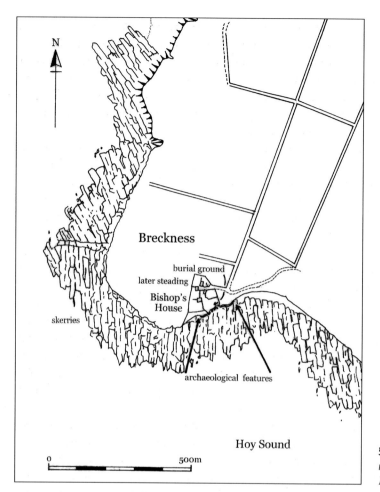

**55** *The location of the threatened features at Breckness*

eroding cliff with its archaeological features can be problematic from one monitoring season to another. Although the monitoring of Breckness has been established and persists through personal interest, the methodologies employed are by no means a best standard. They can be discussed further and improved but their aims can be applied elsewhere.

## Discussion and conclusions

The sea, and other waterways, were probably the most important means of widespread communication and exchange throughout British prehistory. The emphasis on the sea, not just for communication but for the limitless resources it offered, was probably one of the most important reasons for the location of Iron Age settlements along the Atlantic seaboard of northern Scotland. The coastal situation, which was an initial advantage, is now seen as a major threat to the survival of brochs and the wealth of information they contain. They are a finite resource and the information they contain about the Iron Age way of life including diet, constructional techniques, technological developments and farming among others is being removed either persistently or intermittently by the combined effects of sea and wind.

The documentation and research at Breckness has wider relevance. The effects of erosion will be experienced in varying degrees by other Iron Age sites along the west coast and in other exposed littoral situations throughout Orkney and the North of Scotland. Orkney has many vulnerable sites of all periods but is not the only region where sites are threatened (see Church 1998). Breckness has been chosen as an example because it is accessible to this author and because its particular coastal situation was documented during the middle of the nineteenth century. It is also a site where the preservation of the broch and settlement versus its erosion can be evaluated and examined further. Other vulnerable Orcadian sites have been targeted for more detailed funded archaeological investigations, such as St Boniface on Papa Westray (Lowe 1998) and Tuquoy, Westray (Owen 1994). These have tended to be sites with proven research potential, with often deep and complex stratigraphy spanning many periods and linked to visible surface remains, often ecclesiastical. But what of other coastal Iron Age sites?

Coastal erosion has been discussed by Historic Scotland in two publications (Ashmore 1994 and as a procedural paper in 1996). In the latter, four strategies were suggested: long term studies of coastal processes; strategic archaeological surveys; site protection schemes and carefully designed archaeological excavations. Some of these strategies have been undertaken on Iron Age sites on the Northern and Western Isles but there has been little dissemination or debate of the results that could inform the future recording of threatened Iron Age sites and the identification of new ones. The evaluation and protection of sites from further erosion seems only to take place where there is either good research potential, an economic return or an emotional connection; for example, the building of a protective seawall at Warebeth was to protect the cemetery not the broch below.

Through Historic Scotland funding, much of Scotland's coastline has been assessed for archaeological sites, which will allow the identification and prioritisation of vulnerable sites. Although this debate is confined to the Iron Age, the problem of coastal erosion of sites is ubiquitous and Iron Age sites must compete for funding with sites of all periods. It is beyond the means of one government agency to fund and control the adequate recording of all threatened sites with prehistoric and early historic heritage.

Continued monitoring of Iron Age sites is one method of recording and preserving the archaeological heritage. One archaeological body which could carry out this work is that of monument wardens. The wardens already carry out periodic inspections of sites but the collection of data from actively eroding and accessible sites could be emphasised. Visiting archaeologists and museum curators already play their part in the assemblage of data but none of this is managed or prioritised from the point of view of the site, its information, its period or its location. Although recently published reports on excavated Iron Age sites from the Northern and Western Isles acknowledge coastal erosion as a problem, it is rarely discussed as a major issue in terms of its processes, its effects on sites or the rate of information loss. The emphasis is often on accessible sites where the collection and therefore preservation of data is easier, but what of the information lost from less accessible sites?

Breckness, as described above, is by no means set up as an example of best practise, as the monitoring is carried out on an *ad hoc* basis due to personal interest and accessibility. Breckness is simply one eroding complex Iron Age site. Monitoring is a simple method of recording without exacerbating the erosional processes. However, threatened Iron Age coastal sites be evaluated by more traditional archaeological methods using geophysics, selected excavation, or cliff cleaning and recording without causing further significant erosion. They could also be used in association with coastal defence. This combined methodology was attempted in the Western Isles at the broch and settlement at Dun Vulan (Parker-Pearson and Sharples 1999) where protection was added to the coast after the completion of the archaeological investigations. However, the broch remains under threat as the sea has eroded deposits beyond the coastal barrier (Stephen Driscoll pers. comm.).

Other sites have been targeted on the Western Isles such as Galson on Lewis where the identification of principal archaeological features and the sampling and dating of important contexts formed part of the aims of the project (Church 1998). This method presupposes that the contextual importance of features beyond the broch, or the principal structure, within a vertical section can be clearly understood in relationship to the whole site. The complexity of stratigraphy is not necessarily immediately apparent and identification of main features may be impossible.

An evaluation of information collection methodologies (including time and money) versus the potential information yield should be made. Traditional archaeological methods will inform best on the questions concerning the constructional details of brochs and other contemporary Iron Age settlements, their resources and economies, and their social makeup. But traditional methods are both time-consuming and expensive, and will not be possible in all cases because of exacerbating erosion conditions and because of health and safety considerations. An eclectic approach may be the most valuable where at targeted sites simple recording approaches (inexpensive) can be linked with more detailed approaches (expensive) which include cleaning, detailed recording and sampling of the cliff face and cliff top topographic and geophysical surveys when necessary. This could be extended by specific excavation of targeted areas in order to understanding contextual and sample information. However, selected excavation of broch settlement sites is fraught with stratigraphic and other difficulties.

There are possibly as many monitoring and data collection solutions to the problem of coastally situated eroding Iron Age sites as there are sites, leading to the logical conclusion that each site could be taken on its own individual merit. In some instances, effective monitoring may be limited or impossible due to difficulties of access, at others the method used could be adapted and applied to different types of coastline and the potential of the visible features. However, the questions remain as to how do we prioritise sites, and how do we balance targeting selected sites for more thorough investigations and a more general monitoring of sites undertaken on a more regular basis. The emphasis must lie in prioritising sites and in co-ordinating archaeologists, their work and results.

Broch settlements have always been one of Euan MacKie's favourite research topics. The usually exceptional preservation of structures and the good survival of stratigraphy have enabled detailed analysis that can inform on the Iron Age way of life. The traditional excavation of these most difficult sites is restricted by their sheer expense, size and extent and other cultural heritage factors, such as economic return. In a time of increasing economic hardship for archaeological research perhaps the only cost-effective means of gaining new knowledge of brochs is to turn our resources to the ones that are the most threatened, the coastal sites. A consistent monitoring programme at targeted sites may provide much valuable statistical data on how fast the Iron Age cliff edge heritage is dwindling. Without this basic knowledge we cannot adequately plan to save it in the future.

# 15  Pictish pigs and Celtic cowboys

## Food and farming in the Atlantic Iron Age

*J.M. Bond*

## Introduction

Discussion of the nature of later Iron age society in the Atlantic region has, with a few exceptions (e.g. Edwards & Ralston 1997) usually centred on the architectural and artefactual evidence, with little attention being paid to the economic base. This paper looks in detail at the economic evidence for the Northern Isles in the late Iron Age, and suggests that a major increase in agricultural intensification occurred at that time. Childe, writing in 1946, saw in the Scottish Iron age evidence for 'indirectly intensified agriculture and an increased reliance on cereal foods' (Childe 1946, 82). Piggott thought, for good reasons, that Childe was wrong. By that point, in 1958, few rotary querns had been discovered in Northern England or Scotland, apart from some in southern Scotland which appeared to be Roman introductions. The only finds of pre-Roman or non-Roman charred grain known were from south-east England, and it would be another 20 years or so before systematic sampling and sieving would start to alter that picture. Piggott suggested instead that northern Iron Age Britain did not take the same path as the south and intensify its agriculture in the Roman and post-Roman periods, but that there was an alternative type of economy, based on pastoralism with an element of nomadism, which he called the 'Stanwick type' (Piggott 1958, 11-14). This is in many respects the old Classical dichotomy between boring but civilised farmer and savage but exotic pastoralist. Piggott himself recognised this but he was seduced by the idea, as many distinguished archaeologists, working in different places and time periods, have been since. His enthusiasm is obvious in his writing. What had been a dry-toned paper dealing with evidence for agriculture in Scotland explodes into ringing phrases which conjure up a dramatic world of pastoralists, heroes and cattle-thieves. He compares the northern Celts to the warrior Maasai, and says for example:

> There is no doubt that in the cattle-raid of Cooley, and in the other Ulster stories, we are among the warrior aristocracy of a pastoralist economy . . . whatever may have been the status of the lower orders of society, the heroes of the Ulster stories . . . are chariot-driving pastoralists, counting their wealth in flocks and herds.
>
> Piggott 1958, 17, 18

Piggott acknowledged that crops must have been grown in Scotland, but felt the yields could never have been high and that the terrain in the Atlantic Province, where brochs and wheelhouses were to be found, meant that the land was better suited to spade cultivation which would 'prohibit much improvement in agricultural techniques beyond a rather primitive level'. In fact, modern work such as Dockrill's on soils (Dockrill 1994) and the author's research into the historical and ethnographic evidence of barley cultivation show that this sort of intensive spade cultivation coupled with heavy manuring can give very high crop yields (Bond 1994, and see Dockrill this volume). Piggott however felt that true intensification (and perhaps true civilisation) was only to be obtained though the use of a plough. He envisaged Northern Britain as populated, in his now-famous phrase, with 'celtic cowboys and shepherds, footloose and unpredictable, moving with their animals over rough pasture and moorland' who 'could never adopt the Roman way of life in the manner of the settled farmers of the South'.

Until relatively recently, there has been very little work done which would refute Piggott's conclusions. Until the advent of large-scale environmental sampling on modern excavation sites and the dissemination of research on the recovered material, any discussion was based on scarce animal bone data and interpretation of artefacts such as quernstones and stone ard points, along with visible landscape features such as field boundaries. The publication of several major Iron Age sites with environmental data such as Crosskirk in Caithness, Howe in Orkney and most recently Upper Scalloway in Shetland, is changing this picture for the Northern Isles (Fairhurst 1984, Ballin Smith 1994, Sharples 1998) (**46**). The author's own research on the multi-period sites at Pool in Orkney and the ongoing excavations at Old Scatness in Shetland are also providing detailed evidence for this period (Bond 1994, Bond in Hunter *et al.* forthcoming)The debate on the nature of the economies of the Atlantic Iron age was restarted not with the Northern Isles sites, but with a discussion of the site of Dun Vulan, on South Uist in the Western Isles (Parker Pearson *et al.* 1996). Although the present paper concentrates on evidence from the late Iron Age of the Northern Isles, the debate about the nature of the Dun Vulan economy provides a useful comparison with many of the same problems of interpretation.

Parker Pearson *et al*'s paper looked at brochs in the Western Isles and specifically, the broch of Dun Vulan. The authors argued that significant differences could be seen between the economies of the brochs and smaller settlements, and that these differences represented a settlement hierarchy. They suggested that at Dun Vulan the cattle were raised under a 'high input high risk' dairy strategy, and sheep raised as 'low input low output low risk meat strategy'. It is suggested that at Dun Vulan, as at other broch sites, animal bone assemblages are dominated by young pigs and calves, and that a lot of red deer was also being eaten. The authors suggested a parallel with the differences between Medieval English aristocratic and commoner diet, where the aristocracy exercised a monopoly on wild game, and favoured pig as a feasting animal. Although this is a modern interpretation based on new evidence, the faint ghost of Piggott's chariot-driving warrior aristocracy is perhaps still discernable.

A reply to this paper was published in *Antiquity* two years later (Gilmour & Cook 1998). The authors disagreed with several of Parker Pearson *et al*'s conclusions and argued that the midden with the high proportion of pig was not contemporary with the broch but was in fact later in date. Their most serious objection was to the interpretation which the excavators of Dun Vulan put forward for the high numbers of very young calves, arguing that these animals cannot be a consequence of a dairying strategy in the Iron Age. To support their argument, Gilmour and Cook quoted work by McCormick (1991, 1992, 1998). McCormick believes that high proportions of very young calf bones from pre-Medieval settlements cannot represent dairying, because literary evidence suggests that primitive cows would not give milk unless the calf was present and thus killing the calves a few weeks after birth would prevent the cows from being milked. Gilmour and Cook therefore argue that the high numbers of young calf bones present on these sites represent not animals slaughtered to increase the amount of milk available for humans, but those which have either died from stress or which have been killed because there was insufficient fodder available for them. But if the farming system was consistently failing to produce enough fodder to support so many calves, why put the cows through the stress and danger (and increased food consumption) of pregnancy? Why not limit the number of cows put to the bull, and thus reduce the number of calves which would have to be killed soon after birth?

Parker Pearson, Sharples and Mulville responded with a further paper (Parker Pearson *et al.* 1999a) in which they refuted the reinterpretation of Dun Vulan's stratigraphy, restated their view that there was a very high proportion of pig bones, some perhaps from meat joints brought to the broch from elsewhere, and pointed out that there is considerable variation in the age range for culling calves in dairying economies (cf. Parker Pearson *et al.* 1999b).The evidence considered in detail in this paper is for intensification in the post-broch farming economies of the Northern Isles, but the Dun Vulan debate is useful because many of the factors involved (the high numbers of very young cattle with the possibility of dairying, the relatively high proportions of pig bones and the suggestion of power and hierarchies expressed through food and the economy) are strands which are also present in the late Iron Age of Orkney and Shetland. In many ways the Northern and Western Isles are not directly comparable systems: soils, environment and even the building traditions differ, but as island systems in marginal environments there are many similarities in the constraints placed on agricultural intensification (Bond 1998). Studies in island biogeography would predict that in order to avoid risk, economies in both the Northern and Western Isles would be broad-based rather than specialised, leading to an apparent conservatism and a lack of major changes (Bond 1994, 299-304; Bond 1998, 82-3). Given the apparent similarities between the economies of the broch period in the Western Isles and the post-broch period in the North this is evidently true and so, in order to see any intensification or change, it is necessary to look in greater detail at the data for a more restricted area. This paper therefore concentrates on evidence from a single area, the Northern Isles.

## Cattle in late Iron Age Orkney and Shetland

The site of Pool on the island of Sanday in Orkney has produced, like Dun Vulan, a high number of neonate cattle bones: 47 per cent of the mandibles from the late Iron Age/Pictish phases had tooth wear which indicated the animals were under six months old at death (Serjeantson & Bond forthcoming). The proportion of young animals increased again in the succeeding Viking/Norse period, and evidence from epiphyseal fusion of the cattle bones shows the same trend. At Howe broch, Mainland Orkney, there was also a high proportion of neonate and juvenile animals; only a quarter of the cattle reached adulthood (Smith *et al.* 1994, 144). The animal bone work on material from the late Iron Age middens at Old Scatness Broch, Dunrossness, Shetland, is still at an early stage but those assemblages are also producing high proportions of very young cattle (Nicholson & Bond 1999). This pattern seems to be very similar to the evidence from the Western Isles sites. However, Scalloway broch in Shetland produced a different pattern with a peak of cattle killed between 18 months and 2.5 years (O'Sullivan 1998, 127). O'Sullivan followed McCormick's reasoning and argued that it was actually this very different pattern which indicated dairying, with the calves killed after weaning. If this is so, and no allowance is made for different patterns of dairying, what do all the younger calves on the other sites represent? Medieval deposits dating to the mid-thirteenth to late fourteenth centuries from the Bedern in York produced an animal bone assemblage in which the cattle bones were concentrated into two groups: a very young group with the first permanent molar not yet in wear (approximately two to six months old) and an elderly group with advanced wear on all columns of the first molar. Epiphyseal fusion data showed similar results (Bond & O'Connor 1999, 364). This pattern is very similar to that seen at Pool and the other sites (with the exception of Scalloway) under discussion here. The Bedern assemblages were the waste from a religious community; these animals had to have been brought into the city from outlying farms and were therefore the result of deliberate culls rather than large numbers of accidental or stress-related deaths. The authors interpreted the Bedern calves as the by-product of a dairying system, brought to the site to be used either for veal or vellum, or both. There are methods recorded from all over the Old World for persuading more primitive breeds of animals to give milk without the actual presence of their young. Most of these involve visual or sensory stimulation of the animal to make it believe its offspring is present and thus stimulating production of the hormone prolactin to produce the milk. Methods cited by Lucas from the Irish sources include setting the stuffed skin of the animal's own calf in front of the animal at milking time. He quotes Moryson, whose account of experiences in Ireland in the early seventeenth century included a description of how the Irish killed many calves at birth in order to increase the milk yield:

> the calves being taken away, the Cowes are so mad among them, as they will give no milk till the skinne of the calf be stuffed and set before them, that they may smell the odour of their own bellies.
>
> Moryson quoted in Lucas 1989, 51-2

Lucas points out that this practice was obviously considered by writers over several centuries to be one of the 'wonders of Ireland', and was therefore presumably unknown in England by this time. He also includes an account of a similar practice from the Outer Hebrides in 1884, which suggests that such methods were still in use in other areas with unimproved cattle (Lucas 1989, 54). Another method cited by Lucas is 'cow blowing'. First recorded by Moryson in Ireland in the early seventeenth century, Lucas quotes an account by Dinely from his tour of Ireland in 1681:

> In milking of kine when milk doth not come down freely, they are observed in the North of Ireland and elsewhere either to thrust a stiff rope of straw . . . into the cow's bearing place, or else with their mouthes to blow in as much wind as they can, with which doing they many times come off with a shitten nose.
>
> Lucas 1989, 55-6

Lucas points out that these customs have an extremely wide distribution; the calfskin trick is known amongst many Old World pastoralists, for example in India, Mongolia, Tibet, among the Bedouin (who use it with their camels) and in parts of Africa. Cow blowing has been recorded in Africa, China, India, Russia, the Alps and the Pyrenees. Herodotus, writing in the fifth century BC, describes the Scythians using the method with their horses. A milking scene dating from *c.*2500 BC at Al 'Ubaid in Mesopotamia has been interpreted as showing the milkers utilising cow blowing (Lucas 1989, 55-8). Whilst it is impossible to prove that either these or similar methods were used in late Iron Age Scotland, the ubiquity of such practices amongst the owners of unimproved breeds of domestic animals makes it a likely possibility. The simplest explanation for the high numbers of young calves on settlement sites in the Northern and Western Isles is that they are a by-product of milk production.

## Late Iron Age and Pictish pigs

As in the Western Isles, the numbers of pigs found on some Northern Isles sites in the Iron Age is relatively high. At Pool in the late Iron Age they comprise about 15-25 per cent of all mammal bone in terms of minimum numbers, 10-15 per cent by numbers of identified specimens (NISP) (Bond 1994, 278-9 & Appendix B, Bond in Hunter *et al.* forthcoming). Pig-keeping was much less common in the Northern Isles in historical times; The *Statistical Account* of 1791-9 records that on Sanday in Orkney, with a human population of 1772 souls in 349 households, there were but 135 swine (*Stat. Acc.*, 45). At Dun Vulan pig forms 22 per cent of the mammal bone from the first to third century AD midden (Parker Pearson *et al.* 1996, 65). Scalloway broch in Shetland and Howe broch on Mainland Orkney also had relatively high numbers of pigs (O'Sullivan 1998, 108-9, Smith *et al.* 141). At Scalloway, in a faint echo of Piggott, it is said that

> the rise in pig consumption may have been due to changing dietary preferences among the ruling classes . . . contemporary Irish literature makes it clear that pork was the preferred meat of the ruling classes. (O'Sullivan 1998, 109)

A representation of a pig or boar was found at Old Scatness broch in 1998 (**56**). The carving was found on the buried portion of one of the kerbstones around a hearth in a small Pictish-type multicellular building (Bond 1999). This animal bears little resemblance to the classic carvings of boars on symbol stones, but was nevertheless found in a significant position in an undoubtedly Pictish-style building, and though a little stiff in execution, it was probably drawn from life. Several naturalistic details suggest features seen on old breeds, such as the lappet or flap of skin like a chicken's wattle by the mouth, the stiff mane and the straight hairy tail. An old unimproved breed of Irish pig illustrated in Watson (1998) shows similar features. In the eighteenth and nineteenth centuries Orcadian and Shetland pigs were said to be covered in a coarse reddish-brown hair which was long and strong enough to be used in rope-making (Fenton 1978, 496). The position of the Old Scatness boar carving and its careful execution do suggest that the pig had a certain importance to the late Iron Age and Pictish inhabitants of the settlement. Pigs are usually kept essentially as meat providers, so a rise in pig numbers would suggest a rise in meat consumption. It is, though, more difficult to connect this rise in meat-eating to any particular social class, without good evidence from a range of smaller and 'poorer' sites in the Northern Isles.

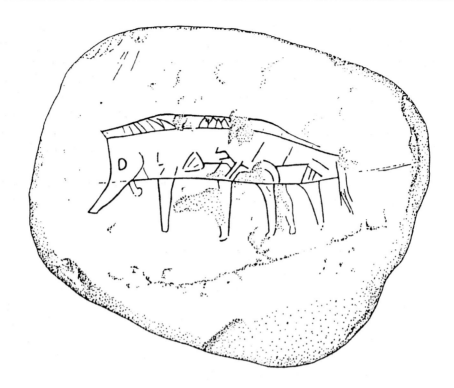

**56** *Hearthstone from multicellular building at Old Scatness, with incised representation of a pig*

## Cereal production

Barley is present as the main crop from the Neolithic period in the Northern Isles, but there is a difference in the concentration of charred grains recovered archaeologically from the broch period onwards (see Dockrill this volume). At the brochs of Howe and Scalloway, large amounts of charred grain were found, some obviously immature (Dickson 1994, 134, Holden 1998, 126). At the non-broch site of Pool, the late Iron Age buildings contained several large dumps of charred grain, giving densities of cereal grains per litre of soil sample as high as 64.4 in one case (Bond 1994, 246). At the Old Scatness settlement in Shetland, Structure 5, the Pictish-type multicellular building containing the boar carving also produced high proportions of cereal grains per litre of soil sample (Bond 1998b, 92). It seems to be generally true that, with the exception of the Neolithic charred grain cache from the Ness of Gruting, Shetland (Milles 1986), large concentrations of charred grain are not found on Northern Isles sites until the middle to late Iron Age. This is not the place to discuss in detail the nature of plant remains assemblages from these sites, but study of these samples has convinced the author that what is happening is a change from small-scale, day-to-day bulk processing of grain for virtually immediate consumption, to a larger-scale processing and storage operation, with the accumulation of grain, perhaps from more than one landholding, in central places. The change from day-to-day to bulk processing would be sufficient to account for the changes in recovery, as larger-scale drying and storage would increase the chances of large amounts of grain catching fire and charring at the same time. As Dockrill suggests (this volume) brochs may well have provided a central storage place, but the phenomenon of high concentrations of grain also occurs in the later Iron Age, at sites like Old Scatness and Pool. It is interesting to speculate whether domestic cats, which appear on Northern Isles sites with remarkable rapidity after their introduction to Britain (Phase 2 at Upper Scalloway, *c.*100 BC–AD 500, O'Sullivan 1998, 110. Phase 6, second and first centuries BC at Howe, Smith *et al.* 1994, 146. Phase 6.3, later Iron Age/Pictish period at Pool, Bond 1994, 274), were not imported and tolerated in order to deal with an increase in pests resulting from bulk storage of grain. At Old Scatness the earliest house mouse (*Mus musculus*) yet found in Shetland has been recovered from the hearth deposits of a late Iron Age wheelhouse, an apparently secure context (Bond 1998b, 93; identification by R A Nicholson). At least one colleague takes a more cynical view and argues that cats are like fleas; they arrive uninvited and are then extremely difficult to dislodge (O'Connor, pers. comm.).

## The introduction of oats to the Northern Isles

An important development in Orkney and Shetland in the middle to late Iron Age is the introduction of a new cereal crop. Cultivated oats (*Avena sativa*) are found in the late Iron Age at Scalloway broch and Howe broch and at Pool, too, cultivated oats (*Avena strigosa*) are a late Iron Age introduction (Holden & Boardman 1998, 99, Dickson 1994, 125, Bond 1994, 180). There are as yet only preliminary results available from Old Scatness, but oats (*Avena* sp., not yet further identified) are present in the late Iron Age samples from that settlement also. The significance of oats as a crop is that they will grow successfully on much poorer land than barley. *Avena strigosa*, the oat identified at Pool and elsewhere, is also known as the 'black oat' and sometimes as the 'sand oat'. Though the grain is very small in comparison to modern cultivated varieties, it is able to live on extremely poor and very sandy soils. By growing such a crop, poorer land unsuitable to the cultivation of barley could be utilised, thus increasing the total area of land available for cultivation and the total yield. The weed assemblages from the sites of Pool and Scalloway bear this out, with the introduction and increase of weeds of poorer land: weeds of light and sandy land at Pool, and species which prefer more acidic conditions at Scalloway (Bond 1994, 193–5, Holden 1998, 126).

As well as being an important human food in the North of Britain, oats have also been traditionally used to feed animals. A crop which not only extended the amount of poorer land available for cereal cultivation, but also provided storable extra winter fodder for cattle and horses, would have been an extremely important innovation in an area with a very limited growing season. Oats were also used in Ireland to fatten pigs (Watson 1998, 64). It may be that horses themselves became more common at some sites, and were introduced at others, only when this agricultural intensification led to the greater availability of fodder; they appear first in the records for Scalloway and Howe in the middle Iron Age, and at Pool in the late Iron Age (O'Sullivan 1998, 110, Smith *et al.* 1994, 139, Bond 1994, 273).The intake of poorer land for oat cultivation would have cut down on the available grazing for sheep. It would have also encroached upon the hill land, which still supported red deer both on the Mainland of Orkney and in the islands; there is no evidence that red deer ever lived in Shetland. Red deer seem to have formed part of the diet at some of the larger Orcadian settlements, though it is interesting to note that the small early Iron Age settlement of Tofts

Ness on the northern tip of Sanday, Orkney, produced no evidence for the eating of deer. The larger site of Pool, on the same island, was however utilising the animal from the Neolithic right through until the late Norse period. It is possible that larger settlements like Pool controlled access to the herds (Bond 1994, 273-4).

## Flax

Another crop, flax (*Linum usitatissimum*), first appears in the environmental record in the late Iron Age phases of some Northern Isles sites. At both Howe and Warebeth brochs on Mainland Orkney and at Scalloway in Shetland flax appears to be a late Iron Age introduction (Dickson 1994, 131-2, Bell & Dickson 1989), though at other multi-period sites such as Pool on Sanday this crop does not appear in the records until the Viking/Norse period (Bond & Hunter 1987). Flax could provide both linseed oil and flax fibre, both extremely useful commodities, but growing and processing is time-consuming and would eat into the good land available for barley production, which may explain why it was not immediately adopted throughout the Northern Isles.

## Just Celtic cowboys?

The modern excavation and sampling methods employed at Iron Age and multi-period sites like Old Scatness, Pool, Scalloway and the Howe mean that it is now possible to begin to distinguish between broch and post-broch material, a division sometimes unclear in older excavations of these extremely complex Northern Isles settlements, as Fojut has recently argued (Fojut 1998). The evidence presented above paints a picture of increasing agricultural intensification in late Iron Age Orkney and Shetland, with the introduction of new crops and subsequent taking-in of extra farmland by settlements, the concentration of storage and bulk-processing in larger settlements, evidence for dairying, the possible use of pigs as a favoured meat animal and the introduction of horses. Surprisingly, the focus of most of this intensification appears to be not in the broch period, but in the post-broch settlements. At first this may seem counter-intuitive. One might expect that intensification and change would go hand-in-hand with the brochs themselves, symbols of local power and patronage. However, the transition from the monumental architecture of broch towers to the outwardly unimpressive post-broch buildings at sites like Old Scatness and elsewhere seems to occur at much the same time as the early stages of state formation and the emergence of distinctively 'Pictish' cultural elements. Perhaps local power (and its expression in the broch towers) counted for less, as developing political ties and contacts were opening up the local economies to longer-distance trade and wider networks of influence. This late Iron Age agricultural intensification could be seen as a direct development from the centralisation begun with the broch farmers (Dockrill this volume). The farmers of late Iron Age Orkney and Shetland were very far from being mere Celtic cowboys.

# 16 Viking and late Norse re-use of broch mounds in Caithness

*Colleen E. Batey*

## Introduction

In 1974 Euan MacKie published his report on the excavations at Dun Mor Vaul on Tiree (Mackie 1974). Amongst the artefactual assemblage, he recorded an antler comb with iron rivets which had been found in association with three fragments of flint blades stained with iron, a whetstone and three tiny hollow bronze hemispheres (MacKie 1974, 143) (**57**). These items are Norse in origin, and may have been related to the event of the deposition of a single inhumation in the central court of the broch which was C14 dated, GX 3426 1145±155BP. The date has been recalibrated to be AD 600–1250 with 95.4 per cent probability (OxCal v3.5 Bronk Ramsey 2000). This is evidence for the presence of the Vikings, perhaps prior to the final stages of the collapse of the broch lintels at Dun Mor Vaul. The precise nature of this presence is unclear, since the burial would seem to have been unaccompanied on discovery and the group of objects, consistent with a grave group, lacks an associated skeleton; indeed it is possible that the comb itself, with its copper-alloy rivet used in repair, was in use in the Late Norse period when grave goods would not be usually be deposited.

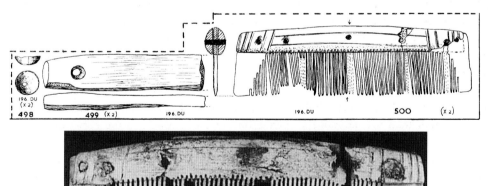

**57** *Finds group from Dun Mor Vaul context 196 DU (after MacKie 1974, fig. 19 and Plate XIII). Composite antler comb (actual length 4.1in), and whetstone. a) line illustration, b) photography of reverse of the comb*

## Northern Scotland

This situation is more marked in Northern Scotland and the Isles, where there has been a long tradition of antiquarian investigation of the many brochs which are a frequent feature of the northern landscape. In Orkney, for example, Viking burials from broch mounds have been recorded at the Howe near Stromness (Graham-Campbell and Batey 1998, 60) and more significantly at the Broch of Gurness. Reconsideration of the available excavated evidence at this site led Hedges to suggest the presence of six or more pagan Viking graves (Hedges 1987, 72-3, 86-7), further to a female burial, discovered in 1932 (Robertson 1969) and distinguished by the presence of a rare Thor's hammer amulet on her neck ring. It is thus clear that at least in the case of the Broch of Gurness, the large structural feature of the broch tower and its later developments were a focus for Viking activities.

## Structural remains: Caithness

The situation in Caithness is potentially similar. Excavations were undertaken by several early workers, most particularly those funded by Sir Francis Tress Barry of Keiss Castle and supervised by John Nicholson of Auckengill. Both Pictish and Norse stray finds and structural fragments were recovered during these campaigns.

There are a small number of examples in Caithness where it is possible that Viking or Late Norse structures may have been added to the top of the broch complexes. This author has written

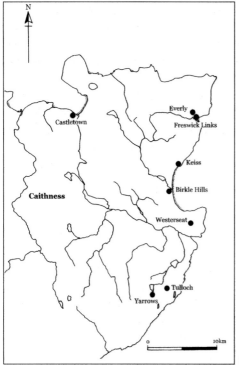

**58** *Location map of sites mentioned in the text*

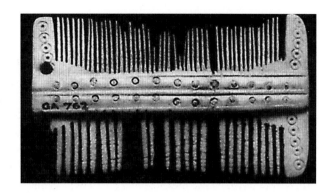

**59** *Freswick Sands Broch antler comb (NMS GA 762).* After Batey 1987a, 208 and Plate 35

elsewhere concerning the possible post-broch structure at Birkle Hills, near Wick, which may have been a building of the Viking or later period (Batey 1987a, 28-9; Batey 1987b, 131). It seems, following the new work undertaken by Dr Andrew Baines at Glasgow University in connection with the Wag constructions of Caithness (Baines 2000), that the Birkle Hills construction would be more likely assignable to the late Iron Age cultural milieu than the Norse. The same situation may also pertain to the site at Tulloch broch, Latheron (Batey 1984, LAT 239; Batey 1987a, 29), and it was clearly the same at Freswick Sands broch (Batey 1987a, 59-60) (**58**).

A small number of Norse finds were recovered from the early excavations at Freswick Sands broch (eg comb 8.9.1 Batey 1987a, Plate 35A, 248) (**59**), which is not unexpected given the proximity of the major late Norse settlement in Freswick Bay (Morris *et al.* 1995), but serious occupation of the mound in the late Norse period is not a viable suggestion. Nearby, at Everly broch, which Tress Barry also excavated, he noted secondary paving in the broch tower and recovered a handled steatite vessel from that campaign (Batey 1987a, 60). Elsewhere, re-use of structures may be suggested at Yarrows, Outbuilding G, where pottery and a steatite vessel were noted by Anderson (1980, 136) and also further south, at Keiss West, where Laing noted in 1866 (1866, 19-20 fig. 25), on a crude section drawing, what may have been a later building seeming to overlie the broch midden (Foster 1989, 196 following Swanson). In 1901, Anderson described an oblong building located between the broch and the church (1901, 131, 139). The survey undertaken by Foster into the late Iron Age activity in Caithness (Foster 1989; 1990) includes other examples of post-broch structures (as well as distinctive post-broch artefactual material), but without excavation dating and cultural affinity of the structural evidence cannot be confirmed at this stage. One area where it is easier to assign a specific cultural identity to material remains is in the pagan burial material recovered from broch mounds.

## Burial remains: Caithness

As long ago as 1883, Anderson noted that there is a distinct favouring by the Norse for burial in a mound (Anderson 1883, 44 fn 1), although flat graves which had surface markers must have been employed at least in cemetery contexts such as Westness in Orkney (Kaland 1993, 312-317). Mounds may have been purposely raised following burial, much as described so graphically by Ibn Fadhlan on witnessing an elaborate boat cremation in his travels amongst the Rus of the Volga Region (quoted in Jones 1986, 435-30), but more locally to be seen in the Isle of

Man for example at Ballateare or Cronk Moar (Bersu and Wilson 1966, Chapter II and III). Pre-existing settlement mounds were also employed, as at Buckquoy where a Norse building had a male inhumation inserted into it following abandonment (Ritchie 1977, 190-1 and 220). Curle notes 'a number of instances [where] human remains have been found on the tops of the mounds covering the ruins (i.e. brochs). The extended burial, and the orientation of the bodies, usually characteristic of these interments, indicate their relation to Christian times' (RCAHMS 1911, xxxiii). More recently, Foster has drawn attention to several examples of inhumations in long cists and short cists which have been placed in the top of broch mounds, such as Dunbeath, Brounabon or Thrumster (Foster 1989, 201), although most are likely to be of similar date (probably later Iron Age) to the excavated examples at Crosskirk (Fairhurst 1984, 101-3). There are a small number of graves of Viking date that have been identified in Caithness and which have made use of pre-existing broch mounds; these are discussed below.

All the evidence for Norse burial in Caithness, from whatever location, has to rely on old excavation records. This is in contrast to the situation in Orkney where recent years have seen modern excavation techniques applied to such sites, as at Westness on Rousay (Kaland 1993, 312-17) or Scar on Sanday (Owen and Dalland 1999). However, although often tantalisingly incomplete, these records do have some merit. The record for Housel Cairn in Halkirk Parish may well be one such rare source of information. The site was recorded by Mr A.O. Curle in his fieldwork for the Royal Commission Inventory of Caithness published in 1911. The entry is brief, but seems a likely description of one or more Viking burials:

> At the edge of a cultivated field about 1/4 mile WSW of Ben Morven Distillery, Halkirk, is a large grassy mound. The mound has been sharply scarped all round and the fragmentary ruins on the top appear to be those of a broch. The construction has, however, been so much pillaged that definite measurements are unobtainable. The O.S. map records that here were found stone cists, containing human remains, bronze rings, iron spear-heads, and pottery.
>
> RCAHMS 1911, 35 no.115

A similar situation may well have pertained at the site of Longhills near Wick (also known as Westerseat), Caithness, where a stone cist was located within a gravel hillock 'a short distance below the broch of Kettleburn', with a pair of oval brooches contained therein, although no skeletal material is noted. Although the actual circumstances of recovery are unclear, with even the date of discovery open to doubt (Batey 1993, 151), this was clearly a Viking deposition.

One of the earlier of these discoveries, to be discussed here in further detail, was made in 1786 in Castletown, on the North Caithness coast, where a female skeleton was discovered accompanied by a small suite of distinctive grave goods (Batey 1993, 148-151) (**60**). Anderson's description of the Castletown (Castlehill) find provides the available evidence and apparently subsequent sources have extracted elements of this account. Firstly in 1874, he records:

> The fine brooch here figured is one of a pair found at Castletown, Caithness, in 1786. It is noticed in the list of donations to the Museum for the year 1787, printed in the Appendix to the Archaeologia Scotica, vol.iii, p 61, as one of several articles presented by James Traill, Esq., among which were:

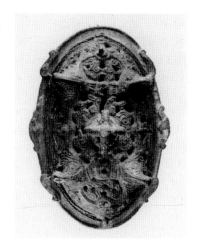

**60** *Castletown oval brooches a) National Museum of Scotland collection (IL 221) (Copyright: Trustees of the National Museums of Scotland), b) National Museum of Denmark, Danish Collections Inventory Nr.10521 (Copyright: National Museum of Denmark).*

two oval brooches of copper gilt, embossed and decorated with rich carvings, each surrounded with a double row of silver cord near the edge, with an iron tongue on the hollow side, much corroded; the length of each brooch, 4.5 inches, the breadth 3 inches. These were, in September last (1786), dug out of the top of the ruins of a Pictish house in Caithness, lying beside a skeleton, buried under a flat stone with very little earth above it.'

One of this pair of brooches was given to Mr Worsaae, on his visit to Scotland, along with other Scottish specimens . . . and I had no difficulty in recognising it in one of the cases of the Museum in Copenhagen (**colour plate 28**).

The notice of the interment with which these brooches had been deposited states that it had been made on the top of one of the mounds covering the ruins of a Pictish broch.

Anderson 1874, 549-50

Writing in 1883, Anderson repeats much of this information, adding something to his description of the decoration:

A pair of oval bowl-shaped brooches of great beauty were found in Caithness in 1786. One of these is in the National Museum . . . it is double-shelled, and the gilding, both on the under and upper shells, is still visible, although the 'double row of silver cord along the edge' which is noted in the first description of the brooches when they were presented by James Traill of Rattar in 1787, is now gone. The centre of the convexity of the brooch is surmounted by a bold ornament, in form somewhat resembling a crown. The ornamentation is distinctly zoomorphic, the four projecting ornaments below the centrepiece being carved into the form of animals' heads.

Anderson 1883, 43-4

The items, excluding the second oval brooch, were given by James Traill in 1787 to the National Museums of Scotland (SAS 1892, 217 and 278) and accessioned as IL 221 (brooch),

FN2 (jet ring) and FN3 (bodkin). Anderson omits in his 1874 reference that the first part of the entry includes 'a black ring or brooch of cannel coal, $2\frac{3}{5}$ inches in diameter, with a slender pin of bone 4 inches long . . . ' as being gifted at he same time and cited specifically as being of the same grave find (Donations 1787, Appendix 2, 61).

It seems that the second brooch was never gifted to the National Museum in Edinburgh, despite Anderson's quotation of the *Archaeologia Scotica* reference. The second brooch, gifted to the National Museum in Copenhagen, has recently been re-identified by Michele Smith of Glasgow University during her Doctoral research, and this author is grateful to her for the following information. The brooch is accessioned as number 10521 and the associated text states that it was the gift of the Duke of Sutherland, one of a pair (the other retained in Edinburgh) found on one of his excavations of 'Pictish Towers'. It was accessioned in 1848.

The Duke of Sutherland had a keen antiquarian interest and wrote to the Royal Society of Northern Antiquaries encouraging them to send a Danish archaeologist to Britain. King Christian VIII sent Worsaae in 1846, and he travelled in Britain for a year. The outcome of his visit was the publication of the volume *An Account of the Danes and Norwegians in England, Scotland and Ireland,* published in 1852, and including an image of one of the Castletown brooches (Worsaae 1852, 255). Although this brooch illustration is not very clear in its reproduction, it is presumably the brooch, which was gifted to him by the Duke of Sutherland. It is naturally very similar to the one retained in Scotland, shown as the image published by Anderson (1878, 329) and there are sufficient differences in the clarity of Anderson's illustration to suggest that this is a different drawing and presumably (not unexpectedly) an image of the National Museum brooch. They were an almost identical pair (the author is most grateful for the help of Brian Smith, Shetland Archives for this information). From this it is clear that the brooches were split at or near the time of discovery, one being given to Edinburgh by James Traill, and the other being retained by the Duke of Sutherland and gifted to Worsaae on his visit to Scotland. To this author's knowledge, it is illustrated here for the first time with the accompanying assemblage.

In the RCAHMS volume of 1911, the brooch illustration used by Anderson is reused and the circumstances of recovery repeated, with the additional information that 'a bracelet of coarse jet, and a bone pin 4 inches in length' were recovered (RCAHMS 1911, 87, no. 320). The unidentified sculptured stone from Castlehill mentioned elsewhere in that volume (op cit, 89 no. 335) cannot be definitively associated with this burial.

In conclusion, it is clear from the material here outlined that there is evidence for the re-use of broch mounds by the Viking and late Norse populations, not just in Caithness but also in Orkney and Tiree. Ongoing excavations by Bradford University and the Shetland Amenity Trust at the site of Old Scatness near Jarlshof may well mirror this situation there, with occasional Norse finds, possible structure and deposition horizons being recovered (S. Dockrill and J. Bond pers. comm.). Unfortunately the methodologies employed by Antiquarians of past centuries have to some extent militated against the full recovery and understanding of any structural remains which may have been Norse in origin – excavation of complex multi-phase stone constructions is a challenge at any time! We are thus thrown back to searching the archives for the distinctive elements of material culture, which was recovered from earlier work on these sites. Fortunately for us, the Vikings were buried in a pagan tradition with accompanying grave goods, and this enables us to match their cultural footprints across parts of the north and west of Scotland.

# 17 Torrs and the early La Tène Ornamental Style in Britain and Ireland

*D. W. Harding*

## Introduction

In a recent summary analysis of bronze-work decorated in the La Tène style in Scotland, Euan MacKie rightly emphasised the limited southern distribution of the main series of scabbards, bridle-bits and penannular brooches, which he believed 'only the most optimistic anti-diffusionist' could deny were the result of a movement of aristocratic groups from the Arras culture region of Yorkshire. The later and even more concentrated north-eastern distribution of terrets and massive armlets he equally regarded as the products of 'Celtic craftsmen, and their local imitators, who fled north with their chiefly patrons after the heavy defeat of the iron age tribes by the Romans at the battle of Mons Graupius in AD 86' (MacKie 1995, 657-59). Before addressing the question of the cultural significance of these finds the question of chronology should be considered, for the great majority of these artefacts, including the higher status products such as weapons and horse-bits, are all late in date, that is, not earlier than the first century AD for the most part. The fact is that Scotland lies effectively on the periphery of the zone of contact with the La Tène cultural distribution, and for much of its early Iron Age, from the mid-first millennium BC, the only manifestations of La Tène material types are a handful of pins or brooches, the value of which as cultural or chronological indices has been greatly over-rated in the past (Clarke 1971).

The late appearance of higher status items should not simply be accepted as a consequence of peripherality, with the built-in assumption of 'time-lag' that characterised diffusionist thinking from Sir Cyril Fox onwards (1932). It must signify a process of rather more complex character and significance. Conspicuous and portable symbols of identity may well have been prompted by the political and economic disruption of the indigenous social infrastructure, which followed the Roman invasion, in Scotland as much as in the regions further south, so that their appearance in southern Scotland need not have been the result solely of refugees or the movement of population groups. And if they were, one need not be an anti-diffusionist, irrespective of mood, to note that Group IV swords have a Brigantian distribution rather than one which correlates with the geographical distribution of the Arras culture of eastern Yorkshire, the most diagnostic characteristic of which, its manner of burial within a square-ditched barrow, apparently made no impact in southern Scotland whatsoever. The recent unique find, seemingly an intact (as opposed to dismantled) chariot-burial, from Newbridge,

Edinburgh has yet to be evaluated fully, but a single, isolated find can hardly transform the general pattern of evidence.

From the inventory of high-status metalwork of late date one group stands totally apart, the Torrs pony-cap and horns. Even in the era of compressed Iron Age chronology, this composite piece was regarded as two or three centuries earlier than the rest, so that its dating and its find-spot in the south-west both seemed anomalous. Stevenson, whose map of Scottish Iron Age metalwork (1966, Fig. 2) resembled the products of the early hyper-diffusionists, dismissed the idea of Torrs being a local product as pleasing but untenable: its potential significance as evidence of Hiberno-Scottish connections was not stressed, since contemporary opinion favoured a direct Continental derivation for the Irish scabbard-style. In consequence his arrow pointing to Torrs derived from eastern England, where Atkinson and Piggott's (1955) study of the find had identified its stylistic affinities. MacGregor too was reluctant to contemplate a local origin which did not seem to offer 'an archaeological background of sufficient sophistication' (1976, 24). Surprisingly, Atkinson and Piggott had not dismissed a local origin in south-west Scotland, though they added emphatically and quite unsustainably that the only likely alternative was Yorkshire. At least a third-century date seemed widely acceptable, but even this was predicated upon the prevailing chronological framework for the British Iron Age and upon the derivative system of classification of insular Celtic art developed by J.M. de Navarro (1952).

## Stylistic considerations

De Navarro based his classification upon Jacobsthal's (1944), so that the insular system was inevitably shackled to the presumption of influence from Continental Europe. Style 1, Jacobsthal's 'Early Style', made no impact in Britain, but Style 2, the 'Waldalgesheim Style' was seen as having an important influence on the Brentford horn cap, the Newnham Croft arm ring, Cerrig-y-Drudion fragments, the Woodeaton and Beckley involuted brooches and other insular pieces. Even Torrs, with its stylistic affinities to Newnham Croft, might be regarded as having sub-Waldalgesheim (Style 2) influences, but at the same time its relief ornament was considered ultimately to be the insular counterpart to the Continental 'Plastic Style', one of the two sub-styles of de Navarro's Style 3. The other sub-style of Style 3, allied to the Continental 'Sword Style', was manifest on the engraved ornament of the Torrs horns (and possibly on the patches of the pony-cap). Yet collectively the Torrs assemblage belonged to de Navarro's insular Style 4, a designation retained by Stead, to which the latter has added a Style 5, represented by the Battersea shield, the Waterloo helmet and the insular mirror series. Inherently this system is flawed, in that it assumes the insular sequence is secondary to and prompted by the Continental, rather than being parallel or cognate to the Continental styles, which in fact themselves display regional variations and a complexity of relationships which Jacobsthal's pioneer classification could take no account of.

Several factors pre-condition any analysis of high-status insular Iron Age metalwork. First, unlike the majority of comparable examples from the north-Alpine European mainland, the British and Irish material comprises in significant proportions stray finds, notably from rivers, and very seldom in association with other artefacts, either in hoards or as grave deposits. Dating therefore has traditionally been dependent upon typological or stylistic considerations rather than upon context and association. Second, even where there are associations these need to be evaluated with caution, since there must be every expectation that prestige goods could have remained in circulation for many generations after they were made, so that the date of deposit may have little bearing upon the date of manufacture. Thirdly, and consequent upon the previous point, such high-status goods might expect to have undergone repair, as was evidently the case with the Torrs pony-cap and horns. The end product studied by the archaeologist may therefore be a composite piece, incorporating elements representative of quite different periods of workmanship. Some crude repairs may be self-evident, but repairs or alterations that are not so obvious would plainly not be beyond the technical capacity of Iron Age craftsmen. Finally, it should not be assumed that prestige artefacts, especially a complex product like a sword scabbard or shield, were necessarily the work of a single craftsman, so that the fact that several hands may be detected need not itself imply that different styles or techniques were not part of the original design. This is most obviously relevant to a consideration of the concurrence of *repoussé* and engraved ornament from Torrs and on several of the south-eastern English finds.

## The Torrs pony-cap and horns

With these qualifications in mind the evidence of the Torrs group can be reviewed. The function of both principal parts, cap and horns, has been the subject of unresolved debate. It is generally assumed that the present position of the horns, mounted on the crest of the cap, is not as the maker intended, though we should not assume this to be true simply because the attachments are self-evidently not original. The horns are plainly a pair, and intended to be used as a pair with the ornamented surfaces, which are on opposite sides relative to the curvature of the horn, facing outwards. With or without the horns, the cap, plainly too small for a *chamfrein* as Atkinson and Piggott demonstrated, could indeed have adorned a small pony, or may have been a prop for some other ritual charade, as Jope (1983) suggested. Considering alternative uses for the horns, Atkinson and Piggott were not persuaded that they could have been terminals for drinking horns, though this still seems to accord best with the evidence for the association of prestige metalwork with fighting or feasting. If the horns were not part of the ensemble, then the only grounds for treating them together with the cap is their supposed associated provenance, and the fact that the small repairs to the cap also display some engraved decoration, though not yet demonstrably by the same hand as represented on the horns.

The first striking feature of the *repoussé* design of the cap (**61**) is its fold-over symmetry, balanced about a central axis from front to back. The design of the larger front section is echoed in that of the rear, the two being joined by unusually angular bridges over the presumed openings for the pony's ears. Both portions centre on an omega motif, from which branch tendrils leading to peltate elements and bossed terminals which, in the rear section, are shaped as birds' heads, but with an exaggerated, cartoon-like quality. The forward omega is balanced by a small pendant pelta, in markedly different proportions, but otherwise stylistically not unlike the *repoussé* component of the upper plate of the Standlake scabbard (**64**). Contrary to conventional assessments, the invocation of lyre-patterns and palmette-derivatives seems illusory. The principal elements seem to be omega motifs, peltae and peltate finials and birds' head or bossed terminals. Given that the original template of the *repoussé* design

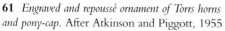
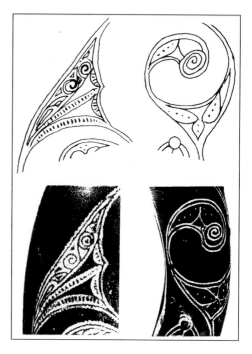

**61** *Engraved and repoussé ornament of Torrs horns and pony-cap.* After Atkinson and Piggott, 1955

**62** *Detail of engraved ornament on Torrs Horn A: note the differences.* After Atkinson and Piggott, 1955

would have been two-dimensional, we might anticipate if the two styles were contemporary, that these motifs might recur in the engraved ornament of the horns.

It has to be remarked that analysis of the engraved designs of the horns has not been well served by the published drawings. Atkinson and Piggott themselves complained about the misleading renderings reproduced by Anderson and Leeds, but their own interpretation was less than accurate in detail, as comparison of their drawings and photographs readily reveals (**62**). The asymmetrical tendril ornament is different in composition on the two horns, and Horn A has additionally been repaired in a quite different technique. Recognising that the design of the replacement section showed a finer line than the original, Atkinson and Piggott nonetheless still insisted that 'stylistically no break can be detected, and the whole design forms a unified and continuous pattern' (1955, 220). In fact, on the repaired section the engraved line describes the design, whereas the original, and Horn B, use a quite different technique in which the background is cut away to leave the definition of the motif upstanding, and creating a much more subtle interplay between foreground and background. This aspect of the engraving requires further study, necessitating the removal of the white paste, which was added in modern times to accentuate the designs. Motifs displayed in the repaired section are essentially just two, the tightly-wound hair-spring spiral, and the leaf with dotting down its spine; neither is used in quite the same fashion on either of the original horns. Both can be broadly matched in the filler motifs of the Irish scabbards (**65**; Raftery 1984, illus 55). At one point near the junction with its original, the repair deploys the leaf motif in a trefoil within a cut-away curved triangle, simulating briefly the style of the original.

The design of the original section of Horn A begins with a circular motif which has something of the character of a yin-yang, but interrupted by a medial line, an unusual device in La Tène art, as Duval remarked (1977, 145), through a central rivet, around which the alternating voids and panels of infilled ornament give the illusion of rotating. From this a tendril leads to a second, smaller, sub-circular device, comprising two opposed peltae, one containing a small face-mask, and a peltate finial. Here too there is a linear transverse bar, but offset, and coinciding with the point of juncture with the repaired section. Among the decorative infilling, a fan-shaped spandrel between the initial circlet and tendril includes a spiral-and-circlet device, and panels of linear rouletting. The decoration of Horn B begins with a similar, sub-circular whorl, with medial line across a rivet. Thereafter, its stringier tendril leads through a flattened, curved triangle to fan-like finials. Infilling includes dotted elements and spirals, though not as tightly-coiled as on the repaired portion of Horn A, and a pelta-within-a-pelta device which also occurs in slightly flattened form on the larger whorl of Horn A.

Comparison between the *repoussé* ornament of the cap and engraved ornament of the horns at first sight might suggest that the two styles have rather less in common than has generally been implied, even allowing for the differences of technique. The pelta, or flattened pelta, certainly is a common element within the tendril composition, and it may be significant that even in the *repoussé* variant there is an a hint at infilling, echoing the main design. Equally, the bossed terminals of the *repoussé* form can be regarded as the equivalent of spiral terminals in the engraved designs; indeed some of the bosses have a visible tendency to spiral. Beyond that, the omega motifs or angular bridges of the cap have no counterpart in the horns. The ornament of the horns is again based upon tendrils, but there are linking devices like the bisected whorls, which are not closely paralleled elsewhere, and leading to terminal finials of fan or 'batwing' form, in the repaired section of Horn A incorporating the use of tightly-coiled hair-spring spirals. The motifs and style of infilling of the horns proclaim them unequivocally as collateral to the insular Scabbard Styles, though whether their affinities lie closest to the Irish scabbards or with the Yorkshire and eastern English series remains to be considered.

## The Newnham Croft bracelet

It has already been remarked that Atkinson and Piggott linked Torrs with Newnham Croft as key examples of their 'early' school of Waldalgesheim-derived insular art, republishing Fox's drawing of the bracelet, which regrettably was no more accurate than their own published drawings of the Torrs horns. Newnham Croft (**63**) is a classic example of an object whose ornamental style invites comparison with the Continental Waldalgesheim style of the fourth century BC, but the dating of which has commonly been retarded to accommodate its apparently later associations. As regards the ornate brooch with its foot cast in one with the bow, Hawkes some years ago (Hull & Hawkes 1987, 147ff) dispelled the myth that this had to be regarded as an exclusively La Tène 3 trait, when other stylistic features are clearly indicative of an earlier period of innovation in insular brooch-making. Every commentator has remarked how very severely worn is the low relief ornament of the arm-ring. This surely was an heirloom, which had been in use for a century or more before it was finally deposited in its presumed funerary context. Its surface shows the much-worn traces of a low-relief tendril design, which twists its course

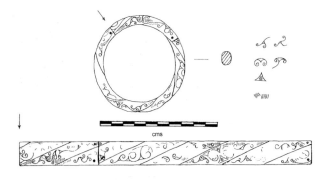

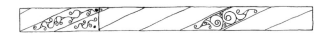

**63** *Newnham Croft,*
*Cambridgeshire, bracelet.*
Drawing D.W. Harding

around the surface divided into a continuous series of diagonal panels, reminiscent of the diagonal bias of Hungarian sword-ornament. Stead (1995a, with his new drawing Fig. 33) correctly reconstructed the better-preserved panels as standard Waldalgesheim tendrils of Verger's (1987) type B, though in one instance at least the vortex or curving triangle which links the dividing arms of the tendril swings the wrong way. Similarities with the Torrs *repoussé* style include this use of curving triangles or flattened peltae, from which branches turn into spiral terminals. However, the very close similarities in the use of these motifs on the Bann 1 scabbard (**65c**) should not be overlooked. These might argue for a very much more complex series of inter-relationships between south-eastern England on the one hand and south-west Scotland and Ireland on the other than the diffusionist tradition admitted.

A distinctive element of the Newnham Croft ornament is its use of background hatching, conventionally regarded by English scholars as a tell-tale sign of insular manufacture, in spite of its presence at La Gorge Meillet (Jacobsthal 1944, 157), on the Erstfeld torcs (Wyss 1975) and on the Borsch flagon handle (Jacobsthal 1944, 383), all from Early La Tène. At Newnham Croft it is certainly not squared hatching of the Borsch or later mirror-style variety, but neither is it quite the alternating, diagonal kind exemplified by the Cerrig-y-Drudion fragments. In places it seems to be simply multiple parallel-line hatching, for which no predetermined provenance nor dating should be assumed. In sum, there seems to be no compelling reason for assigning the Newnham Croft bracelet to a date of manufacture very much later than the currency of its Continental Waldalgesheim antecedents, but rather to somewhere in the early third century BC at latest.

## The Standlake scabbard plate

A potentially early parallel for the relief omega motif and peltate elements of the Torrs pony-cap, which was cited by Atkinson and Piggott, is provided by the upper scabbard plate from Standlake in Oxfordshire (**64**). The Standlake scabbard is again surely a composite piece, so that dating its individual components might be less than straightforward. Its chape end is of La Tène 1 open-ring form, which might alone encourage a dating before 300 BC, whereas the cross-bridge

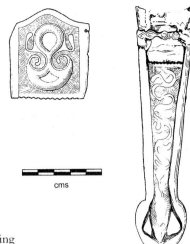

cms

**64** *Standlake, Oxfordshire, scabbard.* Drawing D.W. Harding

reminded Jope of bird-bridges of Swiss Middle La Tène swords, so that a dating for the chape as a whole in the early or mid-third century might be preferred. The sinuous tendril design of the base-plate is closely based upon Continental Waldalgesheim models, but this plate is very severely worn, and the fact that its ornament seems to extend under the side-binding again suggests that it has been re-used, having perhaps originated in the fourth century. The flattened finials of the tendril design, however, are reflected in the spatulate arms flanking the omega relief of the upper plate. This association of relief omega-pelta with a Waldalgesheim-derived motif argues for an early third-century date rather than later, and the combination of background hatching of a kind most closely matched at Cerrig-y-Drudion seems to endorse this conclusion.

## Yorkshire scabbards

Standlake may have been just antecedent to the new series of decorated Yorkshire scabbards, notably Wetwang 1 and 3 and Kirkburn. The ornamental style of these scabbards (Stead 1991) is not directly comparable to Torrs, though they are broadly contemporary. The Yorkshire scabbard style nonetheless enters into the equation because of the long-debated connections with the northern Irish decorated scabbards, with which the Torrs ornament does display elements in common. The ornament of Wetwang 1, essentially a scroll design with balanced alternating tendril-terminals comprising a pair of spirals, one larger and with more coils, the smaller little more than a boss, echoes the *repoussé* motifs on the Torrs cap. Likewise the infilling of the Kirkburn scabbard, mostly linear hatching but with some dot-filled panels, could be paralleled on the Torrs horns, while the fan-finials of Wetwang 3 might be compared generally to the 'batwing' terminals on Horn B from Torrs. But otherwise the balanced structure of the Kirkburn scroll design with alternating tendrils is quite unlike the informality of the designs on Torrs horns. Distinctive of the Yorkshire scabbard series is the creation of negative trumpet voids (one side convex, one concave and the third S-shaped) seen later on the Bugthorpe scabbard as well as in the later Mirror Style, but now demonstrably of an earlier derivation (Stead 1991, Fig. 99). Finally, the border ornament of dot and wavy line of both

Wetwang 3 and Kirkburn may be matched on both the Witham and Wandsworth (round) shields, reinforcing the eastern and southern stylistic affinities of the series.

The relationship between the Yorkshire scabbards and the Irish has been a source of contention at least since Piggott proposed his 'plantation of Ulster' by Yorkshire charioteers 50 years ago (1950). Piggott's case has long been recognised as untenable on the basis of his Group III swords, the Bugthorpe scabbard in particular, the ornament of which hardly afforded a convincing source for the Irish series, and which were probably too late in date anyway. Furthermore the absence in Ireland of cart- or chariot-fittings, and still more an absence of burials of the distinctive Arras culture types, made actual population movement on any perceptible scale improbable. The more recent discovery of swords from Wetwang Slack and Kirkburn, however, has nonetheless caused Raftery to review his position (1994). These new Yorkshire scabbards are essentially of La Tène 1 type, and should be earlier than the Irish scabbards. As well as their affinities in terms of ornament, the mutual use of centrally-located suspension-loops has frequently been remarked, though the Irish chapes are quite different from the Yorkshire series. Following Jope (1954) most authorities recognise that the Irish chapes owe more to the Continental tradition than to the British, and parallels from Champagne to Hungary are really quite striking. Furthermore the Irish swords are relatively short compared with their British or Continental counterparts. Most are less than 0.5m in length, whereas British and Continental swords of the Early to Middle La Tène transition, like Standlake, can be in the order of 0.75m in length. The more recent finds from Yorkshire, however, are not nearly so long, and may serve to underline the tendency for earlier swords to be shorter, and later examples to become progressively longer.

## Irish scabbards

At first sight, the engraved decoration of the Irish scabbards (**65**) seems immensely complex, filling every available part of the scabbard-plate from mouth to chape with intricate free-flowing curvilinear designs. In fact, the designs are very much more regular, even to the point of symmetry, than first appears, and the fundamental designs are very simple, being based upon lyres or S-tendrils or variations on them. Only the secondary foliage, itself rather repet-itive, conveys the impression of complexity, and any departure from symmetry is largely achieved through varying the infilling of these vegetal finials. This principal is best exempli-fied in the British Museum's Lisnacrogher scabbard (**65a**), the basic design of which consists of stacked lyres or opposed S-motifs in mirror symmetry about its central midrib; even the terminal finials are symmetrically balanced, leaving only the filler-motifs to provide an element of variation. A second Lisnacrogher scabbard and Toome 1 (**65b**) are essentially similar, being based upon stacked S-motifs or reversed-S, whereas Bann 1 (**65c**), despite its worn surface, appears to have been based upon a more sinuous wave-tendril design, and certainly incorporates compound peltate elements which bear comparison with Newnham Croft or the relief designs of Torrs and Loughnashade. Among the filler-designs characteristic of the Torrs horns, leaf- or vessica-shaped motifs with dotted infilling and peltae-within-peltae occur on the Irish scabbards, but the commonest element on both is the tightly-wound hair-spring spiral, which of course is also one of the recurrent components of the eastern and south-eastern England series of high-status metalwork.

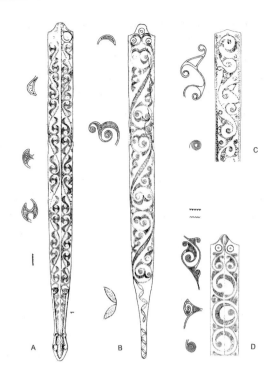

**65** *Irish scabbard ornament: A) Lisnacrogher, Co. Antrim, British Museum, B) Toome, Co. Antrim, C) Bann, Co. Derry, D) Lisnacrogher, Co. Antrim. After Raftery, 1984*

## The Witham shield

In that English group, concurrency of engraved and relief styles is well attested by two prime examples of developed insular art with which Atkinson and Piggott chose to link their later Torrs phase, the Witham shield and Wandsworth circular shield-boss. The Witham shield (Jope 1971; Brailsford 1975) in its secondary form had a central umbo and two terminal roundels, linked by a spine down the long axis. The relief design of the umbo consists of two pairs of opposed looped peltae, not unlike the basic motif of the engraved central panel of Horn A from Torrs. Within the peltae are smaller looped elements, the inner containing a domed stud, the outer a rosette, in which the outer component could be read as an omega springing from a pelta, thus echoing the *repoussé* motifs of the Standlake upper scabbard-plate, or indeed of the relief design of the Torrs pony-cap itself. Between these devices, along the axis of the spine, are opposed pairs of comma-leaves with exaggerated spiral terminals, and leading to lobate tips which point down the spine. Within a central setting are three coral studs, a decorative embellishment which itself has chronological implications, since the use of coral goes out of fashion north of the Alps shortly after the transition to La Tène 2. In the clockwise junction only of comma-leaves and peltae, and thus diagonally-opposed within the total composition are two areas of infilling, which, taken together with the orientation of the lobes pointing down the spine, make it clear that this is *not* fold-over symmetry, as has been claimed, but *rotational* symmetry, and in this respect stands distinct from the style of the Torrs pony-cap.

**66** *Engraved ornament on the Witham, Lincolnshire, shield*. After Jope, 1971

The terminal roundels are a matching pair in terms of their *repoussé* ornament, and are supported by a pair of exaggerated sub-equine beasts. More pertinent in the present context, however, is the engraved ornament on the flat surfaces within the terminal roundels (**66**), comprising conjoined, rather than continuous, figure-of-eight scrolls. These display close similarities to the engraved designs of scabbard ornament, recalling the sub-Waldalgesheim over-and-under figure-of-eight of the Hungarian scabbards. Within Britain a more angular version of the same figure-of-eight theme is represented on the Wetwang 3 and Kirkburn scabbards. The stacked S-designs of the Irish scabbards might be seen as related to the same theme, notably the stacked reversed-S design of Toome 1, which also shares the axillar infillings between S-motifs. The hair-spring spiral with split-palmette or 'batwing' are dominant and recurrent, both key motifs also in the engraved design of the Torrs horns. Both are motifs shared with the main *repoussé* design of the Witham shield, the multiple-leaved palmette amply represented on the equine supports of the end-roundels, the axillar fillings echoing those of the central roundel, so that there is no reason to think of the two aspects of the shield's ornament as being other than part of an integral composition.

This then is important endorsement of the belief that engraved and relief ornament were part of a contemporary unity of design, and not sequential or indicative of later adaptation. By contrast with the Torrs horns, however, what distinguishes the Witham engraved ornament is its sense of formality. In spite of their detailed lack of symmetry, the engraved scrolls are balanced and equally-proportioned around the available surface, and lack the erratic freedom of the Torrs engraving. Piggott saw 'strong Classical influence in the design of the shield' (1970, 4), which he dated to the first century BC. Jope more specifically saw the engraved ornament and the flower of the central boss of the terminal roundels as echoing Hellenistic or southern models (1971; 1978; 2000), but still saw Witham at the head of the insular shield series in the third century.

## The Witham scabbard fragment

One of the most interesting examples of the combined use of *repoussé* and engraved techniques is the Witham scabbard fragment, since it is the only instance apart from the Wandsworth shield roundel in which the engraving is integral to and enhances the *repoussé* design, rather than occupying a vacant flat surface. The diagonal disposition of the ornament is commonly compared to the layout of Hungarian sword ornament, but the Witham example is singular in its design and execution. In fact, from the upper dome, which is located somewhat left of centre, the curvilinear *repoussé* design initially progresses more-or-less centrally down the plate into the second element, which is more eccentrically disposed from left to right. In two dimensions the template might have resembled the tendril-linking-sub-circular-units layout of the Torrs horns or of the engraved ornament on the central boss of the Wandsworth shield roundel. But its *repoussé* format gives the Witham design an altogether more fleshy aspect, though it defies convincing identification in terms of plants or birds. Individual motifs include spirals and split-palmettes, and a fan or 'batwing' device, which has acquired a vessica-shaped bell-terminal, that may be compared with trumpet motifs on the Wandsworth boss. Between the two principal elements of the Witham design is a narrow ridge across which linear hatching recalls the extended parallel hatching on the Newnham Croft armring.

## Wandsworth shields

Finally in this closely-related series of prestige metalwork we should consider the two shield fragments from the Thames at Wandsworth. One of these is the central boss and spine of what must have been a sub-rectangular shield of the Witham type, but significantly smaller, as Jope's reconstruction effectively showed (Jope 1976, Fig.1). The design on its central boss of the Wandsworth piece is essentially composed of *repoussé* birds' heads, opposed with accessories once again in rotational rather than fold-over symmetry. The birds' heads are separated by a raised wavy line, very similar to those that encircled the terminal roundels of the Witham shield, while the balanced composition ends in leaf-like lobes pointing down the spine, again reminiscent of similar elements on the Witham shield. Such similarities of detail, reinforcing a broader comparability of design, are bound to foster the belief that these two shields were the product of a local school of parade-armour craftsmen, even if the Wandsworth shield was produced al generation or two after the Witham model. Given the probable longevity of these prized pieces, it is not necessary to invoke tradition or professional memory to account for specific points of similarity. The rendering of bird's heads on the central boss, and the modelling of the terminal face-masks, are cognate in their bold relief to the continental 'Plastic Style' faces of the third and second centuries. One final, but important, aspect of the Wandsworth mask-shield is its use of fine engraved ornament, and tool-mark bordering. The engraving, which appears on the nose of the face-mask, on the birds' heads and on the lobe-like terminals of the central design, is dominated by tight hair-spring spirals on the central boss sustaining the rotational symmetry of the composition, and perhaps thereby reinforcing its authenticity as part of the original design. The engraved designs, and those elements of the *repoussé* style which recall the Witham shield, argue for a date which could be as early as the second half of the third century BC.

## The Wandsworth shield-roundel

Latest in this series of finds is the shield-roundel from Wandsworth (Brailsford 1975; Jope 1978), consisting of a central dome-shaped umbo, around which a wide circular flange is ornamented in *repoussé* and engraved techniques. Rivet-holes around its perimeter and in a setting of four around the central boss indicate that the roundel was originally mounted on a wooden or stiff leather backing, which Jope believed (2000, 68) was probably of sub-rectangular form. Whilst there are certainly points of comparison with the other major products of the Torrs-Witham-Wandsworth series, a great difference is in the *repoussé* technique itself, in which the outlines of the design are sharply defined in contrast to the higher-relief masses of the Torrs pony cap, for example. This in itself would not disqualify its description as being in the 'Plastic Style' tradition (Jope 1976, 183). The principal elements in the *repoussé* design are two opposed S-scrolls, one end of each curving to form birds' heads. From these heads extend 'wings', one foreshortened, the other more fully developed into a spiral terminal matching that at the base of the original S-motive. These two elements, as on all the southern pieces examined, stand not as mirror-images in fold-over symmetry, but in a relationship of rotational symmetry, or in de Navarro's phrase in circular rhythm (1952). The engraved ornament provides an interesting commentary upon this relationship. The engravings on the birds' heads and longer wings, though different in detail, occupy the same relative spaces, in contrast to the engraving on the foreshortened wing, which occupies the opposite relative positions. The central boss, too, has engraved ornament, in two separate tendrils that have a rotational relationship, though the details of the designs are not identical. The ornament of the central boss and of the surrounding flange appears to be stylistically the same. Birds' heads with wings are more or rather less explicit; both have trumpets with hatched bell-ends. Other motifs include triangles-within-triangles and pelta-within-pelta, and star-rosettes (on the central boss only). Among the infilling of the flange is one panel in which an over-and-under figure-of-eight has a fan or 'batwing' finial balanced by a comma-leaf and pelta-within-pelta finial. Again, these echoes of earlier pieces should argue against an unduly retarded dating, perhaps in the earlier second century BC.

## The Battersea shield

It is not proposed here to examine in detail the design of the Battersea shield, conventionally, and probably correctly, regarded as the latest in the south-eastern series. Nonetheless, the fact must be remarked that the Battersea design does indeed show fold-over symmetry, as do other examples of insular metalwork of the late pre-Roman Iron Age, like some of the south-western mirrors. Stead (1985b) put the case for an earlier dating for Battersea, though the balance of opinion probably still favours a less radical assessment. The conventional dating in the first century BC, however, propounded by Hawkes, Jacobsthal and de Navarro has seemingly now been upstaged by analyses of the 'sealing-wax red enamel' of the Battersea ornament, which on the basis of its chemical composition cannot date later than the second century BC (Jope 2000, 351). Without being distracted by this issue, it is noted that Jope, who above all scholars of early Celtic art stressed the composite nature of these prestige objects, quite deliberately concluded that the enamel was no later than second century, though his chronological chart implied that he also accepted that this was probably true for the shield as a whole. The point as far as an assessment of Torrs is concerned is not that the concept of fold-over symmetry was totally alien to southern and eastern England, which it was not, but that it was not the distinctive style of composition of the Witham-Wandsworth 'school' of prestige metalworking, and in general was not in evidence in southern England until the end of the first millennium and the advent of the Mirror Style.

## The Loughnashade horn-disc and scabbards

The closest parallel to the conception of design of the Torrs cap comes not from finds 200 miles and more to the south, but from just over 100 miles to the west, across the water at Loughnashade in Co. Armagh. Like Torrs, the design of the Loughnashade horn-disc (**67**) is executed in *repoussé*, and like Torrs it is balanced in fold-over symmetry. The principal motifs like Torrs include peltate elements extending into bossed terminals, some of which hint at exaggerated birds' heads, though not so explicitly as Torrs. Double finials are balanced on the opposed side of a curving triangle or vortex by a single bossed finial, a combination also seen on the Newnham Croft bracelet. Dating the Loughnashade trumpet exposes all the traditional inhibitions and prejudices of archaeologists. Though Atkinson and Piggott recognised the obvious affinities, they dismissed Loughnashade as 'the Torrs style in uncomfortable decline' (1955, 231), whilst Megaw suggested that Loughnashade might even be an import into Ireland from Britain (1970, 141), offering in consequence a second or first century BC date. Not surprisingly, Raftery could see little to commend in either of these views (1984, 138), but was cautious in advancing the case for a reciprocal influence from Ireland to Scotland, which he advocated more positively in terms of the influence of the Irish Scabbard Style on the Torrs horns. As to dating, he too was conservative in not advancing a case earlier than the second century BC for Loughnashade, perhaps allowing too much credence to the D-shaped patch on the horn, which was paralleled on cauldrons of the first century AD. Since patches by definition imply longevity of use, the style of the patch is necessarily secondary, and its similarity to repairs on other artefacts can hardly be adduced as reliable evidence of date of manufacture.

Atkinson and Piggott were of course perfectly well aware of the Irish analogues for Torrs, both in the *repoussé* style of Loughnashade and in the engraved ornament of the scabbards, so that to revisit the three-cornered equation is not novel. Unfortunately, Piggott at any rate was unquestionably locked into his view of the Irish material, notably the scabbards, as the product of his 'plantation of Ulster' by Yorkshire charioteers, and most of his contemporaries would in any event have favoured a diffusionist view in which both Scotland and Ireland inevitably would have been regarded as late recipients of influences from southern Britain, or just conceivably from the Continent directly. Time-lag has always been a dubious concept in archaeology, and where prestige goods are concerned there is every reason to believe that it was the 'pulling power' of local elites which triggered innovation from abroad rather than a protracted process

**67** *Horn-disc from Loughnashade, Co. Armagh.* After Raftery, 1984

of diffusion of which they were the passive recipients. Torrs with its relief style pony cap and engraved style horns on the one hand, and Loughnashade and the Irish scabbards on the other, could be broadly contemporary manifestations on opposite sides of the North Channel of a wider tradition of insular and Continental prestige metalwork, sharing with each other as much or more than either have in common with the south-eastern English schools of the period.

## Conclusions

Cross-channel connections between northern Ireland and southern or western Scotland were evidently of long standing, pre-dating by centuries the documented settlement of Strathclyde in the early historic period. Archaeologically these connections are well attested for the early centuries AD, for example, in the distribution of spearbutts and moulds for their manufacture. Recent research (A. Heald, pers. comm.) suggests that the so-called Lisnacrogher and doorknob types may be sequential rather than contemporary, dating from around the turn of the millennium. But there is no reason to regard cross-channel connections as so late a phenomenon. For many years the Bargany House scabbard has been accepted as one of Irish type, and even if Raftery (1984, 70; 94-5) accepted Stevenson's qualification (1967, 24) that it was unlikely to be of Irish manufacture, he nonetheless was prepared to accept it as the product of an Irish craftsman, or at the very least a local product produced under the Irish influence. The sword fragment from Steventon Sands, Ayrshire (MacGregor 1976, no. 139) is another possible Irish piece. The dating of these weapons is doubtless later than Torrs, but they nonetheless reinforce the existence of an Iron Age Hiberno-Scottish relationship in the closing centuries of the first millennium BC, of which Torrs might well be the earliest and most prestigious manifestation. The dating of the Group III swords from the Tweed and south-east Scotland may well be no earlier than the first century BC, and as Euan MacKie suggested, doubtless do represent a northerly extension of the Brigantian cultural tradition.

In effect, and hardly surprisingly if we take the early historic period as a model, southern and western Scotland were subject in the pre-Roman Iron Age to a complexity of cultural influences, which this writer, never having been an optimistic anti-diffusionist, would not wish to deny. The nature of those influences is more difficult to determine. Diplomatic exchange might account for high-status or prestige goods, which might reasonably be regarded as actual imports. Exchange of technical expertise or stylistic influences might be accounted for through social exchange within a system of client relationships. The relatively late appearance of Celtic art on fine metalwork in Scotland could have been triggered by political or social circumstances in which the need to assert identity resulted in the expression of a latent tradition previously manifest through other media in a form which has not survived in the archaeological record. Or, of course, such high-status products may have been triggered by an influx of settlers, perhaps limited in numbers but of influential social status, such as has been suggested to account for the appearance of the La Tène phenomenon in Ireland itself. All of these potential catalysts, and others, should doubtless be considered as contributing to the appearance of metalwork in the La Tène style in Scotland. What is no longer tenable is the simplistic assumption that these items were necessarily imports from, or the product of influences from, any single region or 'school' in southern or eastern England.

# 18  Excavation archives
## preservation and chance

*J.N. Graham Ritchie*

## Introduction

Euan MacKie's contribution to Scottish archaeology has been one that centres on a scientific approach, testing hypotheses, and recording with care in an enquiring framework. The excavation report of Dun Mor Vaul, Tiree, exemplifies this (MacKie 1974), and the material was sufficiently carefully bagged and the archive maintained for re-examination to take place more than 20 years later (MacKie 1997). The present writer edited the latter paper and used the carefully labelled archive set of photographic prints in the Hunterian Museum excavation archive as potential illustrations. The Dun Mor Vaul material is an excellent example of the careful preservation of the evidence from that most unrepeatable activity, namely excavation. There is an element of chance in the survival of archaeological evidence, chance that relates both to the survival of monuments on the ground and to whether the report of a casual discovery reaches the appropriate authority, as well as to the conservation or destruction of the paper or photographic record of early excavations. Guidelines are now in place to ensure that the records of current work are carefully preserved. This personal account of the discovery of less conventional archaeological information is designed to illustrate the variety of such material and some of the more unusual ways that archaeological results have been preserved and discovered.

The nature of physical survival of monuments on the ground is the best understood of these topics and stands at the centre of many discussions of field monuments in the landscape (Stevenson 1975; RCAHMS 1994, 7-11; 1997, 24-9). Particular forces of land use and economic patterns are in play. Agricultural improvement may have swept away standing stones and cairns in some areas of Scotland, but their survival in others may be explicable only in terms of the antiquarian interests of the landowner or his agent, perhaps a matter of chance. Reporting of discoveries has an element of uncertainty, but increasingly, where archaeological liaison with the community is good, the sort of exchange reported years ago at a bridge table in Angus should be a thing of the past:

> Your son is one of these archaeologists isn't he; we had one of those cist things wi' a pot in it last week, but I just got the grieve to get rid of the lot; we didnae want any bother at this time of year.

The material evidence that goes to create the archaeological canon of monuments and artefacts, to say nothing of archaeological theory, has major elements of such cruel chance that a healthy scepticism is perhaps an understandable approach. Nowhere are chance and serendipity better illustrated than in the survival of archaeological records. If the following essay in Euan's honour is anecdotal, it may nonetheless serve to put on record the background to some of the unlikely survivals of information about the archaeology of Argyll, Lanarkshire and Dumbarton, as well as looking at some of the reasons why such evidence is important.

As a young Investigator with the Royal Commission on the Ancient and Historical Monuments of Scotland in the later 1960s the writer had two areas of responsibility; one was to act as a junior fieldworker in the preparation of the Inventory of Argyll, initially in Kintyre, and the other was to act as the archaeologist who was to play a part in the newly formed National Monuments Record of Scotland that resulted from the incorporation of the Scottish National Buildings Record of Scotland with the Royal Commission in 1966 (RCAHMS 1991, xiv). The latter role was not intended to be a large one, as it was clear that the major collections were of an architectural nature, the main archaeological elements being the Royal Commission's own original plans. Junior investigators got all sorts of odd sites to write up, the ones that had been put to one side, and, in the preparation of the Kintyre Inventory, the writing of short entries on the Bronze Age cairn at Balnabraid and on the late Iron Age material from Keil Cave, Southend fell to me.

Some of the material from Mrs Lindsay Galloway's 1910 and 1913 excavations of the Balnabraid cairn was in the Hunterian Museum, and I first experienced Euan's kindness as he looked out the objects and made them available for drawing. I excavated part of the cairn in April 1966, but it helped only a little to elucidate the original excavation report; a ginger beer bottle in one of the empty cists held a message that the site had already been excavated by Mrs Lindsay Galloway and Ludovic McLellan Mann, my first piece of archaeological archive! (Galloway 1911; Ritchie 1967a).

## Keil Cave, Kintyre, Argyll

The excavation of late Iron Age deposits in Keil Cave had been undertaken by J. Harrison Maxwell using Boy Scouts' labour between 1933 and 1935. The available material was unpromising, a number of articles in the Campbeltown Courier and a series of small finds in Campbeltown Museum. But clearly not all the small finds had been deposited there. In 1966 Mr Maxwell was living in Crieff and he was delighted to assist in the preparation of the short Inventory account, to present the remaining small finds to the National Museum of Antiquities of Scotland, and to offer the archive material that he still held on the site, plans, photographs etc, to the fledgling National Monuments Record of Scotland (MS/26). The writer prepared a short account for the *Proceedings of the Society of Antiquaries of Scotland* with Mr Maxwell's approval (Ritchie 1967b). Iron Age cave archaeology is still little understood, and the odd collection of finds, including a triangular weaving tablet, a sherd of Roman colour-coated ware and comb fragments, suggests a third or fourth century AD date, while the quantities of iron slag may imply the activities of itinerant smiths.

Not all the artefacts could be found in Crieff and a bronze penannular brooch was drawn from a photograph. The published account rather coyly reports that it has been drawn approximately to scale, which implies perhaps an imperial scale on the photograph. But this was not so, the brooch had been positioned in wax on the grid created by Ludovic McLellan Mann, who had identified the alpha and beta units of 0.618 inch and 0.553 inch as being crucial prehistoric measurements (**68**) (Mann 1930). Mann had been a mentor to Maxwell and had given

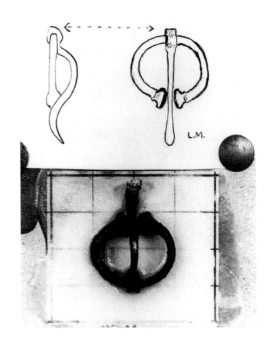

**68** *Brooch from Keil Cave, Kintyre, mounted onto a background of Ludovic Mann's alpha and beta units.* Crown Copyright: Royal Commission on the Ancient and Historical Monuments of Scotland

him copies of the gridded paper he had had printed in order to size up objects accurately to his individual pattern of measurements. Mann was also a predecessor of Euan MacKie as president of the Glasgow Archaeological Society, and more was to be discovered later about his work. But the brooch was illustrated as best fitted onto the Mann grid using a Grant Projector.

The matter might have ended there, but, after Mr Maxwell's death in 1971, his widow found a small tobacco tin among his effects. By chance still having my address, she wrote 'I have found it. I have found the brooch!' A visit to Crieff ensured its donation to the National Museum of Antiquities of Scotland collection (*Proc Soc Antiq Scot*, 105 (1972-4), 325).

'But what should I do with all the glass slides,' asked Mrs Maxwell in despair, 'museum archaeologists have said that I should just get rid of them as no one lectures with $2\frac{1}{4}$ inch square glass slides these days, and any case they will all have been copied from books.'

The glass slides were the basis of Mr Maxwell's many years' work as an Adult Education lecturer on archaeological and historical topics. Some were certainly taken from the volumes of the *Proceedings of the Society of Antiquaries of Scotland* and other published sources and could readily be replicated, but others were less familiar and with a National Monuments Record of Scotland to fill with new material the writer was glad to offer them a new home, so long as the appropriate sorting and, if necessary, disposal of duplicated material was acceptable. It soon became clear that this was a storehouse of information, so nearly lost, with evidence on the cist burials in Lanarkshire, and a strange excavation at Knappers, Clydebank, Dunbartonshire, by Ludovic Mann. There were coloured slides of what seemed to be a notebook relating to the excavation of the crannog at Dumbuck, Dunbartonshire, in 1898, which had been the subject of considerable discussion at the time of the excavation because some of the discoveries were forgeries in the opinion of many scholars. An element of chance, the discovery of a brooch and an address, had added to the National Monuments Record of Scotland a range of archaeological information about several important sites that was entirely unsuspected.

In 1936 and 1939 Mann had excavated several Bronze Age burials and cists at Ferniegair, Lanarkshire. Humphrey Welfare was able to use not only the published newspaper accounts of the time, but also photographs and cuttings from the Maxwell collection in his detailed assessment of the work, which formed the basis of the more summary Royal Commission Inventory article (Welfare 1975; RCAHMS 1978, 72-3, no. 143).

## Knappers, Clydebank, Dunbartonshire

The glass slides contained an extensive coverage of the excavations by Mann at Knappers, in the late 1930s, and gave a clear impression of the complexity of the site and its interest both from an archaeological point of view and also from that of the personalities involved and the impact of the excavations on the public. In collaboration with Helen Adamson, Glasgow Art Gallery and Museum, the available information was gathered, the small finds drawn and an initial account prepared. It seemed likely that George Applebey, who had been Mann's archaeological executor, might have more information. Contact was made and Mr and Mrs Applebey could not have been kinder. Mr Applebey brought out relevant material and allowed it to be copied for NMRS. Mann was a flamboyant presenter of information and held idiosyncratic views on metrology and astronomical interpretations, which, if we were to get to the archaeology which was undoubtedly present, would have to be put to one side but not glossed over. A lecture to Glasgow Archaeological Society followed, which Mr Applebey attended, and I was relieved that he had felt that we had made a fair assessment. The paper was eventually published in the *Proceedings of the Society of Antiquaries of Scotland* (Ritchie and Adamson 1981).

The burials and cists at Knappers, on the east side of Great Western Road, excavated by J.M. Davidson, were published by him in 1935; on the west side of the road the timber settings excavated by Mann remained little understood because the publication of the information was in today's terms 'alternative', if not 'way out': *The Druid Temple Explained*, 1939. Mann, however, caught the imagination of the public through newspaper articles and open days at which he lectured on site (**69**). He also created banks and a central setting of upright posts, which were linked at the top in the manner of Stonehenge, causing *The People* to describe the site as 'the Westminster Abbey of Scottish Druid times' (**70**). *The Glasgow Herald* reported that 'Members of the Glasgow Archaeological Society, with hundreds of other visitors viewed the prehistoric temple at Knappers, near Kilbowie'. The site is difficult to interpret, but the many slides in the Maxwell collection suggest that a series of post circles was indeed present, and they bear testimony to the care with which the excavation was undertaken even if the interpretation that it was a temple to commemorate the victory of light over darkness might not now be accepted. The excavations have relevance to later approaches to the debate about archaeoastronomy, for Mann presented his results by assertion. In the 1970s, following the publications of Alexander Thom, Euan MacKie entered a similar debate through scientific observation, excavation and questioning. There is a telling contrast in approach between the assertions of Mann and their demolition by the 'Establishment', and the work of Thom and the long debate about the implications, in which Euan has played a major part (Ruggles 1999, 9, 10, 28-34).

The users of archive information have a particular duty to use it sensitively, never to use it in a negative way, for donors, archaeologists as well as lay people, will have a reserve about

**69** *Ludovic Mann lecturing at Knappers in 1938.* Crown Copyright: Royal Commission on the Ancient and Historical Monuments of Scotland

**70** *Knappers, Dunbartonshire, with upright canes showing the position of stake-holes.* Crown Copyright: Royal Commission on the Ancient and Historical Monuments of Scotland

putting material into the public domain if allowances are not made for the often erratic ways in which it was gathered in the first place. Attitudes to the use of archival evidence are still ambivalent. The growing professionalism of excavation in Scotland of the post-war era resulted in better excavation reports in journals; almost all the evidence could be published in full, and there might be a few more photographs, but often any residual manuscript material was thought to be superfluous. The published account, where it existed, was the last word. The use of the diaries and day-books from the excavations at Knossos to cast doubt on the find-spots of the Linear B tablets, widely publicised in the press, created a reluctance in the minds of some archaeologists to deposit archive material that might suggest that their published account could be proved wrong or that the work was not up to scratch. The Knossos controversy was also conducted through the pages of *Antiquity* (for example 35 (1961), 4-7, 135-41; 36 (1962), 38-40). Sinclair Hood warned of the problems of using first observations and impressions made in notebooks at an early stage in any excavation that might later be reconsidered (1962, 39).

## Dumbuck Crannog, Dunbartonshire

Mr Maxwell's glass slides of a series of coloured sketches of the excavations of the crannog at Dumbuck in 1898 are perhaps the most remarkable addition to the record (**colour plate 29**). The excavator of the crannog, John Bruce, an antiquary from Helensburgh and a Fellow of the Society of Antiquaries of Scotland, Vice-President between 1919–22, published an account in their proceedings (Bruce 1900). The paper was clearly controversial and unusually there is publication of the discussion of the authenticity of the finds. The slides have thus a significant bearing on the interpretation of the site. They appear to come from a sketchbook belonging to the practical excavator of the site William Donnelly, coupled with photographs of Donnelly himself and of visiting groups. Like the material on Knappers the slides offer insights not only into the archaeological evidence but also into the social impact of the excavations on the Clyde mudflats. Donnelly's artistic skills and precision in recording were in no small measure due to his profession as contributor and illustrator to the *Illustrated London News*. The difficulties of excavating in the tidal mud are graphically shown, but so is the pattern of timbers discovered and the shaped constructional members. The drawings offer an immediacy of recording that is unique, which no suite of photographs could ever match. They show the men at work digging the timbers clear of mud, and the smart fashions of ladies 'Doing the Crannog' (**71** & **72**). The archaeological assessment must be left to others, but the slides offer a remarkable insight into the excavation method and their value in terms of social history is undoubted.

Among news-cuttings books discovered later was a page from the *Illustrated London News* 19 November 1898, 754 (**73**), which admirably demonstrates Donnelly's skill in amalgamating the sketches into a single page illustration, as well as showing some of the obviously fake artefacts that caused scorn to be poured on the whole operation at the time. Bruce is shown at the centre of the group supervising the removal of a canoe and Donnelly may well

**71** *(opposite) Watercolour of work at Dumbuck with annotations, 28 Ocober 1898 by William Donnelly.* Crown Copyright: Royal Commission on the Ancient and Historical Monuments of Scotland

**72** *High fashion on the mudflats at Dumbuck, 'Doing the Crannog', by William Donnelly.* Crown Copyright: Royal Commission on the Ancient and Historical Monuments of Scotland

**73** *Page from Ludovic Mann's Newscuttings Album recording 'The discovery of a crannog on the Clyde: further interesting chapters of unwritten history', drawn by William Donnelly, 1898, with both genuine and fake artefacts. Mann has annotated the illustration to the effect that the cupmarks are natural (NMRS MS/678/1 p.26). John Bruce is supervising the removal of the canoe. William Donnelly may be at the centre of the picture with his notebook.* Crown Copyright: Royal Commission on the Ancient and Historical Monuments of Scotland

be the tall figure with the notebook. The canoe is discussed by Bruce and Mowat (Bruce 1900; Mowat 1996, 26-7), where the surviving remains, in Glasgow Art Gallery and Museum, are described as 'a distorted, shrunken and greatly-split plank'. Andrew Lang who entered the controversy with The Clyde Mystery in 1905 mentions in his preface that 'Mr Donnelly also protests that his records of his excavations were exceptionally complete', and that he 'took daily notes and sketches of all features and finds with measurements' (1905, vi); the notes are illustrated (**71**). Lang feels that he must mention these facts as in the book he implies that Donnelly 'kept no minute and hourly book of his explorations, with full details as to the precise positions of the objects discovered'. Context sheets were a long way off.

The discovery of the slides shows that Donnelly's illustrative talents were fully involved in recording the excavation, and that the notebooks, though we do not know if they have survived, did indeed exist. They take us no nearer to the forger, but in a visual way they demonstrate Donnelly's own skills, which contrast with the crudeness of the counterfeit antiquities. Information about Scottish archaeology was presented to the wider public in such visual formats before the days of photographs in newspapers or television. The glass slides also illustrate another important way in which archaeological information was presented to the public: through organised site visits and lectures, with Donnelly seen lecturing to a group with a small collection of objects at his feet (**74**). As with Knappers, the slides illustrate that the standard of excavation and sketch recording was higher than might have been expected.

John Bruce has been included in the context of archival survival not only as an active partic-ipant in the work at Dumbuck, but also as someone a fragment of whose papers has become known through the merest chance. Some of his papers were discovered on a skip and were iden-tified as being of antiquarian interest; they came to the knowledge of the Society of Antiquaries of Scotland and thus into the public domain through the *Society of Antiquaries of Scotland Newsletter* 10.2 (February 1999). These papers were thus saved, but it can never be known what else was on that skip and how much else that was relevant to this complex site has been lost.

After Mr Applebey's death, Mrs Applebey contacted the writer, and with her son George sought advice about the deposition of further archival material. The scale of the material was quite unexpected, as only relevant portions had been seen on earlier visits. The artefacts were transferred to Glasgow Art Gallery and Museum and the archive to NMRS. Of particular interest are the news-cuttings books, illustrating Mann's long subscription to Durant's Agency (**75**). Mr Applebey had recalled that Mann would prepare a piece for a newspaper, send it round to the editor in the hands of a young lad whose task it was to check that it would be in the next edition, otherwise another editor might be interested. The results of news coverage are clearly seen in the derivative stories carried in later editions of other papers throughout the land. Something of the continuing tradition was sensed when the writer called at the Mitchell Library in Glasgow to check on holdings about the excavations at Knappers. Drawing a blank at first, he ventured that it was sometimes called 'The Druid Temple', 'Goodness, why didn't you say that in the first place,' was the instant response. Newspapers are hard to trawl through, but with the relevant dates, this is made much easier and there is also a much greater understanding of the contempo-rary impact that archaeological discoveries were making at the time than perusal of the pages of a journal may allow.

**74** *William Donnelly addressing a group at the railway bridge near Dumbuck.* Crown Copyright: Royal Commission on the Ancient and Historical Monuments of Scotland

**75** *Page from Ludovic Mann's Newscuttings Album 22 July 1933 recording the work of J. Harrison Maxwell at Keil Cave, Kintyre (NMRS MS/678/13, p.66).* Crown Copyright: Royal Commission on the Ancient and Historical Monuments of Scotland

## Newstead, Roxburgh

Excavation notebooks recording the work of James Curle at the Roman fort at Newstead, Roxburgh, survived not so much through chance, but came to public notice only through the tenacity of the finder, Lady Cameron of Lochbroom. A piece of furniture inherited from a relative was delivered to Edinburgh and was found on inspection to have a number of notebooks in a drawer. That these related to the excavation of Newstead was not in doubt, but when additional information was sought about them, the first professional advice was that, as the excavation had been fully published, they were of no interest. Undaunted Lady Cameron sought advice from the British Museum where by chance a curator, Dafydd Kidd, was doing research on the collection of Gotlandic bronzes that James Curle had sold to the Museum in 1921. The interest of the material was thus identified and knowledge of the notebooks made more widely available (copies in NMRS) (Kidd & Ritchie 1988). They add to knowledge of how the excavation was directed and recorded, as well as offering insights into the character of Curle himself (**colour plate 30**), but without the tenacity of the finder and the unlikely knowledge of the excavator on the part of a curator in a distant museum, the notebooks might still be in a drawer, or indeed discarded.

Something of Curle's care in preparing the report for publication can be gauged by his generous acknowledgement to George (later Sir George) Macdonald, the leading Roman scholar of the time in Scotland, for his help (1911, vi–ix). But there can be strange pointers to the relationships between scholars, for RCAHMS holds the copy of the Newstead report that was owned by Thomas Ross, who prepared all the plans of the site and was a distinguished architectural historian. Ross has annotated his copy in no uncertain terms:

> George Macdonald visited the camp only once, and this just at the conclusion of operations, of which he had no knowledge whatsoever. I suppose he assisted in the preparation of the book. The whole excavations from the beginning to end were carried out by Mr. A. Mackie.

There is no doubt that he was making a statement to future owners of the volume. Little could he have known that after the death of his last daughter, the Royal Commission on the Ancient and Historical Monuments of Scotland, of which he had been a founder Commissioner, would be offered the opportunity to accept books for their Library. Thus his comments entered a more public domain. The photograph that he had stuck into the flyleaf showing 'Mr Mackie and myself at Newstead July 1906' is however less reassuring as to the method of excavation.

## Serendipity and the telephone

Serendipity and chance also play a part in the garnering of archaeological archival material and information. As part of research into the work of Walter Grant on Rousay in Orkney, including the excavation of the broch at Midhowe, we realised that a key player had been David Wilson, Grant's architectural collaborator (Reynolds & Ritchie 1985). His illustrations lie at the heart of the excavation reports, and, although Wilson himself had died many years before, it was possible that his widow might have more information. A tentative telephone call to a likely address did not find the right Wilson, but someone who knew exactly who was meant. Thus the second call made the right connection.

Mrs Wilson had a presentation portfolio of her husband's coloured drawings in a splendid binding. Although most of the illustrations were previously known in published form, the plan of the excavation of a burnt mound at Quandale, Rousay, was a new discovery (**colour plate 31**). These were pioneering excavations of a type of monument that was little understood at the time and the results remain unpublished and unknown apart from this plan (Lamb 1982, 21, no. 65, 40). The portfolio is now in the Orkney Archive (copies in NMRS). Spurred by the success of this telephonic venture, a subsequent object of research, J.M. Corrie, an archaeological investigator with RCAHMS who had died in 1938, prompted a phone call to a Miss Corrie in Dumfries-shire, with the eventual discovery of his granddaughter, who knew of the existence of manuscript notebooks. All the original documentation copied at that time for NMRS is now in the Dumfries and Galloway Archives (Reynolds 1984).

Perhaps the strangest piece of telephonic serendipity was that connected to the illustration of *The Sculptured Stones of Scotland* (Stuart 1856 and 1867). In the course of the preparation of a short paper on the methods of illustration of Early Christian stones and the use of lithography in their publication, I remembered the display of tools of the etcher's craft in Aberdeen Art Gallery, and wondered if perhaps the gallery would know of similar practical displays of tools relating to lithography. A telephone call to the appropriate department found the curator, Jennifer Melville, who had no display of lithographic implements, but who was at that time reading a manuscript life of the distinguished painter Sir George Reid, which detailed for the first time his involvement as an apprentice in the recording of the Early Christian stones for Stuart's volumes (Ritchie 1998, 12-13). Information gathered in this way is not entirely by chance, but it certainly requires an element of luck. The archaeological record would be the poorer without it.

This contribution has been designed to underline that even today the gathering of archaeological evidence is not a quantifiable science. In visual terms it is intended to show that the study of archaeology goes far beyond the dry excavation report, as with William Donnelly's water-colour of the *Wild Boar Hunt at the Crannog* (**76**), the result of the preservation of glass slides. The studious cultivation of the media by Mann may still be paralleled, but rarely will the personal record of it be so comprehensive. The illustrations help to set the archaeology of the period into context in a way that no contemporary run of journals can. This paper is not merely intended to show that what may be taken as archaeological ephemera is an engaging topic, and one designed to amuse a scholar who has consistently challenged mainstream attitudes and has a particular interest in 'fact'. Facets of 'fact' and archaeological information may profitably be mined from the unusual sources explored in this paper, yet the weighing of the 'fact' is a complex matter (Hood, 1962, 39). But we must also evaluate the historical context in which any work was being undertaken. It may be difficult for archaeologists working today to imagine the framework in which Maxwell, Donnelly or Mann were active, let alone even earlier generations, but the information that they recovered is still relevant to the material at our disposal for archaeological study. The information from their archives enhances our understanding of both the material and how it was gathered.

**76** *The Wild Boar Hunt at the Crannog, by William Donnelly.*
Crown Copyright: Royal Comission on the Ancient and Historical Monuments of Scotland

Realisation that elements of chance play a part in the survival of material or information about archaeological work even in the comparatively recent past should have a sobering effect on any evaluation of the generality of the evidence at our disposal and on its incorporation in any theoretical stance. The survival of evidence depends on the regard or lack of regard that society places on the collectors of the evidence in the first place and on the tenacity and faith of the guardians of that record, such as Mrs Maxwell, and Mr and Mrs Applebey. Examples of the deliberate destruction of such records are also known. There is too a parallel in the fickleness of the archaeological evidence itself, where for example material that has been gathered into a chambered cairn may be set to one side or totally discarded to make way for further deposits, which may itself depend on the personal approach of the later users of the monument. The survival of monuments certainly involves wider landscape issues, but there can also be an idiosyncratic human element at work. The deliberate destruction of the Stone of Odin, Orkney in 1814, to prevent people from visiting it, is not without parallel in more recent times. The preservation of even the most unpromising material that records work on archaeological and historical monuments is of great importance: its interpretation is a matter of greater complexity.

# 19  Conclusions

*Beverley Ballin Smith and Iain Banks*

## Introduction

The intention behind this volume is to present a general overview of the state of Iron Age studies in Scotland at the beginning of the twenty-first century. It also marks the retirement of Dr Euan MacKie from his curatorial post at the Hunterian Museum in Glasgow. Dr MacKie has been a major figure in Scottish Iron Age studies and continues to be so. The health of the subject is in no small part due to his contribution and enthusiasm for the subject. While many have not agreed with his arguments, he has often initiated and been at the centre of all the major debates on the Scottish Iron Age, pushing forward the discourses necessary to further our understanding of the period. As this volume is in his honour, we have not sought to constrain the contributors and have instead attempted to obtain a range of opinions about the Scottish Iron Age. We wish therefore, to point out that the views expressed by the individual authors are theirs and not necessarily those of the archaeological academy as a whole. The reader may notice discrepancies in hypotheses and different interpretations of events. These have been deliberately left as they stand to promote future debate.

## Regional research shifts

This volume represents contributions from a significant number of archaeological researchers presently working in Scotland on the Iron Age, on single sites, complex settlements and landscapes. There are some notable omissions of institutions and individuals working in the Western Isles and the Northern regions especially. However, these papers highlight the geographical and funding shift which has taken place over approximately the last 10 years. As can be seen from the distribution of papers, the emphasis now is heavily towards the Western Isles in spite of the often-repeated remark that the Northern Isles, and Orkney in particular, have received the lion's share of activity and government funding. This latter picture was true when a significant number of large excavations were carried out on Orkney in the late 1970s and the 1980s. This does not mean that there has been a complete cessation of archaeological activity in the Northern Isles. It still exists, and while there are perhaps fewer projects, they are still large scale.

The 'rebirth' of the Western Isles reflects the availability of a large landscape with copious archaeological sites that previously lay logistically beyond the interests of most researchers and outside the main thrust of rescue work. Today, many universities with archaeological departments have developed the expertise of their archaeological staff and students on research excavations on Iron Age sites of the Western Isles. Indeed, the situation has probably come full circle since Euan MacKie began his work there in the 1960s. Spectacular discoveries, publicity and publications have all helped to thrust the Western Isles into prominence and rival the lead the Northern Isles established.

What is remarkable in this volume is the paucity of papers on the Iron Age of mainland Scotland. This dearth is primarily reflected in the nature of the archaeological activity, which is often associated with developer-funded projects rather than research excavations. Commercial projects are often undertaken in single seasons and rarely affect known monumental Iron Age structures of any type. This situation lies in direct contrast to work undertaken in other geographical regions, which often targets sites or landscapes with specific archaeological questions. The mainland Scotland Iron Age can therefore be said to suffer from a lack of research due to the general nature of the archaeological work that is undertaken, and the appeal of more geographically remote areas with spectacular but vulnerable coastal scenery.

## Predominant research interests

One of the purposes of this final chapter is to look at the wide spectrum of papers and the views expressed and to try to make some attempt to evaluate the present state of Iron Age studies.

Perhaps more than we would like to admit the archaeological research of today still has much in common with the major trends of the middle to late twentieth century. The contributions to this volume reflect the persistent obsession with structures, usually specific structures, in contrast to the wider Iron Age landscape. Nomenclature is still a preoccupation, as the debates over the usage of terms such as broch and simple/complex roundhouses clearly show. There is still a fixation on the broch as a unique structure (although this is gradually changing), with other monument types suffering by comparison from a lack of interest. The wags of Caithness are an example of this untapped resource despite their complexity (e.g. Baines 2000). There is also a widely held assumption of a hierarchical social structure and of the place of the broch settlement in that structure, although there has been little explicit debate since Barrett's seminal paper about the nature of Iron Age society in Scotland (Barrett 1982). Furthermore, we should question whether one societal model embraces all of the different population groups in Scotland during the period, covering highland, lowland, coastal, inland, riverine and moorland settlements. The position of the broch within these social models is also little debated. Yet can all brochs be unique, and be expressions of high status communities? One paper (see Armit) in the volume begins to ask questions of the equation of brochs with high status individuals, and opens a wider discussion on this issue.

As archaeologists we tinker round the edges of the complex subject of the Iron Age whose monumental expression of the period, the broch, still tantalises us with its uniqueness, its simplicity and its elusiveness: as expressed by Hedges and Bell (1980) it remains 'that tower of Scottish prehistory'. In spite of 40 years' work by archaeologists who have come and gone, we still are unable to adequately discuss what the purpose and function of the broch was. We have broadened our archaeological horizons and with it stretched the terminology that is used. From the broch tower we can now talk of broch settlements within defences, to broch settlements beyond defences and now, even broch field systems. But one questions the potential of more recently introduced terminology such as 'complex and simple Atlantic roundhouses' to be as all-embracing as the word 'broch'.

It is perhaps a reflection of chance, or more likely fashion, that there are very few papers on the environmental and artefactual aspects of the Iron Age. Most present day excavations and other archaeological research closely involve questions about the environmental remains of sites, which have become vital components and essential tools of the archaeologist. The lack of emphasis may indicate that a hierarchy is subconsciously at work in the archaeological mind. Research into the environmental remains of Iron Age sites may not yet have reached its peak, while that of artefactual work may have surpassed it. Many of the important questions concerning regionality, the chronology and contemporaneity of Iron Age sites still rest largely with the environmental and artefactual evidence and it is to them we will turn (again) in the future.

## Missing links

So few broch towers have ever been demonstrably excavated to their foundations, that still we discuss them with the limited knowledge and evidence often acquired from the infancy of broch studies 80 to 100 or more years ago (see Ballin Smith forthcoming). There are few hard facts and figures and this paucity remains one of our more shameful failures. The scientific sampling and procedures we now rigorously apply to middens, fields, landscapes and other deposits are not applied to the excavation of broch towers, simply because broch towers are so very rarely excavated in their entirety. This is not solely the fault of researchers; the willingness is there but the funding is not. Iron Age excavations, especially those of the brochs and duns of the North and Western Isles, still remain some of the most expensive excavations ever funded in Scotland. That very expense is often a hindrance to the furtherance of scientific study and discovery. Other factors such as display and the economic return of sites are also hindering the winning and furtherance of scientific knowledge.

The perceptual landscape of Iron Age studies in Scotland is dominated by elite and monumental stone structures such as brochs and duns. But what was the exact relationship of brochs, duns, vitrified forts, hillforts, promontory forts, crannogs, souterrains and earthhouses to each other? Do we fully understand their interrelationships and functions? The Iron Age is a difficult period for radiocarbon dating, and this may partly be responsible for the lack of chronological definition of the different classes of settlement sites. We have little clear idea about what structures existed in the landscape at any given time and how different sites related chronologically. As our understanding of the chronological relationship of the different settlements and buildings is so poor any statements we do make about the status and social interrelationships are often mere guesswork.

There is generally very little attempt to seek out the ordinary and non-monumental, the sites that would have been largely built of wood. There have been few excavations of the enclosures that litter southern Scotland, and the main impetus for these excavations has been rescue. There has been no structured attempt to determine whether there was an unenclosed population, living in buildings made of organic materials that have left no obvious surface traces. Our analysis of the social systems in Iron Age Scotland are largely written on the basis of evidence from the monumental sites of the Northern and Western Isles, with virtually no attempt to consider whether these models fit the rest of Iron Age Scotland.

At the moment, our model of Iron Age social structure is a strange mix of anthropological equivalences, sociological modelling and parallels from Irish texts of a later period and disputed purpose. This may be adequate, and it may correctly encapsulate the nature of society in the period. However, it is a fairly major assumption that all parts of Scotland would have had identical social systems in the period. Without wishing to re-introduce environmental determinism, it is possible that different conditions created different social structures. The farmlands of eastern Scotland may have more closely resembled the societies of southern England than the societies of the Highlands, while communities living on the coast may have been very different from those located inland. It is possible to argue that the environment was a major factor in the development of Iron Age social systems because it determined the nature of the available resources and the activities that populations could undertake.

Scottish Iron Age studies over the past 40 years have failed to address the notion of a life story for individual sites. The beginnings, middles and ends of sites frequently crossed several generations of human occupation and as such the understanding and perception of a site during its existence will have changed. Structures and settlements, which may to the archaeologist and researcher look the same over time, may have developed and changed functions several times. Sites that resemble one another may not have had the same function, nor are they necessarily of similar dates. In the absence of excavation and of reliable dating evidence, all else is supposition.

Other areas of Iron Age studies are problematic. One important question which often arises is, where are the Iron Age burials? In a reversal of the Neolithic and Bronze Ages where emphasis was laid on the disposal of the dead and the accompanying rituals, the Iron Age dead are conspicuous by their absence. We can encounter the dead in the Roman and post-Roman Iron Age, where long cist cemeteries emphasise the importance of disposing of bodies. However, in the Iron Age there appears to be a fundamentally different approach. Was there a new ideology, or were there significant social factors that account for the paucity of cemeteries? Equally, one might ask where the Iron Age ritual monuments are. Is it a problem of our own making – do we not recognise them – or did they not exist? Are the surviving Iron Age monumental structures simply an expression of the living and the emphasis on life? Are our interpretations wrong?

Another area of neglect is the sea. As the dominant means of communication, with boats as a major means of transportation, the value of the sea as a resource in Scottish Iron Age studies is often overlooked. Rarely have discussions of the potential size of Iron Age populations mentioned the sea in equal measure with the available land resources of sites. The sea and coastal locations are resources of great richness and our emphasis on resources of the land may be erroneous. The predominance of Iron Age settlements close to the coast and to inland waterways suggests that seas and rivers were important elements for communication and social and economic intercourse. The ability to move easily and range over a greater area may suggest that some Iron Age settlements dominated larger swathes of coast through their boats than has hitherto been appreciated.

It has been pointed out (Kenny Brophy's unpublished lecture '*If brochs were Neolithic*' for the Iron Age Student Research Seminar, Glasgow University, June 2002) that post-processual theoretical approaches analysis has not really taken place in Iron Age studies in Scotland. The continued obsession with structural origins and the current definitions of widely used Iron

Age terminology may, according to Brophy, be constraining research rather than aiding it. This is a point of view which may in the future be seen as prophetic, and which may inspire newer researchers to take us in new directions.

## Conclusions

Much has been achieved in the past 40 years, in spite of obvious omissions, and Euan MacKie's contribution remains significant. However, in the need to progress and become more inclusive in our research and debate, some of the attributes of post-processual theoretical modelling may need to be applied to Iron Age Studies in Scotland. We are certain that Dr MacKie would hope that his legacy will form part of the continual development of the discipline as the frontier of knowledge expands, but unless there is adequate research funding for the investigation of a wide range of Iron Age sites, we shall still continue to be in the shadow of the brochs.

# Footnotes

## Chapter 8

**1** The vessel containing 'bog-butter' found at Kyleakin has recently been dated to 1730±35 bp (UB-3186), which at one standard deviation gives a date range of AD 246-346 (Earwood 1991, 233-6 with refs). This, together with the vessel from Kilmaluag (Ritchie 1941, 5-22) is well documented. Less well known is that found at Aird, Point of Sleat in the nineteenth century (Donations, in *Proceedings of the Society of Antiquaries of Scotland* 3, Pt 4, 105). Notice of a fourth discovery, made either towards the close of the nineteenth century or in the early years of the twentieth, has been largely overlooked by archaeologists: 'In the peat moss of Valtos,(Trotternish; centred NG 515 638) several bronze spearheads were found, and a barrel, formed from the hollowed trunk of a tree, filled with what appeared to be tallow, was found embedded in the moss. The police took possession of the barrel' (Mackenzie 1995, 22).

The late Dr Alasdair Maclean recounted that during the early half of the twentieth century a wooden container filled with bog-butter had been found near Ollach in the Braes, to the south of Portree (centred NG 511 365). Few in the community were aware of the find, and the fate of the container is unknown.

Mrs Mary Anne Graham of Peingowan, Kilmuir, told of a second discovery of bog-butter at the moss at Kilmaluag, Kilmuir, North Skye (centred NG 4374). It was found during peat-cutting in the early 1940s, and it was doubtless because of the earlier discovery of a barrel of butter in the same bog, that it was readily identifiable for what it was. Mrs Graham saw the butter and was definite that it had been found as a lump, and not contained within a wooden vessel. This indicates alternative practices for wrapping butter before deposition, which might well affect the chances of recognition and recovery. In this respect Jonathon MacDonald of Kilmuir (whose knowledge of the traditions and history of the area is unrivalled), indicated that his grandmother (born in the 1850s) was familiar at first hand with the practice of wrapping fish and butter in horsehair and burying them in the bog for later recovery. Cheese, it seems, was not so commonly made in Skye at this time as it was in the other isles, and so did not figure prominently amongst such deposits; well-salted 'crowdy' (the strained whey from boiled milk) on the other hand, could be, and was, kept for some months.

**2** The term 'Highland Pantries' includes those spaces within buildings designed to store dairy produce in cool conditions. They emerge in the literature in the sixteenth century, where they are referred to as 'closets', small rooms situated in positions sheltered from the heat of the fire, usually with the intercession of the arrangement of beds. They were, moreover, further subdivided by the addition of wattle screening, which gave rise to subsequent descriptions of aumbries within what are essentially cold store larders.

By the beginning of the nineteenth century many of these closets were being converted into bedrooms (pers. comm. from Ross Noble, Highland Folk Park, Kingussie). Fenton has drawn attention to the subterranean storehouses that 'resemble small souterrains', known in Angus, Roxburgh and Fife in the later eighteenth century and used for the storage of potatoes, turnips and other root crops (Fenton 1976, 121-3 & refs). It is therefore of more than passing interest to hear of the strikingly similar constructions found particularly in those areas of eighteenth- and nineteenth-century colonial settlement in the United States, apparently built as root cellars. (pers. comm. courtesy of Diane Murray; see for example Neudorfer 1979, 79-146).

**3 Single Cups** *Suisgill II, Sutherland* (NC82NE 15); *Mains of Clava, Aberdeenshire* (NJ42SE 16), in side wall; *Culsh, Aberdeenshire* (NJ50SW 1) in side wall; *Pitcur, Perth & Kinross* (NO23NE 1.01) five stones, including two on the underside of the lintels; *Blairs of Airlie, Angus* (NO35SW 19) underside of roof slab; *Elliot, Angus* (NO63NW 7) two stones, incorporated into the floor paving; *Hurley Hawkin, Angus* (NO33SW 7) two stones, a capstone bearing nine cup-marks on its upper face, and a second stone bearing nine cup-marks adjacent to the northern entrance of the souterrain; *Tealing III, Angus* (NO43NW 1) in side wall (see also cup & rings below); *Kilvaxter, Highland* (No.30 above) five stones, including one pinning on the upper-side between the lintels.

**Cup & Rings:** *Ruthven, Angus* (NO24NE 1) in roof; *Tealing III, Angus* (NO43NW 1) in wall (see also cups above); *Ardross, Fife* (NO50SW 12) in side wall; *Carlungie I, Angus* (NO53NW 12) in the backfill from dismantling the souterrain; *Ardestie, Angus* (NO64NW 19) in one of huts associated with souterrain; *Letham Grange, Angus* (NO64NW 19) in wall; *Crichton Mains, Midlothian* (NT46SW 11).

**4** This affinity to water has a striking parallel in the relationship between shielings and stream courses, with a clear premium upon siting next to waterfalls. Proximity to water was an important factor to the dairying activities so well attested at shielings sites, such as, scouring clean the wooden vessel used in the butter and cheese making. It is perhaps with such uses in mind that one must consider many of those casual discoveries of wooden vessels found in boggy upland situations, whose dates range across at least two millennia (Earwood. 1993, 355-62). In a Skye context this would include the wooden bowls from Talisker (Barber 1982, 578-9) and Ghlinne Bhig (Crone 1993, 269-73), both firmly dated to the Iron Age.

| Building aspect | Species identified at Oakbank Crannog |
|---|---|
| Construction timbers | mainly alder, then oak, with a few birch, apple type, willow, elm and ash |
| Construction dowels | at least some were oak |
| Hurdle walls | mainly coppiced hazel with some birch, mostly for uprights |
| Draft exclusion/ miscellaneous packing | weft-forming mosses, bracken, wood-working waste |
| Thatch | uncertain, but probably bracken. Long-stemmed rushes and straw may have had a minor role |
| Floor covering | bracken, long-stemmed rushes and wood-working waste. Probably also hay/straw and wild flowers including meadowsweet |
| Fuel | mostly birch and alder, including wood-working waste. Pine tapers for fire-lighting |
| Bedding | bracken, hay/straw, probably also heather and weft-forming mosses |
| Household implements | many were alder, including bowls, a spoon, butter dish and canoe paddle |
| Rope | twisted birch twigs found. Also probably heather, plus flax or nettle twine |
| Lamp wicks | probably the pith of long-stemmed rushes |
| First-aid | bog moss, with selfheal possibly used to staunch blood flow |

**1** *Summary of plant taxa identified from Oakbank Crannog with their actual and speculated uses in construction of the building*

| Lab. No | Sample context | Years BP uncal | 1σ calBC/AD date range | 2 σ calBC/AD date range |
|---|---|---|---|---|
| GaK-1222 | charcoal from low in fallen rubble of the vitrified fort | 2360 ± 80 | 550-370 BC | 800-200 BC |
| GaK-1223 | charcoal from occupation layer of the vitrified fort | 2270 ± 90 | 410-180 BC | 800-50 BC |
| GaK-1224 | charcoal from planks. Inner wall face of the vitrified fort. | 2540 ± 70 | 700-530 BC | 820-410 BC |

**2** *Finavon radiocarbon dates*

| Lab.No. | Sample context | Years BP uncal | 1σ calBC/AD date range | 2σcal BC/AD date range |
|---|---|---|---|---|
| GaK-1222 | charcoal from low in fallen rubble of the vitrified fort | 2360 ± 240 | 800-200 BC | 1000 BC - AD 200 |
| GaK-1223 | charcoal from occupation layer of the vitrified fort | 2270 ± 270 | 800 -50 BC | 1000 BC - AD 400 |
| GaK-1224 | charcoal from planks. Inner wall face of the vitrified fort. | 2540 ± 210 | 900 - 400 BC | 1300 - 100 BC |

**3** *Finavon radiocarbon dates with increased error ranges*

| Sample No. | Depth | Date BP | Date AD |
|---|---|---|---|
| TL58fa | 0 - 5 cm | 1255 ± 70 | AD 625 - 765 |
| TL59fa | 10 - 15 cm | 1560 ± 80 | AD 310 - 470 |
| TL60fa | 20 – 30 cm | 1220 ± 95 | AD 635 - 825 |
| TL62fa | - | 1330 ± 75 | AD 545 - 695 |

**4** *Finavon thermoluminescence dates*

| Site | Material | Lab number | Radiocarbon date |
|---|---|---|---|
| Dun Bharabhat (Harding and Dixon 2000) | hearth material | GU-2436 | 2550±50bp |
| Coile a'Ghasgain, Skye (Armit 1996) | hazel charcoal | B-66137 | 2370±190bp |
| An Dunan, near Uig Sands (Church and Gilmour 1999) | Charred barley grain | OxA-8478 | 2215±40bp |
| | Charred barley grain | OxA-8479 | 2145±40bp |
| | Charred barley grain | OxA-8613 | 2165±40bp |
| | Charred barley grain | OxA-8480 | 2250±35bp |
| | Charred barley grain | OxA-8575 | 2155±45bp |
| | Charred barley grain | OxA-8577 | 2230±50bp |
| Sollas Site A (Campbell 1991) | pottery residues | OxA-6945 | 1895±50bp |
| | | OxA-6966 | 1575±35bp |
| | | OxA-6968 | 1960±35bp |
| | | OxA-6969 | 2045±35bp |
| Sollas Site A2 (Campbell 1991) | charcoal | OxA-6967 | 1845±35bp |

**5** *Radiocarbon dates for Western Isles sites mentioned in the text*

| Uncalibrated date | Archaeological context | 1 σ calBC/AD date range | 2 σ calBC/AD date range |
|---|---|---|---|
| 2010±50bp (GU-2434) | Secondary occupation destruction layer (charred timber) | 90 - 70 BC (3.0%) 60 BC - AD 60 (65.2%) | 170 BC - AD 90 (93.8%) AD 100 - 120 (1.6%) |
| 2100±50bp (GU-2435) | Secondary occupation destruction layer (charred timber) | 200 - 190 BC (1.5%) 180 - 40 BC (66.7%) | 360 - 290 BC (6.4%) 240 BC - AD 30 (89.0%) |
| 2550±50bp (GU-2436) | Primary or pre-roundhouse (uncarbonised wood) | 800 - 750 BC (23.6%) 690 - 660 BC (9.0%) 650 - 540 (35.6%) | 820 - 510 BC (94.4%) 440 - 410 BC (1.0%) |

**6** *Radiocarbon dates from Dun Bharabhat, Lewis*

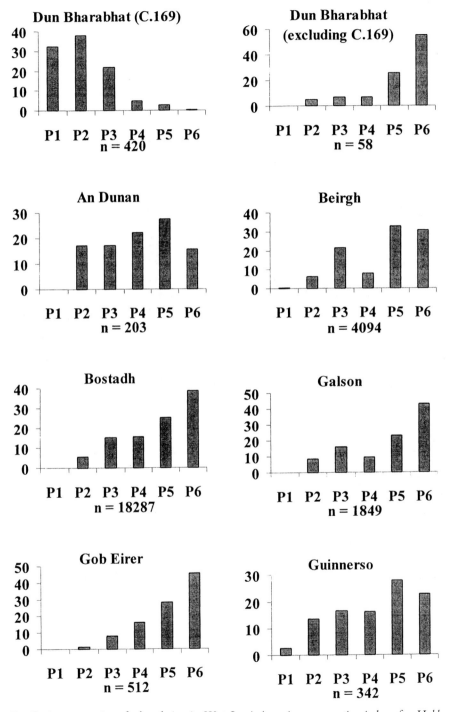

**7** *Grain preservation of selected sites in West Lewis (x axis= preservation index after Hubbard & al Azm, 1990; y axis= percentage of total assemblage.)*

| Context | 169 |
|---|---|
| *Volume (litres)* | *5* |
| | |
| **Cereals** | |
| Barley basal rachis | 34 |
| Hulled barley grain | 77 |
| Hulled barley twisted grain | 185 |
| Hulled barley straight grain | 133 |
| Two row hulled barley rachis internode | 28 |
| cf. Two row barley rachis internode | 28 |
| Two row hulled barley basal rachis internode | 9 |
| Two row hulled barley grain | 4 |
| Two row hulled barley sterile lateral spikelet | 42 |
| Six-row hulled barley rachis | 150 |
| Six-row hulled barley basal rachis | 23 |
| Six-row hulled barley twisted grain | 7 |
| Six-row hulled barley straight grain | 14 |
| Cereal straw fragment | 2000F+ |
| Cereal straw root base | 302 (10F) |
| Cereal straw node | 1299 (55F) |
| | |
| **Wild Species** | |
| Creeping buttercup seed | 1 |
| Bulbous buttercup seed | 1 |
| Common chickweed seed | 10 |
| Ray's Knotgrass seed | 2 |
| Knotgrass (species) seed | 8 |
| Knotgrass (genus) seed | 3 |
| Violet seed | 7 |
| Cabbage family capsule base | 2 |
| Wild turnip seed | 155 |
| Heather capsule | 2 |
| Heather stem/leaf | 3F |
| Ling stem/leaf | 18F |
| Cross-leaved heather stem leaf | 4F |
| Grass grain | 3 |
| Grass floret | 7 |
| Monocotyledon straw root base | 169 |
| Monocotyledon straw node | 109 (13F) |
| Monocotyledon rhizome fragment | 4F |
| Unidentifiable seed | 10 |
| | |
| **Totals** | |
| Total grain components | 420 |
| Total chaff components | 1915 |
| Total cereal components | 2335 |
| Total wild species | 480 |
| Total quantifiable components | 2815 |
| Quantifiable components/litre | 563 |

**8** *Carbonised plant macrofossils from possible thatch, Dun Bharabhat (c.169).*

| Site | Archaeological information | Palaeoenvironmental information |
|---|---|---|
| *Shetland* | | |
| Scalloway (Sharples 1998) | Conflagration of secondary occupation of CAR | Soil micromorphology (Carter 1998) |
| *Orkney* | | |
| Howe (Ballin Smith 1994) | 1. Early Phase 7 – SW building roof fire<br>2. Early Phase 7 – NW building roof fire<br>3. Early Phase 7 – E building *in situ* posts<br>4. Early Phase 7 – 'Broch 2' secondary occupation fire<br>5. Late Phase 7 – 'Broch 2' secondary occupation roof fire<br>6. Late Phase 7 – 'Broch 2' secondary occupation fire | Archaeobotany (Dickson 1994)<br>1. Timbers (willow, spruce), six-row naked barley/heather mixed thatch, *in situ* floor level material<br>2. Closure episode (?), timbers (willow, spruce), six-row naked barley thatch<br>3. Uncarbonised alder posts<br>4. Six-row naked barley straw (stored or on floor)<br>5. Roof timbers (willow and spruce)<br>6. Six-row naked barley crop processing accident leading to fire, roof timbers (willow) |
| *Western Isles* | | |
| Beirgh (Harding & Gilmour 2000) | Primary Cellular *in situ* uncarbonised structural material | Archaeobotany (Church, forthcoming)<br>1. Spruce post<br>2. Coppiced hazel wattlework |
| Dun Bharabhat (Harding & Dixon 2000) | Secondary occupation conflagration | Archaeobotany (Church 2000)<br>1. Timber (spruce, Scots Pine)<br>2. Six-row and two-row hulled barley thatch |
| Bornais (Sharples, DES) | Probable wheelhouse conflagration | Post-excavation work ongoing |
| *Inner Hebrides* | | |
| Dun Ardtreck (Mackie forth.) | 1. Iron Age conflagration<br>2. Medieval (?) conflagration | None |
| Dun Mor Vaul (Mackie 1974) | Possible early Iron Age conflagration | Archaeobotany (Renfrew 1974)<br>1. Carbonised post (indet.)<br>2. Six-row hulled barley cache |
| *Argyll* | | |
| Rahoy (Childe & Thorneycroft 1938) | 1. Vitrified walling in 'fort'<br>2. *In situ* interior posts | 1. Hazel timber<br>2. Oak |
| *Sutherland* | | |
| Langwell (Nisbet 1995) | Atlantic Roundhouse roof fire | None |

**9** *Conflagration levels in Iron Age Atlantic Scotland*

| Site | Gallery length | Sites with greatest gallery width | Entrance position | Souterrain orientation | Gallery termination |
|---|---|---|---|---|---|
| 1 | c.20m | | Stream bank | N-S | Circular chamber |
| 2 | c.23m | | Down slope | NE-SW | Circular chamber |
| 3 | ? | | Stream bank | E-W | Circular chamber |
| 4 | c.17m | | Stream bank | NE-SW | ? |
| 5 | c.9m | | Stream bank | NW-SE | ? |
| 6 | c.8.2m | | Down slope | NE-SW | ? |
| 7 | ? | | Down slope | ? | ? |
| 8 | ? | | Close to stream | E-W | ? |
| 9 | 8.5m | | Down slope | E-W | Butt end |
| 10 | ? | | Close to stream | ? | ? |
| 11 | c.5m | | Close to stream | E-W | ? |
| 12 | ? | | Down slope | ? | ? |
| 13 | ? | | Down slope | ? | ? |
| 14 | c.11m | | Stream bank | E-W | Circular chamber |
| 15 | 8.8m | | Down slope | ?NE-SW | Circular chamber |
| 16 | 11.5m | * | Close to stream | NW/SE | Butt end |
| 17 | ? | | Down slope | ? | Cave |
| 18 | ? | | Down slope | ? | ? |
| 19 | ? | | Down slope | ? | ? |
| 20 | c.4m | | Down slope | N-S | ? |
| 21 | 13m | * | Down slope? | SE-NW | Butt end |
| 22 | ? | | Down slope | ? | ? |
| 23 | 20m | * | Down slope | N/S | Butt end |
| 24 | 29m | | Stream bank | ? | Circular chamber |
| 25 | ? | | Stream bank | ? | ? |
| 26 | ? | | Down slope | ? | ? |
| 27 | ? | | Down slope | NE-SW | ? |
| 28 | 7.7m | | Down slope | NE/SW | Circular chamber |
| 29 | ? | | Down slope | ? | ? |
| 30 | c.17.5m | * | Close to stream | ? | Butt end |
| 31 | ? | | Down slope | E-W NE/SW | ? |

**10** *Souterrain characteristics*

| Site (Ref.No) | Material | Lab.No. | 14C Determination BP | Calibration (to 2 sd) and Median Date |
|---|---|---|---|---|
| Tungadale (9) Primary Hearth | Charcoal (Corylus, Betula, Calluna) | GU3810 | 2150±100BC | 392 BC - 56 AD 168 BC |
| Tungadale (9) Secondary Floor Post-pad | Charcoal (Corylus, Salix, Betula, Calluna) | GU3808 | 2310±70BC | 756 - 178 BC 467 BC |
| Tungadale (9) Secondary Floor | Charcoal (Corylus, Salix, Betula, Calluna) | GU3809 | 2100±70BC | 358 BC - AD 62 148 BC |
| Alt na Cille (16) Souterrain floor | Charcoal (Corylus, Alnus, Salix) | GU3829 | 1890±90BC | 51 BC - 379 AD 164 AD |

**11** *Radiocarbon dates from souterrains*

| Site No. | Height m. OD | Geology | Soils | Land use |
|---|---|---|---|---|
| 1 | c. 20 | Clay | Brown forest soils | Improved grazing land |
| 2 | 75 | Glacial clays on Tertiary basalts and dolerite | Some peat | Permanent pasture with lazy beds a field boundary & rig and furrow |
| 3 | 30 | Clay | | |
| 4 | c. 29 | Basalt | Peaty gleys and Brown forest soils | With Atlantic heather vegetation and With traces of earlier cultivation |
| 5 | c. 100 | Basalt and dolerite | | Extensive remains of later cultivation |
| 6 | 50 | Basalt | | ?Grazing land |
| 7 | 8 | Alluvial gravels caped by windbown sand | | Arable land |
| 8 | 95 | Basalt | | Earlier rig and furrow |
| 9 | c.100 | Basalt | | |
| 10 | ? | | | |
| 11 | 7 | Alluvium | | |
| 12 | ? | Basalt | | |
| 13 | ? | Basalt | | |
| 14 | 80 | Basalt with clay and alluvium | | Formerly extensive cultivation now heather moorland with sheep grazing |
| 15 | ? | Basalt | | Rough pasture, mixed heather moorland |
| 16 | 70 | Basalt and Jurassic sandstone | Brown forest soils and bog | Light woodland and rough grazing |
| 17 | 130 | Jurassic limestones, sandstones and shales | Brown forest soils and bog | Former rig and furrow cultivation |
| 18 | ? | | | |
| 19 | ? | Basalt | | |
| 20 | 85 | Basalt | Brown forest soils | Heather |
| 21 | 30 | Sandstone outcrop | | Grassed |
| 22 | ? | | | |
| 23 | 170 | Jurassic shales | | Gravel pits |
| 24 | ? | | | |
| 25 | 30 | Jurassic shales and granite | | |
| 26 | ? | | | |
| 27 | ? | | | |
| 28 | ? | | | |
| 29 | ? | | | |
| 30 | ? | Glacial clay over Ostracod limestones & rotted stone 'brash' | Brown forest soils | Bent-fescue grassland, heather moor and permanent pasture |
| 31 | 40 | | Bog | Unimproved pasture, abandoned fields |

**12** *Information on the location of Skye souterrains*

| | Udal S A | Udal S B | Udal S C | Udal N XV | Sollas | Eilean Maleit | C. a Chomhalachd | Garry Iochdrach | Cleitraval | B.M.Chonnain D | B.M.Chonnain A | Foshigarry A | Foshigarry B | Foshigarry C | Grimsay | Hornish | W.Gerinish | Drimore I | Drimore II | Kildonnan | Kilpheder | Scalavat | Uamh Iosall | E.Gerinish | Allasdale | Cnip 9-1 | Cnip 9-2 | Cnip 12 | T.nam Berie | T.na Fhearnain | C.na Creagaich A | C na Chreagaich B1 | C na Chreagaich B2 | Wagmore Rigg N | Wagmore Rigg S | Wiltrow | Clickhimin | Bayanne | Stanydale |
|---|---|---|---|---|---|---|---|---|---|---|---|---|---|---|---|---|---|---|---|---|---|---|---|---|---|---|---|---|---|---|---|---|---|---|---|---|---|---|
| | Western Isles | | | | | | | | | | | | | | | | | | | | | | | | | | | | North Coast | | | | | | | | | |
| **Excavation details** | 1 | 2 | 3 | 4 | 5 | 6 | 7 | 8 | 9 | 10 | 11 | 12 | 13 | 14 | 15 | 16 | 17 | 18 | 19 | 20 | 21 | 22 | 23 | 24 | 25 | 26 | 27 | 28 | 29 | 30 | 31 | 32 | 33 | 34 | 35 | 36 | 37 | 38 |
| for Research | | | | | | | | | | | | | | | | | | | | | | | | | | | | | | | | | | | | | | |
| for Salvage | | | | | | | | | | | | | | | | | | | | | | | | | | | | | | | | | | | | | | |
| for Recreation | | | | | | | | | | | | | | | | | | | | | | | | | | | | | | | | | | | | | | |
| Site condition - eroded | | | | | | | | | | | | | | | | | | | | | | | | | | | | | | | | | | | | | | |
| | | | | | | | | | | | | | | | | | | | | | | | | | | | | | | | | | | | | | | |
| **Constructional details** | | | | | | | | | | | | | | | | | | | | | | | | | | | | | | | | | | | | | | |
| Double walling | | | | | | | | | | | | | | | | | | | | | | | | | | | | | | | | | | | | | | |
| Single walling | | | | | | | | | | | | | | | | | | | | | | | | | | | | | | | | | | | | | | |
| Broch inserts | | | | | | | | | | | | | | | | | | | | | | | | | | | | | | | | | | | | | | |
| Piers - free standing i | 11 | 11 | 8 | | 13 | 7<9 | 7 | 7 | 8 | 8 | 2 | | 3<13 | 4<12 | 8 | | | 12 | 3<6 | 6 | 11 | 5<10 | 4<9 | 1<? | 7<9 | 8 | 3<7 | ?2 | | | | | | | | 6<10 | | |
| Piers - butted to wall ii | | | | | | | | | | | | | | | | 5<10 | 9<11 | | | | | | | | | | | | | | | | | | | | | |
| Piers - bonded to wall iii | | | | | | | | | | | | 3 | | | | | | | | | | | | | | | | | | | | | | | | | | |
| Piers - bonded at door only iv | | | | | | | | | | | | | | | | | | | | | | | | | | | | | | | | | | | | | 4<6 | |
| Piers - Triangular v | | | | | | | | | | | | | | | | | | | | | | | | | | | | | | | | | | | | | | |
| Piers - Orthostatic vi | | | | | | | | | | | | | | | | | | | | | | | | | | | | | 7+ | 2? | 2? | | 2? | | 6? | | | 6? |
| Diameter | 10.6 | 10.8 | 7.6 | | 10.9 | 7.6 | 7 | 7.75 | 7.4 | 8.7 | 5.7 | 11 | 11.9 | 10 | 8.5 | 8 | 9.6 | 10.6 | 4.9 | 5 | 8.8 | 8.2 | 8 | ? | 8.2 | 6.7 | 6.7 | 6.7 | 5.5 | 7.9 | 7.9 | 5.8 | 6.1 | 8.8 | 6.4 | 7.5 | 7.5 | 5.2 |
| Radiocarbon dates | | | | | | | | | | | | | | | | | | | | | | | | | | | | | | | | | | | | | | |
| Pottery dating | | | | | | | | | | | | | | | | | | | | | | | | | | | | | | | | | | | | | | |
| Archaeomagnetic dating | | | | | | | | | | | | | | | | | | | | | | | | | | | | | | | | | | | | | | |
| Lintels - in situ | | | | | | | | | | | | | | | | | | | | | | | | | | | | | | | | | | | | | | |
| Lintels - dislodged | | | | | | | | | | | | | | | | | | | | | | | | | | | | | | | | | | | | | | |
| Hearths | | | | | | | | | | | | | | | | | | | | | | | | | | | | | | | | | | | | | | |
| Tanks/sinks | | | | | | | | | | | | | | | | | | | | | | | | | | | | | | | | | | | | | | |
| Twin wheelhouses | | | | | | | | | | | | | | | | | | | | | | | | | | | | | | | | | | | | | | |
| Founding pits | | | | | | | | | | | | | | | | | | | | | | | | | | | | | | | | | | | | | | |
| Entrances | | | | | | | | | | | | | | | | | | | | | | | | | | | | | | | | | | | | | | |
| Satellite cells | | | | | | | | | | | | | | | | | | | | | | | | | | | | | | | | | | | | | | |
| Aumbries | | | | | | | | | | | | | | | | | | | | | | | | | | | | | | | | | | | | | | |
| Door cells ('guard cells') | | | | | | | | | | | | | | | | | | | | | | | | | | | | | | | | | | | | | | |
| Wall corbelling | | | | | | | | | | | | | | | | | | | | | | | | | | | | | | | | | | | | | | |
| Pier corbelling | | | | | | | | | | | | | | | | | | | | | | | | | | | | | | | | | | | | | | |
| Bay kerbs | | | | | | | | | | | | | | | | | | | | | | | | | | | | | | | | | | | | | | |
| Drip courses and gutters | | | | | | | | | | | | | | | | | | | | | | | | | | | | | | | | | | | | | | |
| Aeolianite deposits | | | | | | | | | | | | | | | | | | | | | | | | | | | | | | | | | | | | | | |
| Animal burials | | | | | | | | | | | | | | | | | | | | | | | | | | | | | | | | | | | | | | |
| Bay 'bowl' pits | | | | | | | | | | | | | | | | | | | | | | | | | | | | | | | | | | | | | | |
| Covered drains | | | | | | | | | | | | | | | | | | | | | | | | | | | | | | | | | | | | | | |
| Peripheral postholes | | | | | | | | | | | | | | | | | | | | | | | | | | | | | | | | | | | | | | |
| Obelisks | | | | | | | | | | | | | | | | | | | | | | | | | | | | | | | | | | | | | | |
| Plaster/mortar | | | | | | | | | | | | | | | | | | | | | | | | | | | | | | | | | | | | | | |
| Putlog holes | | | | | | | | | | | | | | | | | | | | | | | | | | | | | | | | | | | | | | |
| Scarcements | | | | | | | | | | | | | | | | | | | | | | | | | | | | | | | | | | | | | | |
| Paving | | | | | | | | | | | | | | | | | | | | | | | | | | | | | | | | | | | | | | |
| Door draw bolt shafts | | | | | | | | | | | | | | | | | | | | | | | | | | | | | | | | | | | | | | |
| Later insertions | | | | | | | | | | | | | | | | | | | | | | | | | | | | | | | | | | | | | | |
| | | | | | | | | | | | | | | | | | | | | | | | | | | | | | | | | | | | | | | |
| **Exterior Associations** | | | | | | | | | | | | | | | | | | | | | | | | | | | | | | | | | | | | | | |
| Enclosures | | | | | | | | | | | | | | | | | | | | | | | | | | | | | | | | | | | | | | |
| Souterrains | | | | | | | | | | | | | | | | | | | | | | | | | | | | | | | | | | | | | | |
| Cremation platforms | | | | | | | | | | | | | | | | | | | | | | | | | | | | | | | | | | | | | | |
| Cultivation furrows | | | | | | | | | | | | | | | | | | | | | | | | | | | | | | | | | | | | | | |
| Human burials | | | | | | | | | | | | | | | | | | | | | | | | | | | | | | | | | | | | | | |
| Brochs | | | | | | | | | | | | | | | | | | | | | | | | | | | | | | | | | | | | | | |
| Other structures | | | | | | | | | | | | | | | | | | | | | | | | | | | | | | | | | | | | | | |
| Landscape (O.G.H) | | | | | | | | | | | | | | | | | | | | | | | | | | | | | | | | | | | | | | |
| | | | | | | | | | | | | | | | | | | | | | | | | | | | | | | | | | | | | | | |
| **Total attributes** | 27 | 26 | 16 | 9 | 24 | 9 | 14 | 12 | 21 | 16 | 10 | 4 | 6 | 8 | 7 | 4 | 14 | 17 | 10 | 5 | 18 | 9 | 9 | 5 | 14 | 12 | 7 | -1 | 2 | 2 | 4 | 2 | 5 | 4 | 10 | 11 | 5 | 2 |
| O.G.H. - Old Ground Horizon | | | | | | | | | | | | | | | | | | | | | | | | | | | | | | | | | | | | | | |

**3** *Wheelhouse attributes by site and region (cont. next page)*

The following table records site attributes (Northern Isles and others), with sites numbered 39–62 across the columns and a Totals column at right.

| Attribute | Levenwick 39 | Brough Head 40 | Ward Hill 41 | Jarlshof 1 42 | Jarlshof 2 43 | Jarlshof 3 44 | Jarlshof A 45 | Old Scatness 5 46 | Old Scatness 6 47 | Old Scatness 7 48 | Old Scatness 11 49 | Old Scatness 12 50 | Old Scatness 14 51 | Old Scatness 15 52 | Mousa 53 | Calf of Eday 54 | Homme Brae d 55 | Homme Brae i 56 | Homme Brae j 57 | Homme Brae k 58 | Broch of Gurness 59 | Burrian of Burian 60 | Burrian Broch Russ 61 | Alt Chroisail 62 | Totals |
|---|---|---|---|---|---|---|---|---|---|---|---|---|---|---|---|---|---|---|---|---|---|---|---|---|---|
| **Excavation details** | | | | | | | | | | | | | | | | | | | | | | | | | |
| for Research | | | | | | | | | | | | | | | | | | | | | | | | | 32 |
| for Salvage | | | | | | | | | | | | | | | | | | | | | | | | | 9 |
| for Recreation | | | | | | | | | | | | | | | | | | | | | | | | | 11 |
| Site condition – eroded | | | | | | | | | | | | | | | | | | | | | | | | | 33 |
| **Constructional details** | | | | | | | | | | | | | | | | | | | | | | | | | |
| Double walling | | | | | | | | | | | | | | | | | | | | | | | | | 20 |
| Single walling | | | | | | | | | | | | | | | | | | | | | | | | | 35 |
| Broch inserts | | | | | | | | | | | | | | | | | | | | | | | | | 10 |
| Piers – free standing i | | 2<? | 3 | 8 | 7 | 3<? | 5<8 | | | | | | | | | | 8-9 | | | 3<7 | | | | | 32 |
| Piers – butted to wall ii | | | | | | | | 6<11 | | | | | 5<6 | | 3<5 | | 4 | | | | 6<12 | 3<7 | | 2<7/8 | 12 |
| Piers – bonded at door only iv | | | | | | | | | | | | 10 | | | | | | | 3<7 | | | | | | 8 |
| Piers – Triangular v | 5 | | | | | | | | | | | | | | | 9 | | | 3<? | | | | | | 8 |
| Piers – Orthostatic vi | | | | | | | | | 6 | 3<12 | 7 | | | | | | | | | | | | 4<8 | | 12 |
| Diameter | 5.2 | | 10.4 | 9.6 | 7.2 | 7 | 11.2 | 11.5 | 7.2 | 10.5 | 6.5 | 10 | 10.5 | 4 | 4.3 | 7.6 | 4.6 | 5.8 | 7 | 10 | 9 | 7.5 | 10.1 | c.7 | 25 |
| Radiocarbon dates | | | | | | | | | | | | | | | | | | | | | | | | | 61 |
| Pottery dating | | | | | | | | | | | | | | | | | | | | | | | | | 7 |
| Archaeomagnetic dating | | | | | | | | | | | | | | | | | | | | | | | | | 48 |
| Lintels – in situ | | | | | | | | | | | | | | | | | | | | | | | | | 2 |
| Lintels – dislodged | | | | | | | | | | | | | | | | | | | | | | | | | 19 |
| Hearths | | | | | | | | | | | | | | | | | | | | | | | | | 14 |
| Tanks/sinks | | | | | | | | | | | | | | | | | | | | | | | | | 28 |
| Twin wheelhouses | | | | | | | | | | | | | | | | | | | | | | | | | 14 |
| Founding pits | | | | | | | | | | | | | | | | | | | | | | | | | 18 |
| Entrances | | | | | | | | | | | | | | | | | | | | | | | | | 3 |
| Satellite cells | | | | | | | | | | | | | | | | | | | | | | | | | 5 |
| Aumbries | | | | | | | | | | | | | | | | | | | | | | | | | 10 |
| Door cells ('guard cells') | | | | | | | | | | | | | | | | | | | | | | | | | 21 |
| Wall corbelling | | | | | | | | | | | | | | | | | | | | | | | | | 15 |
| Pier corbelling | | | | | | | | | | | | | | | | | | | | | | | | | 9 |
| Bay kerbs | | | | | | | | | | | | | | | | | | | | | | | | | 16 |
| Drip courses and gutters | | | | | | | | | | | | | | | | | | | | | | | | | 29 |
| Aeolianite deposits | | | | | | | | | | | | | | | | | | | | | | | | | 8 |
| Animal burials | | | | | | | | | | | | | | | | | | | | | | | | | 1 |
| Bay 'bowl' pits | | | | | | | | | | | | | | | | | | | | | | | | | 4 |
| Covered drains | | | | | | | | | | | | | | | | | | | | | | | | | 5 |
| Peripheral postholes | | | | | | | | | | | | | | | | | | | | | | | | | 17 |
| Obelisks | | | | | | | | | | | | | | | | | | | | | | | | | 2 |
| Plaster/mortar | | | | | | | | | | | | | | | | | | | | | | | | | 5 |
| Putlog holes | | | | | | | | | | | | | | | | | | | | | | | | | 15 |
| Scarcements | | | | | | | | | | | | | | | | | | | | | | | | | 2 |
| Paving | | | | | | | | | | | | | | | | | | | | | | | | | 5 |
| Door draw bolt shafts | | | | | | | | | | | | | | | | | | | | | | | | | 25 |
| Later insertions | | | | | | | | | | | | | | | | | | | | | | | | | 6 |
| | | | | | | | | | | | | | | | | | | | | | | | | | 2 |
| **Exterior Associations** | | | | | | | | | | | | | | | | | | | | | | | | | |
| Enclosures | | | | | | | | | | | | | | | | | | | | | | | | | 2 |
| Souterrains | | | | | | | | | | | | | | | | | | | | | | | | | 9 |
| Cremation platforms | | | | | | | | | | | | | | | | | | | | | | | | | 1 |
| Cultivation furrows | | | | | | | | | | | | | | | | | | | | | | | | | 1 |
| Human burials | | | | | | | | | | | | | | | | | | | | | | | | | 1 |
| Brochs | | | | | | | | | | | | | | | | | | | | | | | | | 19 |
| Other structures | | | | | | | | | | | | | | | | | | | | | | | | | 34 |
| Landscape (O.G.H) | | | | | | | | | | | | | | | | | | | | | | | | | 20 |
| **Total attributes** | 9 | 11 | 3 | 18 | 19 | 11 | 16 | 7 | 12 | 8 | 14 | 12 | 7 | 12 | 13 | 6 | 12 | 11 | 13 | 9 | 9 | 7 | 7 | 4 | |

O.G.H. – Old Ground Horizon

| Site number | Site Name |
|---|---|
| **Western Isles** | **North Uist** |
| 1 | The Udal South A |
| 2 | The Udal South B |
| 3 | The Udal South C |
| 4 | The Udal North (level XV) |
| 5 | Sollas (Middlequarter Machair lots ½) |
| 6 | Eilean Maleit |
| 7 | Cnoc a Chomhalachd |
| 8 | Garry Iochdrach |
| 9 | Clettraval |
| 10 | Bac Mhic Chonnain D |
| 11 | Bac Mhic Chonnain A |
| 12 | Foshigarry A |
| 13 | Foshigarry B |
| 14 | Foshigarry C |
| 15 | Bagh nam Fheadaig, Grimsay |
| | |
| | **South Uist & Barra** |
| 16 | Cnoc Mor, Hornish |
| 17 | A'Ceardach Mhor, West Geirnish |
| 18 | A'Ceardach Bheag I, Drimore |
| 19 | A'Ceardach Bheag II, Drimore |
| 20 | Sligeanach Kildonnan |
| 21 | Burach an Thionail Aird, Kilpheder |
| 22 | Tigh Lair, Scalavat, nr Usinish |
| 23 | Uamh Iosail, Moladh na h-Uamha, nr Usinish |
| 24 | Loch Sheilavaig, East Geirnish |
| 25 | Tigh talmhanta, Allasdale, Barra |
| 62 | Allt Chriosail, Barra |
| | |
| | **Lewis & Harris** |
| 26 | Cnip 9, 1 |
| 27 | Cnip 9, 2 |
| 28 | Cnip 12, Traigh nam Berie |
| | |
| **Mainland** | **Sutherland & Caithless** |
| 29 | Tigh na Fhearnain, Meall Madhnach, Durness |
| 30 | Carn na Chreagaich, Braemore A |
| 31 | Carn na Chreagaich, Braemore B1 |
| 32 | Carn na Chreagaich, Braemore B2 |
| 33 | Wagmore Rigg, Latheron N |
| 34 | Wagmore Rigg, Latheron S |
| | |
| **Northern Isles** | **Shetland** |
| 35 | Wiltrow |
| 36 | Clickhimin |
| 37 | Bayanne, Yell |
| 38 | Stanydale |
| 39 | Levenwick |
| 40 | Brough Head/East Shore |
| 41 | Ward Hill |
| 42 | Jarlshof 1 |
| 43 | Jarlshof 2 |
| 44 | Jarlshof 3 |
| 45 | Jarlshof A |
| 46 | Old Scatness 5 |
| 47 | Old Scatness 6 |
| 48 | Old Scatness 7 |
| 49 | Old Scatness 11 |
| 50 | Old Scatness 12 |
| 51 | Old Scatness 14 |

**14** *List of wheelhouse sites and place names (cont. next page)*

| | 52 | Old Scatness 15 |
|---|---|---|
| | 53 | Mousa |
| | | |
| | | ***Orkney*** |
| | 54 | Calf of Eday |
| | 55 | Howmae Brae d |
| | 56 | Howmae Brae i |
| | 57 | Howmae Brae k |
| | 58 | Broch of Gurness |
| | 59 | Broch of Burrian |
| | 60 | Burrian Broch, Russland |
| | 61 | Hillock of Burroughstone |

**14** *List of wheelhouse sites and place names (cont. from previous page)*

| Site (Ref.No.) | Lab.No. | 14C Determination BP | 1 σ calBC/AD date range | 2 σ calBC/AD date range |
|---|---|---|---|---|
| The Udal S, B *(2)* | Q 3019 | 1950+50 | AD 0 - AD 130 | 60 BC - AD 220 |
| The Udal S, B *(2)* | Q 3111 | 1905+40 | AD 20 - 210 | AD 20 - 230 |
| The Udal S, C *(3)* | Q 3112 | 2000+55 | 60 BC - AD 80 | 170 BC - AD 130 |
| The Udal N, XV *(4)* | Q 3012 | 1869+40 | AD 80 - 220 | AD 60 - 250 |
| Sollas *(5)* | GU 2562 | 1880+50 | AD 70 - 220 | AD 20 - 250 |
| Sollas *(5)* | GU 2564 | 1870+50 | AD 80 -220 | AD 20 - 320 |
| Sollas *(5)* | GU 2565 | 1880+50 | AD 70 - 220 | AD 20 - 250 |
| Sollas *(5)* | GU 2566 | 1670+80 | AD 250 - 530 | AD 130 - 570 |
| Sollas *(5)* | GU 2590 | 1890+100 | AD 0 - 250 | 110 BC - AD 390 |
| Sollas *(5)* | GU 2591 | 2010+60 | 100 BC - AD 70 | 170 BC - AD 130 |
| Kildonnan *(20)* | OxA 3356 | 1670+75 | AD 250 - 530 | AD 210 - 570 |
| Brough Head *(40)* | AA 11695 | 1914+59 | AD 0 - 210 | 50 BC - AD 240 |
| Brough Head *(40)* | AA 11693 | 1777+66 | AD 130 - 350 | AD 80 - 420 |

**15** *Radiocarbon determinations of wheelhouses*

| Site | Technique | Determination | Technique |
|---|---|---|---|
| Sollas *(5)* | Archaeo-magnetic | AD 1 - 100 | AD 50 |
| Kildonnan *(20)* | TL | 1740+380 BP | c. AD 210 |

**16** *Thermoluminescence and archaeo-magnetic dating of wheelhouses*

| Site | Reference | Material | Age Range |
|---|---|---|---|
| The Udal S, B *(2)* | Crawford 1979 | Roman Pot | AD 250 - 300 |
| Garry Iochdrach *(8)* | Robertson 1950 | Roman Coin | AD 337 - 361 |
| Clickhimin *(36)* | Wainwright 1962 | Rhenish Pot | AD 250 |
| Clickhimin *(36)* | Hamilton 1968 | Roman Glass | AD 70 - 140 |

**17** *Imported artefacts from wheelhouses independently dated*

# Euan M. MacKie:
# List of published work
# (to March 2002)

1961a New light on the end of the Maya Classic culture at Benque Viejo, British Honduras. *American Antiquity* 27, 216-24.

1961b Disaster and Dark Age in a Maya city: discoveries at Xunantunich in British Honduras. *Illustrated London News,* Archaeology Section no. 2059 (July 2second), 130-4.

1963 Some Maya pottery from Grand Bogue Point, Turneffe Islands, British Honduras. *Atoll Research Bulletin* 95, 131-4.

1964a Two radiocarbon dates from a Clyde-Solway chambered cairn. *Antiquity* 38, no. 149, 52-4.

1964b The Lang Cairn, Dumbarton Muir. *Proceedings of the Society of Antiquaries of Scotland* 94, 1960-1, 315-4.

1965a Review of *In quest of the White God* by Pierre Honore. *Journal of South African Archaeological Society* 00, 37.

1965b A dwelling site of the earlier Iron Age at Balevullin, Tiree, excavated in 1912 by A.H. Bishop. *Proceedings of the Society of Antiquaries of Scotland* 96, 1962-3, 155-83.

1965c Brochs and the Hebridean Iron Age. *Antiquity* 39, no. 156, 166-78.

1965d The origin and development of the broch and wheelhouse building cultures of the Scottish Iron Age. *Proceedings of the Prehistoric Society* 31, 93-146.

1965e *Excavations on two 'galleried duns' on Skye in 1964 and 1965: interim report.* Hunterian Museum, University of Glasgow.

1966a New excavations on the Monamore Neolithic chambered cairn, Lamlash, Isle of Arran. *Proceedings of the Society of Antiquaries of Scotland* 97, 1963-4, 1-34.

1966b A burial ground of the middle Bronze Age at Girvan, Ayrshire. *Ayrshire Archaeological and Natural History Collections* 7, 1961-6, 9-27.

1967a Iron Age pottery from the Gress Lodge earth-house, Stornoway, Lewis. *Proceedings of the Society of Antiquaries of Scotland* 98, 1964-6, 199-203.

1967b Review of *The Iron Age in Northern Britain,* ed. A.L.F. Rivet. *Antiquity* 41, 238-39.

1967c Review of *The Picts* by Isobel Henderson. *Current Archaeology* 1, no. 5 (November), 127-28.

1967d Review of *Inventory of Peebles-shire* by the Royal Commission on the Ancient and Historical Monuments of Scotland. *Antiquity* 40, no. 164, 320-21.

1967 *Interim Report on Excavations at Dun Lagaidh, Ross and Cromarty, in 1967.* Hunterian Museum, University of Glasgow.

1968a Stone circles – for savages or savants? *Current Archaeology* 2, no. 11, 279-83.

1968b *Excavations on Loch Broom, Ross and Cromarty: second interim report 1968.* Hunterian Museum, University of Glasgow.

1969a Radiocarbon dates and the Scottish Iron Age. *Antiquity* 43, 15-26.

1969b with I.E.MacAoidh Tuineachas Iarunnaoiseach air Tiriodh (An Iron Age settlement on Tiree). *Gairm* 67, 276-81.

1969c Timber-framed and vitrified walls in Iron Age forts: causes of vitrification. *Glasgow Archaeological Journal* 1, 69-71.

1969d Review of *Excavations at Clickhimin, Shetland* by J.R.C. Hamilton. *Proceedings of the Prehistoric Society* 35, 386-8.

1969e The historical context of the origin of the brochs. *Scottish Archaeological Forum* 1, 53-9.

1969f Continuity in fort-building traditions in Caithness. *The Dark Ages in the Highlands.* E. Meldrum (ed.). Inverness, 1-18.

1970a The Scottish 'Iron Age': a revision article on the final prehistoric age in Scotland. *Scottish Historical Review* 49, no. 157, 1-32.

1970b *An Archaeological view of Neolithic astronomy.* Hunterian Museum, University of Glasgow.

1970c The Hownam culture: a rejoinder to Ritchie. *Scottish Archaeological Forum* 2, 68-72.

1971a English migrants and Scottish brochs. *Glasgow Archaeological Journal* 2, 39-71.

1971b The Iron Age pottery of the Western Isles. *Actes du VII ieme Congres Internationale des Sciences Prehistoriques et Protohistoriques* (Prague 1966), 2, 842-6.

1971d Thoughts on radiocarbon dating. *Antiquity* 45, 197-200.

1971e Archaeoastronomy: a review of *Megalithic Lunar Observatories* by A. Thom. *The Listener* 28 January.

1971f Prehistoric Astronomy and Kintraw. *University of Glasgow Gazette* no. 66 (June), 8-9.

1972a Radiocarbon dates for two Mesolithic shell heaps and a Neolithic axe factory in Scotland. *Proceedings of the Prehistoric Society* 37, 412-16.

1972b Some aspects of the transition from the bronze- to the iron-using periods in Scotland. *Scottish Archaeological Forum* 3, 55-72.

1972c Some new quern stones from brochs and duns. *Proceedings of the Society of Antiquaries of Scotland* 104, 1971-2, 137-46.

1973a A challenge to the integrity of science? *New Scientist* (January 11th), 76-7.

1973b Review of *Beyond Stonehenge* by G.S. Hawkins. *New Scientist* (October 11th), 138-140.

1973d Duntreath. *Current Archaeology* 4, no. 1, 6-7.

1974a *Dun Mor Vaul: an Iron Age broch on Tiree.* Glasgow: University of Glasgow Press.

1974b Archaeologicalogical tests on supposed prehistoric astronomical sites in Scotland. *Philosophical Transactions of the Royal Society of London,* Section A, 276, 169-94.

1974d Review of *The sphinx and the megaliths* by J. Ivimy. *New Scientist* (August 29th), 548.

1974e *Excavations at Leckie, Stirlingshire, 1970-73: first interim report.* Hunterian Museum, University of Glasgow.

1975a *Scotland: an Archaeological guide.* London.

1975b The brochs of Scotland. P. Fowler (ed.) *Recent work in rural Archaeology.* Bradford on Avon: Moonraker Press, 72-92.

1975c *Cultoon stone circle: first interim report.* Hunterian Museum, University of Glasgow.

1976a The vitrified forts of Scotland, D.W. Harding (ed.) *Hillforts: later prehistoric earthworks in Britain and Ireland.* London: Academic Press, 205-35.

1976b The Glasgow conference on ceremonial, and science in prehistoric Britain. *Antiquity* 50, 136-8.

1976c Historical parallels for the megalithic yard. 47-8 in Freeman, A., Bayesian analysis of the megalithic yard. *Journal of the Royal Statistical Society* A. 139, part I, 20-55.

1976d Review of *The Iron Age in Lowland Britain* by D.W. Harding. *Scottish Historical Review* 55 (no.159, April), 62-3.

1976e Review of *RCAHMS Argyll: an inventory of the ancient monuments. Voume 2, Lorn.* *Archaeological Journal* 132, 1975, 381-2.

1977a *Science and Society in prehistoric Britain.* London: Elek.

1977b *The megalith builders.* Oxford: Phaidon

1978 The origin of iron working in Scotland. M. Ryan (ed.) *Origins of Metallurgy in Atlantic Europe.* (Proceedings of the fifth Atlantic Colloquium). Dublin: 295-302.

1979 Review: Man's Place in Nature. *Nature* 282 (16 December), 657.

1980 Dun an Ruigh Ruaidh, Loch Broom, Ross, and Cromarty: excavations in 1968 and 1978. *Glasgow Archaeological Journal* 7, 32-79.

1981a Using the MDA cards in the Hunterian Museum. *Museums Journal* 80 no. 2, 86-9.

1981b With Jane Glaister *The Wemyss Caves, Fife.* Hunterian Museum, University of Glasgow.

1981c Wise Men in Antiquity? C.L.N. Ruggles and A.W.R. Whittle (eds.), *Astronomy and Society in Britain during the Period 4000 – 1500 BC.* British.

1982 With R.B.K Stevenson, Kintraw again. *Antiquity* 56 (March), 50-1.

1982 Implications for Archaeology. *Archaeoastronomy in the Old World,* D.C. Heggie (ed): Cambridge, 117-40.

1983 Testing hypotheses about brochs. *Scottish Archaeological Review* 2.2, 117-28.

1984a The Leckie broch, Stirlingshire: an interim report. *Glasgow Archaeological Journal*

1984b With Rona M. MacKie Red-haired 'Celts' are better termed Caledonians. *American Journal of Dermatopathology* 6, Supplement 1 (summer), 147-9.

1984c Megalithic Astronomy: Review of C.L.N. Ruggles 'Megalithic Astronomy: a New Statistical Study of 300 Western Scottish Sites (1984)'. *Archaeoastronomy* (The Journal for the Centre of Archaeoastronomy) 7, nos. 1-4, 144-50.

1985a With P.F. Gladwin & A.E. Roy A prehistoric calendrical site in Argyll? *Nature* 314 (March 14th), 158-61.

1985b *Excavations at Xunantunich and Pomona, Belize, in 1959-60.* British Archaeological Reports (International series), 251: Oxford.

1985c With A.E. Roy Prehistoric Calendar. *Nature* 316 (22 August), 671.

1986a A late single piece dug-out canoe from Loch Doon, Ayrshire. *Glasgow Archaeological Journal* 11, 1984, 132-3.

1986b Review of D. Breeze (ed) *Studies in Scottish Antiquity presented to Stewart Cruden. Glasgow Archaeological Journal* 11, 1984, 134.

1987 Review of H. Fairhurst, *Excavations at Crosskirk broch, Caithness. Antiquaries Journal* 65 no. 2, 500-01.

1988a Review of I.G. Shepherd, *Exploring Scotland's Heritage: Grampian. Glasgow Archaeological Journal* 13, 1986, 87-8.

1988b Iron Age and Early Historic occupation of Jonathan's Cave, East Wemyss. *Glasgow Archaeological Journal* 13, 1986, 74-7.

1988c William Hunter and Captain Cook: the 18th century ethnographical collections in the Hunterian Museum. *Glasgow Archaeological Journal* 12, 1985, 1-18.

1988d Investigating the prehistoric solar calendar. C.L.N.Ruggles (ed.) *Records in stone: papers in memory of Alexander Thom.* Cambridge: Cambridge University Press, 206-31.

1989a Leckie broch: impact on the Scottish Iron Age. *Glasgow Archaeological Journal* 14, 1987, 1-18.

1989b Comment: Dun Cuier again. *Scottish Archaeological Review* 2, 117-28.

1989c Review of J. Barrett, A.P. Fitzpatrick & L. McInnes (eds.), *Barbarians and Romans in North-west Europe. Glasgow Archaeological Journal* 14, 1987, 73.

1991 With A. Davis New light on Neolithic rock carving: the petroglyphs at Greenland (Auchentorlie), Dumbartonshire. *Glasgow Archaeological Journal* 15, 1988-89, 125-56.

1992 The Iron Age semibrochs of Atlantic Scotland: a case study in the problems of deductive reasoning. *Archaeological Journal* 149, 1991, 149-81.

1993a Review of C. Renfrew (ed) *The Prehistory of Orkney, Glasgow Archaeological Journal* 16, 1989-90, 89-91.

1993b *Lismore and Appin: an Archaeological and historical guide.* Glasgow.

1994 Review of R. Feachem *Guide to Prehistoric Scotland. Glasgow Archaeological Journal* 17, 1991-2, 91-2.

1993 The ethnographical collections in the Hunterian Museum, Glasgow. *Pacific Arts*, 8, 35-41.

1994 Aspects of the origin of the brochs of Atlantic Scotland. J.R. Baldwin (ed) *Peoples and Settlement in North-west Ross*: Edinburgh, 15-42.

1995a Gurness and Midhowe brochs in Orkney: some problems of misinterpretation. *Archaeological Journal* 151, 1994, 98-157.

1995b The early Celts in Scotland. Miranda Green (ed.) *The Celtic World*. London: Routledge, 654-70.

1995c Obituary: Sir Grahame Clark. *Glasgow Herald* 30 September, 20.

1996a Three Iron Age rotary querns from southern Scotland. *Glasgow Archaeological Journal* 19, 1994-95, 107-9.

1996b Review of P. Ashmore, *Calanais: the standing stones*. *Glasgow Archaeological Journal* 19, 1994-95, 116-17.

1996c Review of P. Barker, *Techniques of Archaeological Excavation*. *Glasgow Archaeological Journal* 19, 1994-95, 117-18.

1997a Some eighteenth-century ferry houses in Appin, Lorn, Argyll. *Antiquaries Journal* 77, 243-89.

1997b Maeshowe and the winter solstice: ceremonial aspects of the Orkney Grooved Ware culture. *Antiquity* 71 (June), 338-59.

1997c Dun Mor Vaul re-visited, J.N.G. Ritchie (ed.) *The Archaeology of Argyll*. Edinburgh: 141-80.

1998 Continuity over three thousand years of northern prehistory: the 'tel' at Howe, Orkney. *Antiquaries Journal* 78, 1-42.

2000 The Scottish Atlantic Iron Age: indigenous and isolated or part of a wider European world? 99-116, Jon C. Henderson (ed.) *The Prehistory and Early History of Atlantic Europe*. British Archaeological Reports International Series 861: Oxford.

2001 Review: The thinking behind the design: Archaeology in the new Museum of Scotland. *Scottish Archaeological Journal* 23,1, 2001, 75-81.

2002 Excavations at Dun Ardtreck, Skye, in 1964 and 1965. *Proceedings of the Society of Antiquaries of Scotland* 130, 2002, 301-411.

In press, Corpus of Brochs part 1, Orkney and Shetland. British Archaeological Reports, British Series. Oxford.

# Bibliography

Adomnán, Saint. *Life of St. Columba*. London: Penguin (translated by R. Sharpe), 1995.

Alcock, L. The supposed Viking burials on the islands of Canna and Sanday, Small Isles, 293-309 in O'Connor, A. and Clarke, D.V. (eds.) *From the Stone Age to the 'Forty-five*. Edinburgh: J.Donald, 1983.

—, L. Pictish studies: present and future, 80-92, in Small, A. (ed.) *The Picts: a new look at old problems*. Dundee: University of Dundee, 1987.

—, L. and Alcock, E. Scandinavian settlement in the Inner Hebrides: recent research on placenames and in the field. *Scottish Archaeological Forum* 10, 1980, 61-73.

Alexander, D. with Ralston, I. Survey work on Turin Hill, Angus. *Tayside and Fife Archaeological Journal* 5, 1999, 36-49.

—, D. and Watkins, T. St Germains, Tranet, East Lothian: the excavation of Early Bronze Age remains and Iron Age enclosed and unenclosed settlements. *Proceedings of the Society of Antiquaries of Scotland* 128, 1998, 203-54.

—, D. Investigation of a cropmark enclosure at Wet Mains, Lunan Bay, Angus. *Tayside and Fife Archseological Journal* 6, 2000, 18-26.

Anderson, J. Notes on the relics of the Viking Period of the Northmen in Scotland, illustrated by Specimens in the Museum. *Proceedings of the Society of Antiquaries of Scotland* X, 1872-4, 536-94.

—, J. *Scotland in Pagan Times: The Iron Age*. The Rhind Lectures in Archaeology for 1881. Edinburgh: David Douglas, 1883.

—, J. Notices of nine brochs along the Caithness coast from Keiss bay to Skirza Head, excavated by Sir Francis Tress Barry, Bart, MP of Keiss Castle, Caithness. *Proceedings of the Society of Antiquaries of Scotland* XXXV, 1900-1, 112-48.

Armit, I. Broch landscapes in the Western Isles. *Scottish Archaeological Review* 5, 1988, 78-86.

—, I. Re-excavation of an Iron Age wheelhouse and earlier structure at Eilean Maleit, North Uist. *Proceedings of the Society of Antiquaries of Scotland* 128, 1998(a), 255-71.

—, I. *Excavations at Cnip, West Lewis, 1988*. Interim report. Edinburgh, 1988(b).

—, I. (ed.) *Beyond the Brochs: Changing Perspectives on the Atlantic Scottish Iron Age*. Edinburgh: Edinburgh University Press, 1990.

—, I. Epilogue, 194-210, in Armit, I. (ed.) *Beyond the Brochs: Changing Perspectives on the Atlantic Scottish Iron Age*. Edinburgh: Edinburgh University Press, 1990.

—, I. Brochs and Beyond in the Western Isles, 41-70. in Armit, I. (ed.) *Beyond the Brochs: Changing Perspectives on the Atlantic Scottish Iron Age.* Edinburgh University Press, 1990(a).

—, I. Monumentality and elaboration: a case study in the Western Isles. *Scottish Archaeological Review* 7, 1990(b), 84-95.

—, I. Broch-building in Atlantic Scotland: the context of innovation. *World Archaeology* 21, 1990(c), 435-45.

—, I. The Atlantic Scottish Iron Age: five levels of chronology. *Proceedings of the Society of Antiquaries of Scotland* 121, 1991, 181-214.

—, I. *The Later Prehistory of the Western Isles of Scotland.* Oxford: British Archaeological Reports (British Series) 221, 1992.

—, I. Archaeological field survey of the Bhaltos (Valtos) peninsula, Lewis. *Proceedings of the Society of Antiquaries of Scotland* 124, 1994, 67-93.

—, I. *The Archaeology of Skye and the Western Isles.* Edinburgh: Edinburgh University Press, 1996.

—, I. *Celtic Scotland.* London: Batsford/Historic Scotland, 1997.

—, I. Cultural landscapes and identities: a case study in the Scottish Iron Age, 248-53, in Haselgrove, C. and Gwilt, A. (eds.) *Reconstructing Iron Age Societies.* Oxford: Oxbow Books, Oxbow Monograph 71, 1996.

—, I. Excavation of a post-medieval settlement at Druim na Dearcag, and related sites around Loch Olabhat, North Uist. *Proceedings of the Society of Antiquaries of Scotland* 127, 1997, 899-919.

—, I. Human responses to marginality, 31-8, in Mills, C.M. and Coles, G. (eds.) *Life on the edge: human settlement and marginality.* Oxford: Oxbow Monograph 100, 1998.

—, I. Re-excavation of an Iron Age wheelhouse and earlier structure at Eilean Maleit, North Uist, *Proceedings of the Society of Antiquaries of Scotland* 128, 1998, 255-271.

—, I. The Abandonment of souterrains; evolution, catastrophe or dislocation. in *Proceedings of the Society of Antiquaries of Scotland* 129, 1999, 577-96.

—, I. Excavations at Cnip. Forthcoming

—, I. and MacSween, A. Discussion of the pottery. in Armit, I. Excavations at Cnip. Forthcoming.

—, I. and Braby, A. *Vallay Strand Project 1996 Data Structure Report 2, Excavations at Ceann nan Clachan burnt mound and later prehistoric structures,* Centre for Field Archaeology (unpublished report) No. 281.2, Edinburgh: University of Edinburgh, 1996.

—, I., Dunwell, A.J. and Campbell, E. Excavation of an Iron Age, Early Historic and Medieval settlement and metal-working site at Eilean Olabhat, North Uist. *Proceedings of the Society of Antiquaries of Scotland.* Forthcoming.

—, I. and MacSween, A. Discussion on the pottery. in Armit, I. Excavations at Cnip. Forthcoming.

—, I. and Ralston, I.B.M. The Iron Age, 169-93, in Edwards, K.J. and Ralston, I.B.M. (eds.) *Scotland: Environment and Archaeology, 8000 BC-AD 1000.* Chichester: John Wiley and Sons, 1997.

Ashmore, P.J. Archaeology and the coastal zone: towards an Historic Scotland policy. Edinburgh: Historic Scotland, 1994.

—, P.J. Radiocarbon dating: avoiding errors by avoiding mixed samples. *Antiquity* 73, No. 279, 1999, 124-30.

—, P.J., Cook, G.T. and Harkness, D.D. forthcoming *Radiocarbon dates for archaeological sites in Scotland issued before June 1996.*

Atkinson, R.J.C. and Piggott, S. The Torrs Chamfrein. *Archaeologia* 96, 1955, 197-235.

Ballin Smith, B. and Ballin, T.B. Breckness, Stromness Parish, 105. *Discovery and Excavation in Scotland,* 1993. Edinburgh: Council for Scottish Archaeology, 1993.

—, B. *Howe: four millennia of Orkney prehistory.* Edinburgh: Society of Antiquaries of Scotland. Monograph Series, No. 9, 1994.

—, B. Brochs – complex sites with complex origins. Proceedings of the conference 'Tall Stories' on Iron Age settlements, Lerwick, Shetland, July 2000, forthcoming.

Baines, A. *An Archaeology of Iron Age Domestic Settlement in Northern Scotland.* Unpublished PhD thesis, University of Glasgow, 2000.

Banks, I. The excavation of three small cairns at Stoneyburn Farm, Crawford, Lanarkshire, 1991. *Proceedings of the Society of Antiquaries of Scotland,* 125, 1995, 289-343.

—, I. *Rural Society and Settlement: Isolated Monuments and Farming Communities in Northern and Western Scotland in the Late Atlantic Iron Age.* Unpublished PhD thesis, University of Glasgow, 1996.

—, I. Investigating burnt mounds in Clydesdale during motorway construction. *Glasgow Archaeological Journal* 21, 1998-9, 1-28.

—, I. Excavation of an Iron Age and Romano-British enclosure at Woodend Farm, Johnstonebridge, Annandale, 1994 and 1997. *Proceedings of the Society of Antiquaries of Scotland* 130, 2000, 223-81.

—, I. *Motorway to the Past: the Archaeology of the M74.* Forthcoming.

Barber, J.W. Excavations on Iona, 1979. *Proceedings of the Society of Antiquaries of Scotland* 111, 1981, 282-380.

—, J.W. A wooden bowl from Talisker Moor, Skye. *Proceedings of the Society of Antiquaries of Scotland* 112, 1982, 578-9.

—, J.W. *Bronze Age farms and Iron Age farm mounds of the Outer Hebrides.* Edinburgh: AOC/Historic Scotland, STAR Monograph 7. Forthcoming.

—, J.W., Halstead, P., James, H and Lee, F. An unusual Iron Age burial at Hornish Point, South Uist. *Antiquity* 63, 1989, 773-8.

—, J.W. and Crone, B.A. Crannogs: A diminishing resource? A survey of the crannogs of south-west Scotland and excavations at Buiston crannog. *Antiquity* 67, 1993, 520-33.

Barclay, G.J. Excavations at Upper Suisgill, Sutherland. *Proceedings of the Society of Antiquaries of Scotland* 115, 1985, 159-98.

—, G.J. 'Metropolitan' and 'parochial'/'core' and 'periphery': a historiography of the Neolithic of Scotland. *Proceedings of the Prehistoric Society* 67, 2001, 1-18.

Barrett, J.C. Aspects of the Iron Age in Atlantic Scotland. A case study in the problems of archaeological interpretations. *Proceedings of the Society of Antiquaries of Scotland* 111, 1982, 205-219.

Batey, C.E. *Caithness Coastal Survey 1980-82: Dunnet Head to Ousdale.* Durham: Department of Archaeology, University of Durham, Occasional Paper No.3, 1984.

—, C.E. *Freswick Links, Caithness. A re-appraisal of the Late Norse site in its context.* Oxford: British Archaeological Reports (British Series) 179, 1987(a).

—, C.E. Viking and Late Norse Caithness: The Archaeological Evidence, 131-48, in Knirk, J.E. (ed.) *Proceedings of the Tenth Viking Congress, Larkollen, Norway, 1985.* Oslo: Universitetets Oldsaksamling, 1987(b).

—, C.E. The Viking and late Norse Graves of Caithness and Sutherland, 148-164. in Batey *et al.* (eds.), *The Viking Age in Caithness, Orkney and the North Atlantic.* Edinburgh: Edinburgh University Press, 1993.

—, C.E., Jesch, J. and Morris, C.D. (eds.) *The Viking Age in Caithness, Orkney and the North Atlantic.* Edinburgh: Edinburgh University Press, 1993.

Batt, C.M. and Dockrill, S.J. Magnetic moments in prehistory: Integrating magnetic measurements with other archaeological data from Scatness multi-period settlement. *Archaeological Prospection* 5 No. 4, 1998, 217-28.

Beith, M. Destroying island history in the name of research? *The West Highland Free Press,* March 1997, 7.

Bell, B. and Dickson, C. 1989 Excavations at Warebeth (Stromness Cemetery) Broch, Orkney. *Proceedings of the Society of Antiquaries of Scotland* 119, 1989, 101-31, fiche1: C3.

Berry, R.J. *The Natural History of Orkney.* London: Collins New Naturalist, 1985.

Bersu, G. and Wilson, D.M. *Three Viking Graves in the Isle of Man.* Society for Medieval Archaeology Monograph 1, 1966.

Beveridge, E. *North Uist: its archaeology and topography, with notes upon the early history of the Hebrides.* Edinburgh: T and A Constable, 1911

—, E. Excavation of an earth house at Foshigarry and a fort, Dun Thomaidh, in North Uist. *Proceedings of the Society of Antiquaries of Scotland* 65, 1930, 299-357.

—, E. Earth houses at Garry Iochdrach and Bac Mhic Connain in North Uist. *Proceedings of the Society of Antiquaries of Scotland* 66, 1931, 32-67.

Beverage, E and Callander, J.G. Excavation of an earth house at Foshigarry and a fort, Dun Thomaidh, in North Uist. *Proceedings of the Society of Antiquaries of Scotland* 65, 1930-1, 299-357.

—, E and Callander, J.G. Earth house at Garry Iochdrach and Bac Mhic Connain in North Uist. *Proceedings of the Society of Antiquaries of Scotland* 66, 1931-2, 32-67.

Boardman, S. J. Charcoal and charred macrofossils, 149-157, in Branigan, K. and Foster, P. (eds.) *Barra: archaeological research on Ben Tangaval.* Sheffield: Sheffield Academic Press, SEARCH 1, 1995.

—, S. J. and Jones, G. E. M. Experiments on the effects of charring on cereal plant components, *Journal of Archaeological Science* 17, 1990, 1-11.

Bond, J.M. *Change and Continuity in an Island System; the Palaeoeconomy of Sanday, Orkney.* Unpublished PhD thesis, University of Bradford, 1994.

—, J.M. Beyond the fringe? Recognising change and adaptation in Pictish and Norse Orkney, 81-90, in Mills, C.M. and Coles, G.M. *Life on the edge: human settlement and marginality.* Symposia of the Association for Environmental Archaeology No.13. Oxford: Oxbow Books. Oxbow Monograph 100, 1998(a).

—, J.M. Ashes to the earth; the making of a settlement mound, 81-96, in Nicholson, R.A. and Dockrill, S. J. (eds.) *Old Scatness Broch, Shetland: Retrospect and Prospect.* Bradford: Bradford Archaeological Sciences Research 5/North Atlantic Biocultural Organisation Monograph 2, 1998(b).

—, J.M. Late Iron age/Pictish inscribed stones. in Bond J.M. and Dockrill, S.J. *Old Scatness / Jarlshof Environs Project 1998, Interim Report No. 4.* Bradford: University of Bradford/Shetland Amenity Trust, Bradford Archaeological Sciences Research 7, 1999.

—, J.M. and Dockrill, S.J. *Old Scatness/Jarlshof Environs Project 1998, Interim Report No. 4.* Bradford: University of Bradford/Shetland Amenity Trust, Bradford Archaeological Sciences Research 7, 1999.

—, J.M. and Hunter, J.R. Flax-growing in Orkney from the Norse period to the eighteenth century. *Proceedings of the Society of Antiquaries of Scotland* 117, 1987, 175-181.

—, J.M. and O'Connor, T.P. *Bones from Medieval deposits at 16-22 Coppergate and other sites in York.* York: York Archaeological Trust/CBA, The Archaeology of York, 15/5, 1998.

Boswell, J. *Journal of a Tour to the Hebrides.* 1786.

Boyd, W.E. Cereals in Scottish antiquity. *Circaea* 5, 1988, 101-10.

Brailsford, J. *Early Celtic Masterpieces from Britain in the British Museum.* London: British Museum, London, 1975.

Bradley, R. *Rock Art and the Prehistory of Atlantic Europe: signing the land.* London and New York: Routledge, 1997.

Branigan, K. and Foster, P. *Barra: Archaeological Research on Ben Tangaval.* Sheffield: Sheffield Academic Press, 1995.

Breeze, D.J. The logistics of Agricola's final campaign, 7-28, *Talanta* 18/19, 1987/8, (=Breeze, D.J. and Dobson, B. *Roman Officers and Frontiers,* 574-95. Stuttgart, 1993.)

—, D.J. *Roman Scotland: Frontier Country.* London: B.T.Batsford/Historic Scotland, 1996.

Brennand, M., Smith, H. and Parker Pearson, M. *The Norse settlement and Pictish cairn at Kilpheder, South Uist: Excavations in 1998.* Internal report, Sheffield University, 1998.

Bronk Ramsey, C. *OxCal Version 3.5.* 2000 (http://www.units.ox.ac.uk/departments/rlaha/orau/06_ind.html)

Bruce, J. Notes of the discovery and exploration of a pile structure on the north bank of the River Clyde, east from Dumbarton Rock. *Proceedings of the Society of Antiquaries of Scotland* 34, 1899-1900, 437-62.

Burbidge, C. OSL dating of a soil profile from Old Scatness. in Bond, J.M., Dockrill, S.J. and Turner, V. *Old Scatness / Jarlshof Environs Project 1998*, Interim Report No. 2. Bradford: Shetland Amenity Trust /University of Bradford, forthcoming.

Burgess, C., Church, M., Dempsey, J. and Gilmour, S.M.D. An Dunan, Uig Parish, 110. *Discovery and Excavation in Scotland,*1996. Edinburgh: Council for Scottish Archaeology, 1997.

—, C. The Chronology of cup-and-ring marks in Britain and Ireland. in *Northern Archaeology* 10, 1989-90, 21-6.

Burn, A.R. Holy men on islands in pre-Christian Britain. in *Glasgow Archaeological Journal* 1, 1969, 2-6.

Buteaux, S. *Settlements at Skaill, Deerness, Orkney: excavations by Peter Gelling of the Prehistoric, Pictish, Viking and Late Periods, 1963-1981.* Oxford: Archaeopress, British Archaeological Reports (British Series) 260, 1997.

Byrne, F.J. *Irish Kings and High Kings.* London: Batsford, 1973.

Callander, J.G. Notices of a short cist discovered in the Parish of Yester, East Lothian; of a prehistoric burial at Alva, Clackmannanshire; and of an earth house in Skye. *Proceedings of the Society of Antiquaries of Scotland* 48, 1913-14, 200-5.

—, J.G. Report on the Excavation of Dun Beag, a broch near Struan, Skye. *Proceedings of the Society of Antiquaries of Scotland* 55, 1920-1, 110-31.

—, J.G. Earth-house at Bac Mhic Connain, Vallay, North Uist. *Proceedings of the Society of Antiquaries of Scotland* 66, 1931-2, 42-66.

Campbell, E. Excavations of a wheelhouse and other Iron Age structures at Sollas, North Uist, by R. J. C. Atkinson in 1957. *Proceedings of the Society of Antiquaries of Scotland* 121, 1991, 117-73.

—, E. Pottery. in Armit, I. Excavation of a post-medieval settlement at Druim na Dearcag, and related sites around Loch Olabhat, North Uist. *Proceedings of the Society of Antiquaries of Scotland* 127, 1997, 909-13.

—, E. The raw, the cooked and the burnt: interpretations of food and animals in the Hebridean Iron Age. *Archaeological Dialogues* 7 (2), 2000, 184-98.

—, E. Pottery from Barra sheiling sites. in Brannigan, K. (ed.) *Historical sites.* Sheffield: Sheffield Academic Press, SEARCH 6. Forthcoming.

—, E., Housley, R. and Taylor, M. Charred food residues from Hebridean Iron Age pottery: analysis and dating. in Housley, R. and Coles, G. (eds.) *Atlantic Connections and Adaptations: economies, environments and subsistence in lands bordering the North Atlantic.* Oxford: Oxbow Monograph. Forthcoming

—, J.L. *Canna, the Story of a Hebridean Island.* Oxford: National Trust for Scotland/Oxford University Press, 1984.

Cant, R. Norse influence in the organisation of the medieval church in the Western Isles. *Northern Studies* 21, 1984, 1-14.

Card, N. Downes, J. and Gibson, J. Minehowe, St.Andrews and Deerness Parish, 65. *Discovery and Excavation in Scotland*, New Series, 1, 2000. Edinburgh: Council for Scottish Archaeology, 2001.

Carson, M. Iron Age finds from the Isle of Lewis. *Proceedings of the Society of Antiquaries of Scotland* 108, 1976, 370-75.

Carter, S. Red ash micromorphology, 29-31. in Sharples, N. *Scalloway: a broch, Late Iron Age settlement and Medieval cemetery in Shetland.* Oxford: Oxbow Monograph 82, 1998.

Carter, S.P., McCullagh, R.P.J., and MacSween, A. The Iron Age in Shetland: excavations at five sites threatened by coastal erosion. *Proceedings of the Society of Antiquaries of Scotland*, 125, 1995, 429-82, fiche 2: C7-C14.

Cary, M. and Warmington, E.H. *The Ancient Explorers.* London: Harmondsworth, (first edition 1929), 1963.

Ceron-Carrasco, R., Church, M.J. and Thoms, J. Towards an economic landscape of the Bhaltos Peninsula, Lewis during the mid to late Iron Age. in Turner, V. (ed.) *Tall stories; broch studies past, present and future.* Oxford: Oxbow Monography. Forthcoming.

Cheape, H. Food and liquid containers in the Hebrides: a window on the Iron Age, 6-27, in Fenton, A. and Myrdal, J. (eds.) *Food and drink and travelling accessories*: essays in honour of Gösta Berg. Edinburgh: John Donald/National Museums of Scotland/Skansen and Nordiska Museet, 1988.

—, H. 1993 Crogans and Barvas ware: Handmade pottery in the Hebrides. *Scottish Studies* 31, 1992-3, 109-27.

Childe, V.G. Excavations of the vitrified fort of Finavon, Angus. *Proceedings of the Society of Antiquaries of Scotland* 69, 1934-5, 49-80.

—, V.G. *The Prehistory of Scotland.* London: Kegan Paul, 1935.

—, V.G. (1) Carminnow Fort; (2) Supplementary excavations at the vitrified fort of Finavon, Angus, and (3) some Bronze Age vessels from Angus. *Proceedings of the Society of Antiquaries of Scotland* 70, 1935-6, 347-52.

—, V.G. *Scotland before the Scots.* London: Methuen and Co., 1946.

—, V.G. and Thorneycroft, W. The vitrified fort at Rahoy, Morvern, Argyll. *Proceedings of the Society of Antiquaries of Scotland* 72, 1937-8, 23-43.

Christie, P.M. Cornish Souterrains in the Light of Recent Research. *Bulletin of the Institute of Archaeology, University of London* 16, 1979, 187-213.

Christison, D. Account of the excavation of the camps and earthworks at Birrenswark Hill, in Annandale, undertaken by the Society in 1898. *Proceedings of the Society of Antiquaries of Scotland* 33, 1898-9, 198-218.

—, D. The forts, 'camps', and other field-works of Perth, Forfar and Kincardine. *Proceedings of the Society of Antiquaries of Scotland* 34, 1899-1900, 43-120.

Church, M.J. Archaeological evaluation of two subterranean, drystone dwellings exposed by coastal erosion at Galson, Isle of Lewis, November 1997 and August 1998. Edinburgh: Centre for Field

Archaeology, University of Edinburgh. Unpublished, 1998.

—, M.J. Carbonised plant macrofossils and charcoal, 120-30, in Harding, D.W. and Dixon, T.N. *Dun Bharabhat, Cnip, an Iron Age settlement in West Lewis: Volume 1, structures and material culture.* Edinburgh: University of Edinburgh, Calanais Research Monograph No. 2, 2000.

—, M.J. Archaeobotanical remains from Loch na Beirgh, Lewis. in *The Iron Age settlement at Beirgh, Riof, Isle of Lewis: Excavations, 1985-95, Volume 2: palaeoenvironmental and palaeoeconomic investigations.* Edinburgh: University of Edinburgh, Calanais Research Monograph. Forthcoming.

—, M. and Gilmour, S.M.D. Guinnerso, Uig Parish, 106-07, *Discovery and Excavation in Scotland 1998.* Edinburgh: Council for Scottish Archaeology, 1999.

—, M. and Gilmour, S.M.D. Excavations at Guinnerso, west Lewis, 1998. Edinburgh: Department of Archaeology, University of Edinburgh, Interim report. Forthcoming.

—, M.J. and Peters, C. Archaeobotanical taphonomy in Atlantic Scotland. in Housley, R. and Coles, G.M. (eds.), *Atlantic connections and adaptations: economies, environments and subsistence in the North Atlantic Realm.* Oxford: Oxbow Monography. Forthcoming.

Clancy, T.O. and Markus, G. *Iona. The Earliest Poetry of a Celtic Monastery.* Edinburgh: Edinburgh University Press, 1995.

Clarke, D.V. Small finds in the Atlantic Province: problems of approach. *Scottish Archaeological Forum* 3, 1971, 22-53.

Clerk, R. Parish of Duirinish, 322-60. *New Statistical Account of Scotland.* 14, 1845.

Coles, B.J. Trackways across the wetlands: Multi-disciplinary studies in the Somerset Levels of England, 146-167, in Coles, J.M. and Lawson, A. J. (eds.) *European Wetlands in Prehistory.* Oxford: Clarendon Press, 1987

—, J.M., Heal, S.V.E., and Orme, B.J. The use and character of wood in prehistoric Britain and Ireland. *Proceedings of the Prehistoric Society* 44, 1978, 1-45.

—, J.M. and Lawson, A.J. *European Wetlands in Prehistory.* Oxford: Clarendon Press, 1987.

Cooke, I.M. *Mother and Son: The Cornish Fogou.* Penzance: Men-An-Tol Studio, 1993.

Cowan, I.B. and Easson, D.A. *Medieval Religious Houses, Scotland.* London: Longman, 1976.

Cowie, T., Bruce, M. and Kerr, N. The discovery of a child burial of probably Viking-age date on Kneep headland, Uig, Lewis 1991: interim report', 165 72, in Batey, C.E., Jesch, J. and Morris, C.D. (eds.) *The Viking Age in Caithness, Orkney and the North Atlantic.* Edinburgh: Edinburgh University Press, 1993.

Cox, R.A.V. Place-name evidence in the west of Lewis: approaches and problems in establishing a profile of Norse settlement. *Scottish Archaeological Review* 6, 1989, 107-115.

Crawford, I.A. *Excavations at Coileagan an Udail (Solas, N. Uidhist), first interim report.* Edinburgh, 1963.

—, I.A. *A preliminary report of excavations at Udal, North Uist, 1964.* Edinburgh: Edinburgh University, School of Scottish Studies, 1964.

—, I.A. *Excavations at Coileagan an Udail, North Uist 1965, 2nd interim report.* Edinburgh: Edinburgh University, School of Scottish Studies, 1965.

—, I.A. Contributions to a history of domestic settlement in North Uist. *Scottish Studies* 10; 2, 1965, 34-63.

—, I.A. *Excavations at Coileagan an Udail, North Uist 1966, 3rd interim report.* Edinburgh: Edinburgh University, School of Scottish Studies, 1966.

—, I.A. *Excavations at Coileagan an Udail, North Uist 1968, 5th interim report.* Edinburgh: Edinburgh University, School of Scottish Studies, 1968.

—, I.A. *Excavations at Coileagan an Udail, North Uist 1969, 6th interim report.* Cambridge: Christs College, Cambridge, 1969.

—, I.A. *Excavations at Coileagan an Udail, North Uist 1970, 7th interim report.* Cambridge: Christs College, Cambridge, 1970.

—, I.A. *Excavations at Coileagan an Udail, North Uist 1975, 13th interim report.* Belfast: Queen's University, 1975.

—, I.A. and Switsur, R. Sandscaping and C[14]: the Udal, N. Uist. *Antiquity* 610, 1977, 124-36.

—, I.A. *Excavations and research at Coileagan an Udail, N. Uist 1978, 15th season.* Cambridge, 1978.

—, I.A. *Excavations and research at Coileagan an Udail, N. Uist 1979.* Cambridge, 1979.

—, I.A. *Excavations and research at Coileagan an Udail, N. Uist 1981.* Cambridge, 1981.

—, I.A. *Excavations and research at Coileagan an Udail, N. Uist 1983.* Glasgow: University of Glasgow, 1983.

—, I.A. *An t-Udal 1986.* Cambridge, 1986.

—, I.A. *An t-Udal 1988.* Cambridge, 1988.

—, I.A. *An t-Udal 1989.* Cambridge, 1989.

—, I.A. *An t-Udal 1990, 28th interim report.* Cambridge, 1990.

—, I.A. *An t-Udal 1991, 29th interim report.* Cambridge, 1991.

—, I.A. *An t-Udal, interim reports 1992-95.* Forthcoming.

—, J. Archaeological collections from sandhill sites in the isle of Coll, Argyll and Bute. *Proceedings of the Society of Antiquaries of Scotland* 127, 1997, 467-511.

—, O.G.S. Notes and news: recent events. *Antiquity* 13, 1939, 257.

Crerar, R. Sollas, 32, *Discovery and Excavation in Scotland* 1962.

*Críth Gablach* trans MacNeill, E. *Proceedings of the Royal Irish Academy* 36, 1923, Section C, 256-316.

Crone, B.A. *Dendrochronology and the Study of Crannogs.* Unpublished PhD thesis, University of Sheffield, 1988.

—, B.A. A wooden bowl from Loch a 'Ghlinne Bhig, Bracadale, Isle of Skye. Proceedings of the Society of Antiquaries of Scotland 123, 1993, 269-75.

—, B.A. *The History of a Scottish Lowland Crannog: Excavations at Buiston, Ayrshire.* Edinburgh: AOC/ Historic Scotland, STAR Monograph 4, 2000.

Cunliffe B. *The Extraordinary Voyage of Pytheas the Greek,* London: Allen Lane, 2001.

Curle, A.O. An account of further excavation at Jarlshof, Sumburgh, Shetland, in 1932 and 1933, on behalf of the Office of Works. *Proceedings of the Society of Antiquaries of Scotland* 70, 1935-36, 153-69.

—, A.O Account of the excavations of an iron smeltery and an associated dwelling and tumuli at Wiltrow in the parish of Dunrossness, Shetland. *Proceedings of the Society of Antiquaries of Scotland* 68, 1933-4, 224-319.

—, J.A. Roman Frontier Post and its People: the Fort of Newstead in the Parish of Melrose. Glasgow: Maclehose, 1911.

Dalland, M. and MacSween, A. The coarse pottery, 178-200, in Owen, O. and Lowe, C.E. *Excavations at Kebister, Shetland.* Edinburgh: Society of Antiquaries of Scotland Monograph Series No.14, 1999.

Davies, J. and Bunce, F. Kilmaluag, 17, *Discovery and Excavation in Scotland* 1979. Edinburgh: Council for Scottish Archaeology, 1979.

—, J. and Calder, G. Claigan Farmhouse, 14, *Discovery and Excavation in Scotland* 1978. Edinburgh: Council for Scottish Archaeology, 1978.

De Navarro, J.M. The Celts in Britain and their Art, 56-82, in Charlesworth D. (ed.) *The Heritage of Early Britain,* London: G. Bell, 1952.

Dick, A.M. Auchlishie, 12, *Discovery and Excavation in Scotland,* 1996. Edinburgh: Council for Scottish Archaeology, 1997.

Dickson, C. Plant remains, 125-39, in Ballin Smith, B. (ed.) *Howe: four millennia of Orkney prehistory.* Edinburgh: Society of Antiquaries of Scotland Monograph Series No.9, 1994.

—, C. and Dickson, J.H. *Plants and people in ancient Scotland.* Stroud: Tempus Publishing, 2000.

—, J.H. *Bryophytes of the Pleistocene.* Cambridge: Cambridge University Press, 1973.

—, J.H. Bryophyte analysis, 627-44, in Berglund, B.E. (ed.) *Handbook of Holocene Palaeoecology and Palaeohydrology.* Chichester: Wiley and Sons, 1986.

—, J.H. North American driftwood, especially *Picea* (spruce), from archaeological sites in the Hebrides and Northern Isles of Scotland. *Review of Palaeobotany and Palynology,* 73, 1992, 49-56.

—, J.H. and Brough, D.W. Botanical studies of a Pictish midden. *Archäobotanik.Dissertationes Botanicae* 133, 1989, 155-66.

Dixon, T.N. A survey of crannogs in Loch Tay. *Proceedings of the Society of Antiquaries of Scotland* 112, 1982, 17-38.

—, T.N. *Scottish Crannogs: Underwater Excavation of Artificial Islands with Special Reference to Oakbank Crannog, Loch Tay.* Unpublished PhD thesis. University of Edinburgh, 1984.

Dockrill, S.J. *The Human Palaeoecology of Sanday, Orkney with Particular Reference to Tofts Ness.* Unpublished M.Phil. Thesis. University of Bradford, 1993.

—, S.J. Northern Exposure: Phase1 of the Old Scatness Excavations 1995-8, 59-80, in Nicholson, R.A. and Dockrill, S.J. (eds.) *Old Scatness Broch, Shetland: Retrospect and Prospect.* Bradford: Bradford Archaeological Sciences Research 5/North Atlantic Biocultural Organisation Monograph 2, 1998(a).

—, S.J. Tofts Ness, 29, *Discovery and Excavation in Scotland 1988,* Edinburgh: Council for Scottish Archaeology, 1988(b).

—, S.J; Bond, J.M. Nicholson, R.A. and Smith, A.N. (eds) Investigations on Sanday Volume 2: The Tofts Ness Peninsula. Society of Antiquaries of Scotland Monograph Series, forthcoming.-

—, S.J. and Simpson, I.A. The identification of prehistoric anthropogenic soils in the Northern Isles using an integrated sampling methodology. *Archaeological Prospection.* 1, 1994, 75-92.

—, S.J., Bond, J.M., Milles, A., Simpson I and Ambers, J. Tofts Ness, Sanday, Orkney. An integrated study of a buried Orcadian landscape, 115-32, in Rowley-Conwy, P. and Luff, R. *Whither Environmental Archaeology?* Oxford: Oxbow Monograph 38, 1994.

—, S.J., Bond, J.M. and O'Connor, T.P. Beyond the Burnt Mound: the South Nesting Palaeolandscape Project, 61-82, in Turner, V. (ed.) *The Shaping of Shetland.* Lerwick: The Shetland Times, 1998.

—, S.J., Bond, J.M. and Turner, V.E. (eds.) *Old Scatness Broch and Jarlshof Environs Project: Field Season 1999* Interim Report No.5 (Data Structure Report). Bradford: University of Bradford and Shetland Amenity Trust, Bradford Archaeological Sciences Research 9, 2000.

Dodgshon, R.A. Land and society in early Scotland. Oxford: Clarendon Press, 1981.

Donations to the Society of Antiquaries by James Traill Esq. *Archaeologica Scotica* III, 1787, Appendix 2, 61.

Donner, J.J. On the post-glacial history of the grampian highlands of Scotland. *Commentationes Biologicae* 24, 1962, 1-29.

Dumayne, L. *Late Holocene Palaeoecology and Human Impact on the Environment of North Britain.* Unpublished PhD thesis. University of Southampton, 1992.

Dunwell, A.J., Cowie, T.G., Bruce, F.M., Neighbour, T. and Rees, A.R. A Viking Age cemetery at Cnip, Uig, Isle of Lewis. *Proceedings of the Society of Antiquaries of Scotland* 125, 1995, 719-52.

—, A.J. and Strachan, R. Excavations at Brown and White Catherthun, Angus, 1995-7. Forthcoming.

Duval, P-M. *Les Celtes.* Paris: Gallimard, 1977.

Earwood, C. Two early Historic bog butter containers. *Proceedings of the Society of Antiquaries of Scotland* 121, 1991, 231-40.

—, C. The dating of wooden troughs and dishes. *Proceedings of the Society of Antiquaries of Scotland* 123, 1993, 355-62.

Edlin, H. *Woodland Crafts of Britain.* Newton Abbot: David and Charles, 1973.

Edmonds, M., Sheridan, A. and Tipping, R. Survey and excavation at Creag na Caillich, Killin. *Proceedings of the Society of Antiquaries of Scotland* 122, 1992, 77-112.

Edwards, K.J. and Ralston, I.B.M. *Scotland: Environment and Archaeology, 8000 BC – AD 1000.* Chichester: John Wiley and Sons, 1997.

Fairhurst, H. and Taylor, D.B. A hut-circle settlement at Kilphedir, Sutherland. *Proceedings of the Society of Antiquaries of Scotland* 103, 1970-1, 65-99.

—, H. The wheelhouse site at A'Cheardach Bheag on

Brimore machair, South Uist. *Glasgow Archaeological Journal* 2, 1971, 72-106.

—, H. *Excavations at Crosskirk Broch, Caithness.* Edinburgh: Society of Antiquaries of Scotland Monograph 3, 1984.

Fenton, A.S. *Scottish Country Life.* Edinburgh: Donald, 1976.

—, A.S. *The Northern Isles: Orkney and Shetland.* Edinburgh: John Donald, 1978.

Fitzpatrick, A.P. The submission of the Orkney Islands to Claudius: new evidence? *Scottish Archaeological Review* 6, 1989, 24-33.

Fleming, A. and Woolf, A. 1992. 'Cille Donnain: a late Norse church in South Uist', *Proceedings of the Society of Antiquaries of Scotland* 122, 329-350.

Flitcroft, C. *A Preliminary Investigation of the Environmental History of the Loch Ruadh Guinnerso Area, North West Lewis.* Unpublished B.Sc.Environmental Archaeology Dissertation. University of Edinburgh Department of Archaeology, 1997.

Fojut, N. Towards a geography of Shetland brochs. *Glasgow Archaeological Journal* 9, 1982, 38-59.

—, N. Some thoughts on the Iron Age, 47-84, in Smith, B. (ed.) *Shetland Archaeology.* Lerwick: Shetland Times, 1985.

—, N. How did we end up here? Shetland Iron Age studies to 1995, 1-41, in Nicholson, R.A. and Dockrill, S.J. (eds.) *Old Scatness Broch, Shetland: Retrospect and Prospect.* Bradford: University of Bradford/Shetland Amenity Trust/North Atlantic Biocultural Organisation, Bradford Archaeological Sciences Research 5, NABO Monograph No.2, 1998.

—, N. Brochs and timber supply: a necessity born of invention. in Turner, V. (ed.) *Tall stories: broch studies past, present and future.* Oxford: Oxbow Monograph Forthcoming.

Foster, S.M. *Aspects of the Later Atlantic Iron Age.* Unpublished PhD thesis, Glasgow University, 1989.

—, S.M. Analysis of spatial patterns in buildings (gamma analysis) as an insight into social structure: examples from the Scottish Atlantic Iron Age. *Antiquity,* 63, 1989, 40-50.

—, S.M. Pins, combs and the chronology of later Atlantic Iron Age Settlement, 143-74, in Armit, I. (ed.) *Beyond the Brochs: Changing Perspectives on the Atlantic Scottish Iron Age.* Edinburgh: Edinburgh University Press, 1990.

—, S.M. *Picts, Gaels and Scots.* London: Batsford, 1996.

—, S. The strength of belief: the impact of Christianity on early historic Scotland, 229-40, in De Boe, G. and Verhaeghe, F. (eds.) *Religion and Belief in Medieval Europe.* Papers of the Medieval Europe Brugge 1997 Conference 4, 1997.

Fox, A. *South West England.* London: Thames and Hudson, 1964.

—, C. *The Personality of Britain.* Cardiff: National Museum of Wales/University of Wales, 1932

Galloway, T.L. Prehistoric Argyll: Report on the excavation of a burial cairn at Balnabraid, Kintyre. *Proceedings of the Society of Antiquaries of Scotland* 54, 1910-1, 172-91.

The Gentleman's Magazine, 1841, pt 1, 36-7.

The Gentleman's Magazine Library, 1886, Archaeology pt 1, 175-6.

Gentles, D. *Archaeomagnetic directional studies of large fired structures in Britain,* Unpublished PhD thesis, Portsmouth Polytechnical College, 1989.

—, D. Vitrified forts. *Current Archaeology* 133, March/April 1993, 18-20.

Gilbertson, D., Kent, M. and Grattan, J. The Sheffield Environment and Archaeology Research Campaign in the Outer Hebrides, 1-4, in Gilbertson, D., Kent, M. and Grattan, J. (eds.) *The Outer Hebrides: the last 14000 years,* Sheffield: Sheffield Academic Press, SEARCH Volume 2, 1996.

Gillies, D. Geological (and Archaeological) Record of Skye. Manuscript Ms. 9517. National Library of Scotland, 1920-70.

Gilmour, S.M.D. *Iron Age Drystone Structures in Argyll.* Unpublished M.A. dissertation, Department of Archaeology, University of Edinburgh, 1994.

—, S.M.D. Complex Atlantic roundhouses: chronology and complexity. in Turner, V. (ed.) *Tall stories; broch studies past, present and future.* Oxford: Oxbow Monograph. Forthcoming.

—, S. first millennium settlement development in the Atlantic West, 155-170, in Henderson, J.C. (ed.) *The Prehistory and Early History of Atlantic Europe.* Oxford: British Archaeological Reports 861 (International Series), 2000.

—, S.M.D. Atlantic Scotland: evidence and controversy. in Alexander, D., Church, M. and Taylor, M. *Circular Arguments: the archaeology of roundhouses,* Glasgow. Forthcoming a.

—, S. and Cook, M. Excavations at Dun Vulan: a reinterpretation of the reappraised Iron Age. *Antiquity* 72, 1998, 327-37.

—, S.M.D. and Henderson, J.C. *The Atlantic Iron Age in Argyll.* Forthcoming b.

Giot, P.R. *Protohistoire de la Bretagne.* 1979.

Gordon, C. Sailing Directory for the West Coast.1855.

Goudie, G. Notice of excavations in a broch and associated tumuli near *Levenwick, in the parish of Dunrossness, Zetland. Proceedings of the Society of Antiquaries of Scotland* 9, 1870-2, 212-21.

Graham, A. Archaeological gleanings from Dark Age records. *Proceedings of the Society of Antiquaries of Scotland* 85, 1950-1, 64-91.

Graham Campbell, J. Two Scandinavian brooch fragments of Viking age date from the Outer Hebrides. *Proceedings of the Society of Antiquaries of Scotland* 106, 1975, 212-14.

—, J. An unpublished gold finger ring of Viking age date from the Isle of Skye and new light on the 1850 Skye hoard. *Proceedings of the Society of Antiquaries of Scotland* 112, 1982, 568-70.

—, J. A Viking-age gold arm ring from the Sound of Jura. *Proceedings of the Society of Antiquaries of Scotland* 113, 1983, 640-42.

—, J. A late Celtic enamelled mount from Galson, Isle of Lewis. *Proceedings of the Society of Antiquaries of Scotland* 116, 1986, 281-84.

—, J. and Batey, C.E. *Vikings in Scotland: An Archaeological Survey.* Edinburgh: Edinburgh University Press, 1998.

Grieg, S. Viking Antiquities in Scotland. in Shetelig, H. (ed.) *Viking Antiquities in Great Britain and Ireland.* Part II. Oslo: Aschenhoug, 1940.

Gregory, R.A. *Excavations at Hayknowes Farm, Annan: the second season's interim report.* Unpublished manuscript, Department of Art History and Archaeology, University of Manchester, 1996.

Gordon, K. A Norse Viking-age grave from Cruach Mhor, Islay. *Proceedings of the Society of Antiquaries of Scotland* 120, 1990, 151-60.

Haggarty, A. and Haggarty, G. Excavations at Rispain Camp, Whithorn 1978-81, *Transactions of the Dumfriesshire and Galloway Natural History and Antiquarian Society* 58, 1983, 21-51.

Hale, A. Past and present research on the Dumbuck marine crannog. *Glasgow Archaeology Society* 42, 1999, 6-11.

Hall, A.R. Medieval biology: the fossil evidence for plants in medieval towns. *Biologist* 33, 1986, 262-67.

—, A.R. and Kenward, H.K. *Environmental Evidence from the Colonia: General Accident and Rougier Street.* London: Council for British Archaeology, The Archaeology of York 14/6, 1990.

Halpin, E. Harpercroft and Wardlaw Hill, Dundonald, Strathclyde, 121-126, in Rideout, J., Owen, O. A., and Halpin, E. (eds.) *Hillforts of Southern Scotland.* Edinburgh: AOC/Historic Scotland, STAR Monograph 1, 1992.

Hamilton, J.R.C. *Excavations at Jarlshof.* Edinburgh: HMSO, 1956.

—, J.R.C. *Excavations at Clickhimin.* Edinburgh: HMSO, 1968.

Harding, D.W. Changing perspectives in the Atlantic Iron Age, 5-16, in Armit, I. (ed), *Beyond the Brochs: Changing Perspectives on the Atlantic Scottish Iron Age.* Edinburgh: Edinburgh University Press, 1990.

—, D.W. *The Hebridean Iron Age: twenty years' research.* Edinburgh: Department of Archaeology, University of Edinburgh, Occasional Paper Series, No. 20, 2000,

—, D.W. and Armit, I. Survey and excavation in west Lewis, 71-107, in Armit, I. (ed) *Beyond the Brochs: Changing Perspectives on the Atlantic Scottish Iron Age.* Edinburgh: Edinburgh University Press, 1990.

—, D.W. and Gilmour, S.M.D. *The Iron Age settlement at Beirgh, Riof, Isle of Lewis: Excavations 1985-95. Volume 1: The structures and stratigraphy.* Edinburgh: Department of Archaeology, Edinburgh University, Calanais Research Series No. 1, 2000.

—, D.W. and Dixon, T.N. *Dun Bharabhat, Cnip: an Iron Age settlement in West Lewis: Volume 1: The Structures and Material Culture.* Edinburgh: Department of Archaeology, University of Edinburgh, Calanais Research Series 2, 2000.

Harman, M. An incised cross on Hirt, Harris. *Proceedings of the Society of Antiquaries of Scotland* 108, 1977, 254-258.

Harrison, J.G. Dream cottage. *The Scots Magazine* 141, 1994, 348-53.

Haselgrove, C., Armit, I., Champion, J., Creighton, J., Gwilt, A., Hill, J.D., Hunter, F. and Woodward, A. *Understanding the British Iron Age: An Agenda for Action.* Salisbury: Trust for Wessex Archaeology, 2001.

—, C. and McCullagh, R. (eds.) *An Iron Age Coastal Community in East Lothian: The Excavation of Two Later Prehistoric Enclosure Complexes at Fishers Road, Port Seton, 1994-5.* Edinburgh: AOC/Historic Scotland, STAR Monograph 6, 2000.

Hedges, J.W. *Bu, Gurness and the brochs of Orkney Part 1: Bu.* Oxford: British Archaeological Reports (British Series) 163, 1987.

—, J.W. *Bu, Gurness and the brochs of Orkney Part 2: Gurness.* Oxford: British Archaeological Reports (British Series) 164, 1987.

—, J.W. *Bu, Gurness and the brochs of Orkney Part 3: The brochs of Orkney.* Oxford: British Archaeological Reports (British Series) 165, 1987.

—, J.W. Surveying the foundations: life after brochs, 17-31, in Armit, I. (ed.) *Beyond the Brochs: Changing Perspectives on the Atlantic Scottish Iron Age.* Edinburgh: Edinburgh University Press, 1990.

—, J.W. and Bell, B. That tower of Scottish prehistory – broch. *Antiquity* 54, 1980, 87-94.

Hethersall, S and Tye, R. *The lost wheelhouses of Uist.* Isle of South Uist: Robert Tye, 2000.

Henderson, J. Analysis of glass and pigment. in Campbell, E. Excavation of a wheelhouse and other Iron Age structures at Sollas, North Uist by R.J.C. Atkinson in 1957. *Proceedings of the Society of Antiquaries of Scotland* 121, 1991, 164-6.

Henshall, A. *The Chambered Tombs of Scotland.* Volume 1. Edinburgh: Edinburgh University Press, 1963.

Hingley, R., Society in Scotland from 700BC to AD200. *Proceedings of the Society of Antiquaries of Scotland*, 122, 1992, 7-53.

—, R., Moore, H.L., Triscott, J.E. and Wilson, G. The excavation of two later Iron Age fortified homesteads at Aldclune, Blair Atholl, Perth and Kinross. *Proceedings of the Society of Antiquaries of Scotland* 127, 1997, 407-66.

Historic Scotland Archaeological Procedure Paper 4, *Coastal Zone Assessment Survey.* Edinburgh: Historic Scotland, 1996.

Holden, T. Carbonised plant, 125-7, in Sharples, N. *Scalloway: a broch, late Iron Age settlement and Medieval cemetery in Shetland.* Oxford: Oxbow Books/Cardiff Studies in Archaeology, Oxbow Monograph 82, 1998.

—, T. and Boardman, S. 1998. Resource exploitation: crops, 99-106, in Sharples, N. *Scalloway: a broch, late Iron Age settlement and Medieval cemetery in Shetland.* Oxford: Oxbow Books/Cardiff Studies in Archaeology, Oxbow Monograph 82, 1998.

Hood, S. The Knossos Tablets: a complete view. *Antiquity* 36, 1962, 38-40.

Hope-Taylor, B. The 'boat-shaped' house in Northern Europe. *Proceedings of the Cambridgeshire Antiquarian Society* 55, 1962, 16-7.

Hubbard, R.N.L.B. Quantifying preservation and distortion in carbonised seeds, and investigating the history of *friké* production. *Journal of Archaeological Science*, 16, 1990, 103-6.

Hull, M.E. and Hawkes, C.F.C. *Corpus of ancient brooches in Britain: pre Roman bow brooches.* Oxford: British Archaeological Reports (British Series) 168, 1987.

Hunter, J.R. *Archaeological Fieldwork on the Islands of Canna and Sanday, Inner Hebrides, Summer 1994: First Interim Report.* Bradford: Department of Archaeological Sciences, University of Bradford, 1994.

—, J.R. *A Persona for the Northern Picts.* Rosemarkie: Groam House Museum, 1997.

—, J.R., Dockrill, S.J., Bond, J.M. and Smith, A.N. *Archaeological Investigations on Sanday, Orkney.* Forthcoming.

Jacobsthal, P. *Early Celtic Art.* Oxford: Clarendon Press, 1944.

Jennings, A. Iona and the Vikings: survival and continuity. *Northern Studies* 33, 1998, 37-54.

Jervise, A. Notice of the discovery of a Pict's house at Fithie, in the parish of Farnell, Forfarshire, in which Roman pottery and animal remains were found. *Proceedings of the Society of Antiquaries of Scotland* 8, 1868-70, 473-4.

Jobey, G. Excavations at Boonies, Westerkirk, and the nature of Romano-British settlement in eastern Dumfriesshire. *Proceedings of the Society of Antiquaries of Scotland* 105, 1975, 119-140.

—, G. A Souterrain at Milfieldhill, Northumberland. *Archaeologia Aeliana* 5th series, 3, 1975, 215-16.

—, G. Burnswark Hill. *Transactions of the Dumfriesshire and Galloway Natural History and Antiquarian Society,* 53, 1977-8, 57-104.

—, G. and Tait, J. Excavations on palisaded settlements and cairnfields at Alnham, Northumberland. *Archaeologia Aeliana* 4th series, 44, 1966, 5-48.

Johnson, M. in Neighbour, T., Knott, C., Bruce, M.F. and Kerr, N.W. Excavation of two burials at Galson, Isle of Lewis, 1993 and 1996. *Proceedings of the Society of Antiquaries of Scotland.* Forthcoming.

—, S. A Journey to the Western Isles of Scotland, 1775. Menston: Scholar Press, reprinted 1968.

Jones, G. *A History of the Vikings.* Oxford: Oxford University Press, 2nd edition reprinted, 1986.

—, M. Quantification in palaeoethnobotany, 62-80, in van Zeist, W., Wasylikowa, K. and Behre, K.E (eds.) *Progress in Old World Palaeoethnobotany.* Rotterdam: Balkema, 1991.

—, M. Sampling in palaeoethnobotany, 53-62, in van Zeist, W., Wasylikowa, K. and Behre, K.E. (eds.) *Progress in Old World Palaeoethnobotany.* Rotterdam: Balkema, 1991.

Jope, E.M. An Iron Age decorated sword-scabbard from the River Bann at Toome. *Ulster Journal of Archaeology* 17, 1954, 81-91.

—, E.M. The Beginnings of the La Tène Ornamental Style in the British Isles, 69-83, in Frere S.S. (ed.) *Problems of the Iron Age in Southern Britain.* London: Council for British Archaeology, 1961.

—, E.M. The Witham Shield, 61-8, in Sieveking G. de G. (ed.) *Prehistoric and Roman Studies.* London: British Museum, 1971.

—, E.M. The Wandsworth Mask Shield and its Sources of Inspiration, 167-84, in Duval, P-M. and Hawkes, C. (eds.) *Celtic Art in Ancient Europe: Five Protohistoric Centuries.* London: Seminar Press, 1976.

—, E.M. The Southward Face of Celtic Britain, 300 BC to AD 50: Four British Parade Shields. *I Celti e la Loro Cultura nell' epoca pre-romana e romana nella*

*Britannia.* Academia Nazionale dei Lincei 237, 1978, 27-36.

—, E.M. Torrs, Aylesford and the Padstow Hobby-Horse. in O'Connor, A. and Clarke D.V. (eds.) *From the Stone Age to the Forty-Five: Essays Presented to R.B.K. Stevenson.* Edinburgh: J. Donald, 1983.

—, E.M. *Early Celtic Art in the British Isles.* Oxford: Clarendon Press, 2000.

Kaland, S.H.H. The settlement of Westness, Rousay, 308-319, in Batey, C.E., Jesch, J. and Morris, C.D. (eds.) *The Viking Age in Caithness, Orkney and the North Atlantic.* Edinburgh: Edinburgh University Press, 1993.

Keller, F. *The Lake Dwellings of Switzerland and Other Parts of Europe* (Translated by Lee, JE). London: Longmans, Green & Co., 1866.

Kelly, F. *A Guide to Early Irish Law.* Dublin: Dublin Institute for Advanced Studies, 1988.

Kenward, H.K. and Hall, A.R. *Biological Evidence from Anglo-Scandinavian Deposits at 16-22 Coppergate.* London: Council for British Archaeology, The Archaeology of York 14/7, 1995.

Kidd, D. and Ritchie, G. The Curle Collection of Gotlandic Antiquities. Bulletin of the National Art Collection Fund 36 (Summer 1988), 7.

Knirk, J.E. (ed.) *Proceedings of the Tenth Viking Congress, Larkollen, Norway, 1985.* Oslo: Universtitetets Oldsaksamlingen, 1987.

Laing, S. *Pre-Historic Remains of Caithness.* Edinburgh; publisher, 1866.

—, S. On the age of burgs or 'brochs' and some other prehistoric remains of Orkney and Shetland, *Proceedings of the Society of Antiquaries of Scotland* 57-58, 1866-67, 56-100.

Lamb, R.G. *The Archaeological Sites and Monuments of Rousay, Egilsay and Wyre, Orkney Islands Area.* Edinburgh: RCAHMS, Sites and Monuments Series No. 16, 1982.

—, R.G. Papil, Picts and Papar, 9-27, in Crawford, B.E. (ed.) *Northern Isles Connections.* Kirkwall: Orkney Press, 1995.

Lamont, D. Strath in Isle of Skye. Glasgow: Celtic Press, 1913.

Lane, A. *Dark-age and Viking-age pottery in the Hebrides, with special reference to the Udal, North Uist.* Unpublished PhD thesis, University College, London, 1983.

—, A. An Iron Age enclosure at Candyburn, Tweeddale: report of excavation 1979. *Transactions of the Dumfriesshire and Galloway Natural History and Antiquarian Society* 61, 1986, 41-54.

—, A. Hebridean pottery: problems of definition, chronology, presence and absence, 108-130, in Armit, I. (ed.) *Beyond the Brochs: Changing Perspectives on the Atlantic Scottish Iron Age.* Edinburgh: Edinburgh University Press, 1990.

—, A. and Campbell, E. The pottery, in Haggarty, A.M. Iona: some results from recent work. *Proceedings of the Society of Antiquaries of Scotland* 118, 1988, 208-12.

—, A. and Campbell, E. *Excavations at Dunadd: an early Dalriadic capital.* Oxford: Cardiff Studies in Archaeology/Oxbow Books, 2000.

—, A. and Cowie, T. Archaeological collections from

sandhill sites in the Isle of Coll, Argyll and Bute. *Proceedings of the Society of Antiquaries of Scotland* 127, 1997, 467-511.

Lang, A. The Clyde Mystery: A Study in Forgeries and Folklore. Glasgow: Maclehose, 1905.

Lethbridge, T.C. Excavations at Kilpheder, South Uist, and the problem of brochs and wheelhouses. *Proceedings of Prehistoric Society* 18, 1952, 175-93.

Lomax, T.M. *Holocene vegetation history and human impact in western Lewis, Scotland.* Unpublished PhD thesis, University of Birmingham, 1997.

—, T. M. and Edwards, K. J. Pollen and related studies of human impact at Loch Bharabhat, 110-13, in Harding, D.W. and Dixon, T.N. *Dun Bharabhat, Cnip, an Iron Age settlement in West Lewis. Volume 1: The structures and material culture.* Edinburgh: University of Edinburgh, Department of Archaeology, Calanais Research Series No. 2, 2000.

Lowe, C. *Coastal Erosion and the Archaeological Assessment of an Eroding Shoreline at St Boniface Church, Papa Westray, Orkney.* Stroud: Sutton Publishing/Historic Scotland, 1998.

Lucas, A. J. *Cattle in Ancient Ireland. Studies in Irish Archaeology and History.* Kilkenny: Boethius Press, 1989.

McCarthy, M.R. and Brooks, C.M. *Medieval Pottery in Britain AD 900-1600.* Leicester: Leicester University Press, 1988.

McCormick, F. The animal bones from Haughey's Fort. *Emania* 8, 1991, 27-34.

—, F. Early fauna evidence for dairying. *Oxford Journal of Archaeology* 112, 1992, 201-9.

—, F. Calf slaughter as a response to marginality, 49-51, in Mills, C.M. and Coles, G. (eds.) *Life on the edge – human settlement and marginality.* Symposia of the Association for Environmental Archaeology No. 13. Oxford: Oxbow Books, Oxbow Monograph 100, 1998.

MacCulloch, J.A. *The Misty Isle of Skye.* Stirling: Eneas Mackay, 1905

MacDonald, A. Two major early monasteries of Scottish Dalriada: Lismore and Eigg. *Scottish Archaeological Forum*, 1973, 47-70.

—, A. On 'Papa' names in north and west Scotland. *Northern Studies* 9, 1977, 25-30.

McDonnell, J.G. Irons in the fire: evidence for iron-working on broch sites, 150-62, Nicholson, R.A. and Dockrill, S.J. (eds.) *Old Scatness Broch, Shetland: Retrospect and Prospect.* Bradford: Bradford Archaeological Sciences Research 5 / North Atlantic Biocultural Organisation Monograph 2, 1998.

MacGregor, M. *Early Celtic Art in North Britain,* Leicester: Leicester University Press, 1976.

Macinnes, L. Brochs and the Roman occupation of lowland Scotland. *Proceedings of the Society of Antiquaries of Scotland* 114, 1984, 235-50.

MacKie, E.W. The origin and development of the broch and wheelhouse cultures of the Scottish Iron Age. *Proceedings of the Prehistoric Society* 30, 1965, 93-146.

—, E.W. Radiocarbon dates and the Scottish Iron Age. *Antiquity* 43, 1969, 16-18.

—, E.W. English Migrants and Scottish Brochs.

*Glasgow Archaeological Journal* 2, 1971, 39-71.

—, E.W. *Dun Mor Vaul. An Iron Age Broch on Tiree.* Glasgow: University of Glasgow Press, 1974.

—, E.W. The vitrified forts of Scotland, 205-35, in Harding, D.W. (ed.) *Hillforts: later prehistoric earthworks in Britain and Ireland.* London: Academic Press, 1976.

—, E.W. The early Celts in Scotland, 654-70, in Green. M. (ed.) *The Celtic World.* London: Routledge, 1995.

—, E.W. Dun Mor Vaul Revisited: fact and theory in the reppraisal of the Scottish Atlantic Iron Age, 141-80, in Ritchie, G. (ed.) *The Archaeology of Argyll.* Edinburgh: University of Edinburgh, 1997.

—, E.W. Excavations at Dun Ardtreck, Skye, in 1964 and 1965. *Proceedings of the Society of Antiquaries of Scotland* 130 (2002), 301-411.

Mackenzie, W. *Old Skye Tales.* Skye: Maclean Press, 1995.

Maclaren, A. A Norse house on Drimore machair, South Uist. *Glasgow Archaeological Journal* 3, 1974, 9-18.

MacLeod, F.T. Notes on Dun an Iardhard, a broch near Dunvegan excavated by Countess Vincent Baillet de Latour. *Proceedings of the Society of Antiquaries of Scotland* 49, 1914-15, 57-70.

—, R. Parish of Bracadale, *Statistical Account of Scotland* 3, 1792, 245-9.

MacSween, A. The brochs, duns and enclosures of Skye. *Northern Archaeology* 5-6, 1984-5, 1-57.

—, A. *The Neolithic and Late Iron Age Pottery from Pool, Sanday, Orkney.* Unpublished PhD Thesis, University of Bradford, 1990.

—, A. Fabric analysis of coarse ware assemblages: examples from three sites in the Northern Isles of Scotland', Lindahl, A. and Stilborg, O. *The aim of laboratory analyses of ceramics in archaeology. Konferenser* 34, Stockholm: Kungl. Vitterhets Historie och Antikvitets Akademien, 1995, 127-38.

—, A. Bayanne Pottery: narrative and interpretation. Unpublished archive report, 2001.

—, A. The pottery. in Armit, I. Excavations at Cnip. Forthcoming.

Malmros, C. Exploitation of local, drifted and imported wood by the Vikings on the Faroe Islands. *Botanical Journal of Scotland,* 46, 1994, 552-8

Mann, J.C. and Breeze, D.J. Ptolemy, Tacitus and the tribes of North Britain. *Proceedings of the Society of Antiquaries of Scotland* 117, 1987, 85-91.

—, L.M. *Craftsmen's Measures in Prehistoric Times.* Glasgow and London: Mann Publishing Company, 1930.

—, L.M. *The Druid Temple Explained, Glasgow.* Privately printed, 1939.

Marshall, P., Mulville, J., Parker Pearson, M. and Ingram, C. *The Late Bronze Age and Early Iron Age Community at Cladh Hallan, South Uist.* Sheffield: Department of Archaeology and Prehistory, University of Sheffield, unpublished interim report, 1999.

Martlew, R. The excavation of Dun Flodigarry, Staffin, Isle of Skye. *Glasgow Archaeological Journal* 12, 1985, 30-48.

Martin, M. *A Description of the Western Isles of Scotland*

circa 1695. 1716. Edinburgh: Birlinn, reprinted 1994.

Marwick, H. Underground galleried building at Rennibister, Orkney. *Proceedings of the Society of Antiquaries of Scotland* 61,1926-7, 296.

Maxwell, G.S. Excavations at the Roman fort of Crawford, Lanarkshire. *Proceedings of the Society of Antiquaries of Scotland* 104, 1971-2, 147-200.

—, G.S. Settlement in Southern Pictland, 31-44, in Small, A. (ed.) *The Picts: A New Look at Old Problems.* Dundee: Sponsored by Graham Hunter Foundation Inc., 1987.

Megaw, J.V.S. *Art of the European Iron Age, a study of the elusive image.* Bath: publisher, 1970.

—, J.V.S. From Transdanubia to Torrs: Further notes on a gabion of the late Jonathan Oldbuck, 127-48, in O'Connor, A. and Clarke, D.V. (eds.) *From the Stone Age to the Forty-Five: Studies Presented to RBK Stevenson,* Edinburgh: J.Donald, 1983.

Megaw, J.V.S and Megaw R. *Celtic Art: From its beginnings to the Book of Kells.* London and New York: Thames and Hudson, 1989

Mercer, R.J. *Archaeological Field Survey in Northern Scotland volume I, 1976-79.* Edinburgh: University of Edinburgh Department of Archaeology Occasional Paper 4, 1980.

—, R. J. *Archaeological Field Survey in Northern Scotland volume II, 1980-1.* Edinburgh: University of Edinburgh Department of Archaeology Occasional Paper 7, 1981.

—, R.J. *Archaeological Field Survey in Northern Scotland volume III, 1982-3.* Edinburgh: University of Edinburgh Department of Archaeology Occasional Paper 11, 1985.

—, R.J. The excavation of a succession of prehistoric roundhouses at Cnoc Stanger, Reay, Caithness, Highland, 1981-2. *Proceedings of the Society of Antiquaries of Scotland* 126, 1996, 157-90.

—, R. The excavation of an earthwork enclosure at Long Knowe, Eskdale, Dumfriesshire, 1976. *Transactions of the Dumfriesshire and Galloway Natural History and Antiquarian Society* 56, 1981, 38-72.

Miller, J.J. *An Archaeobotanical Investigation of Oakbank Crannog, a Prehistoric Lake Dwelling in Loch Tay, the Scottish Highlands.* Unpublished PhD thesis, University of Glasgow, 1997.

—, J.J., Dickson, J.H. and Dixon, T.N. Unusual food plants from Oakbank crannog, Loch Tay, Scottish highlands: cloudberry, opium poppy and spelt wheat. *Antiquity* 72, 1998, 805-11.

Milles, A. Comparative analysis of charred plant remains from Ness of Gruting, 123-4 and fiche, in Whittle, A. (ed.) *Scord of Brouster: an early agricultural settlement on Shetland..* Oxford: Oxford University Committee for Archaeology Monoograph 9, 1986.

Mitchel, H. The Picts in Athol. *Transactions of the Inverness Scientific Society and Field Club* 8 (1912-18), 8.

Mitchell, A. *Trees of Britain.* London: Collins, 1996.

Moore, H. and Wilson, G. The Bayanne Project: Interim report (1995-97). Lerwick: Shetland Amenity Trust, 1997.

Morris, C.D., Batey, C.E. and Rackham, D.J. Freswick Links, Caithness: Excavation and Survey of A Norse Settlement. Inverness and New York: Highland Libraries/NABO, 1995.

Morrison, I. *Landscape with Lake Dwellings.* Edinburgh: Edinburgh University Press, 1985.

Mowat, R.J.C. *The Logboats of Scotland.* Oxford: Oxbow Monograph 68, 1996.

Munro, Dean. *Journey to the Hebrides.* 1549.

—, R. *Ancient Scottish Lake Dwellings or Crannogs.* Edinburgh: Douglas, 1882.

Needham, S.P. and Bimsom, M. Late Bronze Age Egyptian blue at Runnymede. *Antiquaries Journal* 68, 1988, 314-15.

Neighbour, T. *Excavations at Bostadh Beach, Great Bernera, Isle of Lewis.* Edinburgh: Centre for Field Archaeology internal report, 2001.

—, T. and Burgess, C. Bostadh, Uig Parish 113-14, *Discovery and Excavation in Scotland* 1996, Edinburgh: Council for Scottish Archaeology, 1997.

—, T., Knott, C., Bruce, M.F. and Kerr, N.W. Excavation of two burials at Galson, Isle of Lewis 1993 and 1996' *Proceedings of the Society of Antiquaries of Scotland.* Forthcoming.

Neudorfer, G. Vermont's stone chambers: their myth and their history. *Proceedings of the Vermont Historical Society* 47, No. 2, 1979, 79-146.

Nicolaisen, W.F.H. Norse settlements in the Northern and Western Isles. Some placename evidence. *Scottish Historical Review* 48:1, 1969, 6-17.

—, W.F.H. Place-name maps. How reliable are they? *Studia Onamastia,* 1989, 261-268.

Nichols, H. Vegetational change, shoreline displacement and the human factor in the Late Quaternary history of south-west Scotland. *Transactions of the Royal Society of Edinburgh,* 1967.

Nicolson, A. *A Guide to Skye.* Glasgow: Celtic Press, 1950.

Nicholson, R.A. and Dockrill, S.J. (eds.) *Old Scatness Broch, Shetland: retrospect and prospect.* Bradford: University of Bradford/Shetland Amenity Trust/North Atlantic Biocultural Organisation, Bradford Archaeological Sciences Research 5, NABO Monograph 2, 1998.

Nieke, M.R. Fortifications in Argyll, 131-42, in Armit, I. (ed.) *Beyond the Brochs: Changing Perspectives on the Later Iron Age in Atlantic Scotland.* Edinburgh: Edinburgh University Press, 1990.

Nisbet, H.C. Excavation of a vitrified Dun at Langwell, Strath Oykel, Sutherland. *Glasgow Archaeological Journal,* 19, 1994-5, 51-73.

O'Sullivan, D. The ring-ditch house. in McCullagh, R.P.J. and Tipping, R. (eds.), *The Lairg Project 1988 – 96, the evolution of an archaeological landscape in northern Scotland.* Edinburgh. Forthcoming.

—, J. Excavations on the mill stream, Iona. *Proceedings of the Society of Antiquaries of Scotland* 124, 1994(a), 491-508.

—, J. Excavations of an early church and a women's cemetery at St. Roman's medieval parish church, Iona. *Proceedings of the Society of Antiquaries of Scotland* 124, 1994(b), 327-65.

—, J. More than the sum of the parts. Iona: archaeological investigations 1875-1996. *Church Archaeology* 2, 1998, 5-18.

—, T. The mammal bone, 91, 106-10 and 127-30, in Sharples, N. *Scalloway: a broch, late Iron Age settlement and Medieval cemetery in Shetland*. Oxford: Oxbow Books/Cardiff Studies in Archaeology, Oxbow Monograph 82, 1998.

Ordnance Survey Name Book, 22, 1880. Orkney Stromness (National Monuments Record, Edinburgh)

Owen, O.A. Eildon Hill North, Roxburgh, Borders, 21-71, in Rideout, J., Owen, O.A. and Halpin, E. (eds.) *Hillforts of Southern Scotland*. Edinburgh: AOC/Historic Scotland, STAR Monograph 1, 1992.

—, O.A. Tuquoy, Westray, Orkney: a challenge for the future, 318-339, in Batey, C.E., Jesch, J. and Morris, C.D. The Viking Age in Caithness, Orkney and the North Atlantic. Edinburgh: Edinburgh University Press, 1993.

—, O. and Dalland, M. *Scar: A Viking Boat Burial on Sanday, Orkney*. Edinburgh: Tuckwell Press/Historic Scotland, 1999.

Pankhurst, R.J. and Mullin, J.M. *Flora of the Outer Hebrides*. London: HMSO, 1994.

Parfitt, K. *Iron Age Burials from Mill Hill, Deal*. London: British Museum, 1995.

Parker Pearson, M., Sharples, N. and Mulville, J. Brochs and Iron Age society: a reappraisal. *Antiquity* 70, 1996, 57-67.

—, M., Sharples, N. and Mulville, J. Excavations at Dun Vulan: a correction. *Antiquity* 73, 1999, 149-52.

—, M and Sharples, N. 1999 *Between land and sea: excavations at Dun Vulan, South Uist*. Sheffield: Sheffield Academic Press, SEARCH Volume 3.

Pearce, S. *The Archaeology of South West Britain*. London: Collins, 1981.

Perring, F.H. and Walters, S.M. *Atlas of the British Flora*. Wakefield: EP Publishing Ltd., 1976.

Peters, C., Church, M.J. and Coles, G.M. Mineral magnetism and archaeology at Galson on the Isle of Lewis, Scotland. *Physics and Chemistry of the Earth (A)* 25, No.5, 2000, 455-60.

—, C., Church, M.J. and Mitchell, C. Investigation of domestic fuel sources on Lewis using mineral magnetism. *Archaeological Prospection*. Forthcoming.

Piggott, C.M. The Iron Age settlement at Hayhope Knowe, Roxburghshire: excavations 1949. *Proceedings of the Society of Antiquaries of Scotland* 83, 1948-9, 45-67.

—, C.M. Milton Loch crannog 1. *Proceedings of the Society of Antiquaries of Scotland* 87, 1953, 134-52.

—, S. Native economies and the Roman occupation of North Britain, 1-27, in Richmond I.A. (ed.) *Roman and Native in North Britain*. Edinburgh: Thomas Nelson and Sons Ltd., 1958.

—, S. Swords and scabbards of the British early Iron Age. *Proceedings of the Prehistoric Society* 14, 1950, 1-28.

—, S. *Early Celtic Art*. Edinburgh: Edinburgh University Press, 1970.

Pollack, R.W. The excavation of a souterrain and roundhouse at Cyderhall, Sutherland. *Proceedings of the Society of Antiquaries of Scotland* 122, 1992, 149-60.

Pouncet, J. *Allt Chrisal, Ben Tangaval*. Unpublished interim report for Historic Scotland. 2000.

Raftery, B. *La Tène in Ireland: Problems of Origin and Chronology*. Marburg: the author, 1984.

—, B. Reflections on the Irish Scabbard Style, 475-92, in *Festschrift für Otto-Herman Freyzum 65. Geburtstag*, Marburger Studien zur Vor-und Frühgeschichte 16. Hitzeroth, 1994.

Ramsay, S. *Woodland Clearance in West-Central Scotland During the Past 3000 Years*. Unpublished PhD thesis, University of Glasgow, 1995.

—, S. From out of the ooze: pollen evidence for the landscapes of the M74. in Banks, I. *Motorway to the Past: the Archaeology of the M74*. Forthcoming.

Renfrew, A.C. *Investigations in Orkney*. London: Society of Antiquaries/Thames and Hudson Ltd, 1979.

—, J. Carbonised plant remains, 229-232, in Mackie, E.W. *Dun Mor Vaul: an Iron Age Broch on Tiree*. Glasgow: Glasgow University, 1974.

Reynolds, D.M. Aspects of later timber construction in south-east Scotland, 44-56, in Harding, D.W. (ed.) *Later Prehistoric Settlement in South-East Scotland*. Edinburgh: University of Edinburgh, Department of Archaeology, 1982.

—, D.M. J.M. Corrie, archaeologist. *Transactions of the Dumfriesshire and Galloway Natural History and Antiquarian Society* 59, 1984, 94-107.

—, D.M. and Ritchie, J.N.G. Walter Gordon Grant: an archaeological appreciation. *Proceedings of the Society of Antiquaries of Scotland* 115, 1985, 67-73.

Rhodes, A.N., Rumsby, B.T. and Macklin, M.G. Gallanach Beg, Oban, 121-25, in Walker, M.J.C., Gray, J.M. and Lowe, J.J. (eds.) *The South-West Scottish Highlands: Field Guide*. Cambridge: Quaternary Research Association, 1992.

Rideout, J. (a) The Dunion, Roxburgh, Borders, 73-119, in Rideout, J., Owen, O.A., and Halpin, E. (eds.) *Hillforts of Southern Scotland*. Edinburgh: AOC/Historic Scotland, STAR Monograph 1, 1992.

—, J. (b) Gillies Hill, Stirling, Central, 127-36, in Rideout, J., Owen, O.A., and Halpin, E. (eds.) *Hillforts of Southern Scotland*. Edinburgh: AOC/Historic Scotland, STAR Monograph 1, 1992.

—, J., Owen, O.A., and Halpin, E. (eds.) *Hillforts of Southern Scotland*. Edinburgh: AOC/Historic Scotland, STAR Monograph 1, 1992.

Ritchie, A. Meigle and lay patronage in Tayside in the 9th and 10th centuries AD. *Tayside and Fife Archaeological Journal* 1, 1995, 1-10.

—, A. Excavation of Pictish and Viking-age farm-steads at Buckquoy, Orkney. *Proceedings of the Society of Antiquaries of Scotland* 108, 1976-7, 174-227.

—, J. A keg of bog butter from Skye and its contents. *Proceedings of the Society of Antiquaries of Scotland* 75, 1940-1, 5-22.

—, J.N.G. Balnabraid Cairn, Kintyre, Argyll. *Transactions of the Dumfriesshire and Galloway Natural History and Antiquarian Society* 44, 1967(a), 81-8.

—, J.N.G. Keil Cave, Southend: a late Iron Age cave occupation in Kintyre. *Proceedings of the Society of Antiquaries of Scotland* 99, 1966-7(b), 104-10.

—, J.N.G. Early Settlement in Argyll, 38-66, in Ritchie, J.N.G. (ed.), *The Archaeology of Argyll*. Edinburgh: Edinburgh University Press, *c*.1997.

—, J.N.G. and Harman, M. *Argyll and the Western Isles*. Edinburgh: HMSO, 1996.

—, J.N.G. and Ritchie, A. A long cist at Cnoc Aingil, Islay, Argyll. *Proceedings of the Society of Antiquaries of Scotland* 106, 1975, 205-8.

—, J.N.G. Excavations at Machrins, Colonsay. *Proceedings of the Society of Antiquaries of Scotland* 111, 1981, 263-81.

—, J.N.G. *Recording Early Christian Monuments in Scotland*. Rosemarkie: Groam House Museum, 1998.

—, J.N.G. and Adamson, H.C. Knappers, Dunbartonshire: a reassessment. *Proceedings of the Society of Antiquaries of Scotland* 111, 1981, 172-204.

—, J.N.G. and Welfare, H. Excavations at Ardnave, Islay. *Proceedings of the Society of Antiquaries of Scotland* 113, 1983, 302-66.

Rivet, A.L.F. and Smith, C. *The Place Names of Roman Britain*. London: Batsford, 1979.

Robertson, W.N. A Viking grave found at the Broch of Gurness, Aikerness, Orkney. *Proceedings of the Society of Antiquaries of Scotland* 101, 1968-9, 289-90.

—, W.N. St John's Cross, Iona, Argyll. *Proceedings of the Society of Antiquaries of Scotland* 106, 1975, 111-23.

Robinson, D. Botanical remains, 199-209, in Holdsworth, P. (ed.) *Excavations in the Medieval Burgh of Perth 1979-81*. Edinburgh: Society of Antiquaries of Scotland Monograph 5, 1987.

Robinson, S.W. *A computational procedure for the utilisation of high-precision radiocarbon calibration curves*. Open file report in the United States Department of the Interior Geological Survey, 1986.

Royal Commission on the Ancient and Historical Monuments of Scotland. *Inventory of Monuments and Constructions in the County of Caithness*. Edinburgh: H.M.S.O., 1911.

—. *Inventory of Monuments of and Constructions in the County of Sutherland*. Edinburgh: H.M.S.O., 1911.

—. *Inventory of Ancient Monuments and Constructions of the Outer Hebrides, Skye and the Small Isles*. Edinburgh: H.M.S.O., 1928.

Royal Commission on the Ancient and Historical Monuments of Scotland. *Orkney and Shetland*. Edinburgh: H.M.S.O.

Royal Commission on the Ancient and Historical Monuments of Scotland. *Lanarkshire: An Inventory of the Monuments*. Edinburgh: H.M.S.O., 1978.

—. *Argyll Volume 3: Mull, Tiree, Coll and Northern Argyll*. Edinburgh: H.M.S.O., 1980.

—. *Argyll Volume 4: Iona*. H.M.S.O., 1982.

—. *Argyll Volume 5: Islay, Jura, Colonsay and Oronsay*. Edinburgh: H.M.S.O., 1984.

—. *National Monuments Record of Scotland: A Guide to the Collections*. Edinburgh: H.M.S.O., 1991.

—. *South-east Perth: an archaeological landscape*. Edinburgh: H.M.S.O., 1994.

—. *Eastern Dumfriesshire: an Archaeological Landscape*. Edinburgh: The Stationery Office, 1997.

Ruggles, C. *Astronomy in Prehistoric Britain and Ireland*. New Haven and London: Yale University Press, *c*.1999.

Rye, O.S. *Pottery Technology: Principles and Reconstruction*. Washington D.C.: Taraxacum, 1981.

Rymer, L. The history and ethnobotany of bracken. *Botanical Journal of the Linnean Society* 73, 1976, 151-76.

Sanderson, D.C.W., Placido, F, and Tate, J.O. Scottish vitrified forts: TL results from six study sites. *Nuclear Tracks and Radiation Measurements* 14, 1/2; 1988, 307-316.

Sands, R.J.S. *Archaeological Potential of Toolmarks on Prehistoric Wood, with Special Reference to Oakbank Crannog, Loch Tay, Scotland*. Unpublished PhD thesis, University of Edinburgh, 1994.

Schwankl, A. *What Wood is That?* Norwich: Thames and Hudson, 1957.

Scott, W.L. Excavation of Rudh' an Dunain Cave, Skye. *Proceedings of the Society of Antiquaries of Scotland* 68, 1933-4, 200-23.

—, W.L. The problem of the brochs. *Proceedings of the Prehistoric Society* 13, 1947(a), 1-37.

—, W.L. The Chambered Tomb of Unival, North Uist. *Proceedings of the Society of Antiquaries of Scotland* 82, 1947(b), 1-48.

—, W.L. Gallo-British Colonies, the aisled round house culture in the North. *Proceedings of the Prehistoric Society* 14, 1948, 46-125.

Seaward, M.R.D. Observations on the bracken component of the pre-Hadrianic deposits at Vindolanda, Northumberland. *Botanical Journal of the Linnean Society* 73, 1976, 177-85.

Serjeantson, D. and Bond, J.M. Cattle and sheep husbandry; evidence for increasingly intensive dairying. in Hunter J. *et al.* forthcoming.

Sharples, N.M. Excavation at Pierowall Quarry, Westray, Orkney. *Proceedings of the Society of Antiquaries of Scotland* 114, 1984, 75-125.

—, N. *The Iron Age and Norse Settlement at Bornish, South Uist: and interim report on the 1997 excavations*. Cardiff: University of Cardiff, Department of Archaeology, 1997.

—, N. *Scalloway: a broch, late Iron Age settlement and Medieval cemetery in Shetland*. Oxford: Oxbow Books/Cardiff Studies in Archaeology, Oxbow Monograph 82, 1998.

—, N. *The Iron Age and Norse settlement at Bornish, South Uist: An interim report on the 2000 excavations*. Cardiff: Department of Archaeology, 2000.

—, N. Bornais, South Uist Parish, 90-91. *Discovery and Excavation in Scotland* 1999. Edinburgh: Council for Scottish Archaeology, 2000.

—, N. Review: Later prehistory in the Outer Hebrides. *Antiquity* 75, 2001, 633-5.

—, N. Life histories and the buildings of the Atlantic Iron Age. in Turner, V. (ed.) *Tall stories: broch studies past, present and future*. Oxford: Oxbow Monograph, forthcoming.

—, N. and Parker Pearson, M. Norse settlement in the Outer Hebrides. *Norwegian Archaeological Review* 32:1, 1999, 41-62.

Shiel, R. The soils, in Haggarty, A.M. Iona: some results from recent work. *Proceedings of the Society of Antiquaries of Scotland* 118, 1988, 207f.

Simpson, I.A., Dockrill, S.J. and Lancaster, S.J. Making Arable Soils: Anthropogenic Soil

Formation in a Multi-period Landscape. in Nicholson R.A. and Dockrill, S J. (Eds.) *Old Scatness Broch, Shetland: Retrospect and Prospect.* Bradford: Bradford Archaeological Sciences Research 5 / North Atlantic Biocultural Organisation Monograph 2, 1998 (a).

—, I.A., Dockrill, S.J., Bull, I.D. and Evershed, R.P. Early anthropogenic soil formation at Tofts Ness, Sanday, Orkney. *Journal of Archaeological Science* 25, 1998(b), 729-46.

Sinclair, Sir J. (ed) *The Statistical Account of Scotland 1791-1799.* Volume 13, Angus. Wakefield: EP Publishing, 1976.

—, Sir J. (ed) *The Statistical Account of Scotland 1791-1799.* Volume 20, The Western Isles. Wakefield: EP Publishing, 1983.

—, Sir J. (ed) *The Statistical Account of Scotland 1791-1799.* Volume 19, Orkney and Shetland. Wakefield: EP Publishing, (new edition) 1978.

Small, A. Excavations at Underhoull, Unst, Shetland. *Proceedings of the Society of Antiquaries of Scotland* 98, 1964-6, 225-48.

Smith, A.N. Artefacts and the Iron Age of Atlantic Scotland: past, present and future. Forthcoming.

—, B. Breckness, Stromness Parish, 32. *Discovery and Excavation in Scotland*, 1985. Edinburgh: Council for British Archaeology (Scotland), 1985.

—, B. and Lorimer, D. Breckness, Stromness Parish, 33-4. *Discovery and Excavation in Scotland*, 1987. Edinburgh: Council for British Archaeology (Scotland), 1987.

—, B. Ward Hill, Dunrossness, Shetland Isles, 30. *Discovery and Excavation in Scotland, 1988.* Edinburgh: Council for Scottish Archaeology, 1988.

—, C., Hodgson, G.W.I., Armitage, P., Clutton-Brock, J., Dickson, C., Holden, T. and Ballin Smith B. The animal bone, 139-153, in Ballin Smith, B. *Howe: four millennia of Orkney prehistory.* Edinburgh: Society of Antiquaries of Scotland. Monograph Series, No. 9. 1994.

—, H. The plant remains, 297-335, in Parker-Pearson, M. and Sharples, N. *Between land and sea: excavations at Dun Vulan, South Uist,* Sheffield: Sheffield Academic Press, SEARCH Volume 3, 1999.

Smyth, A.P. *Warlords and Holy Men.* London: E. Arnold, 1984.

Society of Antiquaries of Scotland. *Catalogue of the National Museum of Antiquaries of Scotland.* Edinburgh: Society of Antiquaries of Scotland, 1892.

Sommerfelt, A. The Norse heritage of Canna, 232-237, in Campbell, J.L. *Canna, the Story of a Hebridean Island.* Oxford: National Trust for Scotland/Oxford University Press, 1984.

Spriggs, M. and Anderson, A. Late colonisation of East Polynesia. *Antiquity* 67, 1993, 200-17.

Sheridan, A. Scottish Stone Axeheads: Some new work and recent discoveries, 194-212, in Sharples, N. and Sheridan, A. (eds.) *Vessels for the Ancestors.* Edinburgh: Edinburgh University Press 1992.

Stead, I.M. (a) *Celtic Art in Britain before the Roman Conquest.* London: British Museum, 1985.

—, I.M. (b) *The Battersea Shield.* London: British Museum,1985.

—, I.M. *Iron Age Cemeteries in East Yorkshire.* London: English Heritage/British Museum, 1991.

Stell, G.P. and Harman, M. *Buildings of St Kilda.* Edinburgh: RCAHMS, HMSO, 1988.

Stevenson, J.B. Survival and discovery, 104-8, in Evans, J.G., Limbrey, S. and Cleere, H. (eds.) *The Effect of Man on the Landscape: the Highland Zone.* London: Council for British Archaeology Research Report 11, 1975.

—, R.B.K. Metal-work and some other objects in Scotland and their cultural affinities, 17-44, in Rivet A.L.F. (ed) *The Iron Age in Northern Britain.* Edinburgh: Edinburgh University Press, 1967.

Stuart, J. *Sculptured Stones of Scotland.* Aberdeen: Spalding Club, 1856, and Edinburgh, 1867.

—, J. Note on the preceding communication. *Proceedings of the Society of Antiquaries of Scotland* 8, 1868-70, 23-6.

—, M. *The Encyclopaedia of Herbs and Herbalism.* Novara: MacDonald and Co Ltd, 1989.

Stuiver, M. and Kra, R.S. (eds.) *Radiocarbon* 28 (2b), 1986, 805-1030.

—, M. and Pearson, G.W. High Precision Calibration of the Radiocarbon Timescale, AD1950-500BC. *Radiocarbon*, 28, (2b), 1986, 805-39.

—, M., Reimer, P.J., Bard, E., Beck, J.W., Burr, G.S., Hughen, K.A., Kromer, G., McCormac, J., van der Plicht, J. and Spurk, M. INTCAL98: Radiocarbon Age Calibration, 24000-0 cal BP. *Radiocarbon*, 40 (3), 1998, 1041-1083.

Taylor, K. *Rubus chamaemorus* (L.). *Journal of Ecology* 121, 1971, 293-306.

—, M. The wood, 188-192, in Parker-Pearson, M. and Sharples, N. *Between land and sea: excavations at Dun Vulan, South Uist.* Sheffield: Sheffield Academic Press, SEARCH Volume 3, 1999.

Terry, J. Excavation of a farmstead enclosure, Uppercleuch, in Annandale, Dumfries and Galloway. *Transactions of the Dumfriesshire and Galloway Natural History and Antiquarian Society* 68, 1993, 53-86.

—, J. Bodsberry Hill unenclosed platform settlement, near Elvanfoot, Strathclyde. *Glasgow Archaeological Journal* 18, 1993, 49-63.

—, J. Excavation at Lintshie Gutter unenclosed platform settlement, Crawford, Lanarkshire, 1991. *Proceedings of the Society of Antiquaries of Scotland*, 125, 1995, 369-427.

*The Times*, February 18, 2002 Erosion washes away Orkney's Heritage.

Thomas, C. *The Early Christian Archaeology of North Britain.* London: Oxford University Press/Glasgow University, 1971.

—, Capt. F.L.W. On the primitive dwellings and Hypogea of the Outer Hebrides. *Proceedings of the Society of Antiquaries of Scotland* 7, 1869-70, 153-95.

Tierney, J.J. Ptolemy's Map of Scotland. *Journal of the Hellenic Society* 79, 1979, 132-48.

Tipping, R. The form and fate of Scotland's woodlands. *Proceedings of the Society of Antiquaries of Scotland* 124, 1994, 1-54.

Topping, P.G. Later prehistoric pottery from Dun Cul Bhuirg, Iona Argyll. *Proceedings of the Society of Antiquaries of Scotland* 115, 1985, 199-209.

—, P.G. Typology and chronology in the later prehistoric pottery assemblages of the Western Isles. *Proceedings of the Society of Antiquaries of Scotland* 117, 1987, 67-84.

Triscott, J. Excavation at Dryburn Bridge, East Lothian, 117-124, in Harding, D.W. (ed.) *Later Prehistoric Settlement in South East Scotland.* Edinburgh: University of Edinburgh Occasional Paper No 8, 1982.

Turner, D.J. and Dunbar, J.G. Breachacha Castle, Coll: Excavation and field survey 1965-71. *Proceedings of the Society of Antiquaries of Scotland* 102, 1970, 155-87.

Van der Veen, M. *Crop husbandry regimes: an archaeobotanical study of farming in northern England 1000 BC – AD 500.* Sheffield: University of Sheffield Archaeological Monograph 3, 1992.

Van Zeist, W., Wasylikowa, K. and Behre, K.E. (eds.) *Progress in Old World Palaeoethnobotany.* Rotterdam: Balkema, 1991.

Veitch, K. The Columban Church in northern Britain 664-717: a reassessment. *Proceedings of the Society of Antiquaries of Scotland* 127, 1997, 627-47.

Verger, S. La genèse celtique des rinceaux à triscèles. *Jahrbuch Römisch-Germanische Zentralmuseums, Mainz,* 34, 1987, 278-339.

Wainwright, F.T. Souterrains in Scotland. *Antiquity* 27, 1953, 219-321.

—, F.T. (ed) *The Northern Isles.* Edinburgh: Thomas Nelson and Sons Ltd.

—, F.T. *The Souterrains of Southern Pictland.* London: Routledge,Kegan and Paul, 1963.

—, F.T. The Picts and the Problem, 1-53, in Wainwright, F.T. (ed.) *The Problem of the Picts.* Edinburgh: Nelson, 1955.

Warden, A.J. *Angus or Forfarshire: The land and people, description and historical.* 5 Volumes. Dundee: C. Alexander, 1880-5.

Warner, R. The Irish souterrains and their background, 100-44, in Crawford, H. (ed.) *Subterranean Britain.* London: John Baker, 1979.

—, R. Irish Souterrains: later Iron Age refuges. *Archaeologica Atlantica* 3, 1980, 81-99.

Watkins, T. Excavation of an Iron Age open settlement at Dalladies, Kincardineshire. *Proceedings of the Society of Antiquaries of Scotland* 110, 1978-80(a), 122-64.

—, T. Excavation of a settlement and souterrain at Newmill, near Bankfoot, Perthshire. *Proceedings of the Society of Antiquaries of Scotland* 110, 1978-80(b), 165-208.

Watson, M. The role of the pig in food conservation and storage in traditional Irish farming. *Environmental Archaeology* 3, 1998, 63-8.

—, W.J. *The Celic Placenames of Scotland.* Edinburgh and London, 1926.

Watt, W.G.T. The ruins of Breckness: prehistoric and modern. in Charleston, M.M. (ed.) *Orcadian papers, being a selection from the Proceedings of the Orkney Natural History Society from 1887-1904.* Stromness: Orkney Natural History Society 1905, 12-25.

Welander, R.D.E., Batey, C. and Cowie, T.G. A Viking burial from Kneep, Uig, Isle of Lewis. *Proceedings of the Society of Antiquaries of Scotland* 117, 1987, 149-74.

Welfare, H.G. A bronze-age cemetery at Ferniegair, Lanarkshire. *Proceedings of the Society of Antiquaries of Scotland* 106, 1974-5, 1-14.

—, H. The Southern souterrains, 305-23, in Miket, R. and Burgess, C. (eds.) *In, Between and Beyond the Walls: Essays on the Prehistory and History of North Britain in Honour of George Jobey.* Edinburgh: John Donald, 1984.

Whittington, G. Placenames in the settlement pattern of dark-age Scotland. *Proceedings of the Society of Antiquaries of Scotland* 106, 1975, 99-110.

Whittle, A. (ed.) *Scord of Brouster: An Early Agricultural Settlement on Shetland.* Oxford: Oxford University Committee for Archaeology Monograph 9, 1986.

Williams, B.B. Excavation of a rath at Coolcran, County Fermanagh. *Ulster Journal of Archaeology* 48, 1985, 69-80.

Wood-Martin, W.G. *The Lake Dwellings of Ireland.* London: Longman, Green and Co, 1886.

Worsaae, J.J.A. *An Account of the Danes and Norwegians in England, Scotland and Ireland.* London: John Murray, 1852.

Wyss R. *Der Schatzfund von Erstfeld: Frühkeltischer Goldschmuck aus den Zentralalppen.* Zürich: Gesellschaft für das Schweizerische Landesmuseum, 1975.

Young, A. Excavations at Dun Cuier, Isle of Barra, Outer Hebrides. *Proceedings of the Society of Antiquaries of Scotland* 89, 1955, 290-328.

—, A. An Aisled Farmhouse at the Allasdale, Isle of Barra. *Proceedings of the Society of Antiquaries of Scotland* 87, 1952-3, 80-105.

—, A. and Richardson, K.M. A Cheardach Mhor, Drimore, South Uist. *Proceedings of the Society of Antiquaries of Scotland* 93, 1959-60, 135-73.

—, A. The sequence of Hebridean pottery, 45-58, in Rivet, A.L.F. (ed.) *The Iron Age in Northern Britain.* Edinburgh: Edinburgh University Press, 1966.

# Index

Bold references at the end of an entry denote illustration numbers